# THE
# ECHOES
# OF
# BABYLON

by

*Michael Hastings*

*The Echoes of Babylon*
Copyright © 2016
All rights reserved.

Published by Piscataqua Press
An imprint of RiverRun Bookstore, Inc.
142 Fleet Street | Portsmouth, NH | 03801
www.riverrunbookstore.com
www.piscataquapress.com
ISBN: 978-1-944393-09-0
Printed in the United States of America

# TABLE OF CONTENTS

8/27/16

*To those who still serve.*

Don
— Best wishes and
good luck in your continued
efforts — with all things.

Michael Hastings

# PREFACE

⌑

It is the fate of all societies and of all individuals to become objects of history. Often, this history is written. On occasion it may be spoken. Sometimes it will assume the guise of the myth. Frequently, it may be written by those who live through it, often times with a view to formulate public opinion or to influence what history may say of them. Usually, it will be re-written many years later by those who have the advantage of hindsight. Rarely, if ever, is it written in the present day by those who would offer to chance the consequences which contemporary actions may hold toward the future.

This then shall be the objective of this book. It is the desire of the writer to examine some of the recent actions, events and policies of the present, and to assign to them the viewpoint of the writer many years from now. In order to accomplish this mission, it may become necessary to consult historical tendencies from the past, especially those from societies of a republican nature similar to our own. In addition, in order to completely understand the impacts of current actions or events on the future, it may be necessary to separate this discussion into various topics, much as a current modern society is divided into various aspects, such as the military, political, industrial, or agricultural.

Is there some inherent value to writing a recent history along these lines? I believe so. Unfortunately, many of history's great works revolve around the less pleasant events in the affairs of mankind. We find written in the pages of Edward Gibbon's *Decline and Fall of the*

*Roman Empire*, the tragic story of how the world's greatest and possibly most influential society came to an end. In the more recently completed twentieth century, we become acquainted with the tragic, futile and needless beginnings of the First World War in Barbara Tuchman's *The Guns of August*. Therefore, if it is acceptable to contemplate the mistakes of the past in order to offer to them an assignation of their historical significance, would it not likewise be acceptable to contemplate present actions and to assign to them their historical significance as viewed from the future? Often times, we sit idly by and only after events have transpired we condemn or applaud them after the fact. Perhaps the wiser policy would be to consider what the impact of that action might be before the results of these actions have been allowed to transpire.

History has been written in all time periods, from the time of cave paintings, to the clay tablets, to the age of paper and the printing press, to the recent age of electronics. There will always be the need for mankind to record, and even to explain his actions. In recent years, there has been no end to the books and magazines being published and printed and increasingly recorded electronically. In many instances, this media has been used to attach political importance to an event, and not a historical importance. However, there is a very discernible gulf between political history and actual history. If this were not true, then we would all be afforded the opportunity to choose between different libraries much as we have the ability to choose different political parties. To those individuals who would use their writings to influence current events, I believe they may come up very short if they think they may somehow change future events through the evasion of the truth or even a mild edifying or politicizing of it.

For the student of history, in the form of the college professor or even the casual reader, it will always be noted that the life experiences of the author may hold a serious influence on how history is written. Obviously, the viewpoint of the soldier will be different than the viewpoint of the pacifist, the viewpoint of the lawyer different than the viewpoint of the lawmaker, or politician so to speak. Therefore, it should be the object of the historian to be impartial. If we are to read from Roman history, we find that Gaius Julius Agricola is to be considered as one of Rome's greatest generals. Yet his predecessor in Britain, Suetonius Paulinus, the man who defeated Boudicca and at great odds put down the Iceni Revolt in 61 A.D. is rarely mentioned. Could the fact that Agricola was the father-in-law of the Roman historian Tacitus have something to do with this? Probably so.

There is something else that should be recognized by the reader as well. Americans tend to believe that their history began in 1776 or perhaps in 1607 at Jamestown. But it should be remembered that America was a British colony, and for nearly four centuries Britain was a Roman colony. I do not believe that any American can appreciate their own history, without recognizing the contributions of our predecessors to the society we live in today. Our laws are founded in British Common law, a gift to the world from Henry Plantagenet. Likewise, the efforts of Washington and Jefferson cannot be fully appreciated without recognizing the earlier efforts of Simon de Montfort, John Pym, or Sir John Eliot. To have little or no understanding of Roman or English history, is to have little or no understanding of our own.

Is it the hope of the author to influence current political thought through this work? I sincerely hope not, as there are a sufficient number of individuals and entities engaged in that practice already. The desire of the author is simply that as we engage in this peregrination through past and current events, that this work will at least give cause for readers to consider alternative theories to pre-existing perceptions and patterns of thought.

# Chapter 1

¤

# THE DONATIVE

Since the dawn of civilization there has always been the desire, and to some extent the need, for one or more individuals to control others, to control wealth and resources, and to control events. Why does this need or desire exist? To this question there may be several answers, some within the realm of human understanding, and some excluded from it. Due to the fact that for thousands of years we have lived and at times thrived in complex societies, we seem to consider ourselves as being removed from the animal kingdom. I believe this would be a gross exaggeration and misunderstanding on our part. Human nature is such that we enjoy all of the luxuries of life. We enjoy nice houses with controlled climates. We enjoy relaxation as opposed to hard work, and in fact our societal structure is such that individuals who perform little practical labor, such as entertainers and athletes, receive a greater share of the wealth than the practical laborer, such as the farmer or the carpenter or the mechanic. Be this as it may, there are certain biological facts, certain verities, from which we cannot escape. We know fundamentally that we are in truth frail beings. We know that our very existence depends very much on our environment. We cannot survive without breathable air, drinkable water and nourishing food. We know also that unlike most members of the wild kingdom that there is some need to control our immediate

1

environment. Given the varying climate of the planet upon which we live we also need protective shelter. All of the aforementioned require the distribution, and hence competition for natural resources. Within these needs we find also the basic concepts for the organization of modern societies. We use various forms of currency as a means of purchase and distribution of wealth. We also have laws, civil and criminal, as a means of controlling behavior.

If we are to look further, to find an understanding of how to control the flow of currency, and of controlling laws and behavior, then we arrive with a necessity to control thought. No doubt, many are familiar with the term "the pen is mightier than the sword." This no doubt is in reference to the power of the written word. Also of notable quotation is the statement of Victor Hugo, "Far more powerful than all armies, is the idea whose time has come." Are these concepts valid? Most assuredly they must be, or why else would societies comprised of various forms of government had to have spent several thousands of years trying to control their citizens by use of writings, teachings, various forms of media propaganda, peer pressure and control of financial institutions. We may see and understand the use of military force to control subjects in totalitarian states, but by and large the use of such means are restrained to using them against conquered peoples, and not so much to control persons within the state from which these armies arise.

Equally, and perhaps as importantly, if we search the pages of history for another means of governments controlling their people, we must inevitably arrive at the use of the donativum, or donative. Far more sinister and effective, the use of this means of control usually goes undetected. It is also usually far more effective because it does not place importance on the issue of fact, is not restricted by race or creed or gender, and simply exploits something that all humans are susceptible to, by this I refer to human weakness. What is a donative exactly and how does it work? A donative is simply a donation. Something given to someone or several someone's to curry favor. Historically, the use of the donative does not appear to be restricted in terms of which forms of government engage in its use.

However, it at times appears that Democratic or Republican forms of government tend to rely on it greatly and hence to suffer from its effects more than others.

Therefore, if we now know of the existence of the donative and of its use, can we reference examples of its use from the past, the consequences of this use, and compare them to our own society and times? To this question there must be an affirmative answer. We know that to date, the world's greatest and longest lasting society was Republican and later Imperial Rome. History tells us that Roman emperors were far more inclined toward the use of bread and circus to control their peoples than they were toward using the legions. If we are to believe most contemporary histories of Rome, we know that the citizens of Rome proper did not pay taxes for several centuries. We know also that they were given rations of grain and olive oil, antiquities version of welfare if you will. The purpose behind this practice? It must appear obvious. The right to govern, even in an autocratic society, is dependent to some extent on popularity, much the same as in democratic societies.

I believe that when we speak of Rome today, probably as was also the case in ancient times, the first connotation or image that appears in our minds is of the legionary or the centurion. No doubt this is due in part to the fact that not only did Roman soldiers conquer the Mediterranean world, they also built much of Rome's infrastructure. The Via Appia, the aqueducts, Hadrian's Wall, and Caesar's bridge across the Rhine are all examples of Rome's engineering prowess and a testament to the legionaries skills as engineers. Do donatives have relevance in regard to Roman military institutions? Most assuredly. In the aftermath of Rome's civil wars involving Sulla, Cinna, Caesar and Pompey, it was eventually realized that to seize the imperial purple, one had to control the army. Given human nature, what would be the most efficient means for one individual to control the allegiance of many? The donative. Initially, during the years of the republican armies, this was done by giving grants of land to Roman veterans. Although land grants to Roman colonists had earlier been practiced during the years of Gaius Gracchus and the Sempronian reforms, in the year 100 B.C. the tribune Lucius Appuleius Saturninus and the praetor Servilius Glaucia proposed an agrarian law affording land grants exclusively for the benefit of Gaius Marius veterans. These new veterans' colonies were to be placed in Southern Gaul, Greece and North Africa. Julius Caesar would later expand upon this practice on a massive scale, creating veterans' colonies in Spain, Gaul, Carthage, Corinth, Greece, Syria and the coast of the Black Sea. Octavian, or Augustus, was reportedly responsible for the founding of about 75 different settlements for his 300,000 veterans during the early years of the Roman principate.

Furthermore, if we consult Winston Churchill's work, *The History of the English Speaking Peoples*, we find in Roman Britain, the colony of Camulodunum (Colchester). This colony was the center of Roman authority on the island. It was settled by veterans as well, and was supported by members of the current soldiery, the latter of whom no doubt entertained hopes that they would someday receive land grants of their own. During the later years of the principate, it became the policy of many Roman emperors to establish these colonies all along the frontiers both as a means of controlling the frontiers and of controlling the veterans.

Were other forms of the donative used in regard to Rome's military institutions? When we consult Nigel Rogers' recent work, *Ancient Rome*, we find that it was the practice of many emperors to award a donative to the legionaries after their accession to the throne and occasionally after a great or purported victory. In the first century A.D., aware of his need to retain the loyalty of the army, the emperor Domitian increased legionary pay by one third.[1]

This practice of flattering the vanity of Rome's warrior class was to continue unabated into the second century. Septimus Severus began to allow his legionaries the honor of wearing gold rings, a privilege previously reserved for the wealthy. In addition, Severus began a policy of allowing them to live with their wives in the idleness of their respective encampments. Although there are to be

---

[1] Rodgers, *Ancient Rome*, 74.

found examples of issues with discipline and at times outright revolt in earlier times (in the aftermath of the Varian disaster of A.D. 9, the charming and urbane General Germanicus would be sent to quell a mutiny within the eight legions of Rome's Rhine Command, then the largest within the army), it would be during the years of Severus when we see a general relaxing of discipline and the beginnings of a disregard for authority within Rome's armies.

Much the same as the use of the donative was used to control the armies, their employment was also used to control the behavior of the subject peoples. The distribution of grain, corn and olive oil at no cost to the people, various forms of entertainment such as the circus and gladiatorial games and the use of Salutary Laws were all means used to garner popular support. Grants of land to the warrior and wealthy classes performed this same act with regard to separate classes of citizenry. The intention and the result of all of these actions must be regarded as the desire to sink all subject peoples to a common level of dependence.

Do we find examples of this reliance upon donatives within our society? Most definitely. Long before the time of our Independence we find the use of land grants in action. With the establishment of the Plymouth Colony and the subsequent second plantation in Duxbury in 1632, we find a growing demand for land grants within colonial societies. It is in these instances of course, that we find a combination of the donative used as a means to stimulate economic growth, and hence wealth, as much as to win popular support. This policy would continue after the time of American independence and would play an important part in the concept of manifest destiny and the settling of the American West.

This use of the land grant would not be restricted to the English colonies, as the French applied the same methods with their perspective colonists, known as trente-six-mois (thirty-six months). It is certain that the donative does not always assume the guise of a monetary gift or a grant of land. During the middle centuries when Europe existed under the feudal system, although grants of lands were given to nobles in exchange for fielty, the donative could also be found in titles and privileges bestowed upon noblemen by the various monarchs.

So exactly how would all of these aforementioned examples of various forms of donative pertain to our current society? The answer to this question is probably quite simple, they establish precedent. In the immediate aftermath of America's war for independence, donatives would be used as a form of compensation for individuals to the cause of liberty. Thomas Paine, in recognition of his essays *Common Sense* and *Crisis*, would receive a substantial honorarium from Congress and be given real estate as a gift from the State of New York.[2]

The use of donatives would also be used to spur economic and industrial growth. In the aftermath of the American Civil War, the

*The Roman Centurion, symbol of Rome's power and prestige.*

---

[2] Chernow, *Washington, A Life*, 447

United States Government, at that time dominated by the Republican Party, would, under a series of railroad laws, subsidize railroad construction with loans totaling more than sixty million dollars and gifts of over one hundred million acres of public property. In addition, wartime taxes on coal, iron, and corporations would be repealed. If the intention was to stimulate the economy, these attempts would prove to be highly successful. In the years between 1860 and 1870, the number of manufacturing firms in the United States increased by eighty percent and the total value of manufactured goods by over one hundred percent. Of course this would be a very small beginning to a process by which we have arrived at a time and a place where the United States Government oversees no less than two thousand various social programs. The fact that we now exist as a nation with a staggering fifteen trillion dollar debt may in no small part be attributed to this ongoing habit of using the donative. Does this process seem to be restricted to a singular or a very few segments of our society? I dare say no. Today, we still find use of the land grant at all levels of government, to include state and local. We employ the use of agricultural subsidies. In the wake of the economic downturn in recent years, we see enormous buyouts and grants given to banks and financial institutions and to various industries such as the automotive industry. In fact, if we are to review the federal budget to any great depth, we will no doubt find the use of donatives spread throughout programs involving defense budgets, agricultural programs, social welfare programs, energy programs, transportation programs, and even no doubt educational programs.

Are we to assume, however, that the use of donatives are restricted to the citizens of our own country and with the desire to affect the outcome of events, of elections, or the behavior of individuals within our own society? To answer this question I believe it would be necessary to examine United States foreign policy since the advent of American involvement in world affairs after the Spanish American War. Soon after a peace agreement was reached in Paris between the United States and Spain in December 1898, the tasks of reform, re-organization and development of our new possessions in the Philippines and the Islands of the West Indies would begin under the leadership of individuals such as General Leonard Wood.[3] All of these issues would of course require the expenditure of tax dollars and no doubt would be done with the intention of winning the support of native peoples.

In the wake of United States involvement in World War I there would be a move within American society away from internationalism and toward isolationism. This should in no way be interpreted that there would be no further American involvement abroad and that the use of donatives would be curtailed. During the years between the two world wars, we find the creation of the Young Plan and the Dawes Plan for the settlement of reparations deemed necessary by the Treaty of Versailles. Essentially, the United States was lending money to Germany so that they in turn could pay war reparations to Great Britain and France.

It would be during the years after the second Great War however, when the use of gifts, grants and military assistance would take on an entirely new proportion. We could consider it as being foreign aid on steroids, I suppose. In the aftermath of World War II, being confronted with rebuilding a war torn Europe and the beginning of a cold war with the Soviet Union, the solution to our problems would be found in the creation of the Marshall Plan, named of course after George C. Marshall, then Secretary of State and alumni of the Virginia Military Institute. After being initially proposed during a speech at Harvard University on June 5, 1947, the European nations involved were asked to devise a long term rebuilding plan, which they did in August, asking for an initial 29 billion dollars in aid.[4] This amount would later be reduced to 6.8 billion, being appropriated by Congress in April 1948.[5]

It would be developments in international relations and in the sphere of martial contest around the globe that would lead to the

---

[3] Nevins and Steele, *Pocket History of the U.S.*, 367.
[4] Zelizer, *Arsenal of Democracy*, 11.
[5] Ibid, 75.

ossification of donatives within future United States government budgets. Two wars in the Far East within two decades, Korea and Vietnam, would lead to massive military expenditures, both in terms of spending on our armed forces and in terms of military assistance. During the height of the war in Korea in 1953, defense spending would consume 14.5 % of gross national product (GNP) and would remain as high as 9% by the beginning of the 1960's. In contrast, defense spending in recent years has hovered in the vicinity of 4.3% of GDP. With our current massive debt, it is entirely likely that this figure may, of necessity, be reduced.

Do these facts bear witness to historical examples and can we expect repercussions from them? I would say most definitely so. It was always the policy of Republican and later Imperial Rome to "keep your weapons short and your frontiers long." Wise advice. Yet this would be an advice they themselves would not be allowed to follow. During the years of the late republic, much of this would have to do with public opinion and the attempt to gain and consolidate political power through the process of conquest. The surest way to gain popular support was to increase territory by conquest. This was accompanied of course with certain gifts to the Roman public, such as grain from Carthage or slaves from Gaul. These attempts at conquest would lead Rome to domination of the Mediterranean world. They would also lead to some of the Republic's greatest disasters, such as the loss of the entire army at Cannae in 216 B.C. and the defeat of Marcus Licinius Crassus by the Parthians at Carrhae in 53 B.C. In the case of the latter, due to his reputation for excessive greed, upon his capture by the Parthians, Crassus was reputed to have had molten gold poured down his throat. It is of note however, that at the time of these defeats, Rome was wealthy enough and had military traditions which would allow them to overcome these defeats and go on to heights of greater glory.

It was to be in the later years of Imperial Rome that such was not to be the case. After years of both internal and external warfare, Rome was to acquire huge amounts of debt, which would be accompanied by a drastic demise in its military systems. This military demise would not only include a reduction in discipline, but would also be accompanied by a reduction in the quality of arms and armaments used by the Imperial Roman soldier. To view the Roman soldier of the early principate, we find an individual armed with the gladius and the Pilum, wearing lorica segmentata, led by Centurians and possessing levels of discipline which, when combined in his fighting unit, the legion, would make him superior to all of his enemies. When skillfully led victory could be had at extreme odds, such as when Suetonius Paulinus with less than ten thousand troops crushed the Iceni Revolt of Boudica, with somewhere between 80,000 and 230,000 troops, at odds of almost 23 to 1.

In contrast, by the time of the fourth and fifth centuries, we find the Roman soldier poorly equipped. The gladius, lorica segmentata, the Centurion, the discipline and the expectation of victory were long since gone. The Roman soldier no longer possessed the technological advantage he once held. More often than not, Rome would have to rely on auxiliary troops to fight its wars. During the years of Julius Caesar, 49% of Roman legionaries were true Romans.

By the time of Hadrian, only 10% could claim this status. Eventually, this shortage of Roman troops would become so bad that large numbers of barbarian tribes would be allowed to settle within Rome's borders. They would be given the status of foederati and used as a source of troops for the army.

Naturally the outcome of this policy would lead to utter disaster. In the late fourth century, the Roman General Stilicho would become regent of the Western Roman Empire under the child Emperor Honorius. Of barbarian descent himself, Stilicho would spend much of his time fending off incursions by the Visogothic tribes. He would also spend much time intriguing against his rivals and playing off the Visogothic tribes against the Eastern Roman Empire. Twice he would defeat the Visogothic armies in battle; in Western Greece in 395 A.D. and again in northern Italy in 402 A.D. However, both times he allowed his enemies to escape. These actions would lead to his murder in 408 A.D., after the loss of Gaul to Vandal and Suevian invaders. As a result of his death, many German mercenaries were to

*The Roman Legionary of the early principate, heavily armed and
well protected. When ably led and deployed in battle formation, he
could be expected to win victory even against great odds.*

be slaughtered within the Western Roman armies; thirty thousand
would defect with Alaric, the Visogothic leader.

Within two short years, Alaric would enter Rome at the head of
his armies and sack the city on the night of August 24, 410 A.D. It
would be the fate of Rome's last great General, Aetius, to suffer from
similar consequences. When Attila became co-leader of the Hunic
tribes in 434 A.D., he would immediately set about to become sole
ruler by killing his brother. Shortly thereafter, he would adopt a
policy of extorting tribute from the Eastern Empire through a policy
of terrorizing the region with his three hundred thousand strong
armies. In the year 450 A.D., the Eastern Empire would receive a new
emperor, Marcian, who simply refused, or simply could not pay any

more. Attila immediately set his sights on the Western Empire. When the Western Empire's Emperor Valentian III's sister was caught having an affair with her steward, she was placed in seclusion as punishment. However, she then sent a ring to Attila and asked for his help. Using this rather strange circumstance as an excuse, Attila invaded Gaul and demanded half the empire as a dowry. In his invasion of Gaul, city after city would be sacked. Finding itself financially and militarily weak, the Western Empire would need Aetius as a savior. Gathering what western troops that he could, and combining them with the Visogothic armies of Theodoric, Aetius would meet the Hunic armies at Chalons sur Marne in 450 A.D. After an entire day of combat, leaving the ground covered with Cadavera Vero Innumera (truly numberless corpses),[6] Attila would be defeated for the only time in his life. However, with the death of their King, Theodoric, the Visogothic armies would depart and after having suffered horrific losses, Aetius and Rome would find themselves without an army. Shortly thereafter, Aetius would be assassinated by a jealous Valentian III and Rome would find itself without a defender as well. In the year 455 A.D. Rome would endure a final sack at the hands of the Vandal King Gaiseric, who would take a leisurely fourteen days to do so. Shortly thereafter, in the year 476 A.D., the emperor Romulus Augustus would be deposed by the German Odovacar. The light was to go out on the western world for centuries to come.

So the conclusion that these events would most assuredly lead us to is that massive debt, brought about by the rampant use of the donative, combined with the loss of martial spirit and an inability to financially support adequate armies, would help bring to an end one of mankind's greatest societies.

Undoubtedly there are many gifts that ancient Rome had to give to the western world even after the time of its decline and ultimate demise. However, due to the silent artillery of time, many of these lessons and gifts would either be forgotten or would just simply fail

---

[6] Rogers, *Ancient Rome*, 249.

to be recognized by us in a modern context. Therefore, it may be necessary to examine and compare one of history's more recent examples of decay within a republican or democratic society. This society would emerge over the course of many centuries. It would exist at one time as a portion of the Roman world and eventually grow to become the world's largest empire, governing roughly a quarter of the earth's population, controlling a similar proportion of the earth's land mass and dominating nearly all of its oceans. This of course would be the British Empire.

If we are to compare these two empires, no doubt we will find many similarities and many dissimilarities. Likewise, in their respective rises to supremacy, we will find similar motivations even though the two were separated by over a thousand years as their populations would find themselves with similar needs. Both would become economic powers that would eventually need to import much of their agricultural and mineral resources from colonies and conquered territories. Both would become maritime powers, one reluctantly, the other gladly. One would have its naval triumphs over Carthage and have its Agrippa at Actium; the other, its naval triumphs over Spain and France and its Nelson at Trafalgar. One would rely on the gladius and its civil engineering prowess, the other on the Martini—Henry and Lee—Enfield rifles and on its mechanical engineering prowess. Both would succumb to the effects of massive debt, both would see this debt have a direct effect on their ability to wage war.

In addition, both would find that this gradual loss of military prowess would lead to challenges against their supremacy from former colonies and territories. In the Third, Fourth and Fifth centuries, as Rome would find itself shifting its limited military forces from one area of concern to another, its enemies would adopt a policy of simply waiting until such time as the limitanei and comitatenses were removed from their area, and would then exert pressure on the Roman frontiers. With the British Empire, it would be in the aftermath of two world wars that it would find itself heavily indebted, unable to maintain its perceived naval supremacy and then challenged by its former colonies. In the time of Julius Caesar, Attila the Hun would probably not have been such a threat as he was in the time of Aetius.

Likewise, it would not seem that tiny Argentina would have been quite so bold as to invade the Falkland Islands as it did in 1982 if it were confronted by the Grand Fleet of Jutland or the British Carrier Fleet of World War II. It is interesting to note that on VJ-Day in 1945, the Royal Navy possessed ten fleet carriers and eleven escort carriers serving in the Pacific Ocean alone.[7] For the re-conquest of the Falkland Islands in 1982, it possessed only two operational aircraft carriers in its entire navy, Hermes and Invincible. Combined, the two could put up a scant twenty fixed wing aircraft. Likewise, in 1982, the British Empire's aerial response to the Falkland invasion would consist of seven Avro-Vulcan bombers flown non-stop from Britain to the South Atlantic and back. One must draw the conclusion that whether it is the Visogoths of the Fourth and Fifth centuries or the Argentineans of the Twentieth, the recognized or even perceived loss of military prowess can only invite a certain amount of challenge to authority.

Does there exist some correlation between the Roman practice of using donatives, debt and ultimate loss of military power and the process by which Great Britain was to suffer this same loss of prestige? Historically, I believe the answer must be yes. If we examine Great Britain in the nineteenth Century at the time of Queen Victoria's Diamond Jubilee in 1897, we find soldiers from throughout the empire marching through London in various exotic uniforms in a display of military might. There was also a review of the Grand Fleet at Spithead. This was the age of "jolly little wars against barbarous peoples." This age was to be accompanied by such heroes as General Charles George (Chinese) Gordon, General Herbert Horatio Kitchener of Khartoum renown, and Major General Sir Bindon Blood.

Throughout the years of the 1890s, there would be an attempt to

---

[7] Humble, *Aircraft Carriers, The Illustrated History*, 126.

immerse the minds of Great Britain's young men with the idea of a new imperialism and a pride in British military might. There were popular magazines such as *Chums, Pluck* and *Union Jack*. One issue of *Chums* contained the story "Storming the heights of Dargai," in regard to an incident in 1897 during the North-West Frontier Campaign in which a group of Highlanders rushed a Pathan position, spurred on by the playing of a wounded piper who was later awarded the Victoria Cross.[8] In 1903, Captain F.S. Brereton published *One of Our Fighting Scouts*. At the conclusion of the story, readers were urged "if it is your fortune to take a rifle and go forth to fight for your king and country — may you keep your face to the enemy and ride as boldly as did George Ransome, one of the Fighting Scouts."[9]

This state of mind would of course be subject to change. Even as British fighting men were engaged in combat during the colonial wars of the late nineteenth century, British society and parliamentary practices involving the use of donatives would begin to transform the British mind. This social tug of war, so to speak, can be best viewed during the years from 1868 through 1894, when Benjamin Disraeli and William Ewart Gladstone enjoyed a near dominance of the office of Prime Minister of England. Disraeli, as a conservative, was largely responsible for England's policies toward jingoism and nationalism. Conversely, Gladstone, as a liberal, would put forth many of the measures generally associated with a modern liberal society and was far more inclined toward keeping England out of Europe's affairs. During the years of Disraeli and Gladstone, many salutary laws would be passed in England, to include the Education Act of 1870, an act legalizing trade unions in 1871, as well as a public housing act, a health act and a factory act.

Gladstone and Disraeli would not be the last of England's political leaders to recognize the wants and needs of England's expanding electorate. Ironic it may be that at the dawn of the twentieth century,

---

[8] James, *Rise and Fall of the British Empire*, 207.
[9] Ibid, 209.

a man generally regarded as being a warmonger for much of his life would be instrumental in this continued change in English attitudes. This individual would of course be Winston Spencer Churchill. In the early years of the 1900s, while serving in the British Colonial Office, Churchill would urge South Africans to adopt a program for unemployment compensation. In December of 1907, in a letter from South Africa he would offer proposals for parliamentary bills establishing a minimum wage, insurance against sickness and old age pensions in England.[10] All of these are issues that concern the use of donatives. Furthermore, in the March 7, 1907 issue of the *Nation*, Churchill recommended that men without jobs be "treated as if they were hospital patients". He further urged that the economy of Great Britain be managed through a "network of state intervention and regulation." It is a famous Churchill quote from this period of his life that he saw "little glory in an Empire, which can rule the waves and is unable to flush its sewers."

If it can be stated that actions and reactions within a nation's borders may be relative to the rising or faltering fortunes of a society. It must also be realized that it can be the actions and events external to a society that may ultimately have the greater impact. Much the same as the Edwardian attitudes of Winston Churchill and his fellow Britain's were modifying from their old imperial views of the Victorian Era due to changes within British Society, it would be the events of 1914-1918 that would change the British Commonwealth forever.

It is interesting to note that much as the Roman regent of the Western Empire, Stilicho, had sought to secure Rome's borders through a process of coalitions to play off Roman enemies against each other, it had been the practice of British foreign policy to pursue a similar course. Examples of this can be seen during the time of William of Orange and the First Duke of Marlborough and the Wars of the Spanish Succession. We find it again during the Napoleonic Wars. Each time British forces would be used as part of a coalition;

---

[10] Manchester, *The Last Lion, Vol I*, 403.

each time the purpose of this coalition was to guarantee that no single power would control continental Europe. In this first example, this would be France under the Sun King Louis XIV; in the second, France under the Corsican Napoleon Bonaparte. It would be the example of 1914 to 1918 that would reveal to the world one of history's greatest misconceptions. What would this misconception be? With the surrender of the armed forces of the Kaiser Wilhelm I in November of 1918 and the subsequent Treaty of Versailles of 1919, the common perception was that the "war to end all wars" had left the allied powers pre-eminent and supreme. However, victory in the Great War had cost Great Britain, as well as the rest of the belligerent nations a very great deal. Financially, no combatant power had spent as much on the war as Great Britain. The British expenditure would come in at just under ten billion pounds.[11] Often times we hear of the generation of young men lost to Britain during World War I as the "lost generation." The death toll for the British Isles, not including her dominions, was around three quarters of a million men. This equates to one in sixteen of all British males between the ages of fifteen and fifty. Both of these costs, the financial and the human, would have extensive repercussions in the years between the two world wars.

Paying for the war would lead to a tenfold increase in Britain's national debt. The interest alone on that debt would consume close to half of total government spending by the middle of the 1920's. As a result of these severe economic restrictions, Britain, in regard to its military expenditures, would adopt the "Ten Year Rule." The basic premise behind this rule was the belief that the British Empire would not become engaged in any great war during the next ten years. This Ten Year Rule would be renewed every year until 1932. This is where we find the great irony. In 1919, with the annihilation of Germany as a maritime power and the scuttling of the High Seas Fleet in Scapa Flow, we find England with an overwhelming naval preponderance. At that time, Britain possessed forty-two capital ships; the rest of the

---

[11] Ferguson, *Empire*, 265.

world possessed forty-four. As the second largest naval power, the United States possessed sixteen.

In the use of tanks and armored warfare, we find Great Britain firmly in the lead. Yet all of this was to slip away. In the ten years from 1922 to 1932, the British defense budget would be cut by more than one-third. In contrast, Italian and French budgets would see an increase of 60 and 55 percent.[12] Within the British military the decision to motorize cavalry regiments was not made until 1937. When war was to break out with Germany again in 1939, the British artillerists would find themselves using an artillery model from 1905, with half the range of their German counterparts. Hence the great irony: the perception that Britain was all-powerful, and the stark reality that World War I had left the British Empire more vulnerable than ever before.

---

[12] Ibid, 273.

# Chapter 2

¤

# PACIFISM AND CONTEMPT

With all forms of democratic and republican governments, and in all eras, there seems to be a repeated insistence by the people within these societies to destroy that instrument which has purchased their freedoms, increased their power, their prestige and their wealth. This instrument of which I write is their respective militaries. The reasons for this may be many and varied. In some cases it may be due to a simple power struggle, civilian authority versus military rule. The history of mankind is inundated with examples of ambitious men using a nation's armed forces to gain control of their respective societies. Was it not Julius Caesar who put an end to the Roman Republic with the use of the tenth legion? It is interesting to note that one ambitious man with but a forty-five hundred-man army could bring an empire of twenty million inhabitants to its knees. Shortly thereafter, on February 15, 44 B.C., Caesar would be appointed dictator for life (dictator perpetuus). Approximately eighteen hundred years later, it would be one of the world's greatest soldiers, Napoleon Bonaparte, who would rise to the supremacy of Europe by use of a "whiff of grapeshot." This would occur on the night of October 4-5,1795 when, serving as Director of Military Plans at the Bureau Topographique, the young brigadier general would quell a right-wing coup in the streets of Paris using cannon. As a reward for his services, the French Directory would award him the rank of General de Division and give him command of the Arm'ee de l'interior. Shortly thereafter, on March 2, 1796, the twenty-seven year old Bonaparte would be appointed Commander-in-Chief of the Arm'ee de l'italie. It would be this command and the subsequent victories he would gain with it which would lead to a nearly twenty-year domination of Continental Europe.

Of course, these are only two of the more prominent examples of individuals employing their nation's military to rise to power. If we were to scan the entire length of recorded history, up to modern times in some of the less stable areas of the modern world such as the Middle-East and Africa, we could no doubt fill entire books, and no doubt entire volumes, with the stories and facts of the military coup.

There are other historical instances of military interference within government that give cause for alarm to these governments and to the governed. Perhaps one of the more notable, and more notorious, would be the Imperial Roman Praetorian Guard. First established under the Emperor Augustus as an elite bodyguard, the Praetorians would later increasingly wield political power in the appointments of emperors. Their rise to influence would begin under the direction of the prefect Aelius Sejanus during the reign of Tiberius. Their influence would end in the year 312 A.D. when Constantine the Great would rout the armies of his rival Maxentius at the Battle of the Milvian Bridge. The list of injuries perpetrated by the Praetorian Guard is long. The list of the injuries caused by the Praetorians with regard to the issue of financial gain is probably just as long. On January 24, 41 A.D., the Emperor Caligula, of whom history does not speak well, would be the first of the Imperial Roman Emperors to be assassinated by the Praetorians. This plot against Caligula would teach all future conspirators a very valuable lesson: before all else, establish the support of the Praetorian Guard.

This lesson was almost immediately seized upon by Caligula's uncle, Claudius. Popular legend has it that the Praetorian Guard, after having dispensed with Caligula, discovered Claudius hiding behind a curtain and declared him the new emperor. The historical truth is no doubt more complicated and prosaic. Shortly after the assassination of Caligula, the Roman Senate convened a meeting at which proposals for a return to Republican government were entertained. However, most, if not all of the Praetorian privileges were owed to the imperial system. One can therefore conclude that a return to senatorial rule would not be in their best interest.

Praetorian involvement in the death of Caligula and the naming of Claudius as emperor was to be only the beginning of a lengthy Praetorian involvement in Imperial Roman politics. During the year of the four emperors in 68-69 A.D., the Praetorian Guard would initially support the seventy year old Galba. This support would last only until Galba, confronted with the less than desirable state of Roman finances, cancelled loyalty payments promised to the Praetorians for their support. On December 15, 68 A.D. the Praetorian Guard along with other elements of the Roman Army would declare Otho the new emperor. The emperorship of Otho would last only three months, as Aulus Vitellius would form a coalition of legions from Rome's Rhine command and defeat the forces of Otho at the Battle of Bedriacum, outside present day Cremona. Within months, on July 1, 69 A.D., Vespasian would be proclaimed emperor by the Roman armies occupying Egypt, Judea and Syria. These armies would be followed by the Balkan legions in the provinces of Pannonia, Illyricum and Moesia. In short order Vespasian's men would secure Rome, stab Vitellius to death, cast his body into the river Tiber and secure for Vespasian the emperorship of Imperial Rome. It may be found both interesting and sad that the society which was able to produce great citizen soldiers such as Cincinnatus and the Scipios during the years of the Roman Republic, would find itself possessor of individuals who would increasingly come to rely on the Praetorian Guard and the Roman legions as power brokers. It is noteworthy that Vespian himself dated his rule not from any date when the people of Rome or the senate voted for his confirmation, but rather as from July 69 A.D., when he was proclaimed emperor by his troops.

As often happens when individuals or groups of individuals are given power, their next desire seems to be to acquire even more power. And so it was to be with the Praetorians. On the last day of 192 A.D., the emperor Commodus, son of Marcus Aurelius, was reputedly poisoned by his wife, Marcia. In the power vacuum that followed, the Praetorian Guard would overplay its hand as power broker. Due in large part to the fact that the murder of Commodus was unorganized and an impromptu event, there existed no plan for succession in advance. Thus it would be the elderly Helvius Pertinax, twice consul of Rome and a general of Marcus Aurelius, who would be approached for the job of emperor. His appointment would follow on New Year's Day 193 A.D.[13] His appointment would prove to be very brief, ending after only eighty-six days. As emperor he proved to be a severe disciplinarian, never a popular thing. In addition, the Praetorians were very resentful that palace staff were responsible for the removal of an emperor whose behavior and eccentricities had worked to their advantage. In March of 193 A.D., a group of 300 Praetorians stormed the imperial palace and killed Pertinax. In the days which followed, as once again there existed no plan for succession, the royal diadem would basically be placed up for auction. The winner of this auction would prove to be a very wealthy senator named Didius Julianus. All that would be necessary for Julianus to acquire the emperorship of Rome would be a much larger accession donativum than his rivals. The tradition of emperors offering a donativum to the Praetorians and to the legions had existed since the time of Tiberius. However, these circumstances were different, would prove to be far more openly corrupt, and would prove to have severe consequences to both Didius Julianus and his Praetorian conspirators.

The events that were to follow the succession of Didius Julianus were much the same as those of the succession of Galba during the year of the four emperors in 68-69 A.D. Shortly after Julianus was appointed as emperor, three provisional governors, all with the

---

[13] Potter, *Emperors of Rome*, 138

support of the respective legions in their respective provinces, would claim the throne of Rome. Of the three, Clodius Albinus in Britain, Pescennius Niger in Syria and Septimus Severus on the Danube in central Europe, Severus would find the most support, as the armies on the Danube consisted of ten legions. On April 9, 193 A.D., Severus would be proclaimed emperor at Carnuntum, in what is now lower Austria. Given that Severus possessed clear superiority in terms of the number of legions he controlled, there was probably little that Didius Julianus could do. He was soon to be dispatched by a member of the Praetorian Guard. In this instance, their betrayal of an emperor would do them no good. Soon after his consolidation of power in Rome, Septimus Severus would dismiss them and appoint members of his army of the Danube to replace them. If we are to consult the work of Edward Gibbon, we find it written in Chapter Five of his multi-volume, *Decline and Fall of the Roman Empire*, that "the Praetorians had violated the sanctity of the throne by the atrocious murder of Pertinax; they dishonoured the majesty of it by their subsequent conduct."

Given this almost continuous habit of Praetorian interference within the political spheres of Rome, and given that the Praetorian Guard was derived from the Roman armies, and as such closely associated by the populace with it, can there be any doubt as to why eventually the Roman people would come to resent the very institution which made them great, which engineered their transportation systems, viaducts and public water supplies and maintained the frontier garrisons which would protect them from the barbarian tribes?

This resent of military institutions may be more evident when viewing the composition and numbers of troops maintained by Rome during the Republic through the time of the principate and thence to final collapse. While it is a commonly known and recognized historical fact of Rome's sack at the hands of Alaric in 410 A.D. and its eventual destruction again in 476 A.D., what many people may not be as familiar with is the rise and fall of Rome's military fortunes centuries before that. During Rome's formative years, shortly after conquering the Etruscan city of Beii in 396 B.C., Italy would be invaded by a horde of Gauls, barbarous souls of Celtic origins. In the year 390 B.C., Rome would send its entire army, at that time a force of some 15,000 men, to confront this danger.[14] This force would be completely destroyed by the Gaullic army, which was twice its size. Shortly thereafter, the now defenseless city would endure a general massacre and be burnt to the ground.

Nevertheless, Roman arms would soon recover from this disaster. Rallied by Marcus Furius Camillus, the city would be rebuilt. In the year 378 B.C., the Servian Walls would be built to protect the city. This initial protective structure would stand twelve feet high and enclose roughly 1,000 acres. From the time of the construction of the Servian Wall, Rome itself would not fall to a foreign conqueror for a period of eight hundred years.

During the decades and centuries to follow, Roman military fortunes would continue to rise and fall, always after each fall to rise again to greater glory. During the Samnite Wars, which lasted more than forty years, Rome would suffer some very humiliating defeats, such as at the Battle of the Caudine Forks in 321 B.C., after which Rome was forced to accept an armistice under very unfavorable terms. They would suffer defeat again at Lautulae in 316 B.C. These defeats however, would lead to a complete reorganization of the Roman military system and the construction of the Via Appia in 312 B.C., thus giving the Romans a logistical advantage over all of their Latin enemies.

These military reorganizations would serve Rome well in the future. In the year 310 B.C., a Roman army under the command of Q. Fabius Rullianus would defeat the Etruscans at the Battle of Lake Vadimo. In 309 B.C., L. Papirius Cursor would defeat a Samnite army in the decisive battle of the war at Bovianum. Due to these victories all of Rome's enemies would be forced to make peace in the year 304 B.C.

This peace, brought about by the use of Roman arms, would prove

---

[14] Rodgers, *Ancient Rome*, 25.

to be short lived. During the years 298 to 290 B.C., Rome would be confronted by a revolt and forced to fight against a combined army of Gauls, Umbrians, Etruscans and Samnites. In the year 293 B.C., these combined forces would be defeated by Manius Curuis Dentatus at the Battle of Aquilonia. It is interesting to note that in a farsighted diplomatic move, in recognition of their gallantry, the Samnites would be permitted to enter into the Roman confederation with the status of allies, and not as a conquered peoples.

This pattern of defeat, frustration, and ultimate victory would continue for Rome in its next series of contests for the domination for the Italian peninsula. In the years 285 B.C. to 282 B.C., there would be another revolt, this time of Etruscans and Gauls, and another Roman defeat, at Arretium in 285 B.C. Once again, Rome would reverse its fortunes, and victories would be won at Lake Vadimo in 283 B.C. and at Populonia in 282 B.C.

Within one year of the end of final Etruscan resistance, Rome would again find itself at war, this time against the city-states of Tarentum and Epirus. The Epirote king, Pyrrhus, with his twenty thousand infantry, three thousand cavalry, and a very judicious use of war elephants, would establish himself as master of the Greek cities of Southern Italy. He would inflict on Roman arms successive defeats at the Battle of Heraclae in 280 B.C., and again at the Battle of Asculum in the year 279 B.C. At each of these battles, though victorious, Pyrrhus would lose a sizeable contingent of his men.

It is reputed that after Heraclea, with the loss of eleven thousand men, that Pyrrhus is supposed to have said: "One more such victory and I am lost." It is from the Battles of Heraclae and Asculum that the term, "Pyrrhic victory" was derived. These losses in battle would cause Pyrrhus to spend the years 278 to 276 B.C. in Sicily. Upon his return to Italy in 275 B.C., Pyrrhus would be forced to meet another Roman army, commanded by the earlier victor at Aquilonia, Manius Currus Dentatus. At this battle, Beneventum, Roman arms would prevail. Pyrrhus would soon depart for Greece. Upon his departure, it is alleged that Pyrrhus would exclaim: "What a fine field of battle I leave here for Rome and Carthage."[15]

If not successful in his war against Rome, Pyrrhus was most certainly correct in his prediction of future conflict between the two Mediterranean powers. Within one decade of Pyrrhus' defeat at Beneventum, the First Punic War would erupt.

It would be during the years of the three Punic Wars that Rome would continue its ascension to domination of the Mediterranean world. The pattern of military success and military defeat would continue with Roman arms securing great victories while at the same time suffering humiliating defeats. Interestingly, the origins of these Punic Wars did not originate with a direct contest between Rome and Carthage. Rather, the initial stages of this war would begin with a contest between the Mamertines of Messana and the forces of Hiero II of Syracuse. It is also interesting to note that while Rome is usually regarded as a land-based military power, that this first Punic War would see the rise of Rome as a naval power. After some initial success on land at the outbreak of hostilities between the two Mediterranean powers, Rome and Carthage, Rome would suffer an initial naval defeat at the Battle of the Lipara Islands in 260 B.C. However, within this same year, a new Roman naval squadron under the command of C. Dullius would win a decisive victory over the Carthaginian fleet at the Battle of Mylae. This victory would wrest control of the seas from the Carthaginians. Four years later an entire fleet of 330 Roman vessels under the consuls M. Atulius Regulus and L. Mantius Volso would depart from Sicily with a force of 150,000 soldiers with the intention of invading Africa.[16] This fleet would defeat a Carthaginian fleet of 350 ships in a hard fought battle off the coast of Sicily. These naval victories for Rome could be attributed to the Roman tendency toward innovation and to one of history's first truly "secret" weapons. Realizing that Roman vessels were not as maneuverable as those of Carthage, and that the Roman sailors did not have the maritime skills of their Carthaginian enemies, the

---

[15] Dupuy, *Encyclopedia of Military History*, 59.
[16] Ibid, 61.

Romans simply decided to create an environment at which they excelled, to basically create land war at sea. In order to do this they began a crash shipbuilding program by copying examples of the Carthaginian quinquireme. Additionally, a corvus (raven) was added to the Roman vessels near the bow of the Roman galleys. This corvus, a combination between a grappling hook and a gangway, was simply a narrow bridge approximately twenty feet long. When a Roman vessel engaged a Carthaginian counterpart, this corvus could be pivoted around and released to come crashing down onto the enemy deck where it would be held in place by a large spike attached to its underside. This would allow a boarding party of Roman soldiers and sailors to enter onto the enemy vessel and to basically fight a land war on the enemy vessel. So as to assist in this process, fighting turrets were installed fore and aft of the Roman vessels, thus allowing additional soldiers and sailors armed with missile weapons to assist the boarding party while at the same time discouraging enemy attempts at boarding their own ship. Additionally, Roman fleets adopted the habit of castrementation to their naval tactics. Basically, the Roman fleets would be beached at shore every night so as to protect them from storm damage. An entrenched camp was then constructed on the shoreward side so as to protect both men and vessels.

As the fortunes of Roman armies ebbed and flowed on land, so this same pattern would mirror Roman naval fortunes as well. After the victories at Mylae in 260 B.C., and at Cape Ecnomus in 256 B.C., a Roman fleet of 364 ships would be caught in a storm between Africa and Sicily, losing 284 ships and costing Rome approximately 100,000 of its best soldiers and sailors. In the year 249 B.C. another Roman fleet of 200 warships would suffer a defeat at the Battle of Drepanum. Just before this battle the Roman consul P. Claudius Pucher is said to have attempted to invoke the blessing of the gods by placing sacred chickens on deck, where they were supposed to eat grain placed before them as a favorable omen. When they refused to eat, Claudius had them thrown overboard with the comment "Then let them drink."[17] During the battle, the Roman fleet was defeated with the loss of 93 ships and twenty-eight thousand casualties; eight thousand killed, twenty thousand captured. Perhaps the historical lesson for Claudius Pucher would be to pay less attention to omens and more attention to sacred chickens.

Ultimate victory in the First Punic War would certainly come to Rome. At the Battle of the Aegates Islands in 241 B.C., Rome would secure the ultimate victory when its navy would defeat a Carthaginian fleet of 200 ships in Sicilian waters. In this battle, 70 Carthaginian ships would be captured and 50 of them sunk. As a result, Carthage would be forced to make peace, Sicily would become a possession of Rome and Carthage would agree to pay an indemnity of 3,200 talents (95 million) over ten years.

The conditions of this imposed Peace would ultimately prove to be somewhat more than the Carthaginians could stand, much the same as the peace imposed upon Germany by the victorious allies with the Versailles Treaty of 1919. In the latter case, upon hearing the terms of the imposed peace, Marshall Ferdinand Foch would observe; "This is not peace. It is an armistice for twenty years."[18] In the case of the former, it would be exactly twenty-two years before the re-opening of hostilities in the year 219 B.C. Rome would find in this second Punic War its greatest enemy, Hannibal Barca. Rome would also experience two of its greatest defeats, at the Battle of Lake Trasimene in April of 217 B.C., and again at Cannae in August of 216 B.C. At Lake Trasimene, about 30,000 Roman troops were killed or captured, including their commander Gauis Flaminius. At Cannae, approximately 60,000 Romans, again to include their commander Aemilius Paulus, lay dead on the field at the conclusion of the battle. Never before, nor since, has a nation or state survived after such crushing defeats in rapid succession. Having lost the first three major battles of the war at Trebia, Lake Trasimene and Cannae, and having lost such large numbers of troops should have spelled the demise of

---

[17] Ibid, 61.
[18] Dupuy, *Military Heritage of America*, 409.

the Roman state. However, the opposite would prove true. Upon hearing of the disaster at Cannae, although there most assuredly must have been more than a few faint hearts, Rome as a whole determined to persevere towards victory. The Roman Senate would appoint M. Julius Pera as dictator. All able-bodied Roman men were to be mobilized, regardless of age or occupation. A new field commander, Marcus Claudius Marcellus, would be appointed. Within a year of the disaster at Cannae, Rome would have a new army in the field comprised of 140,000 soldiers. With these new troops, Marcellus would force Hannibal with his 40,000-50,000 troops into a stalemate in Campania. Within two years, Roman armies would grow to 200,000 men. With these armies, Rome would devise a new tactic against its most feared enemy, to engage in a war of attrition.

These years of crisis for Rome would also lead to the emergence of one of its greatest soldiers, Publius Cornelius Scipio, known to history as "Africanus." Scipio Africanus' father, Publius Scipio, had been killed in 211 B.C. during a battle in the Upper Boetis Valley in Spain, fighting against Hannibal's brother, Hasdrubal. Upon Publius Scipio's death, his 25-year-old son was sent to assume command of Rome's armies in Spain. Within two years, the younger Scipio would re-establish Rome's dominance in Spain and would capture the Carthaginian capital of New Carthage. In the year 204 B.C., the younger Scipio, as proconsul, would sail for Africa with a magnificently trained and equipped army of 30,000 men. Two years later, Scipio would meet and defeat Rome's greatest enemy at the Battle of Zama. During this battle, 20,000 Carthaginians would be killed and 15,000 would be taken prisoner. As a result of this victory, Carthage would be forced to agree to another peace. The terms of this peace were such that Carthage would surrender all of its warships and war elephants. In addition, Carthage would agree to pay Rome 10,000 talents or around 300 million, over a period of fifty years. Also, the terms of the peace included a concession that Carthage could not make war without the permission of Rome. As for Rome's feared enemy, Hannibal, upon accusations by Rome that he was planning to violate the provisions of peace, in 196 B.C., he would flee Carthage.

While being pursued by the Romans in Bithynia in the year 183 B.C., Hannibal committed suicide; thus ending any serious threat to Roman control of the Mediterranean world.

The third and final Punic War would occur during the years 149-146 B.C. As compared with the previous wars between Rome and Carthage, this war would prove to be very ephemeral. The war would begin as a local contest between Carthage and the aged Numidian King Massinissa. Intervention by Rome, led by Carthage hater Marcus Porcius Cato, was to include terms that Carthage surrender hostages to Rome; that it would disarm and dismantle the city's fortifications. The final demand provided that the city be abandoned and the population moved inland. It would be this final demand that would give rise to war.

Perhaps this war should be noted for only two reasons. First, its brevity, and secondly, for the appearance of another of history's great citizen soldiers, Publius Scipio Aemilianus, adopted grandson of Scipio Africanus. In the year 147 B.C., Scipio Aemilianus would begin a land and naval blockade of the city of Carthage. One year later, an all out assault of the city would take place. When all was said and done, nine-tenths of the Carthaginian populace would perish by means of battle, starvation, or disease. By order of the Roman Senate, and against the advice of Scipio, the city would be completely destroyed and its remaining populace sold into slavery. Most assuredly this would be the reason for the historical term "Carthaginian Peace."

Albeit, in another of history's great ironies, victory in the Punic Wars would bring about conditions which would contribute to the end of the Roman Republic. Beginning in the mid-second century B.C., there would exist the beginnings of a serious decline in Roman military capabilities. This decline would be accompanied and perhaps caused by political, social and economic unrest. In the political sphere, the Roman Senate was not yet familiar with the policies needed to govern the newly acquired empire. In its administration, inefficiencies were rampant and corruption was rife. In the social sphere, large estates, made possible by the slave labor acquired by

*Greatest soldier of his age: Publius Cornelius Scipio Africanus and his Carthaginian opponent Hannibal just before the Battle of Zama in 202 B.C. In 190 B.C. Rome would lose his services after he was falsely accused of misappropriating booty from the army's campaigns in Syria.*

military contest, replaced the small farm and the sturdy peasantry which had constituted the backbone of the Roman military system. These newly pauperized citizens would be forced to either relocate to the cities and become partially dependent on handouts from the state, or they could join the newly formed professional armies. Basically, there would be a transformation from citizen soldier to mercenary army.

These new soldiers of the late Republic lacked the traditional Roman discipline. They generally owed their allegiance to their commanding generals, and were motivated simply by financial gain rather than patriotic ardor or loyalty to the state.

This decline in martial ability would lead to a near collapse of law and order, repeated slave insurrections, to an increase and near domination of the Mediterranean by pirates, and to civil strife and political discord. Some of the historical events accompanying these societal tendencies were the Servile Wars of 135 to 132 B.C., the assassinations of all three of the adopted grandsons of the conqueror of Zama; first, Tiberius Gracchus in 133 B.C., then of Scipio Aemilianus and Gaius Gracchus, as well as the revolt of the Italian allies such as the Fregellae in 124 B.C.

It would be during the years at the beginning of the first century B.C. that we find a transformation of Roman arms from a multi-based system dependent upon the citizen soldier to the more mercenary concept of a standing professional army. During the years 109-104 B.C., there would occur a migration of Cimbri and Teutones south from modern day Switzerland into Southern Gaul. In response to this perceived invasion, Rome would send an army of 80,000 men to confront it. This army, commanded by M. Junius Silanus, would be nearly annihilated at the Battle of Arausio. This battle would prove to be one of the worst disasters to ever befall Roman arms, as nearly forty thousand non-combatants would be killed in addition to the loss of most of its army.[19]

As a response to this defeat, another successful Roman general, the man who had led Roman arms to victory during the Jugurthine War of 112-106 B.C., would institute a series of military reforms. Gaius Marius, a former tax collector-turned soldier would be made consul of Rome in the year 104 B.C. Using the sweeping power he was given, he altered the composition of the Roman legion by introducing the cohort consisting of six centuries. He established the tradition of presenting each legion with a silver eagle, an emblem, which in the future would become of tremendous importance. In addition, he abolished the system of property qualifications, thus opening the ranks of the Roman legions to the landless poor. He adopted the pilum, or throwing spear, with a soft neck that would bend on impact, thus rendering an enemy's shield useless. It would be during these reforms that a complete and revised manual of drill regulations would be created by one of Marius' colleagues, Publius Rufus. Also, the previous aristocratic distinctions between militia classes would be abolished, as were distinctions of age and experience.

The reorganization and transformation of Roman arms would take

---

[19] Dupuy, *Encyclopedia of Military History*, 91.

place in the army cavalry contingent as well. The old Roman cavalry, consisting of equites or nobility was to disappear from the scene. It would be replaced by cavalry units recruited from Rome's allies, with a heavy reliance placed upon mercenaries. During the years of Marius, the cavalry units would come mostly from Thrace and Africa, sometimes from Spain. During the Gallic wars of Julius Caesar, the cavalry contingent would consist mostly of Gallic and German mercenaries.

These military reforms would also have an impact on the overall structure of Roman society. Whereas in earlier times the Roman legionary had been a landholder, now the average legionary was an Italian peasant or lower-class city dweller. If one desires to have larger armies, then it becomes of necessity to have a larger population from which to draw recruits. Hence, the granting of the franchise and the giving of citizen status to all Italians had received much of its initial impetus by Marius. This practice could be compared with the desire to have large numbers of immigrants move into an industrial society so as to provide labor for the factories.

The results that these military reforms on Rome's military institutions would be dramatic. During the years of Rome's rise to pre-eminence in the Mediterranean world, Roman armies would expect success due to five factors. These factors included: regularity, discipline, training, flexibility and a firm reliance on the efficacy of taking the offensive during campaigns. Also, since the average legionary was a land-owning Roman citizen, there could always be expected of him a high degree of patriotism and loyalty to the state. In contrast, upon completion of the Marian reforms, the legionary who in the past owed his allegiance almost exclusively to the state, now tended to owe it to his general or commander. Much of the former discipline was now gone. During the years of the militia system, there existed a higher level of competence within military leadership. Under the more professional system created by Marius, military leadership was often granted to professional politicians who avoided the hardship of the campaigns experienced by the legionaries and junior officers. This created a lack of experience within the upper ranks of command. In addition, due to the fact that most troops were now recruited from the lower elements of society, there existed a general lack of trustworthiness in them, and a lack of confidence between the commander and the commanded. In turn, this lack of mutual confidence led to a tendency for the legion to fight in a more defensive posture, the grouping of troops in tighter formation. This led to a decrease in the tactical superiority of the legion over its oftentimes more numerous enemies, and as a result contributed to a number of Roman defeats.

In the centuries to follow, this decline in the martial and moral health of the late republic, and later the principate, would prove to have dramatic repercussions. Primarily, the cost of maintaining large standing armies, as opposed to reliance upon a strong militia system, eventually leads to a necessary reduction in the size of one's armies. As early as the reign of Augustus, due in large part to the limited finances available to the principate, the standing army was limited to 25 legions. With this force comprising roughly of 300,000 men, Rome had to defend a frontier of nearly 4,000 miles. This simple financial fact would create a certain dilemma of defense. Should the Roman armies be preclusive, preventing invasion by using all available manpower on a heavily fortified border, or should there be a firm reliance on the defense in depth. This concept of a defense in depth was subject to a certain Achilles heel. At that time, a Roman legion with all its armaments and baggage could march only about fifteen miles per day. Any event on the Rhine frontier would necessitate a 67-day march from Rome. A similar journey to Antioch in the east would require a journey of 124 days. Fortunately for Imperial Rome, throughout the years of the Pax Romana, roughly 1-200 A.D., no great threat to Roman military supremacy existed. It was during these times that one could boast that a typical Roman citizen had no more need of arms when close to the frontier than they did amongst the streets of Rome itself.

This scenario would certainly change. In response to this dilemma of defense, static defense or defense in depth, a new military system would arise during the years of the tetrarchy. This transformation would come in the form of the creation of distinct separation of troops into two different categories; the limitanei, lightly armed garrison troops along the frontiers, and the comitatenses, heavily armed and superior mobile troops. Of course the issue here would be multi-faceted. The reasons for much of Rome's success, the legion as a fighting unit, the iron discipline and the leadership of the centurions, the advantage in weapons, the pilum and the gladius, were all to be discontinued within the Roman military establishment. The new legions, instead of being the self-sufficient unit of the past, would be reduced from 5,000 men with auxiliary cavalry, to a unit of about 1,000 men. On paper, this would give the appearance of martial strength. The reality of course, would be much different. Also, the quality of the legionary would be much diminished.

After the opening of the ranks to all classes of citizenry during the Marian Reforms, and with the tendency to recruit more and more troops from within the captured provinces, true Romans just simply lost the interest and the inclination to serve. The concept that if a country is worth living in, it is worth fighting for, vanished. During the Punic Wars, Rome was consistently able to recruit armies of 40,000 to 80,000 men, even after huge losses and repeated defeats. If an army was lost, Rome simply recruited a new one. Yet, when Aetius met Attila at Chalons sur Marne in 450 A.D., the Roman army consisted of about 40,000 men and Aetius was forced to rely on his Visogothic allies and their King Theodoric to succeed in this battle. When Attila returned to invade Italy one year later, Aetius had no troops at all.

It is interesting to note that when Rome was sacked in 410 A.D., it would be at the hands of the Visogoths, troops formerly in the pay of the Roman emperor. This policy of relying on foederati (those who have made foedus or treaty), was no doubt a direct attempt to circumvent the problem that most true Romans were disinclined to defend themselves. Initially, this policy was successful to some extent. However, the problems with this policy were soon to become evident and acute. During the reign of Constantine, so many German foederati were allowed to join the Palantinae, which replaced the old Praetorian Guard, that Constantine was accused of "barbarizing" the

*The Roman Empire at its height with the destruction of its legions and its farms*

army. It would not be until the aftermath of Andrianople in 378 A.D., that the real impact of this policy would be recognized.

During the years of the late fourth century A.D., due to pressure for available land in Ukraine and in response to a migration of the Huns from Eastern Asia, the Ostrogoths themselves migrated into the Roman Empire in 376 A.D. In response to this latest migration and invasion, the emperor Valens led an army of 60,000 men to confront an army of Visogoth-Ostrogoth warriors, numbering somewhere between 100,000 and 200,000 men. If Valens, emperor of the Eastern Roman Empire, had awaited the arrival of the Western emperor Gratian and his army, all might have been well.

However, on August 9, 378 A.D., Valens unwisely attacked the larger Gothic army. The outcome of this battle was a total defeat for the Roman army, with Valens himself being among the 40,000 Roman dead. This last great climatic defeat of the legions would force the new Roman emperor of the east, Theodosius, into a policy of appeasement. Accordingly, the Visogoths were allowed to settle in Pannonia, the Ostrogoths in Moesia. As a result of Roman losses at Adrianople, Theodosius would allow Goths into the Roman army, not in small groups, but rather in the form of entire tribes. In addition, they would be commanded not by Roman officers, but rather by their own chieftains, men like Alaric, Gaiseric, Recimer, and Odovacer. Whereas Armenius had betrayed Rome in 9 A.D. and destroyed the three legions of Augustus at the Tuetoberg Forest, these new foreign warriors would extinguish the Western Roman Empire, as well as the light of the western world.

To many, this cycle of military reform and misfortune would seem as an isolated incident that transpired many centuries ago, and hence not relevant to the affairs of our time. However, to those more familiar with military affairs, there are certain historical tendencies which give cause for alarm. Often times, it is the perception of weakness, as much as weakness itself that may cause a hostile nation to attack one of its neighboring states. Just as the barbarian tribes of the Roman world would act upon the perception of Roman weakness, so also do modern peoples and states. In the years prior to the events of 1939-1945, it would be the failures of British and French diplomacy and the adopted policy of appeasement that would lend impetus to the actions of the nazi and fascist regimes of Germany and Italy. In the years between the two world wars, many steps had been taken to avert another such conflict. Yet the Washington Naval Treaty of 1922, the Kellogg-Briand Pact of August 1928, and the Locarno Conference of October 1925, all helped to guarantee the eventuality of future war.

In addition, diplomatic and policy failures would be compounded by a complete disregard by the governments of the western democracies to ensure that the armed forces of their nations maintained levels of discipline and élan, which would allow them to engage their future enemies on equal terms. Just as Rome had deluded itself into believing that watering down its legions with the creation of the limitanei, that relaxing the iron discipline of the republican armies, that opening the ranks of the legions to all and any who would don the uniform of the legionary, and that creating fictitious lists of non-existent legions would save them from their enemies, so too would the western democracies learn this lesson prior to the events of 1939. France was regarded as having the largest and most modern army in the world prior to World War II. Yet the refusal of the French government to expel the Wehrmacht from the Rhineland in March 1936 only confirmed what Adolf Hitler already suspected, that the French army was largely a paper tiger and that it could be beaten, with the German army and air force needing but forty-three days to do so.

Great Britain would be guilty of many of the same sins as well. In the aftermath of the Washington Naval Treaty, Britain would enter into the Anglo-German Naval agreement, a diplomatic maneuver that would allow Germany to build certain types of warships, to include submarines, at levels not to exceed 35 percent of British naval tonnage. This move helped to estrange France from Britain. During the 1935 Ethiopian Crisis, which followed the Italian invasion of that African nation, Britain would assume guidance of the League of Nations. However, the British refusal to impose any meaningful sanctions (such as those on oil), would signal a failure of British resolve as well. Moreover, the willingness of Prime Minister Neville Chamberlain to allow the amputation of the Sudetanland from Czechoslovakia in 1938 announced to the world just how severely the island nation had slumped into a pacifistic dream. With little or no army and a fleet of aging warships, the results were inevitable.

During the years of crisis between 1919 and 1939, America was not without its share of guilt along these lines. With the failure of Congress to recognize the significance of Woodrow Wilson's Fourteen Points and its refusal to join the League of Nations, the stage was set for future hostilities. When Brigadier General William Mitchell challenged traditional military views held by the army and naval hierarchy and advocated for the expansion of American airpower, he was first demoted to colonel and later court-martialed by order of President Coolidge. Mitchell would subsequently be found guilty, suspended from rank and removed from duty for a period of five years. On December 7, 1941, it would be Japanese airpower that would eliminate American naval power in the Pacific.

Then again there were the Nye Committee Munitions Investigations from 1934-1936. This series of investigations portrayed to the American public that U.S. entry into World War I had been to save the banking and business sectors and to protect the arms trade. Although largely fictitious, they did assist in driving America into a deeper form of isolation. The Nye Committee Munitions Investigations were accompanied by the Neutrality Act of April 1935, which forbade Americans from furnishing arms or loans to belligerent nations, including those that would in the future be the victims of Nazi and fascist aggression. American isolationism and pacifism was so entrenched during the inter-war years that in September of 1941, two years after the beginning of World War II and two months before the Japanese attack on Pearl Harbor, that the Renewal of Selective Service Act passed the House of Representatives by a single vote.

There is also the issue of American attitudes toward the U.S. military following the Cold War and during the more recent war on terrorism. To consult the works of Theodor Mommsen and his epic, *The History of Rome*, we find that just prior to the end of the Roman republic there existed an all out assault on Roman agriculture by the forces of commerce. We find also that around this time true Romans were becoming less concerned with their own defense and increasingly larger numbers of their Latin allies were being allowed into the legions at a ratio of almost two to one. We also know that by the time of Hadrian, only one in one hundred legionaries was a true Roman. Is this trend any different than what we see in America today, where only one percent of American youth choose to serve in the military? There is the assault on discipline as well. At those institutions where our officer corps is trained, such as at West Point and the Virginia Military Institute, the intense physical training and the iron discipline of the past are now swept away under the pretense of sexual equality and technological advancement. The ordeal of basic training that was once used to indoctrinate the common enlistee is also gone, replaced by something both shorter in longevity and abbreviated in discipline as well.

Of concern also must be the policies of the civilian government, which not only decides how large our armed forces will be and how they will be equipped, but also where and when they will be employed. Rome and England exhausted themselves with endless cycles of conquest and war. In the twentieth century the involvement of the First and Second World Wars has led to conflicts in Korea, Vietnam, and Kuwait, as well as Afghanistan and Iraq after the terrorist attacks of September 11, 2001. In the twenty-first century, as we see the emergence of China as a first class power, with other heavily populated nations such as India following suit, our own legislative bodies are emulating the French government of the 1930s and issues such as weapons procurement now take a back seat to issues such as open homosexuality being condoned within the battalions of the Army and Marine Corps. If historical precedent is any indication of our fate, one must be concerned.

# Chapter 3

¤

# GREAT BRITAIN'S ROMAN EXPERIENCE

It is perhaps another one of history's great ironies that a colony of the world's first great republican empire would over the course of several centuries become the second such empire. After the light was extinguished in the Western world in 476 A.D., it would take a very long time for another nation to become as commercially successful, and as militarily predominant as ancient Rome. While the first empire was Peninsular, its offspring would be insular. While the predecessor would prove to be a land-based military power with a strong navy when needed, the second would be a naval power with a strong land army, when needed. Both would prove to be commercially successful and would rely heavily on colonies, both for imports and exports. Both would engage in the use of slavery. In time, each would become progressively liberal in their respective governing policies. Each would, in time, grant an increasing level of self-government to those colonies, regardless if they were acquired by conquest or by alliance. Both, over time, would become familiar with the exorbitant cost associated with empire building and of defending these colonies in the military sphere. They would also be faced with a similar challenge to authority from these colonies and would become familiar with the challenges of nationalism within populations that were largely multi-cultural. While the one would enjoy domination of the western world for several centuries, the other would only enjoy this status for several decades. This second empire would, of course, be the empire of Great Britain.

In the aftermath of Rome, and from within its fragments, there would be those who would attempt to resuscitate western civilization. All would meet with varying levels of success. Most were either unsuccessful in their efforts, or their success would prove to be short-lived, or even stillborn. Most, if vaguely known to history, have long since been forgotten. A few, however, are worthy of mention for their efforts. Within the same generation of those who would see Rome's eventual fall, one man, Clovis, King of the Salian Franks, would become the founder of one of the nations known to us to this day; this nation being present-day France. Fifteen years after the final destruction of the Christian city, Clovis would come to inherit the throne of his father, Childeric. Clovis' grandfather, Meroveus, had fought with Aetius at the battle of Chalons. Clovis himself would grow to become a gifted soldier. Due to his admiration of Roman military systems, he would instill in the comparatively small Frankish armies a greater degree of order and discipline than could be found in the armies of his opponents. After an initial conflict with Syagrius, a holdover from the old Western Roman Empire who had established himself as a ruler of North Gaul, Clovis would form an alliance with the brother rulers of Burgundy, Gundobar and Godegesil.

As a means of cementing this alliance, Clovis would marry Clotilda, niece of the two Burgundian brothers. At this time, the Franks were still pagan in their worship. The Burgundians, however, were Catholic. In time, Clotilda would facilitate Clovis' conversion to Catholic Christianity. This would in time prove to be a matter of great political importance, since it would gain for him much popular support in his later conquest of Gallo-Roman Gaul.

In the year 496 A.D., the Ripuarian Franks would call upon Clovis to assist them during an Alemanni invasion of the Kingdom of Cologne. At the Battle of Tolbiac, Clovis would break the power of the Alemanni west of the Rhine River. His actual conversion to Catholic Christianity is by legend attributed to this battle, as Clovis called upon Clotilda's God during a critical juncture during this campaign.

In the year 500 A.D., Clovis would be called upon to intervene during a dispute between his wife's uncles, the Burgundians Gundobar and Godegesil. Choosing to act on behalf of the latter, Clovis would defeat Gundobar at Ouche. Following a prolonged siege of Gundobar at Avignon, and possibly due to other issues of greater importance, Clovis would grant peace without final conquest. As a condition of peace, the Burgundians would become nominal vassals of the Salian king.

In the years to come, Clovis would continue to war against the Alemanni, eventually breaking their power east of the Rhine River. In the year 507 A.D., Clovis and his Frankish army would find themselves again at war, this time with the Visogoth's of Alaric II of Toulouse. Although outnumbered by the more numerous Visogoth's, due to superior discipline and training, Clovis would prove triumphant with a victory at Vouille. By this victory, Frankish authority would be extended as far south as the Pyrenees. In addition, another implication from this victory was the assurance that Catholicism would prove triumphant over Arianism in Western Europe.

For a period of roughly one hundred years, Frankish expansion would continue unabated. This would prove to be possible through a combination of military prowess, able leadership, amazing vigor and a continued level of support from Clovis' fellow-catholic Gallo-Roman allies. In addition, it can be noted that very much unlike the invasions of the barbarous tribes, which were actually mass migrations of displaced peoples more than actual invasions, Frankish military expeditions were just that, unencumbered by large numbers of non-combatants with large amounts of personal possessions. While these Frankish expeditions were successful, their gains would ultimately be eroded by dynastic struggles brought about by the Frankish custom of division of the realm amongst the surviving sons of the king.

Moreover, there seems to be no historical record of any type of commercial base to help maintain the cost of supporting armies. Clovis' short-lived Frankish kingdom would survive for some number of years under the longest-lived of Clovis' sons, Clotaire I. Perhaps the most significant contribution to western society by Clovis' successors would be the series of great battles which occurred in central Germany, resulting in the halt of western migration of the Avars, a mongoloid people, akin to the Tartars and Huns.

While the Merovingian kingdom of the Franks would remain intact in the century and a half after the passing of Clovis, and while much of their vigor and bellicosity would remain, the gradual decline and diminishing of the ruling Merovingian family would invite conditions favorable to the establishment of a new set of rulers. Early in the seventh century, Pepin I would acquire the reins of leadership when he assumed the position of mayor of the palace. This act would be accompanied by an interval of anarchism and violent civil war. Ultimately, Pepin would be succeeded by his son Pepin II. While the reign of Pepin II would prove to be far less eventful than that of his father, by the beginning of the eighth century, he would succeed in passing his authority to his son, Charles Martel, better known to history as Charles the Hammer.

In the eighth century, Europe would see the first of Moslem incursions into the West. It would be the responsibility of Charles Martel to end these uninvited incursions. After more than two decades of almost constant warfare, one of the decisive battles of history would be fought in 732 A.D. near Cenon, on the Vienne River. This battle, known to some as the Battle of Tours, to others as the Battle of Poitiers, would stem the westward movement of Moslems and procure to Christian Europe several centuries of growth and development. In this battle, Charles Martel, realizing that his enemy lacked heavy cavalry and did not carry the weight to deliver a sufficient shock against a strong defensive force, simply allowed his enemy to repeatedly attack his forces and hence to be repeatedly repulsed; a type of victory by exhaustion if you will. At nightfall, learning that their leader Abd-er Rahman had been killed during the battle, the Moslem army seemingly panicked and left the field to their foes. When Charles the Hammer formed his army the next morning, he found his enemy departed. Not wanting to spread out his army in pursuit, he decided to err on the side of caution. Western Europe would not face similar threats from the pagan world until the 13th and 15th centuries.

Upon the death of Charles Martel, the authority he had cemented at Tours would be passed along to his son Pepin III. Pepin would, in the years to come, succeed in driving the Moslems back over the Pyrenees. In addition, after serving for more than a decade as actual ruler of France with the title of Mayor of the Palace, Pepin would put an end to the Merovingian Dynasty by deposing its last king, Childeric III. This act would establish a new Carolingian dynasty. With the death of Pepin III, his kingdom, according to Frankish tradition, would be divided between his two sons, Charles and Carloman. With the death of Carloman in 771 A.D., Charles would become the sole ruler of the Franks, thus laying the basis for the establishment of the Holy Roman Empire.

Charles, known to history as "The Great", or Charlemagne, would establish this new empire through cultural, economic, political and judicial accomplishments. If we consult the works of Edward Gibbon, he informs us that, "The appellation of great has been often bestowed, and sometimes deserved, but Charlemagne is the only prince in whose favor the title has been indissolubly blended with the name."[20] Gibbon also informs us that of his moral virtues, chastity was not the most conspicuous, as he ultimately possessed nine wives. Any weaknesses aside, Charlemagne would arise out of a time of barbarism, and with his passing and the ultimate end of his empire under his offspring, the western world would descend into the dark ages.

The basis and foundation of Charlemagne's empire would be his founding of a new military system. Although crude when compared to the earlier systems of the Macedonians and the Romans, this new system would prove a departure from the military anarchy prevalent

---

[20] Gibbon, *Decline and Fall of the Roman Empire*, 844.

to Western Europe for the preceding four centuries. According to Gibbon, Charlemagne would engage in "three and thirty" campaigns. During these campaigns, Charlemagne would adopt the use of heavy cavalry as demonstrated by his previous enemy, the Lombards. In fact, after defeating them in two brief campaigns, he would use them in his army much the same as the earlier Romans had used Germans, Gauls and Goths as foederati.

In the years prior to Charlemagne, his predecessors found it very difficult and expensive to maintain armies in the field for long periods of time. Charlemagne would find a solution to this problem through a system of calling men to service through his noble vassals, improving the quality of his soldiers while at the same time not denuding the Frankish provinces of the individuals needed to preserve law and order. A logistical system was also established so as to end foraging and plundering. The habit of foraging in one's own territory tends historically to embitter the civilian populace, while foraging and plundering in enemy territory tends to disperse ones forces into smaller groups, which leaves them open to defeat at the hands of concentrated enemy forces. This new logistical system would also allow Frankish armies to remain in the field during the winter, something not considered as being possible since the demise of the Roman legions.

Charlemagne would also re-establish the practice of maintaining a siege train, weapons capable of dealing with enemy fortifications. Much the same as the Romans had employed frontier fortified posts, such as along Hadrian's Wall, Charlemagne instituted a system of "burgs." These posts were constructed along the frontiers of every conquered province and were connected by a system of roads, a concept similar to the Appain Way. The burgs were stocked with supplies, thus allowing the new, more disciplined Frankish cavalry to both patrol newly conquered territory and to project Frankish power forward into areas not yet conquered.

As is generally considered, discipline is a main ingredient in any successful military system. In accordance with this theory, Charlemagne would codify his armies through the issuance of imperial ordinances. Five of these imperial decrees would be issued between 803 A.D. and 813 A.D. This codification would prescribe the duties of his vassals in preparing forces for the field, would establish property qualifications for individual call-ups, list equipment to be carried by individual soldiers, describe organization of individual units and contain a list of punishments for any and all disciplinary infractions. It would be in large part due to these military reforms that Charlemagne would be able to become successful in his operations against hostile armies.

A brief list of Charlemagne's successes would include his campaigns against the Saxons from 772 A.D. to 799 A.D., his defeat of Desiderius, last king of the Lombards, in 773-774 A.D., and the Frankish conquest of Northern Spain. This Spanish campaign would result in the forcing of the Moslems to an area south of the Ebro River in 780 A.D. In 787 A.D., the Frankish armies would campaign against the Duke of Beneveto in Southern Italy. In 787 A.D. and 788 A.D., Charlemagne would manage to re-conquer Bavaria and one year after, occupy Istria. From 791 A.D. to 796 A.D., Charlemagne and his son Pepin would engage and defeat the Avars in the central Danube Valley. During these campaigns, the Franks would establish their authority over parts of Croatia and Slovenia.

Not all of Charlemagne's accomplishments would occur in the sphere of military operations. His military successes would be accompanied by the foundation of schools, the introduction of arts, the reformation of manners during a barbarous time and even attempts to improve the efficiency of farms within the Frankish kingdom. In terms of laws and civil jurisdiction, this portion of Frankish government would be entrusted to the clergy. It should be noted that at the height of his powers, Charlemagne's kingdom would include two-thirds of the former Western Roman Empire. Present day France, Italy, Germany and Hungary were subject to his authority. Unfortunately for the Western World, in terms of the succession of power with the passing of Charlemagne, the Frankish custom of division of the kingdom amongst the surviving sons followed. This would of course lead to chaotic dynastic disputes, and within the latter half of the ninth century authority would devolve into the hands of the dregs of the Carolingian race, individuals with such unpleasant epithets as the bald, the stammerer, the simple and the fat.

And what of Britain during these years of Western European supremacy, demise, decline and finally temporary resurrection? Britannia first arises to the attention of the ancient world during the summer of the Roman year 699 A.D. This is the date at which time Gaius Julius Caesar, having recently subjugated much of Gaul, turned his gaze toward the island to the North. Caesar was by this time familiar with the island peoples of Britannia. In the previous year, he and his fearless legions had encountered British volunteers fighting alongside the now conquered Veneti on the coast of Brittany. To an individual who had recently so greatly expanded Roman control of the western portion of the continent, who had a reputation for being fiercely competitive in battle and in the political sphere, there could be but one course of action. Long ago it was wisely observed, that in matters of military conquest, all conquest must prove to be ineffectual unless they can be made universal. This proves true because as the circle of conquest expands, so does the sphere of hostility. Into this circle Caesar would be drawn. To be historically accurate, there were other motivations associated with Caesars decision to invade an island which had for so long remained aloof from the pages of recorded history. Politically, Caesar's personal competition with his contemporaries in the first triumvirate must have added its weight. Pompey had already added to his fame in 67 B.C., when he cleared the Mediterranean of pirates who had attempted to alleviate Rome of its corn supply. Crassus, the man famous for having suppressed the gladiatorial rebellion of Spartacus in 73 B.C., was at this very time initiating a campaign against the Parthian's who were in his line of advance toward Mesopotamia.

Whereas the Roman mind was always captivated by conquest, a man of Caesar's stratospheric ambition would no doubt lose sleep at the thought of being upstaged by a rival. And so it came to pass that in the year 55 B.C. Caesar would withdraw from the Germanic frontier and would turn his attention to the island in the west. In August of that year, he would set sail from the shores of Gaul with two legions and eighty transports for an initial visit to the little known island.

Commercial interests were involved as well, as Britannia was home to a tough, insular people who possessed a particular value as potential slaves. From the peoples of Brittany came rumors of a pearl fishery, and more importantly, of gold to fill Rome's coffers and to finance further conquest.

While Rome had never been a conspicuous maritime power, an amphibious assault of an entire hostile island did not come to pass without incident. As Caesar's fleet approached England near the White Cliffs of Dover, he found that his antagonists were gathered and waiting for him. Therefore, he simply anchored his ships until the tide turned and then sailed further along the coast, eventually reaching a shelving beach between Deal and Walmer. Nevertheless, the Briton's, fleet of foot and having chariots, were waiting for him here as well. Perhaps not aware of the capabilities of the legionary system, the Briton's waded into the surf to engage the invader. In the events that followed, the aquilifer, or eagle bearer, of the tenth legion leapt from his ship and charged toward the awaiting enemy. The Roman legionaries, always fiercely loyal toward their sacred emblem, followed their eagle bearer's lead and forced their way onto the beach, simultaneously causing the Britons to take flight. And so, the Roman occupation of the Island of Britannia, which would last for approximately four and a half centuries, would begin. Lacking adequate supplies to remain for very long, and with many of his ships in desperate need of repair, Caesar would impose only nominal terms on these few conquered Britons and would gladly sail away with some captives to return to mainland Europe.

Seeking to expand upon this initial foray, Caesar would return the next year with five legions, plus additional cavalry, transported by a fleet of eight hundred ships. Although his landing was unopposed by the islanders, the ever harsh Atlantic would assail his ships. For ten days, Caesar's legions would expend their energies hauling the

Roman fleet onto shore and then enclosing it within a castramentation. This done, Caesar would march inland and confront the hostile islanders. The Britons, having chosen as their great captain the Chief Cassivellaunus, would engage Caesar's forces during a period of skirmishes and retreats. Cassivellaunus, realizing that he could probably not hope to defeat his enemy in a pitched battle, chose to negotiate with his enemy instead. A surrender of hostages was agreed to; there was a promise of tribute to be paid and a promise to remain submissive. Thereupon, Caesar and his legions would proclaim victory and again set sail for the continent. For the next one hundred years no invading army would again set foot on British soil, leaving Cassivellaunus and his peoples to engage in feuds of their own and of their own making.

The next significant chapter in British history would begin with an incident almost farcical in nature. In March of 37 A.D., the emperor Caligula would ascend to the throne of Imperial Rome. Great-grandson of Augustus and son of the much-loved general Germanicus, this third member of the Julio-Claudian dynasty would initially prove to be a very popular leader. However, shortly after assuming power, Caligula would become very ill. Upon recovery, for some unknown reason, his demeanor and behavior had transformed dramatically. What was viewed as an initial streak of extreme extravagance transformed into an eventual paranoia and uncontrolled brutality. Long before the outlandish behavior of Commodus in the second century, Caligula would himself host extremely spectacular gladiatorial games, even appearing at times in the guise of gladiator himself. He threatened at one point in time to appoint his favorite horse, Incitatus, to the position of Consul of Rome. As his relations with the Roman senate continued to decline, he took the dramatic step of dismissing both of the acting consuls for what he considered as treachery. In the summer of 39 A.D., he had a bridge of boats two miles long constructed across the Bay of Naples. To culminate his success, he drove a chariot across it. If he considered this perhaps as some sort of parallel to Caesar's bridge across the Rhine, he was probably alone in his belief. In the autumn of that same year, he would visit his legions on the Rhine and would then decide to lead them west to the channel coast for an invasion of Britain. However, once upon the French coast, he ordered his legionaries to fire their various catapults and projectile throwing weapons into the sea. This was accompanied by having his foot soldiers collect seashells as a form of war trophy. This "victory" over the sea god, Neptune, would be followed by his return to Rome and a personal determination to be worshipped as a god. In fact, he even had a temple built to honor himself and forced some senators to serve as the temple's priest. At this point or sometime shortly thereafter, the courtiers and officers who had served him had had enough of his eccentricities. On January 24, 41 A.D., the emperor Caligula was assassinated.

Following this event, popular history tells us that Caligula's uncle, Claudius, would be discovered by the Praetorian Guard hiding behind a tapestry. As Claudius was the only Julio-Claudian available to them, they appointed him as the new emperor. Perhaps we should consider Claudius as the Harry Truman of his time, as his appointment probably surprised him as much as it did the rest of the Roman world. Also, much the same as Harry Truman would come to surprise his critics, detractors, and those who had no idea who he was, thus also would be the case with Claudius. Although cursed with a stammer and a tendency to dribble, Claudius was regarded as being intelligent in his time, even quite bookish. It is even believed that he had written historical works of his own, although if indeed these did exist, they have since been lost to the world. The complete opposite of his predecessor, he adopted a policy of trying to work with the Senate and not in opposition to it. However, in a very Roman world where much if not all of the authority of a ruler depended upon the support of the army, Claudius possessed no military training or experience whatsoever. To his advantage, his brother Germanicus had been one of Rome's greatest warriors. Therefore, in 43 A.D., Claudius would order the invasion of Britain. The invasion force would consist of four legions, the 2nd Augusta, the 14th Gemina, the 20th Legion and the 9th Hispana. Accompanying these legions would be dozens of auxiliary cavalry and light infantry units.

Sometimes in the course of human events, misfortune can prove to be very fortunate. With an invasion force of forty-thousand men and several thousand cavalry horses and pack animals needing transportation across the English Chanel, much time was spent constructing a fleet of transport ships and an escort of warships. With the coming of spring and hence the campaigning season, the Roman legions were ready to march. Nevertheless, they did not. The reason they did not was not because they could not, but rather because they would not. It seems that as part of a pagan society, Roman legionaries tended to be a very superstitious lot and having heard rumors of all the terrors that awaited them on an island outside of the then known world, the Roman rank and file remained in the relative safety of their camps and declined to participate in this undertaking. In the interim, the tribal warriors of Britain had amassed along the English coast. Having heard rumors from Gallic traders of the gathering of Roman arms and the construction of the invasion fleet at the port of Bononia, the chiefs of the various British tribes summoned their warriors to contest this new invading force. Being a far more primitive society than the invading Romans, the British tribes did not maintain standing armies. Their Achilles heel was to prove to be their agricultural crops. As the tribesmen gathered and waited along the English coast for their expected foe, this would prevent them from being able to plant and tend to their yearly crops. For weeks, the British warriors waited and for weeks, no invasion took place. Finally, believing that this invasion would follow the course of Caligula's farcical invasion four years earlier, they dispersed to tend to their crops. In response to the refusal of his fearless legions to undertake the channel crossing, Claudius would order a member of his staff, Narcissus, to travel to Bononia to negotiate with the legionaries and resolve this impending problem. However, the legionaries would prove to be not at all responsive to the pleas of a freedman, someone they considered as little better than a former slave. Their general, Plautius, would have better luck. Either by threat or by promise of a substantial bonus to those who would undertake this task, the legions were finally convinced to move.

And so, in the late summer of 43 A.D., an invading army consisting of four Roman legions would land on an undefended British coast. One of the leaders in this invasion would be none other than Titus Flavius Vespasianus, the future emperor Vespasian. Vespasianus would command the 2nd Augusta legion. The unprepared Britons would be led in this contest by two brothers, Togodumnus and Caratacus. These two brothers were the great grandson's of Julius Caesar's adversary from one century before, Cassivellaunus. In the campaign which followed, the tactically superior and mechanically efficient Roman legions would prove vastly superior to their British adversaries. Much of the Roman army's advantage could be attributed to technology. According to Stephen Dando-Collins in his work, *Legions of Rome*, the British tribesman of the time "was not equipped with armour or helmets. Most of the ordinary tribesmen came armed with the simple framea, or spear, and a large, leather-covered rectangular wooden shield. Often barefoot, the Briton habitually went into battle stripped to the waist, some even went naked."[21] Against this foe, the Roman legionary went into battle armed with his lorica segmenta, and his Imperial-Gallic helmet with protective cheek flaps and a horizontal shield in back to protect his neck. For armaments he carried two or three pilum, a form of javelin, his short stabbing sword, or gladius, and a short dagger or pugio, which was worn in a scabbard on his left hip. For personal protection, and joint protection when in formation with his fellow legionaries, he carried the scutum, a curved elongated shield about 4-feet long and 2½ feet across. In the center of the shield facing the enemy was a bronze or iron boss intended to deflect blows from enemy weapons. This shield was also used as a form of unit insignia. Much as the modern armies engage in the use of paint schemes on aircraft and armored vehicles, or unit insignia worn on uniforms, the scutum was usually painted with an emblem specific to that cohort or legion. The Roman legionary could also count on support from heavy cavalry

---

[21] Collins, *Legions of Rome*, 291.

units which were superior to any possessed by the Britons and he could count on ballista and catapults, the artillery of that era.

In the fighting to follow, the Britons would prove to be fierce. However, in terms of organization and efficiency, they were simply overmatched. During an ill-conceived attack led by Caratacus, the Britons would receive terrible punishment from their adversaries. In a subsequent attack led by Togodumnus, many more Britons would meet their fate and Togodumnus himself would be severely wounded, to die of his wounds a few days later. Shortly thereafter, the various British tribes began to seek conciliatory terms with their new Roman masters. In subsequent engagements near the Medway and Thames Rivers, Roman arms would again prevail. As with after the initial Roman victories, more and more British tribes chose to submit rather than face the continued onslaught of Roman steel.

Once terms had been established with the majority of the now conquered tribes, the overall Roman commander, Aulus Plautius, would send word to his master in Rome. With an escort of several thousand Praetorians under their prefect Rufrius Pollio, the emperor Claudius would arrive at Camulodunum to receive the formal British surrender. At this ceremony, the men of three legions and their auxiliaries would present themselves in formation dressed in parade dress, as Claudius, sitting on a raised tribunal, would receive the formal surrender of eleven kings from the various British tribes. After some subsequent mopping up operations by Vespasian and his 2nd Augusta legion, all four of the invading legions would settle into permanent fortifications and become an occupying force. And so, the legions had come to stay, or at least for the next four centuries, anyway. Combined with other conquests in Mauratania, which is in North Africa, and Thrace in the Balkans, the conquest of Britain would make Claudius the most expansionist emperor since Augustus, and would gain for him the support of both the Roman people and the Roman army.

And what of the years of Rome's occupation of Britain? There were times of contention and conflict to be sure. We know of the failed Boudican Revolt of the Iceni in 60-61 A.D. and of the great victory won against overwhelming odds by Gaius Suetonius Paulinus at the Battle of Watling Street. Shortly after the suppression of this revolt, Roman general and governor of Britain, Gnaeus Julius Agricola, would complete the Roman conquest of Britannia by occupying Wales and then advancing north into Scotland. Against the iron discipline and methodical practices of the legions, the Caledonian tribes could mount but a piece-meal effort against him. Finally, after seven years of campaigning, Agricola would end British resistance at the Battle of Mons Graupius in 84 A.D. From this point forward, the tribes of Britain would be reconciled to the Roman system and the Pax Romana would remain in force.

Although the first few centuries of the first millennium were a tumultuous and barbarous time, life in Roman occupied Britain settled into a comfortable, civilized time. For the Britons, Roman occupation would bring Roman laws and some semblance of stability. Roman technology would improve the lifestyle of the islanders. There were baths, and with the invention of the hypocaust there was heat and warmth added to their individual dwellings. With the departure of Roman authority around the year 400 A.D., British citizens would not again see baths or central heating for a period of 1,500 years, until roughly the time of Queen Victoria.

Shortly after Agricola's victories completed Roman conquest, there would be a tendency to replace Roman Troops with those recruited almost exclusively from among the Britons themselves. These troops, who would for years maintain the defenses of the Hadrianic and Antonine Walls, were regarded as being the equal of any others found anywhere throughout the empire, except for perhaps the Illyrians. Of the forty-five provinces of the empire, the British would assimilate to the Roman system with a great deal of aptitude. If we are to agree with Churchill in his work, *History of the English Speaking Peoples*, we find that with the Britons "there was a sense of pride in sharing in so noble and widespread a system. To be a citizen of Rome was to be a citizen of the world, raised upon a pedestal of unquestioned superiority above barbarians or slaves."[22] There was to be some measure of self-government for the Britons. During the years of the principate, Roman imperial policy was an attempt to create a commonwealth of self-governing cantons. Whereas those areas along the frontiers which existed under the threat of barbarian invasion or civil uprising and required the occupation by Imperial garrisons would fall under the supervision of the emperor; the more secure provinces without garrisons were generally left under the guidance of the Senate. Each of the provinces was usually organized as a separate unit, and within the borders of these provinces individual municipalities would be given their individual charters and rights. Much the same as the Roman military would adopt the practices and weapons of its opponents when they were found to be of use, so also would Roman civil government adopt those policies as well. Within Roman government in the provinces, there were to be no prejudices based upon race or religion or language, and the only divisions which could be found were those based upon Roman social structure. There were Roman citizens, both wealthy and not so fortunate, there were larger numbers of non-Roman citizens, and then there was the servile class, albeit, upward mobility was possible within this social structure through combinations of luck, skill, or at times, through service in the Roman armies.

As always in the history of our species, where forces exist that tend toward the advancement of mankind, there are often as many forces that combine to suppress this advancement. And so it would be with Roman Britain. With their arrival, the legions had brought peace and stability to Britannia. In their footsteps would follow Roman commerce, culture, schools, baths, an adoption of Roman language and an adaptation to the influence of Roman fashion, such as the wearing of togas. There were improvements in architecture and in transportation, a stabilization of the frontiers, a more orderly administration of those primitive industries that existed, such as the

---

[22] Churchill, *History of the English Speaking people*, 101.

mining of lead and tin, and the laying out of Britannia's first cities by the Roman military engineers. But there was one very critical ingredient missing from the successful future of Roman Britain. This ingredient would prove to be the lack of any extensive technological improvements to the agricultural systems already practiced by the Britons. There was known to the Roman world the existence of a powerful Gallic Plough, which was mounted on wheels. However, this plough was never adopted for use in the new province. Therefore, the levels of productivity and of income derived from the soil would remain basically the same as they were during the time of Caesar's principal antagonist Cassivellaunus. Not only would agricultural productivity remain the same, this inability to expand upon the food supply would cause population levels to remain fairly static. The cities would be born, but they would essentially be stillborn as there was no permanent means for their continued growth. The urbanization of Britain would not be a failure of existence; it would be a failure of dilation.

This failure of agriculture was not to be a regional problem exclusive to Britannia; it seemed to have been an issue endemic to the entire Roman Empire. Rome itself was founded as an agricultural society. At the time of its economic zenith, around 100 A.D., almost 85% of its population lived upon and worked the land. Initially, at the time of the early republic, Roman farmers worked and owned small parcels of land. The great citizen soldier Cincinnatus was said to have had a farm encompassing four acres, just enough to enable him to claim the rights and privileges of a landowner. In the years after the Punic and Macedonian Wars, two factors would combine to change Roman agriculture. First, many of Rome's land-owning soldiers were lost in the wars, leaving many abandoned and neglected farms about the landscape. Secondly, there was a large influx of slave labor. Together these factors allowed large landowners to consolidate larger and larger tracts of land into larger and larger farms. By the second century A.D., these large agricultural estates, known as latifundia, became increasingly common. However, the same society that would prove to be the light of the western world and that would adopt new engineering techniques and new technologies for its armies, never discovered any great technological advances that would increase the productivity of the soil. There were to be no steam engines or center pivot irrigation in the Roman world. Oxen would remain the principal draught animal, and spades, sickles, scythes and saws the arsenal of the farmer. Without new technological developments in the sphere of agriculture, the only way to increase the productivity of the land was to increase the productivity of the worker.

Taxation would also play a significant role in the demise of Roman-British agriculture. In the later years of the empire, the constant cycle of dynastic civil wars and the never ending cost of defending the provinces from the incursions of the barbarians created a very onerous tax burden to all classes of citizens. Those who could no longer afford the cities sought the refuge of the country. Urban life declined. Rural life would decline as well. With the creation of the latifundia in the early centuries of the first millennium, most of the agricultural lands were farmed by tenant farmers who worked for the larger landowners. As the tax burden increased, many of these tenant farmers became impoverished and the land simply fell into disuse. By 400 A.D., almost one-third of the agricultural land in Africa had gone out of cultivation. In Britain, where areas of the Cambridgeshire fens were once drained to produce cereal crops to feed Rome's soldiers on the Rhine, this agricultural decline must have proven to be most painful.

Whereas both agriculture and urban life continued its decline in Britannia in the third and fourth centuries of the first millennium, it would be the continuous dynastic struggles which would lead to Britain's separation from the Roman world. In the year 367 A.D., the Pictish peoples, the Scots and the invading Anglo-Saxon tribes combined to fall together upon Britannia. In response, the Emperor of the West, Valentinian, sent a new general named Theodosius to reorganize the defenses of the province against this new onslaught. Theodosius would not disappoint his emperor and for some years a degree of stability would reign over the island. Coastal defenses would be strengthened and garrisons would once again maintain

Hadrian's Wall. But the memory of the island's people would prove to be ephemeral in regards to the potential dangers from the outside world. In the year 383 A.D., the commander of Roman Britain, a Spaniard named Magnus Maximus, would declare himself emperor of the Western Roman Empire. This claim would however be contested by the then emperor Gratian. Gathering together all the troops he could muster, including the troops maintaining the wall and the coastal defenses, Maximus would depart from Britannia for Gaul. With his departure, Britannia would be left almost entirely defenseless. In the events that would follow, Maximus would defeat Gratian near Paris, then be defeated himself by Theodosius, the savior of Britannia two decades earlier.

This cycle would repeat itself again twenty years later. If the memory of the Britons had been ephemeral during the first cycle of events, it would prove nonexistent in the second. During the years after Maximus' departure, the defenses of Hadrian's Wall would again be breached. Theodosius would send his most capable soldier, Stilicho, to the island. Stilicho would expel the invaders and once again repair the defenses. Britannia could again be grateful.

Stilicho, now the virtual regent of the West, would return to Rome. In the year 402 A.D., he would be forced to defend the Italian Peninsula from an invasion by Alaric and the Visogoths. At the Battle of Pollentia in that same year, he would prove successful in this endeavor. However, soon after his victory over Alaric, a new multiracial host under a new leader, Radagaisus, would sweep down upon him. As twice before, he would again prove successful.

But this cycle of new invaders would not desist. No sooner had Stilicho defeated this second host, than a confederation of Avars, Vandals, Suevi and Burgundians would break through the Rhine frontiers and occupy Northern Gaul. In an example of the worst possible timing, as Stilicho was concentrating all of his energies to meet this new threat, under the guise that their province was being neglected, the Britons would put forth a new, rival emperor named Marcus. Within weeks he would meet his untimely demise, only to be replaced by a Briton named Gratianus. Gratianus would survive weeks, but not months. In turn, the Britons would submit another pretender to the throne, this one bearing the famous name of Constantine. But instead of doing as the Britons intended and defending the island, Constantine, like all ambitious men, would attempt to defend his claim to the throne of the Western Empire. As Magnus Maximus had done before him, Constantine would drain Britain of all of its defenses and set off for Boulogne.

In the end, Constantine would, as Maximus before him, be captured and executed. Thus, in the final half of the fourth century and in the early years of the fifth, Britannia would be stripped of all its defenders in an attempt to defend the empire and to overcome it. Within years, all vestiges of Roman government would disappear. One world had ended; a new world was to begin.

# Chapter 4

¤

# THE LONG RISE TO PRE-EMINENCE

The Roman abandonment of Britannia would create within the island something that we in modern times would refer to as a "power vacuum." Quite literally, there existed no government capable of enforcing its authority over the inhabitants, or of defending those inhabitants from all things external. Into this vacuum would come the Saxons. Unlike the various incursions that were suffered by the Britons in the fourth century, this new Saxon threat would reveal itself as a mass migration. Its origins would lie within the power struggle between the British chieftains after the decay of Roman authority and also through the use of the Roman practice of employing mercenary armies against one's rivals. It would seem that somewhere around 450 A.D., one of the British chiefs would seek to establish himself over his rivals and would invite a group of mercenaries from over the seas. However, once established, these mercenaries would betray their host and would provide the bridgehead for the follow up of their brethren. Soon, entire shiploads of these foreign invaders would descend upon the island, using the coast as points of debarkation and the rivers as avenues of approach. Initially their inroads would meet with much success. However, as with all things historical, fate and perhaps faith would intervene. If the *Anglo-Saxon Chronicle* of the ninth century is historically accurate, then we know the name of the deceived chief to be Vortigern and the name of the deceiver to be Hengist. We also know, if this early text is correct, that a great victory would be won by the Britons over the Saxon invaders at a location known as Mount Badon. The name of the great British warrior responsible for this victory is taught to us more by means of legend than recorded history. This legend is of course that of King Arthur. Irregardless whether we choose to accept the King Arthur legend or not, what we can accept on a reliable basis is that the battle did take place and that its effects would be to stem the tide of Saxon invasion for a period of roughly fifty years.

Although the victory at Mount Badon stemmed the advance of the Saxons, it did not remove them from the island. In the centuries to follow, England would become divided into seven Anglo-Saxon kingdoms.[23] For many years there would be violent struggles for both survival and supremacy between these various kingdoms. However, no great captain would arise to superimpose his will upon his neighbors and there would be no great technological advancement to allow one kingdom to arise pre-eminent. In the years after Hengist and Horsa, and of Arthur to those who believe in him, warfare had regressed into something tribal in nature and not a competition between organized armies as with Rome and Carthage. There was in all likelihood no teaching of strategy or tactics, as writing had virtually disappeared as a medium of teaching or communication, with the exception being that most unwarlike institution, the church, which at this time became a virtual citadel of learning.

Among this heptarcy of seven kingdoms of varying strength, two would prove to be of slightly greater importance than the others. These would be the kingdoms of Northumbria and Mercia. Northumbria, its name vaguely betraying its geographical location, was a Christian kingdom. Mercia would occupy what many today might refer to as the British Midlands. In the year 633 A.D., King Penda of Mercia would form an alliance with Cadwallon, the Christian British King of North Wales. The object of this newly

---

[23] Dupuy, *Encyclopedia of Military History*, 202.

formed alliance was to challenge the suzerainty of Edwin, the Northumbrian king. Ever since the time of the Saxon invasion of Britannia, the island populace had by virtue of dissimilarities in culture and race separated; Britains to the West, Saxons generally in the East. With the opening of this contest between the rival states we find the first instance of Britons and English fighting side by side. The contest would be brief, its consequences fatal to the Northumbrian King Edwin, who would be defeated and slain. In a gesture not to be unexpected in such a barbarous time, his head would be displayed on the ramparts of the former home of the Roman legionaries, York.

If however there were thoughts circulating amongst the Britons that this victory over the Northumbrians might signal a return of British superiority and a return to the pre-Saxon times, these thoughts would prove to be very short-lived. The repaying of old debts was not to be. Edwin's successor, Oswald, would meet Cadwallon and his British followers within one year of Edwin's death. At a battle, which took place somewhere along the wall constructed in the time of Hadrian, Cadwallon would suffer a fate similar to that which he had inflicted upon Edwin. Saxon power had come to dominate the British Isles and the Saxon invasion could now be considered as complete.

The removal of the Britons from the scene would not bring about an end to the struggles between the seven kingdoms of the heptarcy. Soon, the war post would be struck again. This time the conflict would be between resurgent Northumbria and King Penda of Mercia. For seven years the conflict would ebb to and fro. Penda would in time defeat and decapitate Oswald, much the same as he had done with his predecessor Edwin. But Oswald's younger brother, Oswy, would return the favor shortly thereafter. Although Oswy had the ability to avenge the defeat of his predecessor, what he did not have was the ability to end the cycle of violence. This cycle of long and continuous rivalry for leadership between the various kingdoms would continue throughout the seventh and eighth centuries.

Eventually, this period of ceaseless warfare would come to a conclusion. The eventual domination of Saxon England would shift back to Mercia. Two individuals would arise to control Mercia and to gain ascendency over most of the island. These two Mercian Kings, Ethelbald and Offa, would dominate affairs from 716 to 769. The first would lay a firm foundation upon which the second could stand. Ethelbald would lead successful invasions of both Wessex and Northumbria. Given time, he may have gone further. But in an act heralding back to the days of the old Roman Caesars and the Praetorians, he would be assassinated by his own guards. In the struggle to follow, his cousin Offa would succeed him and after a series of hard fought campaigns, establish the first recognized unification of England in the post Roman world.

The reign of Offa would coincide with that of "Carolus Magna", better known to history as Charlemagne. The importance of Offa in regards to the history of Great Britain is that it would be he who led Britain out with its post-Roman isolation and was able to re-establish ties with mainland Europe. This re-uniting of mainland Europe would come about as a result of a dispute between Charlemagne and Offa over the arrangement of marriages between their offspring. In a move no doubt inspired by political considerations, Charlemagne wished to have one of his sons married to one of Offa's daughters. Not to be outdone, Offa decided that if this was to be the case, then one of his sons should in turn be allowed to marry one of Charlemagne's daughters. To this request Charlemagne responded in the negative. But Offa was not to be so easily denied. He contrived to place a trade embargo on continental goods being imported onto British soil. This embargo had the desired effect and soon the reciprocal marriages would take place. In addition, there would occur further trade agreements between the two monarchs.

The trade agreements and the marriages were very significant events at a time when all things in the British world were fluid, nothing solid. A great deal of prestige was added to the regency of Offa. He even affixed to himself the title of Rex Totius Anglorius Patriae, "king of the whole land of the English," He would justify this title by his actions. In the years to come he would suppress the lesser kings of the Severn Valley, defeat the West Saxons in the province of Oxfordshire, and subjugate Berkshire. He would eradicate the monarchy that had existed in Kent since the time of Hengist, and would put down a subsequent uprising with severe levels of brutality. If any one individual could lay claim to, or be justified as having earned the title of being the first of the English kings, it would probably have to be Offa. Whereas we may choose in modern times to consider Offa as the first of the English monarchs, we should probably not consider him as being one of the Island's greater men. In addition to his suppressions of rival power in Kent, Berkshire and Oxfordshire, Offa would also have the King of East Anglia beheaded.

Although this may have been considered the political norm in the eighth century, I believe today it would simply reveal to us that within Offa there did not exist any particular spark of genius that would allow him to gain and consolidate his authority throughout the island by the use of political skill or non-violent means. If however, the actions of Offa are indicative of the violence of the times, the English countryside was soon to become acquainted with far worse.

In the latter years of the reign of Charlemagne, Viking depredations would begin in Western Europe. The Vikings, also known to history as Norsemen or Northmen, were essentially maritime raiders who were seeking plunder and not settlement. This is not to say however, that they did not establish settlements if needed. In fact, in 841, they seized and fortified Dublin, Ireland, and the Norse chieftain Thorgest at one time ruled half of Ireland proper. Shortly thereafter, they would also seize islands along the Scottish and English coast to use for their assault on Britain itself. The first Viking settlement was located on the Isle of Thanet. They then established another permanent base on Sheppy Island at the mouth of the Thames River. What would begin as basic piracy and search for plunder carried out by individual shiploads of Danish raiders or small groups of ships, would eventually reach a torrent where fleets consisting of three to four hundred ships full of Norse raiders would ply the coast and rivers of Britain. In the decade between 865 to 874, Norsemen would engage in the conquest of Northumbria, Mercia and East Anglia. It is some irony that the Saxon invaders of the fifth century would find themselves on the receiving end of a similar treatment in the ninth. Danish lore would have it that much of the Viking conquest's in England would be attributed to one Ivar "the Boneless." Ivar's father was the famous Viking Ragnar Lodbrok, known to history also as "Hairy breeches." Ragnar had engaged in rapine and plunder in France in 845, advancing as far as Paris. At Paris, Ragnar and his fellow raiders would suffer defeat and an onset of the plague. Not one to flinch from adversity, Ragnar simply turned his attention north to Britain. In a raid against the Northumbrians he was captured by King Ella, who would, as payment for his sins, have him cast into a snake pit to die. As he lay dying amongst the adders he would call upon his sons to avenge his death. The prescribed vengeance would be something known to the Vikings as the "Blood-red Eagle," whereupon the flesh and ribs of the victim would be cut and sawn in an aquiline pattern and the still breathing lungs would be ripped out. Such would be the fate of King Ella. While Ivar would gain his revenge upon much of England, he would not live to enjoy this revenge upon all of England. After the conquest of Northumbria and Mercia, and with the defeat of King Edmund of East Anglia, Ivar would depart England along with his fellow chieftain Olaf for Dublin where he would meet his eventual demise in the year 872. The final score between the Saxons and the Vikings would have to be settled by other parties.

In every age, fate or perhaps destiny, brings forth a great man to be defender and deliverer of his people. To the Saxons of England, this deliverer would be Alfred the Great. In the years after the demise of Ivar "the Boneless," the Danish invaders would turn their gaze upon the last of the Saxon kingdoms, Wessex. Wessex was ruled by its king, Aethelred, who in battle was usually joined by his brother, Alfred. With the Danish invasion of 870-871, Aethelred and Alfred would prove victorious in the initial battle at Englefield in December 870. One month later they would be badly defeated at Reading. That same month, January 871, would see the fortunes of Aethelred and Alfred reversed again, and this time, at Ashdown, a sizeable victory would be won by Saxon arms. Nevertheless, the Danish army did not dissolve and throughout the year 871 the armies would meet at repeated engagements. The fortunes of each side would vary and reverse until eventually a five-year truce would be agreed upon after the Danish victory at Wilton. By this juncture of the war, Aethelred, who had fallen ill, died. Alfred, at twenty-four, as brother of the deceased king, would assume his title. This five-year truce with the Danes was a much needed respite which would allow him to consolidate his resources. War would resume in the year 876. For the Danes, there would be a new leader, Guthrum, and after an initial foray back into the English Midlands and a removal of their king, Burgred, there would be a renewed assault upon Alfred and his people. This new contest would be punctuated by perjury and deceit. Twice, Alfred would force his enemy into a compromised position; twice they would agree to a truce, and twice that truce would be broken. Then unfortunate circumstances would lead Alfred into the darkest of times. In January 878, while Alfred and his entourage were at Chippenham celebrating Twelfth Night, a religious feast, the Danes swept down upon them. The entire army was put to flight, as was their king. From January to May of 878, Alfred would be forced to live as a fugitive. But just as fortunes had proven so fickle before, so they would again. In May of 878, Alfred would fight again at Edington, winning what would prove to be a decisive victory. Guthrum would sue for peace and this time the Danes would agree to cease any further hostilities against the kingdom of Wessex. As a further penalty in defeat, the Danish army was required to submit to Baptism. Even after being twice deceived by his foes, Alfred still sought to have a lasting peace with Guthrum and the Danes.

It was at this time that Alfred would set in place various institutions which would have a major impact on the future of English history. Recognizing that much of the problem arising from the Viking invasion was due to the lack of a Saxon, or English navy, Alfred would begin to build such an entity. It was recognized that "to be safe in an island it was necessary to command the sea. He made great departures in ship design, and hoped to beat the Viking numbers by fewer ships of much larger size."[24]

The second major contribution brought forth by Alfred would be his book of laws, also referred to as dooms. The origin of this term is probably the earlier arrived at Gothic term of doms, which translates literally as judgment.

This attempt at jurisprudence was not the first set of laws known to the British Isles. For the first four centuries of the first millennium, the island's inhabitants lived under the protective umbrella of Roman Laws. Across the English Channel, Charlemagne had established laws for the Franks during the days of Carolingian dominance in France, just a few short decades before the arrival of Alfred. But what may be most important about his efforts are the fact that he attempted to establish order on the Island where for over four hundred years piracy, invasion, and the decapitation of one's political rivals were considered to be the norm. Alfred's new laws would also reflect the importance of the Christian religion on the inhabitants of that time. There was a simple inversion of the Golden Rule; "Do unto others as you would that they do unto you," became, "What ye will that other men should not do to you, that do ye not to other men."[25] This new Golden Rule set forth in Saxon England sounds basic enough, but during an age where with the exclusion of the church writing was almost nonexistent and distances were prohibitive to the vast majority of the populace, it was a start.

The story of Alfred the Great and his competitions with the Danes would continue on, even to extend some number of years after his demise. In the year 885, a Viking fleet ascended the Seine River in France containing an army of approximately forty thousand men. For more than one year they would lay siege to Paris, and for a period of six years they lashed out in all directions on mainland Europe. Paris, under the leadership of its governor, Count Odo, would not succumb. Nor would mainland Europe. As a response to this stiffening resistance on the mainland, the Vikings would turn their attention

---

[24] Churchill, *History of the English Speaking Peoples*, 101.
[25] Ibid, 103.

once more to the island to the north.

In the autumn of 892, no doubt much to the chagrin of the British peoples, an armada of two hundred fifty ships carrying the Viking army descended upon English shores. Soon after, a second armada of an additional eighty ships would arrive. Kent, the southeastern-most of the Saxon kingdoms, would bear the brunt of this onslaught. Alfred, equally adept at diplomacy as well as the use of the sword, would try to buy them off. To his disappointment, the new Viking chief, Haesten, would afford to him the same treatment as Guthrum in the previous war. Haesten would accept the bribes and then continue to raid as well. In 893, many of the Danes who had earlier settled in Northumbria and East Anglia joined in the assault, sailing around the islands southern coast and laying siege to present day Exeter. Fortunately for the Saxon kingdoms, Alfred was father to a very capable and valiant son. This son, known to us as Edward the Elder, would follow in his father's footsteps. Edward, first with the assistance of Alfred and then on his own upon Alfred's demise, would engage the Danes for the next twenty-one years, finally defeating the Viking chief Guthrum II in 918 at the Battle of Tempsford. In the immediate aftermath of Tempsford, all of the Danes of East Anglia submitted to Edward and accepted him as their new Lord and protector.

As with all monarchies, upon the death of Edward, the Saxon crown would be passed to the next in line of the House of Wessex. This new monarch, Athelstan, would seek to continue the forward progress initiated by Alfred and Edward. He would make every attempt at harmonious relations with the now established Danes, while at the same time seeking to further his influence into Scottish Strathclyde, where the kings of the Scots agreed to pay him tribute. This forward progress would be interrupted in 937 when rebellion was initiated by the peoples of North Britain, to include those of Celtic, Danish and Norwegian origins. Constantine, King of the Scots, not to be confused with the fourth century founder of Constantinople, was to be joined in his rebellion by Olaf of Dublin, along with a fresh contingent of Viking warriors from Norway. This most recent contest between the Saxons and the Danes with their new found allies would not be so prolonged as those in the past. Within months the antagonistic parties would meet at Brunanburg. The result would be an overwhelming Saxon victory. The Norse chieftain would return to his base in Ireland and Athelstan would receive homage from the Britons of Wales and of Constantine III of Scotland. Of importance during this conquest would be the use of the new Saxon navy in their conquest of Scotland, setting the standard for the English navy of centuries to come and from this point, Athelstan would begin to fashion himself Rex Totius Britannia.

The achievements of the House of Wessex would continue. The succession from Alfred the Great, to Edward, Athelstan, Edmund, Edred and thence to Edgar would see the establishment of many of the foundations of English society familiar to the Englishmen of present day. The organization of the shires would take place. The further subdivision of the shires into the hundreds, and of the hundreds into the burghs (borough) would occur as well. In the shires, hundreds and burghs a system of courts would be established and maintained. As officers of these courts, sheriffs or reeves would be appointed, although they would be responsible to the Crown as well as the courts. There would be the establishment of a common language, a King's English, if you will. Although no doubt varying a great deal from modern English, this new attempt at literary uniformity would be something all educated men could write. This would of course be a departure from the past, where the ability to read and write were a domain almost exclusive to the church. With the establishment of a single monarch over the majority of the island nation there would also be the establishment of a single coinage, and a single system of weights and measures. Perhaps the accomplishments of the Saxon House of Wessex were best stated by Winston Churchill, "From whatever point of view we regard it, the tenth century is a decisive step forward in the destinies of England." Despite the catastrophic decline of the monarchy that followed the death of Edgar, this organization and English culture were so firmly rooted as to survive two foreign conquests in less than a century.[26]

It has always been another of mankind's historical experiences that sometimes a good or even a great people may come to naught due to a progressive weakening of their leadership. Likewise, it is also true that at times a good or a great leader may meet with an unpleasant fate due to a progressive weakening of the subject peoples. With Saxon England, the next step in the long march toward political and military mastery would be a case of the former. With the death of Edgar in 975, the long line of Saxon kings was to be supplanted by an individual with the less than flattering sobriquet of Ethelred the Unready. History does not reveal to us the meaning of this name, whether given to imply that he was unready for leadership or given to indicate that he was unready for the invasion to come. Perhaps the reference is to both. With the year 980 approaching, there would be new assaults on the island kingdom from Scandinavia and Denmark. The towns of Chester, Thanet, Cornwall and Devon would fall victim to sword and slaughter. In the years of Alfred, the Saxon's response would have been a combination of arms when possible and money when necessary. Ethelred would abandon the former and rely exclusively on the later. The resultant sequence of events would bear a striking resemblance to that of the late Roman principate and its response to the barbarian invasions of the fourth and fifth centuries.

In the year 991, Ethelred would pay these new Danish invaders ten thousand pounds of silver, plus rations to quell their other appetite. In 994, the new national ransom would be sixteen thousand pounds. In 1002, the bribe would increase to twenty-four thousand pounds of silver. At this point, with the policy of appeasement becoming less profitable or productive, Ethelred decided to take action. His retaliation may have been driven by false bravado or possibly the result of poor counsel from his advisors. In their time of ruin and decay, the Saxons had allowed into the "fryd", or militia, a large number of Danish mercenaries. This was a repeat of Roman policies in their days. In a repeat of the purge of the Roman army after the

---

[26] Ibid, 114.

assassination of Stilicho in 408, Ethelred decided upon a policy of slaughter of all Danes in the south of England. This purge would not only be of those in his pay, but would extend to those Danes who had peacefully settled on the land since the days of the first Viking invasions. The aggressive act occurred on St. Brice's Day and would claim among its victims the wife of a Viking chief named Gunnhild. As fate would have it, Gunnhild's wife would be the sister of Sweyn Forkbeard, King of Denmark. Retribution would be swift. For two years, Sweyn, along with his son Canute, would exact from the impoverished and the war weary islanders a heavy toll. According to Churchill's *History of the English Speaking Peoples,* the retaliation was so widespread and the landscape so devastated that the Danish army could no longer subsist upon it. Sweyn and his invaders would depart for Denmark in 1005, only to return the next year to resume where they had left off. This time, Ethelred would be forced to pay an additional ransom of thirty-six thousand pounds of silver, three or four times the equivalent of the Saxon kingdoms yearly income.

The truce that was purchased with all this treasure would prove to be very short lived. In 1009, the Danes would return. Ethelred, in a gesture far to ineffective and far too late, had a new fleet hastily constructed to meet this new threat. That portion of the fleet not destroyed in battle would be damaged by storm or deserted by its crews. In the year 1012, another payment was required by the Viking raiders, this time amounting to forty-eight thousand pounds. Again this tribute would serve to ill effect. In 1013, Sweyn would return with his eldest son Canute. This time the Vikings would not be bought off. Sweyn would subdue Yorkshire, Northumbria and Mercia. Ethelred would take flight and seek sanctuary with the Duke of Normandy, brother to Ethelred's wife.

With the departure of Ethelred, Sweyn would be proclaimed as king of the former Saxon kingdom. Sweyn would not enjoy the taste of his conquest long, dying at the beginning of the year 1014. The Anglo-Saxon people would turn to their former regent to fill this void. Ethelred would lead an abortive attempt to regain his throne from Canute, but he would die in London while awaiting the approach of

Canute and his army. However, the dynastic dispute would continue. The eldest son of Ethelred, known to history as Edmund Ironside, would carry on his father's campaign against Canute. A series of battles would be fought. First, Edmund Ironside would win at Pen in Somersetshire, then a draw would be the result of the next battle at Sherston in Wiltshire. After that, Canute would prove victorious at Assandun in Essex. At this point, for whatever reason history does not reveal, Canute and Edmund Ironside agreed to a partition of England, Canute reigning in the north, Edmund in the south. As with all agreements between the Saxons and the Danes, this arrangement would not last especially long either. Shortly after the agreement was reached between the two parties, Edmund would die. Canute would then be elected King of England by the Witan, the ecclesiastical aristocracy of the time. The last descendants of the House of Wessex left England to seek safety in other lands. Thus, much as the Saxons had managed to claim the island nation from the Britons, now the Danes had accomplished the same from the Anglo-Saxons.

The Danish over-lordship of England would not last long. In 1035, Canute would die, and much as was the case with Charlemagne, his empire would soon die with him. Canute had left three sons. Two would be of Elgiva of Northampton and a third, Harthacanute, from his marriage to Emma, former wife of Ethelred. In addition, two sons of Emma from her marriage to Ethelred could also lay claim to the throne. Initially, two of Canute's sons from Elgiva would succeed their father, Harold Harefoot, between 1035 and 1040, and Harthacanute, between 1040 and 1042. At this time politics would become involved in the succession to the throne of England. Of the two sons of Ethelred and Emma, the elder, Alfred, "The Innocent Prince," had earlier been blinded and lived out his remaining days in a monastery at Ely. The younger would return from exile in Normandy to become Edward the Confessor. Edward the Confessor would serve as King of England for nearly a quarter century. There would be peace at last, but little stability. Edward the Confessor is regarded by history to have been a very pious man. He is also regarded as being very weak. The Danish aristocracy of this time was controlled by a Wessex Earl by the name of Goodwin. Goodwin would receive his initial appointment from Canute. He had played a major role in the decision to have Edward the Confessor return from exile to claim the throne. When Edward returned from Normandy, he brought with him an entourage of Norman advisors. In the year 1051, this Norman party in the king's court would succeed in driving Goodwin from the realm, though this exile would be temporary. Goodwin, with the assistance of his son Harold, would raise an armed contingent in Flanders, and would influence Edward to receive them back into the royal court. Turnabout would be fair play and it would soon be the Normans who were forced to flee. Within seven months of his return from exile, Goodwin would expire and Harold would replace his father as the king's principal advisor. It would seem that at some time during the reign of Edward the Confessor, he had assured his prior protector, William, Duke of Normandy, that he would receive the English crown upon Edward's demise. However, in a reversal of policy, he later chose Harold, son of Goodwin, to assume this post. Thus, the stage would be set for an event that would forever change England and send it, in its new form as an Anglo-Saxon-Norman nation, to a leadership and mastery of the world more extensive and complete than that of Rome.

With the passing of Edward the Confessor on January 6, 1066, a series of events would unfold that would bring to mind the dynastic disputes of the Roman Principate. Soon after Edward's death, Harold would be elected King of England by the Witan. Across the English Channel, William of Normandy would regard this act as a usurpation of his rightful claim to the throne of the island kingdom. He would begin his preparations for an invasion of Southern England. In the interim, Harold would be forced to defend his new kingdom from external threats led by his brothers Tostig and Harold Hardrada, King of Norway. Harold, not of Norway, but of England, would prove worthy to his task. On September 25, 1066, he would meet his enemies at Stamford Bridge. In this engagement, both Tostig and Harold Hardrada were killed. More importantly, the housecarls (soldiers) of Harold's Saxon army suffered heavy casualties. Three days later, the

Norman invasion of England would begin when William, soon to be known as the conqueror, landed at Pevensey in Sussex.

The ensuing engagement, known to most as the Battle of Hastings, to others as Senlac, would occur on October 14, 1066. Never has such an important event been accompanied by so many twists of fate. Upon hearing of Harold's election to the throne of England, William immediately began to assemble an army of mercenaries and feudal contingents for his proposed invasion. By midsummer, he was ready to sail for England. However, much the same as the legionary revolt had postponed the Emperor Claudius invasion of Britain in 48 A.D., poor weather and unfavorable winds would defer the invasion of William. This would prove fortunate for Harold, as it would allow him time to deal with his difficult brother and the Norwegian King of his own name. With the changing of the winds on September 27,1066, William would finally set sail. Upon arrival on the English coast, he began building a very strong defensive position complete with wooden fortifications. Harold, after his victory at Stamford Bridge, would begin his march south, covering the 200 miles from York to London in an astounding 5 days. At London, he would rest his army for the next five days, gathering additional troops and supplies for what he must have known would be an inevitable fight. He would then march his army to Senlac, covering the 56 miles in about 48 hours. Upon arrival, he would establish his army upon a ridge eight miles northwest of Hastings. Here, with an army of approximately 20,000 men, he would await history's verdict. Having already been involved in the recent engagement at Stamford Bridge, where much of his army was lost, and having since marched several hundred miles to meet the invader, Harold decided to assume a defensive posture. William, with fresh mercenaries and a larger force, would assume the offensive. Throughout the day of battle, the Saxon housecarls and soldiers of the fyrd  would face alternating assaults from William's archers and crossbow men and his heavy cavalry. Throughout the day, the Saxon army under Harold would defy and repulse all of these repeated assaults. Once again fate would intervene. After several hours of combat, William would order his archers to unleash their arrows in high-angle fire. The Saxon line still held firm. Finally, in mid-afternoon, a chance arrow would strike Harold in the eye, inflicting a mortal wound. Now virtually leaderless, the Saxon line would finally break under the weight of repeated Norman assaults. A few of the braver housecarls would remain on the ridge with the body of their mortally wounded king. They too would eventually give ground. By nightfall, the Battle of Hastings was over, the Norman conquest of Britain was about to begin.

William the conqueror would reign over England and Normandy for an additional period of twenty-one years. This new conquest would prove to be lengthy and complicated. Added to this would be the fact that William would continue to be involved in disputes with the king of France on the mainland, as the border of the Norman province was a mere twenty miles from Paris. In conquering this new land one must remember that for centuries prior to the Norman arrival, there had been almost continuous combat between the Saxons and the Danes. Essentially, to conquer one island, William had to subjugate two populations. There would be revolts and challenges to his authority. After the Battle of Hastings, one particularly stubborn Saxon leader, named Hereward the Wake, would not be subjugated until the year 1071, a period of five years. In 1075, another revolt, this time involving disaffected Norman knights with the assistance of the Saxon leader Woltheof, would break out. But in the end, the conquest of the English by the Normans would be completed and a series of Norman castles would ensure the compliance of the English people and towns.

With the completion of the Norman conquest of England, a system of land tenure based upon military service was created. Whereas the Normans comprised a distinct minority on English soil and had removed and replaced the Saxon ruling class, it would be essential for the new king to maintain a standing army to ensure his stability and survival. With this new system of land tenure, a small but effective armed force could be assured through knight service and quotas of men received from each of the king's feudal vassals. This new system would not be completed without complaints from the former Saxon inhabitants of the land, however. This inquiry would see the establishment or creation of what has become known to us as the Doomsday, or Domesday Book.

This Domesday Book was, in effect, a survey of all England, listing all the landowners and showing the value and extent of their land holdings. The name chosen was to be symbolic of the fact that it supposedly judged all men without bias, similar to the Last Judgment. The names of many of the English villages still present today can be traced back to an entry in this first extensive land survey completed by William the Conqueror. The completion of this survey would be accompanied with an act, which would be repeated by the Fuhrer of the Third Reich, nearly a thousand years later. As a means of ensuring the loyalty of his knights and feudal vassals, all would be required to swear an oath to William personally, much the same as all the soldiers of the Third Reich were required to swear a personal oath to Adolf Hitler upon entering service.

While the initial Norman conquest of England would be done in brutal fashion, with much of the landscape being made desolate, eventually the occupation would undergo the softening effects of time. There would be an assimilation of cultures between the two races. Much the same as the Britons had been forced to learn Latin and then these Roman Britons would be forced to learn Saxon, now much of the English population would learn French. The earlier establishment of Saxon local government, the shires and the hundreds and the burghs, would prove useful to William and therefore would remain intact.

As with all of history's great men, William the Conqueror would meet his maker. He died on September 9, 1087. His death would come as the result of injuries sustained when thrown from a horse during one of his numerous forays against the King of France. Having three sons, the lands of William the Conqueror would be divided. William III, known also as Rufus, would rule over the king's lands in Britain. Robert, a warrior at heart, would inherit Normandy. The youngest of the three, Henry, would receive only five thousand pounds of silver and the hope that one day he might preside over a once again united

Anglo-Norman kingdom. As always, dynastic disputes would be exacerbated by another issue. It would seem that many of the Norman Barons would own lands on both sides of the English Channel, thus requiring that they owe fealty to two different lords, to them a terrible inconvenience. In the disputes to follow, they would adopt a policy of dividing the lords wherever possible and whenever it served their own interest.

Initially, competition between the rivals would be avoided, as Robert, ever the warrior, would leave Normandy to play a role in the First Crusade, answering the call of Pope Urban II in 1095. In his absence, he would leave Normandy pawned to William II for a loan of 10,000 marks. Also in his absence, William II, or Rufus, would extend his father's domains on the island, acquiring both Cumberland and Westmorland. In continuing the policies of his father, he would provoke and alienate many of the baronage. In August of the year 1100, in another act harkening back to the days of the praetorians, he would be mysteriously shot through the head by an arrow while out hunting.

With William II now dead, and Robert in the Holy Land in the service of the Pope, the youngest of the three brothers would now find himself in control. He would waste no time in establishing his authority, his first act being that of seizing the Royal treasury. His second of many farsighted acts upon his accession was the establishment of a charter. The purpose of this charter was to conciliate both the forces of the Church and of the Baronial class and to assure them of their due powers within the state. Henry would then, in an attempt to both placate and assimilate the conquered Saxon population of England, enter into a marriage with Matilda, a descendant of the Old English line of kings. With the intermarriage of the Saxon line of kings and the mollification of the Church and the Baronial class accomplished, Henry would be ready to face his brother Robert upon his return from the crusades. This showdown between the two sons of William the Conqueror would begin in September 1100 and end almost exactly six years later. In the initial phase of this contest, Henry would be forced to defend his claim in

England, facing off against the House of Montgomery through a series of systematic sieges. Henry would overcome the strongholds of his brother's allies. This being accomplished, the next logical step would be to reverse the acts of his father and invade Normandy from England. In September of 1106, Henry would have his Hastings. At the Battle of Tenchebrai, Henry would defeat the forces of Robert, and Robert would be led away to his imprisonment in England. The Saxons who served under Henry, now joined to the Crown through process of marriage, would enjoy a reversal of fortune and transition from being the conquered to being the conqueror. There seems to be no end to the many ironies of history.

The years of Henry I of England are important to us today because of two entities that would be created during his reign. These would be the Curia Regia and the Exchequer. The first body, the Curia, was simply a council consisting of the feudal lords who would come together when summoned by the king. In the Curia, we find the beginnings of a civil administrative body. From the members of this Curia, an official class would be established and from this official class there would in the centuries to come arise a ruling class. The Exchequer, which still exists today in its more modern form, was simply a body of individuals similar to the Curia, but having the sole purpose of overseeing the collection of taxes and fees due to the Crown. In a feudal state, all is based upon ownership of the lands. The king is of course the principal landowner, and in return for their service, the feudal lords are granted lands by the Crown and these lords further divide these lands to the servile class, who in return work these lands for their respective lords. From serf to feudal lord, all owe taxes to the king, with the local sheriffs of the various counties acting as tax collectors. The Exchequer was simply a new civil body established to oversee the transactions of the various sheriffs. To consult Webster's dictionary, the definition of Exchequer is "an administrative and judicial state department in charge of revenue, so called from a table marked into squares, on which accounts of revenue were kept with counters."

The many accomplishments of Henry would go far to establish a further solid base of support for the Norman kings. The hand of fate would soon intervene. Henry would possess but a single son to inherit his crown and his authority. This young prince, aged 17, was to suffer an early demise, compliments of the English Channel. In 1120, while returning from his father's lands in France, the ship upon which he had embarked struck a rock and floundered. All but one drowned. The young prince would not be that one. The Anglo-Norman state would now become the scene of dynastic dispute. Before his death, Henry would seek to establish his daughter, Maud, as successor to the throne. The concept of female rule was not an accepted norm within the age of feudal states. Salic laws had long been established to exclude women from inheriting lands during a time when states were organized according to land tenure and military service. In the latter years of Henry's life, while he sought to establish the hereditary right of his daughter to assume the throne, the baronage and other parties would plot to assure otherwise. In addition to Maud and the baronage, there also existed another potential successor to the throne, Stephen of Blois, grandson of William the Conqueror. With the death of Henry I in December 1135, posturing and intrigue would begin.

While Maud, the only legitimate daughter of Henry had earlier been betrothed to Henry V, Holy Roman Emperor and King of Germany, she would not be present on English soil at the time of her father's death. In her absence, Stephen of Blois would waste no time in establishing himself as King of England. Stephen's brother Henry was Bishop of Winchester, and with his assistance, he would acquire the support of the Church. In a further move of strictly political motivation, he would acquire the support of the baronage by agreeing to relax the severe central controls which his predecessor has placed upon them. These measures were sufficient to ensure that he would be anointed as King Stephen. Whereas his initial actions were wise enough to allow him to attain the support of the Church and the nobles, his subsequent actions would be unwise enough to cause him to lose it. He would imprison the family of Roger, Bishop of Salisbury, thus offending many prelates by violating clerical privilege. In his willingness to accede authority to the barons, there was to grow within their ranks a loss of respect for him and a belief that the time had come to promote their own interest. With this perception of English decay, many of Stephen's enemies would advance into Northumbria. The Archbishop of York would also advance against him. Stephen would prove himself able to survive these challenges to his authority.

If Stephen believed with his victory at Northallerton over his combined rivals that things would soon get better, he would be much disappointed. In 1139, Maud would disentangle herself from her commitments on the continent and would return to England to claim the rights that her father had wished her to receive. Initially, Maud would receive the support of the Church and of many of the parties disaffected by Stephen. In 1141, general rebellion would break out against the rule of Stephen and Maud, though uncrowned, would become virtual monarch of the island. Maud would prove as politically unadroit as Stephen, and within a year she would find herself equally unpopular. With neither antagonist for the Crown able to gain a majority of support, all of the advances of Henry I would be squandered and his realm would descend into degeneracy and chaos. For the next six years there would be neither law nor order and the only thing that would prevail on the island kingdom would be endless civil war.

As with all cycles in history, the cycle of civil war would come to pass. In the aftermath of Maud's marriage to the Holy Roman Emperor Henry, she had remarried, this time to Geoffrey of Anjou. This marriage would produce a son, another Henry, in a time that seemed to be predominated by them. This son would adopt as his emblem the broom, or Planta Genesta. Thus was born to history one of the greatest of England's Kings, Henry Plantagenet. In 1147, while barely fifteen years of age, young Henry would begin his quest for the English crown. Initially, his attempts would meet with failure. Again in 1149, young Henry would campaign for the throne, this time his efforts being carried forward by David of Scotland and the Earl of Chester. Again these attempts would prove fruitless. In 1150, Henry would become Duke of Normandy and with his father's death one year later, Count of Anjou, Touraine and Maine, all provinces in France. This would effectively lead him to pay homage to his new lord, the King of France.

It would be in his travels to Paris to pay homage that one of the most politically significant and astute events of the Middle Ages would occur. At this time the throne of France was occupied by Louis VII, a man given to the ways of the Church. Much the same as Edward the Confessor of England, he would be devout and pious in all his actions. His queen, Eleanor of Aquitaine, was less than impressed by his ways. When young Henry presented himself before the French king to pay homage, he must have left a definite impression, if not on the king, then on his queen. Within short order, Eleanor would receive a divorce from Louis VII under the auspices of consanguinity. Soon thereafter, two months to be more precise, Eleanor would marry the young Henry. With her departure from the French king would go also many of the provinces of Western France. Thus with the marriage of Henry and Eleanor, the lands of Normandy and Anjou would be joined by those of Poitou, Saintonge, Périgord, Gascony, Angoumois, Limousin, as well as claims of suzerainty over Toulouse and Auvergne. If ever history has provided for a successful coup, to the medieval world this must have been it. Such a convulsive act in the feudal world could not go unchallenged. Soon Henry and Eleanor would find themselves under assault from the King of France, Stephen of England, the Count of Champagne and Henry's brother Geoffrey.

In the contest to ensue, Henry and Eleanor would be the beneficiaries of the Norman army, at that point in time probably the best in Europe. This would allow Henry to defend his realm and eventually to turn his attention north to the island. In January 1153, he would return to England to join battle against Stephen. In this contest much blood would be shed, with neither side able to gain a clear advantage. Eventually, an agreement would be reached at Winchester in that same year. Under the provisions of this agreement, Stephen would make Henry his adopted son. This temporary expedient would end the bloodshed and allow Stephen to temporarily remain as King of England. Temporary would prove to be quite temporary. Within one year, Stephen would die and England would soon have seated on its royal throne a new king whose bloodlines could be traced back to William the Conqueror and through his grandmother Matilda, to the now vanished Anglo-Saxon line of kings.

This new collection of lands, which were together inherited by Henry Plantagenet, are known to history as the Angevin Empire. To Henry II, there are due many credits. He was the first of the English monarchs to bring England, Scotland and Ireland into a more axial relationship. In the aftermath of the civil wars of the preceding decades, he re-introduced a unified judiciary and re-established the authority of the Exchequer. Henry Plantagenet is also known to us for his Constitutions of Clarendon, through which he attempted to establish a proper relationship between the powers of the Church and the powers of the state. With these Constitutions of Clarendon, he sought to have the Church submit itself to the laws of the state. It would be these attempts, plus the issue of Investiture, which would lead to the now famous dispute between Henry Plantagenet and the Archbishop of Canterbury, Thomas Becket.

Much of the conflict between Henry II and Becket centered around the concessions made by Henry's predecessor, Stephen, upon his accession to the throne. Henry was much of the temperament of his illustrious relative William the Conqueror. Henry believed the state to be supreme. Much of his energies would be spent in trying to regain what he believed to be lost rights which were rightfully his. His first step in this process was to appoint his servant, Thomas Becket, as Archbishop of Canterbury in 1162. His second step in 1164, was the publication of the earlier mentioned Constitution of Clarendon, a decided step toward the restoration of lost rights. But Henry had entirely misjudged his opponent. Becket and the Church were in no mood to give ground. Added to this conflict was the issue of Investiture. At this point in European history, the bishops were of similar stature to the earls in terms of power and wealth. Bishops were holders of extensive lands, they possessed the ability to place armed forces in the field and they held within their grasps the power of the Church, and hence the ability to excommunicate their perceived enemies. Henry sought to establish the right to have the bishops appointed by the monarch instead of by the Pope. If this right could be established, his hope would be that the bishops would then consider themselves as duty bound to him, a great advantage where there existed discrepancies between the state and the Church.

With the advantage of hindsight, all is known to us now. Initially, Becket would leave England and seek refuge on the continent, remaining there for a period of six years. Eventually, there would be a reconciliation between Henry II and Becket, who would return to England, exclaiming "I go to England, whether to peace or to destruction I know not; but God has decreed what fate awaits me."

That fate would not be pleasant. On December 29, 1170, by an act reminiscent of Caesar, of Stilicho, of Aetius, and of so many others, Becket would be cut down by four knights at his cathedral in Canterbury. The repercussions of this act would be terrible to the reign of Henry. Perhaps it was with the memory of Henry Plantagenet and Becket that our own founding fathers would institute a new form of government in 1787, based upon the concept of a separation of Church and state.

Following the assassination of Becket, Henry would continue to rule England for a period of another eighteen years. He would continue in his policy of establishing the rights of the monarch over those of the baronial class as initiated by his grandfather Henry I, and he would give to England a gift which endures to this day. Trial by jury would not be an invention of Henry II, the Carolingian dynasty of France had initiated this concept several centuries before. But to Henry II, must go much of the credit for establishing a "common law" as a replacement for the former system of Roman law based upon trial by duel and ordeal.

*England of Henry Plantagenet*

In his attempts to re-establish his authority over the barons, Henry would rely upon the old Saxon concept of the King's Peace. According to this concept, all Englishmen had their own peace and it was a criminal act to violate this peace. This so called peace also contained a social element. The more socially elevated the individual, the graver the infraction when this peace was violated. As the most socially elevated individual in the realm, the King's peace was regarded as the most sacred, and a violation of this peace was entitled to be tried in the King's court, as opposed to the baronial, or manorial courts. Gradually, Henry's policy was to bring more and more cases before the King's court, thus extending the King's peace over all of England. Civil cases were brought into the King's court by using the right of appeal in those instances where there existed a perception that justice had been denied to protect individuals in the possession of their lands and estates. This process was to be brought about gradually and without the use of legislation so as to not broadcast its effects. Under the manorial system of justice, determinations could vary from shire to shire, based upon any nature of events or conditions, including the political learnings of those who would sit in judgment. By offering defendants and litigants the perception of a more level playing field, the hope was to have more and more individuals inclined towards a judgment by the King's court. This would of course tip the balance of power towards the king and away from the barons in the judicial sphere. So as to make this new judicial concept available to his subject peoples of England, Henry Plantagenet would establish six assizes, or circuits, as they still exist to this day.

There would be other judicial reforms as well. To establish a legal basis which would allow individuals the right to remove their cases from the manorial courts and to bring them forth before the King's court, a system of writs, royal writs in this particular case, were established. Although these royal writs were originally few in number, so long as an individual could establish a relationship between their particular case and a royal writ, this could be considered as grounds to have their case heard before one of the

King's courts. It would also come to pass that with the establishment of Henry Plantagenet's courts we would find the initial uses of precedents and of case law. With case law, if an individual could show that in previous cases of a similar nature there existed an established custom or tendency in the rulings of the judge, then current judges would be more inclined to rule in this manner as well.

For all his greatness and his contributions toward the advancement of Western European society, Henry Plantagenet would fall victim to his successors much the same as Charlemagne had before him. Like so many of the other notable men of history, Henry would also fall victim to the allure of a woman other than his wife. Henry's relationship with this woman, known to history as "fair Rosamund," would of course strain his relationship with his wife, Eleanor. She would depart from England for the Angevin capital at Poitiers, where she, along with two of Henry's three surviving sons, Richard and John, would endeavor to undermine his rule. Upon the death of Henry's eldest son, the expectation arose that the next eldest, Richard, would be nominated as his successor. This, Henry refused to do, leaning instead toward the younger and more favored John. In 1188, under the influence of Eleanor, Richard was persuaded to pay homage to King Philip II of France. Shortly thereafter, this combination of Philip, Richard and Eleanor would launch an assault against Henry's dukedom of Anjou. During the course of this revolt against his father's authority, Richard would be joined by his younger brother, John. Being in the latter years of life, this strife brought about by the former queen and his two rebellious sons would sap Henry of much of his desire to live. Henry II, founder of the Plantagenet line of kings, would pass away at Chinon in Normandy on July 6, 1189. Soon his kingdom in England would return to the turmoil known to an earlier generation during the years of Stephen and Maud.

Richard would succeed his father to the throne of England. He is regarded at times as one of the great soldiers of his age, although this is at times disputed. His preoccupation with the third crusade would consume much of his time and most of his king's wealth. Having spent his formative years in France, he did not even speak the language of his English subjects. On the whole, history probably would consider him a weak king. The third crusade to which he devoted much of his time was no great success. Unlike the First crusade, Jerusalem would not fall and Richard the Lionheart would not become the great romantic warrior as had Godfrey of Boullion. He would defeat the armies of Saladin on the battlefield and he would win concessions, which would allow pilgrims access to holy places. But there would be no great or historic victory by which we would remember his name. In his absence from England, the brother who had joined him in the revolt against Henry II would now conspire against him as well, forming an alliance with King Philip II of France. Realizing this challenge to his authority, Richard, Coeur de Lion, would depart Palestine for his island kingdom. It would be during this journey home that Richard would be captured and turned over to the Holy Roman Emperor for ransom. Already crushed by the weight of taxes to pay for the crusades, the English people would now be taxed even more to ransom their king.

The rather prodigious ransom demanded by the Holy Roman Emperor for the release of Richard I was 150,000 marks, or roughly twice the annual revenues of the Crown. John and his allies, not especially keen to see the king released, would offer to the Holy Roman Emperor an equal amount to turn Richard over to them.

At this time, the Holy Roman Empire consisted of much of present day Germany. However, the Emperor stuck to his original bargain and the English people on the whole would remain loyal to their long absent king. The Church, having sanctioned the Third Crusade, would fulfill its obligations toward this ransom, even going so far as to sell off holy ornaments from the cathedrals. A new "scutage" would be collected and all laymen would be asked to forfeit one quarter of their movables to free their king. Even with all of these drastic measures for the collection of revenue, the required sum of 150,000 marks could not be attained. However, satisfied that he could at that time receive no more than was collected, the Holy Roman Emperor contented himself with an initial installment and Richard I was released to return home. This return home would not prove especially productive or lengthy. For the remaining five years of his reign, Richard would be forced to defend his domains in France from the determined efforts of Philip to gain them. It would be during these campaigns that Richard would meet his demise by means of a bolt from a crossbow. After receiving the fatal wound, and as he lay on his deathbed, Richard would name his troublesome brother John as heir to the throne and would ask all of his subjects present to swear fealty to him. As for the archer who had inflicted the fatal wound, Richard would have him brought before him, pardoning him and awarding him a monetary gift. Unfortunately for the archer, with the king's death, his successors would not be so forgiving and this man would be flayed alive.

If the reign of Richard the Lionheart was troubling to England, that of his successor John would be a disaster. Although King John was known to possess several abilities, political savvy would not be one of them. Much the same as the Roman Emperor Claudius, John was an ardent bibliophile and treasured his library of books to a great extent. He was capable of being kind and of being extremely cruel. It would be this cruelty and a tendency toward mischief that would lead to an accretion of various forces against him. Ultimately, this combination of forces would force upon John the Magna Carta, usually regarded as a milestone toward the rights of the English people and a new balance between the common people and the Feudal monarchs.

From the very beginning of his reign, King John would find himself under a constant challenge to his authority from a number of quarters. Richard's older brother, Geoffrey, had left a son by the name of Arthur, who was also considered as being an heir to the throne. Also, King Philip of France demanded that John pay fealty to him in regard to John's continental possessions in France. John immediately assumed the position that as King of England he could not possibly submit himself before the French king.

Each monarch would persist in their respective positions on this issue. Using John's refusal to appear before the French court as a form of legal justification, the French king would invade Normandy. In addition, all of King John's other possessions on the continent would be stripped from him. In 1202, King Philip of France would knight the young prince Arthur and would award to him all the fiefs formerly belonging to John. This act by Philip of France would prove fatal to the young prince, Arthur. During the contest to follow, the young prince would be captured by John at the castle of Mirebeau in Poitou. Joining the young prince in capture would be several hundred knights and a number of barons who had revolted against John and had sided with the sixteen-year-old Arthur. The young prince would be imprisoned first at Falaise and later at Rounen. The exact fate of this young man is not known to history, other than the fact that he was not to be seen again.

If it was the intention of King John to solidify his position on the continent and to regain his French provinces, he was soon to be disappointed. Within a year of Arthur's death, the remaining provinces in France would revolt against John. Philip would seize upon this opportunity and during the year 1203 would seize many of the Angevin fortresses. In March 1204, King Richard's prize possession, the Chateau Gaillard, would fall to Philip as well and possession of Normandy would finally revert back to France.

This would not be the last of the unfortunate series of events to set upon King John. In 1206, King John would become involved in an imbroglio with the Church. In that year Hubert Walter, Archbishop of Canterbury, would pass away. In a repeat of the earlier contentions of Henry Plantagenet over investiture, Pope Innocent III would send Stephen Langton to England to assume this post. John would reject his appointment. In addition, John would escalate his disagreement with the Church and begin to confiscate Church property in 1209. His reward for this act would be instantaneous excommunication, no small matter in medieval Europe. This would lead to dissention amongst both the baronial class and his overtaxed common people. In 1213, John would yield to the authority of the Church, going so far as to offer England as a fiefdom to papal authority.

For King John, the problems would only continue. His kingdom would be invaded by the Welsh of Llywelyn the Great, and shortly thereafter Philip of France would defeat John's German allies at Bovines. Having lost all faith and respect for their sovereign, the barons would fly into open revolt against his authority. For his earlier rejection as Archbishop, Stephen Langton would gain his revenge by suggesting openly to the barons that a charter similar in concept to that of Henry I should be forced upon their current king. In the year 1215, in a meadow referred to as Runnymeade, which sat astride the Thames River, John would be compelled to affix the king's seal upon this new magnificent charter or Magna Carta. Not nearly as familiar to history as the Declaration of Independence or the Constitution, this new document would in time serve as the embryo of democratic government in the Western World.

The democratization of England would continue under John's successor, the nine-year-old Henry III. The young king's accession to the throne would be enacted by his guardian, William Marshall. Upon John's death in 1216, it was Marshall who would rush the boy to Gloucester Abbey to have him crowned with the necessary approval of the Church. Three years later Marshall would die and the young king would receive a new overseer, Hubert de Burgh. Hubert would endeavor to return England to the path set forth by Henry II and would attempt in the aftermath of John to re-establish a centralized and capable civil administration. Initially, he would meet with some level of success.

In 1236, the twenty-nine-year-old Henry III would marry the thirteen-year-old Eleanor, daughter of Raymond of Provence. It would be this marriage that would set in motion a chain of events which would lead England to its first parlement, or parliament. With the addition of Eleanor to the king's court, there would come also four of her uncles and a additional entourage of court favorites. Increasingly these "foreigners" would come to fill ministerial and administrative offices and bishoprics. Whereas these positions had previously existed as the domain of the baronage, much discontent would be created within their ranks.

As a further complication to an already tense situation, there would exist a papal dispute with the Holy Roman Emperor, Frederick

II. This dispute would require the need for finance. Therefore, Pope Gregory IX would enter into a policy of exaction, demanding one-fifth of all the rents and movables of the English Church. Although this policy would meet with opposition from the English clergy, the papal emissary, Otto, would return to Rome in 1241 having accomplished his task. Salt would be introduced into an open wound when in recognition of this financial feat, the Pope would decree that the next three hundred vacant benefices would be rewarded to the Italian clergy; thus, a non-violent invasion of both English government and English Church.

In 1247, this non-violent invasion would continue when Henry III's half-brothers, from King John's Queen Isabella's second marriage, joined the royal retinue. As with all coteries, this ever-increasing group of non-English courtiers would scheme toward the advancement of their own interest. In earlier years it had been their efforts that had caused a breach between the young king and Hubert de Burgh. Their next object of intrigue would be Simon de Montfort, son of a soldier of France and husband to the sister of Henry III. Simon de Montfort had served as governor of English lands in Gascony and by his strength, energy and efficiency had earned for himself the jealousy of the king's alien entourage. In 1252, he would be brought to trial and although acquitted would agree to vacate his office. It was about this time, in 1253, that the military ambitions of King Henry III would be re-kindled and that he would seek to recover the English territories in France that had been lost by his predecessor King John. The raising of revenue for this campaign was entrusted to Henry's brother, Richard of Cornwall. In an already over-taxed kingdom, he would not readily meet with success in his endeavors. He then summoned a parlement, or discussion, composed of barons, bishops and for the first time, shire representatives.

Unfortunately for Henry III, this new concept of a parliament would be repeated in the near future, this time its intent was to limit his powers and not to increase his royal revenues. In the aftermath of Henry's less than successful campaign against France, the Pope would intimate to Henry that it might be a wise policy if Henry's son

Edmund and brother Richard could become the kings of Sicily and Rome respectively. The acquisition of these two thrones could be had for the then unheard sum of almost 135,000 pounds, nearly as much as had been asked for the ransom of Richard I. Exercising all of the influence at their disposal, a number of the baronial class united behind Simon de Montfort and refused to partake of this new round of taxation required for the acquisition of the two thrones. They would take their demands one step further than just refusal and would demand of the king new concessions. The result would be the so-called Provisions of Oxford, which were established in 1258 and later accompanied by the Provisions of Westminster. Included in the demands of these provisions were that the alien or foreign component of the king's council be excluded from the affairs of the state and that papal emissaries and foreign bankers be limited in their influence as well. In addition, a new council comprised of fifteen members, to be elected by two members of the baronial party and two from the king's party, would be formed to sit above the king's council of twenty-four. Naturally, this council was to be directed by Simon de Montfort himself. The king would make all attempts to reject the provisions. Easter of 1261 would find Henry III freed from the provisions of Oxford and Westminster by decree from the Pope and as a result, Henry would depose those ministers elected by the barons. Within a year, general insurrection would result. In this contest for control of English affairs, the feudal elements of English society would side with the king. To de Montfort would go popular support. Also to Simon de Montfort would go victory, attained at the Battle of Lewes in the summer of 1264. As a result of this battle, both Henry III and his son Edward would be captured by forces loyal to Simon de Montfort.

As his nature inclined him more towards being the chivalrous soldier and less toward being the astute politician, Simon did not seek unlimited authority with his victory. Instead, he signed a treaty with the captured king allowing for the continuance of the rights of the Crown, albeit with limited authority. One month after his victory over Henry at Lewes, Simon would call for a meeting of a new parliament, to consist of two knights from each shire and two elected burgesses from each city. This new parliament, which met in January 1265, is generally considered as being England's first true parliament.

Unfortunately, this new concept of government to include the participation and consent of the governed would prove to be short lived. Whereas Simon had succeeded in uniting the baronial class against the king, as soon as the barons found themselves in charge, they reverted to their former level of behavior and began to squabble amongst themselves. It would take but one year before Simon de Montfort would find himself in a battle against royal authority again, this time meeting Henry's son Edward of Evesham. There is an old saying that fortune has her favorites. In the wake of Evesham, fortune would offer no favor to Simon de Montfort, as his forces would be defeated and he himself would lose his life on the field of honor. As a warning to all others who might be so inclined as to challenge royal authority, Simon would be dismembered and have his head placed on a spike. Edward would call into place a new parliament and would use its proceedings as an avenue to repeal many of the provisions brought forth by earlier parliaments of Simon de Montfort. In the context of their times, the Magna Carta and de Montfort's parliament could not be regarded as the paramount events of their times. Yet, in the centuries to come, they would become the basis of the western governments as we know them today.

# Chapter 5

¤

# FROM CONTINENTAL POWER TO WORLD POWER

Following the magnificent Charter and the beginnings of parliamentary proceedings in England, there would be a period of expansion, civil war, further expansion, and further civil war. Ultimately England would supplant Imperial Rome as being the greatest empire known to the history of mankind. There would be many actors upon this stage, both men and women. However, if one were to span the entire six centuries that would be required to complete this process, there would be two implements of war associated with it and most responsible for its success. These two implements would be the English Longbow, and the warship in all of its various technological forms, from man o war, to dreadnaught, to the aircraft carrier. In some instances, the success of England in its rise to near world domination would be the result of the internal and external policies of its own government. In other instances, this success would be the result of geographical circumstances and advantages. For many centuries, England would find itself allied to or in opposition with other continental powers, such as Holland and France. All three nations would at some time exist as maritime powers. In regard to England's eventual naval superiority over France and Holland, "The strength of the latter was nearly exhausted by the necessity of keeping up a large army and carrying on expensive wars to preserve her independence; while the policy of France was constantly diverted, sometimes wisely and sometimes foolishly from sea to projects of continental extension."[27]

Another of the reasons for England's near world domination would be a simple physical property, buoyancy. As an island nation, much of England's economic survival would depend upon trade. Whereas most of this commercial and economic expansion would occur before the industrial revolution and the technological advances of steam or internal combustion engines, there existed the simple issue of ease of movement. Buoyancy allowed for the building of larger and larger ships to carry more and more goods, and sail power would prove to be the ultimate means of economically efficient travel. Given the fact that there were few, if any roads, and in the absence of bulldozers and motor graders to maintain them, it follows that England would eventually become dominant in a maritime sense.

There could be one other natural factor involved with England's rise to pre-eminence. As an island nation, England would be removed from the need to maintain large standing armies or static defenses to protect its borders. Essentially, it would be free to concentrate all of its efforts on maritime affairs. If the need arose for a large army, it could with little difficulty raise one. However, its need for armies would be more a matter of convenience than of national survival.

Being of insular origins, much of England's success would also arise from a sound foreign policy. Whereas continental Europe has always been comprised of many city states, nation states and ethnicities, when compressed into a limited geographical area, it would only be natural that issues of contention would arise. The dynastic dispute and the need for "Lebensraum" would always guarantee an abundance of armed conflicts. The two greatest and most destructive wars ever fought would both occur in England's back yard. Being of limited territorial expanse and hence of limited population and natural resources, the only way England could survive against more powerful and more populated nations, or combinations thereof, would be to enter into alliances and form

---

[27] Mahan, *Influence of Seapower Upon History, 1660-1805,* 33.

coalitions of weaker nations to combat the more powerful states. Prime examples of the success of this policy would be during the years of the War of Spanish Succession when King Louis XIV of France dominated continental Europe, and during the Napoleonic Wars when the Corsican Napoleon Bonaparte did much the same. In the Twentieth Century, this policy would remain very much unchanged, though in an ever-expanding world this policy would now include the nations of the new world as well. Eventually this policy would be adopted by England's offspring, the United States, which would eventually supplant England as the leader of the free world.

Long before the advent of the Dreadnaught and the Atom Bomb, and changes in the interrelationships of nations that would be brought about with their creation, it would all be reduced to a single weapon in a much simpler time to allow England to continue its genesis as a world power. As the Plantagenet aristocracy had given to England its first notions of government by the governed, the English would also be inheritors of a new political philosophy. In the latter years of the Roman Republic, it was generally recognized by ambitious men that the support of the people was usually accompanied by a demand for military success in the field. If possible, this success was to include the conquest of other peoples and the seizing of their lands and wealth. This tendency would arise in the English peoples as well. A chronicler of the Anglo-French world of his time, Froissart would write "The English will never love and honour their king unless he be victorious and a lover of arms and war against their neighbors."[28]

With the passing of the English Crown from Henry I to Edward I, there would be almost immediate adoption of this attitude and policy. Within three years of his 1274 coronation, Edward I would begin the most costly military enterprise to take place in the British Isles to that date. The pretense for the invasion of North Wales would be a refusal upon the part of the Welsh sovereign, Llywelyn ap Gruffudd, to pay

---

[28] Jenkins, *Short History of England*, 91.

homage to Edward at his coronation. In this campaign, noted more for its brutality than its success, a force of 15,000 professional soldiers would be employed. In a reminder of the methods of legionary tactics one thousand years before, this army would be accompanied by transports on the coast, as well as by road builders and a complete baggage train.

The English army would sustain itself by means of harvesting Welsh crops along its path of approach. With no sufficient fighting force with which to defeat this invasion, Llywelyn surrendered without bloodshed and agreed to pay the required homage to Edward, but this was not enough to satisfy Edward's appetite. A fine was imposed upon the Welsh rebels of 50,000 pounds. The fine would go unpaid and soon Llywelyn's brother Dafydd would go into rebellion as well. In 1282, ap Gruffudd would die in battle. His less fortunate brother would be captured, hanged, then drawn and quartered, a fate similar to that of Simon de Montfort and typical to those times.

When in 1286 the King of Scotland, Alexander III died, Edward would use the issue of succession as a basis to acquire Scotland as well. In this competition for the Scottish crown, the contestants would be John Balliol and Robert Bruce. Since the time of the Saxon kings, the Scottish kings had regularly paid homage to the English, thus establishing a level of English sovereignty north of the English-Scottish border. Edward would seek to re-establish this policy by supporting John Balliol. The Scottish barons would be so infuriated by this move that they would seek the assistance of France. In order to finance this new campaign against the combination of Scottish barons and French might, in 1290 Edward would expel the entire Jewish population of England and seize their property, as well as the property of anyone indebted to them. This he did by means of an edict of expulsion. The dire need of finances for his wars would lead him to take further action as well. He would convert his personal wardrobe into a new privy chamber, thus allowing for the creation of a privy purse to be overseen by a privy council. Realizing that the high levels of taxation placed upon the English people in recent years had often sown the seeds of discontentment, Edward would be the first of England's monarchs to realize that there was a close relationship between finances and consent. For this reason, in 1295, he called into being a new parliament, to be referred to as the Model Parliament, with the sole objective of voting money to finance his Scottish and continental wars. The importance of the new parliament was not so much its purpose, as its structure. This Model Parliament was to be the first bicameral parliament.

The upper house would consist of earls, barons, bishops and abbots in a baronial chamber and the lower House of Commons would consist of 292 representatives selected from the seventy boroughs. If their designated purpose was to vote the approval of funds for war, they would be very busy; Edward I was expending approximately one quarter of a million pounds per year on his wars.

If conquering Wales had proven a relatively easy feat of arms, Scotland would be much the opposite. In 1296, the individual who Edward I had chosen to succeed to the Scottish throne, John Balliol, was forced by his barons to renounce his homage to the English Crown. In retaliation, Edward would destroy the border town of Berwick and seize Balliol as a captive, removing him to England along with his crown, scepter and orb, as well as the Stone of Scone, also known as the Stone of Destiny. These acts would lead to the revolt of the Scots under the leadership of the Scottish nobleman William Wallace.

Finding himself now confronted by the situation that all nations fear, and trying to avoid a war on two fronts, Edward would come to realize that he had little chance of financing both and no chance of winning both at the same time. He therefore devised a new scheme so as to obtain his objectives. By means of a double marriage between himself and King Philip of France's sister Margaret, and of his son and heir Edward, to Philip's daughter Isabella, a peace with France was to be obtained. This would allow him the opportunity to concentrate his efforts and finances on the threat closest at hand, Scotland. Initially, Edward would meet with much success in his new campaign. When Edward I returned from France and hastened to his new theatre of operations, he would take no chances, bringing with him the entire feudal levy of England. At the Battle of Falkirk in 1298, Edward would take personal command of his armies. Realizing that Wallace had few cavalry and fewer archers, Edward would use his abundance of both to advantage. When the English heavy cavalry was initially repulsed by the spearmen of Wallace's Schiltrons (defensive circles, similar to the English defensive squares at Waterloo in 1815), Edward would simply use his archers to rain down death upon the unprotected Scots. This may have been a lesson kept in mind by Edward's grandson at Crecy. The results were very devastating and the grounds of Falkirk would be littered with fallen Scots. The remnants of the Scottish army would be scattered to the four winds and eventually their leader, Wallace, would be captured in 1305. His fate would be much the same as Simon de Montfort before him; similar fates to similar men from the same man. But Falkirk would not be the end of Edward's Scottish rebellion. One year after Wallace's death, Robert the Bruce would take up where Wallace had left off, crowning himself as King of Scotland.

Edward I, also known to history as "Longshanks" and "Hammer of the Scots," would murder every one of Bruce's relatives known to be in England. The sixty-eight year old warrior would set out to meet his new enemy, but would meet his demise along the route to battle.

Unfortunately for England and fortunately for Robert the Bruce, Edward II was not the soldier that his father was. In the summer of 1314, Edward II would lead an army of twenty-five thousand men to the relief of his forces besieged by Bruce at Sterling Castle. Being heavily outnumbered, Robert the Bruce would establish a defensive position south of Sterling to await the English onslaught.

He would select as a sight for the battle a position that would ensure that the flanks of his smaller army were secure, with an impassable morass on his left and a thick forest on his right. To his front, he would have his men dig several pits to be concealed with small branches and grass as obstacles against the more numerous English cavalry. Having failed to learn from his father's success at Falkirk, Edward the Second would send his heavy cavalry to engage the Scottish Schiltrons, only to see them repulsed. Other assaults would follow, to include the use of English archers who would in the confusion of battle hit more of the English soldiers in the back than they would of the Scots in the front. In the aftermath of a feigned flanking attack on the English left, Edward II would lose his nerve and flee the scene of battle. The remnants of his army would follow. Bannockburn has come to be regarded as one of the worst defeats of English arms ever and the worst to be suffered on English soil.

To the casual historian, one might actually regard Bannockburn as being England's Cannae. This victory, coupled with a second English defeat at the Battle of Byland in 1322, would result in the peace of Northampton in 1328 and the recognized independence of Scotland.

It would be by his general incompetence and perceived weakness in battle, having fled the field at Byland as he had at Bannockburn, which would lead to an accretion of further troubles for the ill-starred Edward II. His decided effeminacy would also lead to troubles. During the reign of Edward I, there existed a slightly too close relationship between Edward II and one of his advisors, a certain Piers Gaveston. This relationship would eventually cause Edward I to drive Gaveston into exile. With Edward I's death, the newly crowned Edward II would obtain his return. However, the king's council would adopt a similar attitude toward Gaveston and would banish him as well. When the king and Gaveston declined the opportunity for separation, it would lead to Gaveston's being seized and put to death. How the king's wife Isabella regarded this situation would be revealed to us by her future acts.

After the Peace of Northampton and following the loss of his most affectionate friend Gaveston, the king would add to his council the two Despensers, father and son, both bearing the name of Hugh. It would be the younger Despenser who would replace Gaveston as the object of Edward II's affection. It would be the actions of both that would incite another baronial war against the king. It would seem that the younger Despenser had been granted an Earldom of Gloucester with extensive lands in Glamorgan and Carmarthen. He would then be given the approval of the king to seize other baronial properties, in this case those of the De Claire family in Gower and Usk.

It would be this threat to the inheritance of land which would spark the new revolt. The leader of this revolt would be Roger of Mortimer, who would eventually be captured and forced to flee to France.

Once again, it would be circumstances in France that would interject themselves into the affairs of England. In the year 1324, there would occur in the Province of Gascony a dispute which would lead Charles IV of France to seize this duchy. Edward II's wife Isabella, in the same way disgusted with the king's affections toward Hugh Despenser as she had been with Piers Gaveston, would use the Gascony dispute as reason to leave England and negotiate with her brother Charles over the Gascony issue. While in France Isabella would become acquainted with and become a willing confederate of the exiled Roger of Mortimer. Soon the two lovers would be joined in France by the young Prince Edward, heir to the throne. With the approaching year of 1326, and in a repeat of the act of William the Conqueror, Isabella and Mortimer would return to England, landing initially in East Anglia. The man who had fled at Bannockburn and Byland would again flee, along with his councilor Hugh Despenser. Both would meet their ends by acts of signal brutality dispensed by "the she-wolf of France." Despenser would be captured "strung up, castrated, forced to watch his genitals being burned, hanged and while still (amazingly) conscious, disemboweled and quartered."[29]

For his earlier offenses against his queen, Isabella would force Edward II to abdicate, on condition that the young Prince Edward would acquire the throne. This condition would be met. With the coronation of the new king, Edward II would be removed to Berkley Castle, where he would die within the year. Popular lore has it that as possible reparation for his perceived or even perhaps real homosexual tendencies that his bowels were burned out by use of red hot irons.

---

[29] Ibid, 87-88.

The years of the two Plantagenet kings, Edward I and Edward II, were to be accompanied by a shift in the balance of power and a transformation in the means of government. In the early years of Edward I, the balance of power and form of government was between the baronial class and the Crown. This of course explains the actions of Simon de Montfort and of Roger of Mortimer, with the baronial class struggling against perceived abuses by the Crown. It would be during the Plantagenet years that the "king's wardrobe" would gain in importance. To consider this in a modern sense, we might compare the king's wardrobe with the executive office of the United States, where you have a president with his various secretaries who combine to formulate public policy. This policy of course requires a level of consent from the Senate. In Plantagenet England, the baronial class would begin to see this increase of influence within the "king's wardrobe." This increase in influence would parallel the later years of the Roman Principate, where various chamberlains, oftentimes eunuchs, would increasingly control the affairs of government in the absence of strong leadership.

In the years of Henry II, it would be the so-called "aliens" or foreigners who would wield increased authority. Yet as able administrators of increasingly complex state governments, the energies and abilities of these administrators were necessary for the operations of government. Therefore, in the later years of the Plantagenet dynasty it would increasingly become the policy of the barons to either choose or to have influence in the appointing of these offices of the Household. An open avenue in this process would be the use of the parliament. As evidence of the importance and growth in influence of Parliament, during the years of Edward II's reign, Parliament would be called into session at least twenty-five times.

With the ascension to the throne of Edward III of England, there would exist a few quiet years, as this new king would initially govern only by the consent of Isabella and Mortimer. By 1329, the seventeen-year-old king would be married; a year later his new wife would give him a son. In years past, the English realm had seen steady conflict between the barons and the kings. This time there would be a union of barons with the new king, with the intention of removing Isabella and the despotic Mortimer from control of English affairs. In October of 1330, Parliament would be called into session at Nottingham Castle, to be joined there in attendance by the Queen mother and Mortimer. While at Nottingham Castle, the two acting rulers would be seized by agents of the young king who had gained access to the castle by means of a secret underground passage. In an act far more generous than Mortimer and Isabella had dealt to Despenser and Edward II, Mortimer would be tried and condemned to death by the lords and hanged on November 29. The Queen mother would be consigned to captivity for life.

At this time, a new phenomenon would appear within the more democratic system allowed with the creation of a stable and influential parliament. This new phenomenon would be the use of Parliament as an avenue for the mercantile and commercial class to intervene in the policies and affairs of the state. The root cause in this new trend would lie in the wool trade. It would seem that about this time in European history that the Flemish towns of the Low Countries were engaging in a new form of economic development based upon the weaving of cloth. This new weaving of cloth was dependent upon wool being raised in England. However, the still feudal courts of Flanders nursed only antipathy for this new industry, considering only that the increase of wealth and power of this new merchant class would conflict with their own wealth and power. The nobility of the Netherlands would seek to curb the influence of the new cloth merchants by a policy of placing obstructions upon the wool trade, Fourteenth Century economic warfare if you will. These new policies would only act to incite the enmity of the mercantile element in the English Parliament.

The new mercantile crisis being contested over the wool trade would also be complicated by dynastic dispute. In 1328, Charles IV of France would die without leaving a legitimate heir. Edward III's mother, Isabella, being the king's sister, would claim the throne for her son. Also laying claim to the vacant throne would be Philip VI of Valois, Charles' cousin. The combination of these events would touch off the Hundred Years War. In its initial phase, the English navy of Edward III would defeat a French fleet in the English Channel, thereby assuring the possibility of an English invasion of France. Edward, in accordance with his naval powers, would be afforded the title "King of the Sea." It is important to note that in this naval battle, the English Longbow would play a crucial role, allowing a smaller English force of about 180 vessels to defeat the larger French navy of about 190 vessels. As a result of this battle, Philip of France would sign a two-year truce with Edward III.

As they had in the past, it would be the French Provinces that would bring about a renewal of hostilities between the English and French monarchs. During the years of 1345 and 1346, Brittany and Gascony would be the scene of renewed conflict. This would lead Edward to invade France wholesale in the year 1346. Departing Portsmouth in July of that year, Edward would set sail with an invading force of about 3,000 knights, 10,000 English archers and 4,000 Welsh light infantry.[30] Following his landing at La Hogue, Edward would march inland via Carenton and St. Lo, names now associated with a much larger invasion some five centuries later, with the avowed purpose of liberating, and not conquering France.

After a month of campaigning in and around France, Edward would select a site suitable for a major engagement near Crecy-en-Ponthieu. It is estimated that in the battle to come that with re-enforcements, Edward's army would comprise about 20,000 men, divided into three groups referred to as "battles." This English force, in hostile territory, would be met by a French army of 60,000 fighting men, including 12,000 heavy cavalry. While numbers would favor the French, there was a certain advantage for the forces of Edward. Edward's force was a professional army, English soldiers enlisted for the duration of the conflict. While the army of Philip of France did enjoy an enormous advantage in numbers of cavalry, many of the soldiers of France were either Genoese mercenaries or communal levies. In addition, the archers of Edward possessed the longbow,

---

[30] Dupuy, *Encyclopedia of Military History*, 354.

those of Philip the much less capable crossbow.

The Battle of Crecy was to begin almost accidently, much like the Battle of Gettysburg during the American Civil War. On August 26, 1364, while advancing along the route of march, the army of Philip would accidently bump into the English line around 6:00 p.m. It was the intention of Philip to give battle the next day. However his undisciplined troops would have none of this. During the next several hours, fifteen or more separate waves of French crossbowmen and mounted knights would assault the English lines, only to encounter a hailstorm of arrows from the English archers. Each of the French assaults would end with the heavy loss of life. By nightfall, 1,542 French knights and more than 10,000 other French soldiers would be dead on the field. English losses are recorded as 2 knights killed, with about 200 archers and infantry killed.[31] Crecy is regarded as one of the more decisive engagements ever fought. The one thousand year dominance of mounted cavalry that had begun with the Gothic victory over the Roman legions at Adrianople in 379 A.D. was now reversed, to remain so until the modern armored formations of the twentieth century.

The Battle of Crecy would result in a truce being signed between Edward and his French antagonist. This truce would not come as a consequence of victory or of need. It was around this time that a pestilence far greater than war was descending upon Europe; the Black Death or Bubonic Plague. This disease was ravaging the populations of both countries so severely that a "time out" was called by both sides. If ever ill-effects were gained by international trade, this would be the prime example. Carried to England along the trade routes from the Far East by means of one of mankind's closest associates, the rat, the Black Death would deprive England of nearly a quarter of its population.

Tragically the plague was to have an upside. With the loss of so many laborers, wages in England nearly doubled, and while there were fewer bodies to occupy dwellings, rents decreased dramatically.

---

[31] Ibid, 356.

In turn, these wage increases were to have another consequence, similar in nature to what was to transpire in the Western World with the Industrial Revolution. Whereas the population decreased dramatically, there was now a surplus of food and a resulting decline in prices. The practice of arable farming, raising food crops has been until recent times very labor intensive. With an increase in wages, many farmers who were suffering from the ill effects of lowering food prices simply left the farms for easier work and more wealth in other occupations. No nation has ever experienced positive gain due to a negation of its agricultural abilities.

Plague or no plague, Edward's foreign policy of waging war in continental France would resume. Almost exactly ten years after Crecy, a new campaign and a new battle would be fought which would go a very long way in testifying to the intransigence of mankind. In 1355, Edward III would send his two sons, Edward the Black Prince, and John of Gaunt, across the channel to raid across Northern France.

A new French king, John II, would be present to contest this new series of raids. Once again a larger French army would be assembled to repel a smaller English one. And once again, the large French army would pursue the English across France. In a repeat of the Crecy battle, the armies would again meet accidentally, this time the English stumbling into the French. As at Crecy, the French army would have a very heavy contingent of mercenaries. And again, the larger French army, although this time dismounted, would assault the English lines. The outcome of this new battle, Poitiers, fought September 19, 1356, would be the same. The English Longbow would devastate the French armies again and the new King of France, John, would be captured and taken to England as a captive.

Following this second major contest of the Hundred Years War, a new treaty would be signed. With the Peace of Brétigny in October of 1360, France would cede to Edward III the possessions of Calais and Ponthieu. In return, Edward relinquished control of Normandy, gave up all claim to the French crown and King John was ransomed for 3 million gold crowns.

It would be during Edward III's campaign against France and in the aftermath of Crecy and Poitiers that new political developments and social ideas would arise. Ever since 1253, when Henry III's brother, Richard of Cornwall, had called for a "parlement" to authorize funds for Henry III's campaign in France, it had become customary for English Parliaments to grant funding for the wars of the English kings without dissent. This would now change. Showing signs of increased authority, Parliament would now seek political concessions from the king in exchange for appropriations for war. It would also be during the years of Edward III that Parliament would become recognized as two separate bodies, the Lords, who regarded themselves as counselors to the Crown, and the Commons, who were to become associated with the granting of taxes and the presenting of petitions for the redress of grievances, both locally and nationally.

In the aftermath of Crecy and Poitiers there would occur within the English mindset a change in attitude towards its armies, similar to that which occurred in the American people following the victories of World War I and World War II. Initially English armies were called into action for defense against invading enemies, the Romans, Saxons, Danes and Normans. There existed always the question of who would prevail, as many times it was not the English.

After Crecy and Poitiers, the English armies themselves were at times the invaders, with victory expected. However, an issue would arise in England during these years, which is associated with our own wartime efforts. While the English were often enthusiastic about the exploits of their soldiers, they were rarely as enthusiastic about the accompanying taxes to support those engagements. Often this lack of enthusiasm bordered on outright resent; so too with the American public in the aftermath of the victories of the World Wars. There is always a willingness to send military troops afar with the expectation of immediate and overwhelming success, to be accompanied with a resentment of taxation to support modern, integrated, combat forces.

There would at this time occur a brief interlude in England's continuous cycle of the use of combined land and naval forces of war against their neighbors across the channel. The accretion of various events and conditions that had placed a severe strain on the English economy, now manifested itself in the form of a popular uprising, or peasant's revolt. When wages soared following the plague, or Black Death, it became possible for the more servile class to rid themselves of class barriers and seek employment with the highest bidder. In reaction to this trend, Parliament in 1351 would pass the Statute of Labourers, an attempt to fix wages at earlier pre-plague levels to limit the migration of workers from their established types of employment, and to enforce the age old feudal contracts.

To this list of grievances would be the creation of a poll tax, levied at the rate of four pence on every English person over fourteen years of age. This poll tax was the brainchild of John of Gaunt, son of the now debilitated Edward III and uncle to England's next king, the ten-year-old son of the Black Prince. After the coronation of Richard II, this poll tax would increase to a shilling a head in 1381.

What was to follow these parliamentary actions is often referred to as the Peasant's Revolt. This revolt would be the precursor of the demonstrations we see intermingled throughout our own American history, such as the Boston Tea Party, or the Civil Rights riots of the 1960s. An armed rebellion with the intention of deposing the existing form of government it was not.

Some acts of violence were to occur, such as the burning of manorial properties and taxation records. The revolt was largely unorganized, although history affords to us the names of Wat Tyler, Jack Straw and John Ball as individuals who would play active roles during this revolt. Eventually the displeased and disparate groups comprising the rebellion would march on London, consigning the city to three days of anarchy in June of 1381. At this point in time, the rebellion would descend into a period of escalating violence. Records exist describing foreigners being murdered. Two members of government, the Archbishop of Canterbury, Simon Sudbury, and the treasurer, Sir Robert Hales, were dragged away by the mob and beheaded on Tower Hill. As further proof of their displeasure with current affairs, the palace of the Regent John of Gaunt was burned. In response to this escalation of violence, the fourteen-year-old king would ride out to the mob, meeting their leaders at Smithfield. The demands placed upon the young king were generally mild. They asked for repeal of the poll tax and of other oppressive statutes, as well as the abolition of Villeinage and a division of Church property. It would be during these negotiations that Wat Tyler, while approaching the King, would be knocked down by the Mayor of London and then killed by one of the king's attendants. In the following pandemonium, the young king would cry out "I will be your leader. You shall have from me all that you seek."[32] This declaration was no doubt to appease public opinion, unlike the actions that were to follow.

As so often proves the case when an unorganized revolt is confronted by organized authority, all and any concessions granted would later be cancelled as having occurred through an underage king under duress. In time the new king would be considered to have made the remark, "Rustics you were and rustics you are still. You will remain in bondage not as before, but incomparably harsher."[33] The consequences of this challenge to English authority were severe. Approximately one hundred fifty executions took place, all to occur by hanging after trial by jury. In January 1382, a general amnesty was proclaimed by Parliament, although this did little to assuage the anger of the lower class, or to mitigate the fear of further rebellion in the upper class.

If the actions and statements of Richard II were baffling and troubling to the masses of the Peasant's Revolt, much worse was to come. In the year 1397, Richard would seek to restore the pre-eminence of the King's prerogatives by using a new Parliament to cancel and repeal the majority of rights and privileges of the lower class gained during the previous century. Richard would accomplish this feat by stacking the Parliament with individuals sympathetic to his cause. However, what the Parliament did not realize was that as they were busy repealing all of the advantages of democracy

---

[32] Churchill, *History of the English Speaking Peoples*, 315.
[33] Jenkins, *Short History of England*, 103.

conceded through the generosity of the two great Edwards or gained by the profligacy of John and Edward II, they also were guaranteeing the reduction of their own authority. Richard II was not the first individual to employ this method of seeking absolute power, nor would he be the last. What he would be was one of the more successful kings in his attempts. After completing its task of reversing all the beneficial gains of an entire century, this Parliament would consign itself to oblivion by allowing for a committee of eighteen selected persons to complete the remainder of its work as soon as Parliament dispersed. Never has a legislative body been as destructive of its own ends. One would think, and hope, that this lesson might reverberate down through history to the more democratic peoples of our times, though such does not appear to have been the case.

Fortunately for English society and history, Richard's thirst for power would exceed his abilities in retaining it. Once the rights of the common people and the inconvenience of having a Parliament to contend with were removed, Richard would seek to remove himself of any possible rival to the throne. Henry Bolingbroke, as son of John of Gaunt, would be the next logical successor to the throne of England in Richard's absence. A quarrel would arise between Henry of Bolingbroke and Thomas Mowbray, Duke of Norfolk. At issue was the perception of treasonable language used by the latter. The issue would be brought before a reconvened Parliament, where each party would give the lie to the other. In the absence of a possible verdict, trial by armed conflict, a duel of sorts, seemed to be the only solution. However, seeing opportunity and seizing the initiative, Richard would forbid this contest from occurring, opting instead to exile Thomas Mowbray for life, Henry Bolingbroke for a decade. This calculated move, intended only to remove a possible rival, would set in place a chain of events that would guarantee that within the span of one year, Richard II would see his fortunes decline from absolute power to absolute ruin.

Without the authority or the ability to contest the decree of Richard II, Henry Bolingbroke would remove himself to France. In his absence, the populace of England would awake from its period of somnolence to realize that a servile Parliament had gambled away many of their hard earned rights. To complicate this situation, in February of 1399, Henry Bolingbroke's father, John of Gaunt, would pass away. By hereditary right, this would secure for Henry the vast estates of his father. But Richard, seeing the opportunity to add substantial money to his more than substantial power, employed the use of a technical legal seizure of John's Lancastrian estates and declared Henry as being disinherited. By this act, he unwittingly challenged the right of all property-holders and incited the enmity of the old baronial class. Having now been able to rid himself of all political inconveniences and rivals, Richard II decided that his next move should be an expedition into Ireland to re-assert royal authority on the island.

In his absence, Henry would return to England, where the disaffected segments of English society would rush to his side. The series of events to follow are almost an exact parallel of the return to England of Isabella and Mortimer three quarters of a century prior. Death by hanging would be the reward for a number of Richard's ministers, and hence accomplices. Richard himself would hasten home from Ireland, only to find that as a political force he was now a non-entity. At Flint he would submit to England's new monarch, Henry Bolingbroke, now referred to as King Henry IV. History does not bestow upon us the reason of Richard's death shortly thereafter, although it does hint at the possibility of starvation, either inflicted or self-inflicted. It is a great irony however that the man who sought to remove from the people their hard earned rights and Parliamentary institutions, was to become in his time, a martyr to the common people.

While fortune may have favored Henry Bolingbroke in his contest against Richard II, it would soon desert him. Regarded as a generous and amicable man, the stresses and strains of kingship would wear on him heavily, eventually leading to a severe decline in his health. He would come to be afflicted with a severe disorder of the skin and also develop a heart condition, which would cause him fainting spells. It is with his reign however that western society will always associate a development toward a more democratic relationship between legislatures and heads of state. Before Bolingbroke, Parliaments had been used by the various monarchs as a means to legally generate tax revenues. A new relationship and practice was now to begin. In addition to the raising of revenues, Parliament would now be granted the authority to become involved in tracking tax expenditures, something which prior kings would never consent to. This practice of financial audit and oversight would eventually become an established practice within western democratic societies.

Perhaps the greatest gift that Henry IV was to bestow upon his realm, however, was his eldest son, the Prince of Wales. In the centuries recent to Henry Bolingbroke, many of the more gifted and able English kings would have the efforts of their energies and lifetimes wasted away due to successors less than able to do their task. Edward I would fall victim to this trend through the failures of Edward II. Likewise, Edward III would suffer a similar fate due to the inabilities of Richard II. Such was not to be the fate of Henry Bolingbroke. In his eldest son, England would find the qualities and abilities that all subject people wish for in their monarch. Henry V would become king at the early age of twenty-six. However, much of his early life had been spent in close proximity to the dealings of his father's court. He had already fought in battle, at Shrewsbury in July of 1403.

In addition to his growing perchant for armed conflict, Henry V would display signs of political ability, as well as indications of knowing recent English history. It had been the realization and thus the policy of Edward III to divert the energies, intrigues and rivalries of the nobles away from internal issues by unifying them in the purpose of a foreign war. Such was now to be the adopted policy of Henry V, to lead the English people away from internal discord by means of foreign conquest. Whereas it was the norm for Parliament to acquire and approve the expenditure of funding for foreign wars, Henry V would first have to win the approval of this body. This would be accompanied by political means. As a concession to the commons, he would declare "that no law should be passed without their assent."[34] He would also declare a general pardon as a means of assuaging issues from the past. The body of the deposed yet extremely popular Richard II would be brought to London for re-internment at Westminster Abbey in a further attempt to gain favor.

Thus with funding assured and popular support garnered, Henry V would begin preparations for a new cross-channel assault. Henry would initiate a new policy in regard to the English navy. Whereas in the past it had been the policy to seize and then arm private ships during times of crisis, Henry would now initiate the policy of building specialized warships for the Royal Navy. The number initially chosen for this new naval construction was at least six, a number familiar with the United States Navy during its formative years, when the U.S. Congress would authorize the construction of six frigates. There would also be some modifications to the English army. At Poitiers, the French had chosen to fight dismounted due to the devastating effects of the longbow on cavalry. Therefore, in this campaign, Henry's six thousand archers would also be armed as infantry. This cross training of arms would play a decisive role in the upcoming campaign.

The prelude to war would assume the guise of a French dynastic dispute. In 1407, conflict would erupt in France between the Orleanist and the Burgundians after the murder of the Duke of Orleans, due entirely to the instigation of the Duke of Burgundy. In this contest, the Orleanist would gain the upper hand, forcing the Burgundians to seek assistance from across the Channel. Again displaying adroit diplomatic skills, Henry would be all too happy to oblige. In May of 1413, Henry secured the neutrality of John the Fearless, Duke of Burgundy. This agreement between Henry and John entailed a promise from John of neutrality in exchange for increased territory as Henry's vassal. With this assurance of non-interference from John, and with his preparations for war completed, Henry sailed for Normandy with his newly formed army in August of 1415.

---

[34] Churchill, *History of the English Speaking Peoples*, 338.

After capturing the city of Harfleur and losing many of his troops to the soldier's most dreaded enemy, disease, Henry would begin his march into the interior of France. In a series of events and marches very much similar to those of his grandfather, Edward III, Henry and his army eventually made contact with the much larger French force near the Castle of Agincourt.

In the advance of the battle, Henry, who found himself outnumbered by a margin of 3-1, would attempt to avoid battle through negotiation. However, the French, confident against Henry much as they had been against Edward III before Crecy, would decline to parle. Therefore, with his army starving and his line of retreat to the French coast blocked by the French army, Henry would opt for battle. He would initially deploy his forces much the same as his grandfather had at Crecy, with archers formed into wedges with heavy infantry in the gaps between. It was the hope of the French commander, D'Albret, that in his youth, Henry would be rash and launch an assault against the French lines. However, Henry would decline to do so. Shortly after 11 o'clock on the morning of October 25, St. Crispins Day, Henry would feign an attack against the French lines, marching forward approximately a half mile to confront the French. They would then halt their advance and quickly pound stakes into the ground to act as a counter to French heavy cavalry. As had happened at Crecy, this feigned attack would cause the overconfident French to assault the English lines. The heavily armored French foot soldiers would move ponderously forward, with the French heavy cavalry moving around their flanks to assault the English. Once again the authority of the longbow would be felt upon the battlefield, as all of the French heavy cavalry would be cut down. In spite of this, the French heavy infantry pressed on, closing with the English line and threatening to overcome it. At this point, as they had been trained by Henry to do so, the English archers would lay aside their longbows and take up their swords and battle-axes. The result would be the utter destruction of the French first line of battle. A second French assault was to follow, only to meet with the same unfortunate results.

At this point in the battle, a very unfortunate and unchivalric event would transpire. While away from their camp engaging the French foe, word was to reach Henry at the front that his camp in the rear was being assaulted. Fearing that his already heavily outnumbered forces were about to be attacked from the rear, Henry ordered that all French captives be put to the sword. As events would unfold, this event would prove to have been brought about by false information, as the feared assault on his camp was merely a case of depredation by French peasants seeking plunder. In the aftermath of this most unfortunate event, Henry would secure victory over the French with a cavalry charge, which he led himself. Victory was complete, over 5,000 French, including D'Albret and many of the Orleanist leaders were killed. English losses were reported as 13 men at arms and 100-foot soldiers killed during the battle.[35] The supremacy of the Burgundians in France was assured and Henry V would henceforth be regarded as King of England and of France.

Henry V had now led England to the height of its power over continental France. Now the English were to discover the lesson administered to their Roman overlords from fourteen centuries before them that, while it may be possible to conquer a foreign land or defeat the enemy's armies, it is rarely possible to subjugate the conquered peoples of such lands. Shortly after his overwhelming victory at Agincourt, Henry would march his victorious army to Calais and then depart France altogether. It is known that during his campaign in France that the French peasants had engaged in the use of guerilla tactics against his forces. He may have also been concerned about Genoese fleets in the Channel preventing either reinforcement of his army or of his return to England.

With Henry's withdrawal from the continent, certain facts became known to him. One of his primary realizations was of the importance of controlling the seas. Before his invasion of the continent, Henry had inaugurated a program of building purpose-built warships for his navy. This concept was now to be expanded upon. For his recognition of the importance of the seas and also of his steps to build then state

---

[35] Dupuy, *Encyclopedia of Military History*, 415.

of the art warships, Henry V would be regarded by some historians as the father of the modern Royal Navy.

There were other contributions and flaws, which Henry would contribute to his island nation. Henry V is regarded as having been the first English king to use the English language as his primary means of communication, unlike many of his Plantagenet predecessors who predominately spoke French. His armies were generally recognized as being comprised of English troops, not of Normans, Saxons or Danes. His reign was sustained by a Parliament that could claim to speak for an entirely English populace, not a section of the people according to social class or ethnicity. On the down side of affairs, his lengthy and costly campaigns back in France after a second invasion in 1417, would deplete the country's finances and lead to a cooling of the nation's war-like spirit, much the same as America's protracted wars in Iraq and Afghanistan have done in the twenty-first century.

For all Henry V's greatness and all the successes he gained for his nation by means of both diplomacy and war, nearly all of these gains would be lost or squandered by his successor following the King's demise in 1422 from dysentery and in his absence. As had proven the case with Henry Plantagenet, Edward I and Edward III, a reign that was pregnant with glory and possibilities was to be succeeded by another of almost unmitigated disaster. After his victories over Charles of France, Henry had married Charles' daughter, the princess Catherine. Through this marriage, Henry V received a son. It would be this ten-month-old infant on whom the weight of the combined crowns of England and France would fall. To a man such as his father, this weight would have been an opportunity. To the son, this weight would press upon him extremely so, leaving his people and his realm as hapless victims.

The reign of Henry V would forever become associated with the loss of France to the English Crown and with what might be considered as England's first Civil War, the Wars of the Roses. With the ascension to the throne by a ten-month-old boy, the French would see weakness and opportunity, much the same as the barbarian peoples would see weakness along the frontiers of the Roman Empire with the disappearance of the legions. Almost immediately after the deaths of Henry V and Charles VI of France two months later, many factions in France would recognize Charles' son, the Dauphin, as rightful King of France. This move was an obvious breach of the earlier Treaty of Troyes, through which Henry V or his heir were to be recognized by France as their rightful king upon the death of Charles VI. Hostilities were soon to begin.

It would be upon this stage of events that we find one of history's great anomalies. Since the time of Edward I and the first use of the English longbow, English armies had been masters of the European battlefields. In France, the English victories at Crecy, Poitiers and Agincourt had established a long tradition of English mastery over their French antagonist. In the initial years of this new phase of Anglo-French warfare, the theme was often repeated. Under the able leadership of John, Duke of Bedford, brother of Henry V, the ascendancy of English arms in France was continued. At Cravant in August 1423, a French force aided by a strong contingent of Scots was destroyed by yet another hailstorm of English arrows. At Verneuil a year later, the long list of English victories was continued. In this battle, a Scottish contingent of at least five thousand men lead by Douglas, Constable of Scotland, was utterly destroyed.

Events and technology were now to intervene against English mastery. From the fringes of the Vosges Forest would arrive a 17-year-old peasant girl who would convince the Dauphin that she had been divinely inspired to guide him to the throne of occupied France and to assist him in the expulsion of their mutual English foe. Persuasive in her arguments, the Dauphin would entrust her with an army to relieve the besieged city of Orleans. This decision would no doubt incite the jealousies of the members of the Dauphin's court, which would probably play a part in Joan of Arc's ultimate fate. The inspired leadership of Joan would help the French army lift the siege of Orleans, ending the mythology of English invincibility and leading to a chain of subsequent French victories. As Joan of Arc had earlier prophesized, the Dauphin would be coronated at Rheims as King

Charles VII. It is truly ironic and tragic that after her "twenty victories" and the coronation of Charles VII, Joan would somehow view her mission as being completed and would ask to be allowed to return to her farm.

Perhaps we should not associate with Joan of Arc the notion of sainthood, but rather we might consider her as the Cincinnatus of her time. Soon, fate would afford to Joan of Arc a very cruel turn of events. With her victories and with the new king's coronation, it would become evident that her allegiance was to God and country, not to the Church or the Orleanist party. With her arrival on the stage of events, a new nationalism was to be born into the French mind. This new nationalism was to be very inconvenient to the particularistic interest and those who formerly gave Joan their allegiance, were now compelled to give her only their scorn.

In May 1430, an English force under the Duke of Bedford would besiege Compiégne in an effort to re-assert English control of the Seine Valley. To the relief of this city, Joan would lead a force of six hundred men, who would attempt a cavalry sortie across a long causeway over the river and into the besieged city. But the English would put up a stiff resistance and in the ensuing encounter Joan would be captured by the Burgundians, who would in turn sell her to the English.

Whereas Joan may have been regarded as a patriot and saint by the French, to the English she bore epithets of a far less pleasant nature. However, as was customary at the time, the English would view her as an asset and would attempt to ransom her back to the French. To the amazement of the English, the French would decline and the peasant girl who had saved France would be left to her fate. Her fate was to be especially vindictive. That which had worked for her, claiming that she was a visitant sent by God to assist her king and her country, would now work against her, as she was condemned as being a heretic by her English captives and sentenced to death by fire. On May 29, 1431, Joan of Arc would be staked atop her own funeral pyre in the marketplace of Rouen. Although she would not live to see it, she would have her revenge upon the English.

Following Joan's execution, skirmishing would continue between the English and French forces. Finally, on April 16, 1444, the Truce of Tours would signal a five-year cessation of hostilities. During these five years, the French army would be extensively modernized. For many years the English Longbow was the master of the battlefield. In an attempt to offset this tactical advantage, France would now organize a professional army, to be accompanied by the adoption of cannon into the world's first efficient artillery organization. With a population of over fifteen million citizens, as compared to only two and one-half million citizens of England, France not only possessed superiority of numbers, but a technological advantage as well.

In 1449, the Truce of Tours would expire. Hostilities would resume with the French re-conquest of Normandy. For the next four years, France would prove victorious on the battlefield. Finally at the Battle of Castillon in July of 1453, English forces, under the Earl of Shrewsbury, would be decisively defeated by French artillery fire, thus effectively ending the Hundred Years War and removing English influence from the French provinces for good.

England would now descend into years of internal unrest and continuous conflict during the Wars of the Roses, which was essentially a civil war fought between two political entities, the Lancastrians and the Yorkist. For thirty years England would be engulfed in bloodshed, with approximately one third of England's 150 noble families being almost extirpated. Perhaps the only thing provided by these fruitless and sanguinary wars was the lesson learned by the Romans during the years of the principate, this being the insecurity of hereditary rule. The Wars of the Roses would alternate along with the fortunes of the various contestants. In turn, Henry VI, Richard, Duke of York, Henry VI again, Edward IV, Henry VI again, Edward IV again, Edward V, and finally Richard III would sit upon England's throne.

To those only familiar with the more recent crimes of history, such as the actions of the dictators, nazism, facism, communism and the many acts of genocide involved with them, they may take some consolation in knowing that even during the more chivalrous years of the middle ages, there would be those still capable of the worst forms of human behavior. King Richard III is regarded as the last of the Plantagenet kings. Known also to history as Richard of Gloucester, he was the brother of Edward IV. During the reign of that king, he was involved in the murder of the unfortunate Henry VI and of their brother Clarence. Upon the death of Edward IV, Edward's twelve-year-old son would become king, with Gloucester acting as regent. What was to follow were acts of regicide and infanticide. Upon hearing of his brother's death, Gloucester would invite Edward's wife Elizabeth, along with the young king and his brother, the prince, to London.

The new king, Edward V, was to be found at Ludlow, under the care of Queen Elizabeth's brother, Earl Rivers. The Queen herself, along with the nine-year-old prince and her other children, perhaps realizing the nature of the new Regent, found sanctuary at Westminster Abby. For a number of weeks, the sides would negotiate. Finally, Rivers, his nephew Grey and two thousand horsemen would depart for London with the new king. At Northampton they would be intercepted. Rivers and Grey would be led away to their ultimate execution, the two thousand horsemen dismissed from further service. The young king was now under the control of Gloucester.

Worse was to come upon arrival in London in May 1483. The young king would in fact receive the fealty of his lords. However, he would then be led away to the Tower of London for his own safety. The next victim of Gloucester's intrigues would be Lord Hastings. Hastings had been a Lancastrian during the Wars of the Roses. Perhaps being one of the first to recognize the inherent danger of Gloucester's actions, he acted as council for the Queen's party at Westminster. His reward for loyalty to the Queen Mother and the young king was his seizure in Council on June 13 and his subsequent beheading that same day, without trial.

The next logical step in this procession of evil incarnate was to be the seizure of the young nine-year-old prince from the Queen Mother at Westminster. To this end, Gloucester would use the king's own council, now purged of the influence of Lord Hastings. Arguing that it would be the best for the young king to be in the company of his brother, Gloucester asked the council to request that the Queen surrender him to Gloucester's care. They would comply. So, unfortunately, would the Queen. The nine-year-old prince and the twelve-year-old king would never be seen again. Years later, during the reign of Charles II, the bones of the two young boys would be discovered in a walled up staircase in the Tower of London.

Having removed the prince's from public view, Gloucester would then seek to have Parliament, by means of his associate the Duke of Buckingham, declare the young princes as illegitimate. This would be done by means of several arguments, chief amongst them was that the marriage of Edward IV to Elizabeth Woodville was null and void, as she was already married at this time. In a move indicative of the occasional unwisdom of the times, one of the more vile elements in English history would be then coronated as King Richard III.

Fortunately for England, the reign of Richard III would last but two years. Although history does not always afford justice to some of the perpetrators of mans greatest crimes, in the instance of Richard III, it would. Shortly after Richard's coronation, his principal accomplice in the usurpation of the English Crown would begin to have second thoughts. Eventually there would be a separation of affection between Richard III and the Duke of Buckingham. With the realization of Richard's ambitions, and in the knowledge that he himself was of royal blood and as a descendent of Edward III could be considered as a rival to the throne, Buckingham sought to distance himself from events. Eventually he would begin to conspire against Richard, acting in concert with another possible claimant to the throne, Henry Tudor, Earl of Richmond. In October, a general rising against the usurper king was planned only to be greeted by ill weather and unfortunate events.

This challenge to authority would be met with vigor and violence. All of the uncoordinated uprisings would be suppressed by Richard and his army. A price was placed upon Buckingham's head, and ultimately he would be betrayed. Buckingham would be seized and slaughtered. Just for good measure and as a warning to other possible conspirators, Richard would add to his already lengthy list of crimes, and others would meet a similar fate.

Although the fates of the young king and his brother were as yet unknown, there existed widespread suspicion and mild trepidation within the realm as to their whereabouts and survival. These suspicions would gain momentum in September 1483, when Richard would have his only son anointed as Prince of Wales. Once again, the schemes of the usurper would be derailed. In April of the following year, this newly created Prince of Wales would die at Middleham. Complicating issues further, Richard's wife Ann was incapable of bearing additional children. The Queen herself would also pass away in short order, succumbing to ill health in March of 1485. Now without wife and child, Richard III would himself begin to suffer from his actions, becoming tormented by the sudden realizations that those loyal to him were so only out of fear, and those who associated with him did so only out of hope of kingly gifts and rewards.

Deliverance and the end to the Wars of the Roses would arrive from across the Channel. As had William the Conqueror, as well as Isabella and Mortimer, Henry Tudor would challenge the sitting king by means of an invasion launched from French soil. In August of 1485, Henry Tudor would depart Harfleur with an army of Yorkist, Lancastrian and French troops, arriving at Milford Haven six days later.

The two antagonists were soon to meet on the field of battle. Theoretically, all the advantages belonged to Richard III, as he had a larger army, which was comprised of professional soldiers. Henry Tudor would possess an army only of about five thousand rebels, half the number available to Richard III. Nevertheless, fate would intervene. Richard III had always ruled by means of fear. Prior to battle, he would seize as a hostage Lord Strange, the eldest son of Lord Stanley. This was done as a means to assure the loyalty of his Yorkist nobles and their red-coated mercenaries.

The battle itself was fought near Market Bosworth August 22, 1485. This particular battle was neither especially long, large, nor costly in terms of lives lost. The aftermath and its ramifications though, were enormous. The three hundred-year reign of the Plantagenet line of kings would reach its end with the death of Richard III during battle. Henry Tudor would prove victorious and would establish the Tudor line of kings as Henry VII. It would be this Tudor line, to include Henry VIII and Elizabeth I, that would usher in an English domination of affairs that would last for centuries.

Of interest, it would be the defection of Richard's ally, the Earl of Northumberland, and Lord Stanley and his three thousand red-coated troops switching sides during the battle that would give Henry Tudor the victory. These redcoats would of course long be associated with the English army during its years of mastery over the rest of the world.

# Chapter 6

¤

# THE BROADSIDE AND THE BULLET

It has often been surmised that man's knowledge triples every ten years, although to the student of history, by virtue of mankind's innumerable errors, one often wonders if we have ever learned anything at all. If perhaps there is truth to this supposition of the advancement of man's knowledge, science and technology must be viewed as the indication of this event. Often this transmutation of science and technology can be subtle and unobtrusive. On occasion, the advancement of science may be far less subtle and far-reaching in its effects on society.

Such was to be during the years of the Tudor monarchy. Although the Tudor monarchy would last for a period of one hundred eighteen years, from the coronation of Henry VII in 1485 to the death of Elizabeth I in 1603, the Tudor world would see the invention or adoption of many technological innovations. These innovations would have dramatic effects on society, on warfare, and on the monarchs themselves.

It can also be argued that these technological advancements and the impact they wrought, would be the driving factors behind the policies which would lead England to near-world domination. Shortly before Henry Tudor's victory at Bosworth, the printing press would establish itself within medieval Europe and would continue to add to the spreading of ideas. With this spreading of ideas would come an ever-increasing thirst for knowledge. Whereas education had once been restricted to the clergy, now it was to be expanded upon to include lay scholars and the gentlemen of the upper class. Within Europe at this time there existed sixty universities to assist in this new concept of dissemination of knowledge.[36] This dissemination of knowledge would occur within all occupations. We find proof of its existence in many forms, from the thesis of Martin Luther, which would lead to the Reformation, to the treatises on war and on chivalry written by Christine de Pisan. There had always existed within England those who felt a compelling need for knowledge, Alfred the Great for instance. Now, with the invention of the printing press, the ability to plant the seeds of knowledge within a far greater portion of society would exist.

There would, during the Tudor years, be another invention, which would dramatically alter the nature of warfare and magnify its effects in regard to the interrelationships of nations. Gunpowder and gunpowder weapons had existed for many years. However, in their infancy, gunpowder weapons existed merely as iron tubes capable of launching a projectile. The weapons were slow to load and fire and difficult to aim. As such they could not gain ascendancy over such dominant weapons as the English longbow. During the later years of the Hundred Years War, this would begin to change. Just as England had been irrestible at Crecy, Poitiers, and Agincourt, when the scales had tipped away from the longbow to the cannon, France would reverse its past failures and afford to the English the treatment the English had once afforded to France. In fact, it would be at the Battle of Castillon in July of 1453 where accurate French artillery fire would smash the English army and virtually end the Hundred Years War.

With all things mechanical, technological advancements would also lead to improvement. Whereas early firearms could be considered as producers of noise more than lethal weapons, sometime around the mid-fifteenth century this would change with the invention of the matchlock and an accompanying trigger

---

[36] Churchill, *History of the English Speaking Peoples*, 221.

mechanism. This matchlock was simply an S-shaped arm that held in place a section of burning cord which, when released forward by the trigger, would ignite a priming powder contained in a small pan-shaped piece located at the rear side of the barrel. This priming powder when ignited would travel by means of a touchhole, igniting the powder charge in the barrel and propelling the projectile out at the desired target. Sometime shortly after the invention of the matchlock, a curved wooden butt piece would be added to these weapons. From this butt piece, to be held against the shoulder when aiming the weapon, would come the term, "arquebus," which translates in French as "hookgun." In time, this new weapon, when accompanied by new infantry tactics, would entirely transform the nature of warfare. Eventually, armed conflict would become the "sport of nations," and not the "sport of kings."

To an island nation such as Britain, it would be the advancement of the cannon as a naval weapon that would ultimately steer its course to becoming the naval and commercial super power it would arise to be. During the Hundred Years War, cannons were used in land warfare primarily as a means to destroy the walls of castles, no doubt further expediting the end of feudal societies. It would naturally follow that if a cannon could reduce the walls of a castle, it could also reduce the sides of a ship. Prior to the Tudor kings of England, naval warfare had been fought much the same as it had been at Octavian's victory at Actium in 31 B.C., and before that at the Greek victory over the all-powerful Persians at Salamis in 480 B.C.

Naval warfare was simply a series of small land battles at sea. Without artillery, the ships would maneuver alongside each other, sending boarding parties across in hopes of capturing the enemy's ship. This would all change with a number of minor inventions. The "gunport," which was initially designed with the intent of allowing the storage of cargo in the hull without the need to hoist it over the side, was of French origins. When the Tudor King Henry VIII decided upon a new plan of naval construction to consist of heavy warships carrying artillery or cannons, English shipbuilders would use this new device as a means to allow cannons to be fired at enemy ships from the lower decks of their own ships. Therefore, this relatively simple device, a hinged port in the side of a ship, allowed many cannons to be carried on board a ship with the weight safely distributed below the center of gravity. When these larger ships, armed with cannons and specifically designed for war, were coupled with the power of the sail, the means would be brought forth for the discovery of the New World.

The English would not be the only nation to seize upon these advances in naval technology. Spain would soon follow the English example and in time would establish a fleet of "galleons." It would be the galleon that would lead Spain to become the naval power of the sixteenth century and which would also lead to its near dominance of the New World.

The galleon would prove in time to be the centerpiece to one of the more conclusive events of English history. In the aftermath of reformation and the counter-reformation, religious tensions were found to exist between a Protestant England and a Catholic Spain. The beheading of Mary, Queen of Scots, in 1586 after having been found guilty of treason, did little to assuage these religious tensions. Coupled with these tensions, an English expeditionary army was sent to the Netherlands in 1585 to fight against Spanish interests there. If these two conflicts of religion and territorial dispute did much to bring about war, there would also be the issue of privateers.

In the aftermath of the Spanish discovery and economic exploitation of the New World, vast amounts of treasure were being transplanted from the mines of Mexico and Peru back to Madrid. This vast influx of wealth was to allow King Philip II of Spain to increase the size of his army and navy beyond all proportion to the other nations of Europe.

For England, there could be but one course of action in response to the growing might of rival Spain. During the reign of Henry VIII, the Royal Navy was increased in size from five ships to thirty.[37] this policy of naval expansion was to continue during the years of Queen

---

[37] Jenkins, *Short History of England*, 131.

Elizabeth I. While lacking the number of ships possessed by Spain, and recognizing that Spanish bases now controlled the major sea routes, Elizabeth, not actively seeking war, would simply turn a blind eye or engage in outright denial when some of her sea captains, such as Sir Francis Drake and John Hawkins, would engage in piratical behavior masked behind royal authority for exploration. Drake more than all others would begin to realize that the power and the tactics of the broadside would give England a clear-cut superiority over its naval rivals, to include Spain and Portugal.

In response to the issues of piracy, continental rivalry, and the beheading of the Catholic Mary, Queen of Scots, Philip II of Spain would begin preparations for a naval expedition to the island. Drake, always one to seek the initiative, would sail into Cadiz Harbor in the spring of 1587, destroying 33 Spanish vessels and delaying the onslaught to come. This delay would prove to be of vital importance, as in the interim Spain's greatest naval commander, Admiral Marquis de Santa Cruz, would pass away in January 1588 before the expedition could set sail. His replacement, the Duke of Medina Sidonia, although being brave and able, possessed no experience in naval warfare.

When the showdown between the Spanish Armada and the English fleet did occur, there would be no decisive battle. Instead, what would transpire was a prolonged series of skirmishes lasting more than two months. Numerically, the two opposing fleets were approximate in numbers of ships, although the Spanish had a numerical superiority in cannons; 2,400 as opposed to approximately 1,800 for the English. However, all of the English guns were heavy cannons, mostly long range culverins. Contrary to popular history, the English fleet was not commanded by Sir Francis Drake. This honor would fall upon Lord Howard of Effingham, although Drake did play an active role by commanding a squadron of 34 ships. Ultimately, after two months of inconclusive skirmishing, nature would secure for England the victory, as most of the Spanish Armada would be destroyed in a storm. Many more vessels and men were lost in the long voyage home to Spanish ports, a voyage which would take the Spanish Armada completely around the British Isles during its long retreat.

Socially, there would be changes within the Tudor realm with which the average American of this day can associate, and from which there are lessons to be learned. When Henry Tudor ascended to the throne of England, the land was occupied by a number of small urban communities. Agriculture, and in this case its close associate the wool trade, were of paramount importance. To this general rule there would be one exception. This exception was the Tudor center of government, London. In 1335, the city had accumulated three times the wealth of any other English community. By the year 1520, this ratio had increased to fifteen to one.[38] London would not only see a tremendous influx of wealth, it would also see a tremendous influx of population. A city of approximately 50,000 people in 1500 had grown to be a metropolis of close to 200,000 by the end of that same century. Apparently, the agricultural issues which had prevented the growth of British cities during the years of the Roman occupation, had been resolved.

This enormous population growth was to have another effect upon English society. Prior to the Tudor years, England had existed in its feudal state with power being shared by the various monarchs and the feudal barons. During the years of the War of the Roses, many of the members of the baronial class had removed each other from the stage by means of internecine warfare. With the majority of the barons gone, a power vacuum was created, and into this vacuum would slip the expanded populace and wealth of London.

There would be a geographical shift in political influence as well. With the beginnings of the Danish invasion of England in 835, the balance of power had shifted from the Old Roman colonies of the South into the Northern kingdoms of Northumberland and Mercia. There it had remained for several centuries. Now, with the emergence of London as the commercial and political capital of England, the pendulum would swing south again. Accompanying this explosive

---

[38] Smith, *This Realm of England*, 89.

growth in the political and commercial sector, London would also see an increase of influence in legal affairs. London and its suburbs were to become the homes of the royal court and the courts of law. This trend would be accompanied by a tendency for the offspring of the gentry to attend the law colleges of London. Eventually, Tudor England was to become a society wherein litigation would be regarded as an indispensable pastime. These trends should be familiar to the Americans of this day, as they are reflective of the transformation we have seen within our own national capital, Washington, D.C., and within our current judicial system.

The Tudor years and the conflict with Spain were to have an even greater effect on the development of the Island nation than any at that time could have foreseen or have intended. As a result of Ferdinand and Isabella financing Columbus' voyage to the New World, Henry VIII granted letters patent to the Venetian explorer John Cabot (Zuan Caboto), granting to him, "full and free authority, faculty and power to sail to all ports, regions and coast of the eastern, western, and northern sea, under our banners, flags and ensigns... to find, discover and investigate whatever islands, countries, regions or provinces of heathens or infidels, in whatsoever part of the world placed, which before this time were unknown to all Christians."

It is of some matter of importance that reference is made to religion by use of the term, "Christians." Not only was the English mindset one of conquest, it was also a mindset that whereas Catholic Spain intended to create a Catholic empire, England had a similar intent to offset this by creating its own Protestant empire.

In the race for empire to ensue, geography and ocean currents were to play an important part. The Atlantic Ocean is dominated by currents which have a clockwise rotational flow. Its currents flow west from Northern Africa until they reach the New World, at which time they flow north along the coast of North America and then flow Northeasterly on their return to Europe. What all this means is that Spanish ships had the advantage of sailing West with the currents and prevailing winds, whereas ships departing England for the New World would be sailing against the currents. These currents would also tend to affect the locations of landfall for the various ships of exploration. To Spain would go Central and South America, to England would go Newfoundland and North America. In its discovery of Central and South America, Spain would be blessed with the acquisition of precious metals, gold and silver, as well as the more densely populated areas of the New World. England would also sail forth in pursuit of precious metals. What they would discover were the cod fisheries of the North Atlantic and regions which were arable, but would take several centuries to develop.

The Atlantic currents and the nature of the natural resources possessed by the regions discovered and exploited by the two infant empires were to affect the nature of the conflict to ensue. For Spain, the mines of Mexico and Peru would produce vast amounts of silver to fill the coffers of the Spanish Crown. Wealth was immediate, and this wealth could allow a Spanish monarch who ruled supreme without the hindrance of a Parliament to build a rapidly expanding empire, based not only upon wealth, but also upon military might. Codfish, while useful, could produce no such immediate result. The result of this imbalance of incoming wealth was that by the time of Henry VII's granddaughter Elizabeth, piracy would become the accepted means of dealing with Spain's increasing wealth and influence. When Sir Francis Drake circumnavigated the globe between 1577 and 1580, he would use raids against Spanish and Portuguese colonies as a means of re-supply and finance to accomplish his mission. In 1585 he would lead further raids against Cartegena and Santo Domingo. He would not be alone in these ventures. In 1595 Sir Walter Raleigh sailed to Trinidad where he raided the Spanish base at San Jose' de Oruna. During this raid, Raleigh would take captive the man he believed to know the whereabouts of the mythical El Dorado, Antonio de Berrio. Sir John Hawkins attacked the Azores in 1581. This English foreign policy of smash and grab would continue almost unabated for another century. In December of 1663, the Welshman Henry Morgan sailed across the Caribbean to raid the Spanish outpost of Gran Grenada. This raid would be followed up by raids against El Puerto del Principe in Cuba,

Portobelo in present day Panama, the island of Curacao in Venezuela, and the 1670 capture of the island of Old Providence, which would lead to the capture of Panama itself.

Eventually, this policy of piracy would end. Mines and the extraction of their wealth are finite in their capacities to produce. Whereas the English supposed that they had initially discovered and then established poorer colonies, they now discovered that their lands were suitable for arable forms of agriculture. Even more important, this new agriculture would not only produce vast amounts of wealth in the form of sugar and tobacco, but this wealth had the ability to regenerate itself, unlike the mineral deposit that, once depleted, could be used no more. This transformation from piracy to agriculture would be slow and arduous. England's first colony in America, at Roanoke Island, south of Chesapeake Bay in Virginia, would survive barely one year. With the establishment of the Virginia Company in April 1606, a second try at colonization would be attempted one year later, this time at Jamestown. In England's second attempt at colonization, the use of the donative was to be employed. Under a "headright" system for the allocation of land to prospective settlers, each settler was to receive fifty acres of land for each dependent accompanying him to the new land. This use of the donative would assist in the need to find colonists willing to attempt the perils of re-locating across the Atlantic to a yet untamed land. The discovery in 1612 that the soils of Virginia were conducive to the growing of tobacco would also help to insure the survival of this new colony. What had initially been viewed as a weed would within ten years see an export rate grown to roughly 350,000 pounds per year.

There are several historical parallels and a certain significance to be found in the process by which England came to colonize North America. In the early years of the Roman Principate, it would be the military-minded and the legions which would lead the way toward colonization. When Caesar conquered Gaul, it was as much with the desire for wealth as it was the desire for conquest. The Roman colonies in North Africa and Egypt were used as agricultural areas from which to supply Rome with the grains necessary to sustain its populations. Rome would use the land grant, generally allotted to the veterans of the legions, to encourage the spread of colonization. Where the Roman military and the desire for wealth would lead, Roman civilization would follow; so too, with England in the New World. It would be the desire for wealth, silver and gold, that would lead the military-minded such as Drake, Raleigh and Morgan to set out for the New World. Where they would lead, English civilization would follow. It is interesting to note, however, that the results would differ slightly. Rome's colony in Britain would be established but it would never thrive. Although there were no doubt several factors involved in this failure, it is generally accepted that the failure of Roman agriculture to take root in Britain did restrict the growth of the Roman-British cities. In North America, this would be different. Agriculture would not only survive, it would thrive. Tobacco, corn, potatoes, timber, fish and many other products would ensure a stable economy and a rapidly expanding population. Roman-Britain would eventually fade due to agricultural failure. British-America would not fail because agriculture succeeded.

To those familiar with the Malthusian cycle, the Tudor years of England might justifiably be regarded as the pinnacle of its upward swing. Conversely, the years of the Stuart Kings to follow might be regarded as the inevitable downward thrust of this cycle. On March 24, 1603, Good Queen Bess, Elizabeth I, would pass away. As England was at this time a hereditary monarchy, she would decree before her death that none but the Protestant son of Mary Queen of Scots should succeed her. This new thirty-six year old king, James I, would begin his reign with the best of intentions. Intentionally or unintentionally, he sought to reform several aspects of English society, to include its foreign policy and its relations with Spain and its religion. He fostered the arts of England, and he also sought to reform the relationship between King and Parliament. In these attempts he would meet with both success and disaster.

In terms of English relations with Spain, barely one year after his coronation, James I would reach an agreement with Spain with the completion of a conference at Somerset House. The conditions of this new peace agreement were such that Spain would relinquish its demands for a Catholic restoration in England if the English would in turn end their policy of piratical attacks on Spanish interests in Europe and the Americas. While peace is generally conducive to societies and to prosperity, in this particular instance it would have unfortunate consequences to those who had formerly been regarded as England's heroes. Sir Walter Raleigh, formerly a favorite of Elizabeth, would find himself imprisoned in the Tower of London in 1603 for high treason. By 1617, Raleigh would convince the new king to release him. With his newfound freedom, he would raise 30,000 pounds and assemble a new fleet of ships. Almost immediately he would return to his piratical ways, using this new fleet to attack the Spanish controlled town of Santo Tome. In this fight, Raleigh's son Wat would lose his life, and after having been denounced as pirates by the Spanish Ambassador, Raleigh himself would be executed by James upon his return to England.

As a boy, James had been crowned King of Scotland. With his coronation as King of England in 1604, he would unite the two crowns, declaring a united monarchy of England and Scotland to be known as Great Britain. In addition to this newly named nation, he would also bequeath to England a new flag, the Union Jack, long to be associated with its empire. But his union of crowns would also meet with unforeseen consequences. With this new union of crowns of England and Scotland, internal frontiers would be eliminated, and the need for a standing army would be curtailed. This resulting reduction of the Crown's forces would bring about a shift in the balance of power away from the King and towards Parliament. The effects of this power-shift would not bode well for the future Stuart monarchs.

A well-intended design to end conflict between the various religious sects of England would meet with unfortunate results as well. In 1604, James I summoned representatives from the Church of England and from the Puritans to Hampton Court to hear their various concerns. However, while willing to hear Puritan concerns, it would seem that James had his own concerns. Just as Elizabeth before him had regarded Puritanism as a threat to her authority, so too would James.

During the time of Elizabeth, a Puritan crisis arose in the year 1586, with the introduction by the Puritan faction of Cope's Bill and Book, which called for the abolition of the state episcopacy and the Anglican Prayer Book and their ultimate replacement with a Presbyterian church, along with a new Puritan Creed. Finding this intolerable, the Supreme Governor ordered their withdrawal from the House of Commons. In response, ten articles would be submitted to the House by Peter Wentworth, who argued that the removal from the House of Cope's Bill was an infringement of constitutional privilege and of free speech. He even went so far as to insinuate that anyone who violated the liberties of Parliament was an enemy to God. This audacity would of course lead to his imprisonment in the Tower of London.

James, although cautious of Puritanical sentiment, would at least seek to be more diplomatic in his approach. Although bishops were entrenched, there would be some compromise on issues such as baptism, ordination, and the civil role of the Church of England. Also, it is King James I to whom credit must go for the new translation of the bible. First published in 1611, this new English translation of the bible was completed by a committee of scholars who were divided into "companies," two each at Oxford, Cambridge and Westminster. Each "company" was to complete a portion of the text, each portion to be reviewed by the other committees. When all portions of the text had been reviewed, they were submitted to an additional committee of twelve for a final revision. What may have been unique about his process was that all of the members of the various committees were chosen without regard to theological bias.

Fiscal reform and the fatal inability of the Crown to practice fiscal restraint were also issues to plague the new Tudor monarchy. As the balance of power was now shifting towards Parliament, friction between the two sides would only increase over the issue of how money would be spent, and who should be responsible for carrying the burden of supporting the costs of government. Other financial frictions existed within English society as well. Whereas the Saxon and Plantagenet years had seen the majority of wealth concentrated in the hands of Feudal barons, by the time of the Elizabethan age, commercial interest had attained a new supremacy through the use of monopolies. The sale of many of these monopolies was used by the Crown as a means of attaining income. It would be through the use of these monopolies that immense amounts of wealth would be garnered for the select and favored few. This of course would be greeted with the unfavor of the unfew.

The issue of wardship would bring about hard feelings as well. With the coronation of James I, the Crown began a systematic investigation into the nature of all land tenure. It was the Crown's assertion that whereas an earl might be a royal ward, the yeoman who possessed but a few acres might be a ward as well. This issue would lead to the establishment of a Court of Wards in 1540. The legal experts of James I would expend much energy to prove that any given subject's lands were held according to a feudal knight's fee. If the existence of this knight's fee could be proven, then the Court of Wards could administer the lands being held in trust and could act to protect the interest of the ward. Often as not, the government would sell these interests to speculators and royal officials who then held the right to manage these lands and estates with the eventuality that the ward himself would end up in complete penury.

Purveyance was also an issue at this time. Purveyance, the right of the Crown to purchase provisions for the army, navy and royal household at a fixed price, would create dissention between the Crown and the merchants. In an era given to inflation, the right of the Crown to purchase supplies at a rate far below the fair market value created possibilities for corruption, as by the re-sale of these supplies at market value, huge profits could be obtained.

The national debt and an increased reliance on the use of donatives presented themselves to be of issue as well. From his predecessor, James had inherited a very costly war in Ireland, a war that would continue to be inflamed by Spanish interference and Spanish money. A debt of 422,000 pounds would continue to grow, due in large part to the fiscal irresponsibility of the King.[39] There existed a sixteenth century maxim "Bounty is an essential virtue of the king." Having come to England from Scotland and no doubt being regarded by many as a foreigner, James would seek to purchase his popularity. Between the time of his coronation in 1604 and the year 1608, wardrobe expenses would quadruple. In addition to money being dispensed to buy personal favor, large amounts of debt were forgiven, to the tune of 176,000 pounds in the same four-year period. As always, the government sought new sources of revenue, such as updating tariffs on imports and exports and imposing new tariffs on goods that were heretofore untaxed. However, the appetite for increased government spending could not be curbed, so that by the year 1618, the annual deficit was 50,000 pounds and the king's debt had more than doubled to 90,000 pounds. The human tendency toward jealously would also play a part. In the year 1611, the king personally gave away 90,688 pounds. Of this figure, nearly 70,000 pounds were given to eleven of James' cronies back in Scotland, much to the chagrin of his new English subjects. One might actually state that foreign policy was for sale.

The result of the disagreements between Parliament and the Crown over these fiscal issues should be familiar to Americans of our own age. Particularist interest, the interest shown toward the good of a segment of society instead of concerns over the welfare of society as a whole were partly responsible. During the years of Elizabeth there had existed a growing pressure from the Crown for more revenue to cover the growing costs of government and of foreign war with Spain. In response to this pressure, local tax assessors simply removed the names of individuals from the tax lists or grossly undervalued the worth of their estates. Therefore, a large number of constituent taxpayers had for years avoided paying any tax at all, and were therefore opposed to any extension of tax rates. It is the same imbalance of taxation we see within our own society, and it is the same reluctance we find on the part of many to contribute their share

---

[39] Ibid, 228.

during the years of fiscal crisis we experience today.

Additionally, there existed another issue with the Stuart monarchs. It had come to be recognized that taxation and the right to raise revenue were the responsibility and the right of Parliament. James I would seek to alter this relationship by means of raising revenue through other means; means which were regarded by many as being unconstitutional. Essentially, the need for sound fiscal policy and the desire to act in the interest of society as a whole became secondary to the need of either Parliament or the Crown to establish their authority in regard to monetary issues. Again, we see similarities within our own fiscal crisis. If particularist interest, party interest, or the competition between legislative authority and executive authority could be removed, we ourselves might find an easier path to fiscal harmony.

As so often proves to be the instance throughout history, although James I set about his path with the best of intentions, events well beyond his control would prove to undermine his efforts and would prove to be the undoing of his successor. In the aftermath of James' attempts at conciliation towards the various religious factors at Hampton Court, England and Protestants in particular would become afflicted with Millenarianistic thought. Millenarianism, the belief that Christendom and the English Commonwealth would suffer defeat at the hands of evil forces before the final triumphant second coming of Christ, would play a role in events to come. James was of course the son of the martyred Mary Stuart, leader of the Catholic Counter-Reformation. With his leanings toward religious tolerance, with his exclusion from Hampton Court of Catholics, and with the completion of peace with Spain, Catholic extremists believed that their efforts to restore their old faith and the proper devotion of England to the Pope were to end in failure. As a result, a small group of these radical Catholics decided to strike against what they regarded as a heretical government.

The principal agent of this plot was Robert Catesby. Guy Fawkes, the Timothy McVeigh of his time, and a handful of co-conspirators decided that the time and place to strike was the opening of the new session of Parliament. King, Lords and Commons could all be destroyed with one blow. The date of this plot to blow up Parliament was set for November 5, 1605. However, in their desire not to injure other Catholics, news of the plot was leaked when one of the conspirators warned a friend to stay away on that given date. Subsequently, Parliament was thoroughly searched and Guy Fawkes was discovered hiding in the basement of Westminster Abbey with forty barrels of gunpowder. Retribution was to be swift and absolute. All of the conspirators were hunted down, hanged, dismembered and beheaded. They would not be the only victims in the plot's aftermath. Soon there would be a very strong anti-Catholic, anti-Puritan sentiment unleashed in England. The Church of England would exploit this sentiment to its advantage, thereafter identifying uniformity of Church with the security of the State. This new wave of religious persecution would be one of the factors involved in the colonization of North America, as, by the end of James I's reign, over eighty thousand English people had crossed the Atlantic in search of religious freedom.

Upon his coronation, James I had achieved a singular foreign policy success, this being peace with Spain. He had also achieved by his demeanor and his spending habits a sense of disassociation with Parliament. Time would see a complete reversal of both, and once again it would be the age-old competition between nations that would bring about this change. In 1623, Prince Charles and the Duke of Buckingham sought to further cement goodwill between Protestant England and Catholic Spain. Both would journey to Madrid in hopes of winning favor with the Spanish court and of securing the marriage of Charles to the Spanish infanta. They would succeed in neither. Spain had already determined its course to support Hapsburg authority in Germany and from this course of action they simply would not deviate. Upon their return to England, Charles and Buckingham would become violently anti-Spanish, encouraging the aging James to go to war with that Catholic nation. Whereas Parliament could in the past find little upon which to agree with James, they now found themselves much in favor of war with Spain, even granting him substantial funds for the waging of that war. Such were to be the beginnings of the Thirty Years War.

As much as James had escaped the repercussions of his earlier actions, he now escaped the repercussions of war. On March 27, 1625, James passed away at the end of a twenty-two year reign, which had for the most part been peaceful. The throne of England and all the problems of power to go with it, were handed to James' son, who would become King Charles I. If issues had existed between Parliament and sovereign during the time of James I, these issues would only be magnified under Charles I. Prior to Charles coronation, as part of the attempts by Charles and George Villiers, Duke of Buckingham, to involve France in the Thirty Years War, Charles would become wed to Henrietta Maria, the fifteen-year-old daughter of the French King. As Henrietta was a practicing Catholic, this would of course lead to ill feelings from the now predominately Protestant population of England.

Financial issues would also arise once more. Whereas James had aroused the enmity of Parliament by his extravagant spending, his son failed to learn from this lesson, instead demanding even more financial resources than his father. To make matters worse, the war that Charles and Buckingham had helped bring about was proving to be more costly than anticipated and slightly less than successful. Angered by what was perceived as a resurgence of Catholicism under the king's wife, and infuriated by what it considered as mismanagement of the war effort, Parliament began to withhold the necessary funding needed to pay for the war. After having initially been in favor of the war, Parliament now only voted to approve 140,000 pounds to finance it, thus effectively curtailing any sizeable war effort. In addition, Parliament acted to suspend the granting of "tonnage and poundage" to the new king. It had been by means of collecting tariffs on the import and export of commodities that had allowed James I to circumvent the need of seeking authority from Parliament to raise revenue. Charles I would view this as a personal insult to his authority. In a further act to assert its authority, Parliament sought to impeach the king's closest and most trusted advisor, Villiers. Holding the Duke of Buckingham personally responsible for the Catholic resurgence that accompanied the King's marriage to the Catholic princess, and taking into account that the Royal Navy was performing poorly under his leadership as Lord Admiral, Parliament felt they had all the justification needed for his removal. In response, and as a means of protecting his closest associate, the king resolved to dissolve Parliament, the second instance of his having done so.

The descent toward chaos would continue. With no parliament and no tariff revenue, the king was forced to secure a sizeable loan from the propertied and mercantile classes to further finance the war. Several would refuse to participate in this loan, including twenty-seven who were former members of Parliament. For their efforts, they would be imprisoned, an act by the king that only further alienated his propertied and mercantile classes. Five of these individuals would file suit against the Crown for what they viewed as arbitrary arrest and an infringement against the writ of habeas corpus. When the courts sided with the king, the propertied classes were further alienated, questioning whether the courts were capable of rendering a requisite level of justice.

The ill-starred and ill-fated Villiers would now complicate matters even further for his sovereign. Being already engaged in war with Spain, Buckingham would cause England to become further involved in a war against France. The events that were to follow would prove to be very unfortunate for Charles and Buckingham, but altogether fortunate for the future of Western democracy. Just as Buckingham had proven to be militarily inept during the raid against Spanish Cadiz in 1625, the next expedition sent to France in 1627 to assist the French Huguenot rebels in their war against the French Crown would end in unmitigated disaster as well.

Repeated failure abroad and contempt for the authority of Parliament at home would now inflame the passions of the Lords and Commons, leading to the creation of the Petition of Right in 1628. This new Petition of Right was sponsored by Sir Edward Coke, the Lord Chief Justice who had earlier been sacked by James I for his view that royal absolution was in violation of common law. This new Petition declared that the king could not imprison persons without trial, and he could not levy taxes without the consent of Parliament. He was also forbidden to support any standing army to impose martial law during times of peace or to billet troops in private homes. All of these prohibitions were an obvious threat to the authority of the king, who simply disregarded them under the pretext that "kings are not bound to give account of their actions but to God alone." This very defiant tone would prove disastrous for Charles I and the events to follow would forever alter the relationship between the Crown and Parliament.

In the aftermath of the Petition of Right, Charles would initially consent to their conditions, and in the spirit of compromise Parliament would vote for further subsidies for the war, with the exception of tonnage and poundage, which they held in reserve. Charles may have believed he had attained some breathing space, however Commons would come forth with further demands. They would at this time voice complaints against a perceived Popery and Arminiansim in high offices, and also about the conduct of the war and the wisdom of retaining Buckingham in a position of authority after so many failures. In response, Charles would again dissolve Parliament.

The downward spiral of affairs between the Crown and the Parliament would now be temporarily interrupted by the murder of Villiers. Having seen his fortunes fall and his influence decline, The Duke of Buckingham decided to reverse his fortunes by personally leading a fleet of 90 ships and 10,000 men to the relief of the French Huguenots of La Rochelle who were still under the assault of the French forces under the leadership of Richelieu. However, before he was able to embark at Portsmouth in his second attempt at the relief of La Rochelle, he would be stabbed to death by a fanatical naval lieutenant who was sympathetic to the views of John Eliot, John Pym, and the other independent leaders of the Commons. With the death of Buckingham, there would be temporary relief in the antagonism against the Crown.

Issues of taxation would end this brief period of respite. Whereas the agreement signed by Charles I where the Petition of Right had withheld tonnage and poundage, the King had continued to collect them through his officers. "Ship money," was a tax levied against coastal towns as a means of acquiring money for their defense. Charles now decided that this should be expanded into a national tax. Over time, this continued collection of taxes without the approval of the now dismissed Houses would become public knowledge. To add further agitation to an already volatile situation, the relief effort to France, which had sailed without Buckingham, now met with continued misfortune. In its failure La Rochelle would fall to the forces of the French King. In 1629, when Parliament was recalled, it became immediately clear that this new session would become increasingly critical of Charles and his policies, both foreign and domestic.

Immediately the Commons would by means of resolution declare that any individuals associated with Popery should be declared enemies of the State. Also to be included in this category were any of the king's ministers who assisted in the collection of taxes without Parliamentary consent, and any individuals who would pay such taxes. In response to this further assault on his Prerogative and policies, Charles would again order the speaker of the House of Commons to dissolve Parliament. In an act of open defiance, as the speaker rose to leave the chamber, he was forcibly held down until the resolutions were read by Eliot and then voted upon. This could be construed as a further challenge to the relationship between the king and Parliament, as Parliament now indicated a desire to either prorogue or dissolve itself.

With continued animosity between himself and the House now the prevalent theme, Charles I decided upon a course of self-rule, which was to last eleven years. With self-rule there would be one major restriction, no Parliament and little if any available funding. This condition would be accompanied by some very interesting restrictions, and results. First of all, with no extensive treasury on which to rely, there could be no further wars on the continent, a circumstance understood by the rulers of the warring nations on the continent and exploited by them to the fullest. Also, in the absence of Parliament there would need to be an efficient, cost effective system of administration to carry out the affairs of government. As Parliament was now discontinued, the King sought to find able ministers from within its former ranks. Many of the Parliamentarians remained firm in their stance, even to the extreme of finding themselves locked in the Tower of London, as was the case with John Eliot. However, a few would break ranks and serve the king. William Laud and Thomas Wentworth, Earl of Strafford, would be chief amongst them. Finances in absence of Parliamentary approval were also necessary. To this end, the Crown would resort to the further extension of "fiscal feudalism," rummaging through long disused medieval contracts with the explicit desire to attain money.

In addition to fiscal feudalism, an ancient law of England, in practice since the time of the Saxon King Alfred the Great, allowed for the collection of duties from coastal communities for the upkeep of the fleet. Charles and his new ministers would now extend this duty so as to make it a national tax. This process was begun in 1635.

The immediate result of this new, leaner and more tax efficient government was an overall increase in productivity and expansion within the non-governmental sphere of the Stuart realm. Agricultural productivity increased, leading to stabilization of prices. Poor laws, first enacted in 1536 for the relief of the less fortunate, were newly extended and more humane. This should strike us as an interesting concept within the financially troubled times within which we now exist.

As usually proves the case with history, external rather than internal affairs would propel events forward along a more discordant path. As Charles' father had united the English and Scottish crowns, Charles now sought to unite this new union of nations under a similar religion. The instigator and spearhead of this new attempt at religious conformity was William Laud, who had in 1633 been promoted to the position of Archbishop of Canterbury.

As such, and with the consent of the Crown, Laud would oversee the creation of a new Prayer Book to regulate the forms of public worship in Scotland. In 1637, Laud would try to impose the use of this new prayer book on his Stuart king's Scottish subjects. This, coupled with the earlier Act of Revocation, which sought to remove from the nobles all the Church lands they had acquired in the aftermath of the reformation, drove the Scots into open rebellion.

To this error in policy would now be added the error of judgment. In response to the policies of Laud, the Scots would first bring forth a Petition, or Grand Supplication, for the withdrawal of Laud's Prayer Book. In 1638, this would be superseded by the signing of a covenant, which was read in the Churchyard at Edinburg and then signed by a long list of Scottish nobles. In an act of further defiance of Charles I, the Scots agreed to convoke a general assembly, the Committee of the Covenanters. In an attempt to diffuse this volatile situation, Charles sent the Marquis of Hamilton north to attempt reconciliation with the disgruntled Scots. If reconciliation were to fail, Charles' orders were to assemble troops and put down the rebellion with all forces necessary. Reconciliation would fail, and Hamilton would order the Assembly to dissolve by order of the King. The Assembly refused the king's order and the path to civil war now lay open. Both the Scots and the King would hastily gather forces for the possible conflict to come, with the Scots able to amass the larger force.

Quite mistakenly, as the Scottish forces descended toward English soil, Charles believed that if he assembled Parliament that they would rise to the occasion to meet this new threat. He could not have been more wrong. As a means of purchasing much needed time, he would agree upon the "Pacification of Berwick," which called upon the Scots to disband their army if he would agree to call for a General Assembly and a Parliament in the year to come. The same levels of suspicion that had always existed between Charles and Parliament now prevailed in regard to the relationship between Charles and the Scots. In distrust Charles would hasten to restore royal fortresses along the frontier and the Scots would establish a new and powerful representative committee.

With his northern dominion in open revolt, the need for revenue to quell this revolt necessitated organizing a new Parliament. When assembled, only one quarter of its members were of the assembly disbanded by King Charles eleven years before. However, one member in particular did return, Pym. This new Parliament, known to history as the "Short Parliament," simply refused to grant new funds for the king. Instead they simply re-stated all of the grievances from years past. Finding no comfort and little consort in this Short Parliament, it was dissolved by Charles within days of its first meeting.

For centuries England had experienced invasion from the continent to the south. Now it would face a similar prospect from the north. Confronted by a strong Scottish army to his north, Charles would again call into session a new Parliament. This "Long Parliament," would again prove antagonistic to its king. Once assembled, this Long Parliament called for the removal of all the king's ministers, to include Wentworth and Laud. The wiser of these ministers would flee England for the safety of other lands. The unwise would remain. Fortune would turn especially unfortunate for the Earl of Strafford. Members of the new Parliament would seek to have him found guilty of treason against England. In court proceedings, they would fail in their attempts. They therefore decided to convict him by an Act of Parliament through means of a Bill of Attainder. This bill would pass the Commons, although clearly in contradiction, that "the law must precede the offense." Fearing that the King might attempt to use the Earl of Strafford against the House in the future if they released him, the Commons sought his execution, no doubt in recognition that "stone-dead hath no fellow." Eventually Laud would be attainted as well. The Earl of Strafford would become headless shortly thereafter; Laud would languish for another four years before meeting his execution as well.

It is important to recognize and to realize that this Long Parliament would now force upon the king a set of statutes that would forever alter the balance of power between the Crown and Parliament in English society. The possibility of Personal Rule by a monarch was ended by means of a Triennial Bill, which called for the summoning of Parliament at least once every three years, with or without the consent of the Crown. In addition, Parliament would henceforth have the authority to control the Church, appoint judges and ministers, and be responsible for the conduct of the army and navy. In all, this Grand Remonstrance contained two hundred clauses. Already having sacrificed his ministers, Charles would view the acceptance of this Grand Remonstrance as the sacrificing of himself.

Perhaps hesitantly, perhaps defiantly, Charles now fought to save his crown and possibly himself. On January 4, 1642, Charles stormed into the chamber where Commons sat accompanied by 400 armed "cavaliers." He demanded that Pym and four others be handed over to him for arrest. However, Pym and his four associates had already fled. Charles was left with no other option but to retreat from the chamber. Now faced with increasing levels of hostility in London, the Queen departed for the safety of Holland while Charles fled to more favorable elements in the north. In a move every bit as contentious and no doubt with the same intended design as the Austro-Hungarian ultimatum that would lead to the hostilities of World War I, Parliament now sent Charles a list of Nineteen Propositions, which further increased their own powers while further reducing the authority of the king. To the King, there now existed but two options: either "live as a king" or die as a gentleman. Once again in the affairs of mankind, passion would prevail over reasoning, and violence would become the means to resolve differences of opinion.

The events to follow the political break between Charles I and the Long Parliament are generally regarded as the English Civil War. These events, which occurred from 1642 to 1660, have been attributed to many causes. History's scholars generally tend to ascribe to these events causes that may be social, economic, geographical, or political in nature. Perhaps it is not so much the nature of the causes, but rather it may be that nature is the cause. In a modern organized society, social, economic, geographical and political threads are generally woven into one cloth. These threads, while separated to one extent or another, are all influenced by one factor, which is common to the entire history of mankind. This factor is the tendency of mankind to seek improvement, this improvement generally wearing the disguise of technological advancement. As technology advances, there is always an accompanying need for social change, such as the tendency toward urbanization. Political institutions must change as well, and there is always a need to legislate and to create laws in regard to how this technology may be applied. Technological advancements have a direct impact on economic trends, both in terms of how products are manufactured, and also as to how and where they are marketed. Even geography is affected by technology, as advances in agriculture and irrigation may turn deserts into agrarian regions, and vice versa.

To this question, was there rapid technological advance in the years prior to the English Civil War, there can be but a single answer: yes. We have already discovered that during the years of the Tudor monarchy, that society was affected by the development of the printing press and its accompanying effects on education; that gunpowder and gunpowder weapons had affected how wars were fought, who would win those wars, and also the construction of the naval vessels which would assist in the discovery of the New World.

Whereas Tudor monarch Elizabeth I had encouraged exploration of the New World in hopes of discovering gold, it would be black gold – coal, that would help England become the dominant economic force of Europe within a century. The burning of coal would not only assist in the heating of homes, it would help bring about an explosion in the production of iron. In the century between 1540 and the sitting of the Long Parliament, iron production would increase in England five-fold.[40] Coal mining productivity increased from 20,000 tons annually to more than 1.5 million tons. From soap to beer, consumer products were readily produced and readily available. This availability of produce, consumer and agricultural, would help assist with the continued populating of cities. The London of Henry Tudor was home to fifty thousand inhabitants. With the death of the last Stuart monarch, Anne in 1714, London had become a city of nearly five hundred thousand people.

---

[40] Ibid, 266.

Such a massive influx of souls would easily outpace the ability of any government to regulate or control such growth. Once rural, England was now rapidly on its way to becoming urban England. Naturally, social, political and economical institutions would be stressed in an attempt to catch up.

In the twentieth and twenty-first centuries we have been familiarized with a new concept, that of the mythology of perpetual economic growth. This emerging concept has arisen out of the more densely populated areas of the earth. Its proponents seek to make us aware that it is not physically or humanly possible for the limited amount of geography and natural resources of the earth to support population growth indefinitely. It would no doubt be suicidal and very unwise to believe that somehow it could.

England during the years of Charles I was experiencing symptoms of this exact phenomenon. Simply stated, population growth had far outdistanced the ability of the economy to employ it fully. In an attempt to control these growth issues, James I had been more or less laissez-faire in his policies. Charles I would institute a different approach. A new system of government paternalism would be born. This new system would involve a Book of Orders set in place by Charles and his Privy Council. Accordingly, this Book of Orders hoped to correct what the government now believed had been neglected by local government institutions, to include the enforcement of apprenticeship regulations, systematic relief for the poor and the organization of public works projects for the benefit of the communities, and as a way of ensuring sufficient employment. These policies, although no doubt well intended, could not overcome the various European and Colonial economic pressures of the day. Perhaps these huge sways of uncontrolled booms and busts were further inducement for those who sought a new life in the New World.

The social policies of Charles I were also to play a part in the antagonisms toward the Crown and toward authority. With London's explosive population growth came new zoning proclamations which were often enforced not so much as a means to control growth, but rather as a means to extract money from contractors. Enclosure laws were also created to prevent landlords from evicting tenants, auspiciously in an attempt to prevent the social evil of homelessness. In reality, these Enclosure Laws actually added to the number of unemployed, landless farm laborers and general vagabonds. There existed one other evil associated with the Enclosure Laws as well. Much the same as zoning proclamations had become a means of extracting money from contractors the Enclosure Laws would now be used as a means of funding the State through the use of fines imposed by the courts. These fines increased the wealth of the government by an estimated 30,000 pounds or more per year. The government's need for money had superseded the need of goodwill towards the governed. Political friction and social bitterness were the natural children of these ill-advised policies.

It can be accurately stated with a degree of certainty that all of history's great events require the participation of great or at least controversial individuals. Into the limelight of the English Civil War would now step such a man, Sir Oliver Cromwell, who was not an especially well-known individual prior to the events of 1642-1660. The man who would one day become the only soul of non-royal blood to ever head the English State, was born on April 25, 1599 into a family of East Anglican gentry given to hardships. Unlike his father, Oliver would receive a grammar style education beginning around age seven. Contemporary accounts of Sir Oliver in his early years describe him as dynamic, energetic, and difficult to control. He was not afforded in early life any spectacular degree of wealth, essentially being the only surviving son of the younger son of a knight. He would in the aftermath of his grammar education go on to attend Sidney Sussex College, although he would leave in June of 1617 without receiving a degree. As with many of history's greats, he would endure the years of hardship prior to his years of success. There would be a time for him of personal crisis during the years of the late 1620s and early 1630s, as he would during these years seek help for Valde Melancolicus, severe depression.

For whatever reason fortune seems to always have its favorites. In

1636, Oliver Cromwell's fortunes would begin to change. In 1636 he inherited control of various properties in Ely from an uncle on his mother's side. He would also inherit his uncle's job as collector of tithes, which would bring with it a resulting increase in salary. Within two years of this reversal of fortune, Oliver Cromwell would be elected to Parliament as a member from Huntingdon. Historical accounts of his term say only that he made little impression, and only one speech. When Charles I disbanded Parliament in 1629 to begin his eleven years of self-rule, Cromwell would find himself removed from further service.

With the "Bishops War" instigated by Archbishop Laud and with Charles again facing the need to call a Parliament to vote on funding for the external threat being imposed by the Scots, Oliver Cromwell would seek re-election to this body, soon to be known as the Short Parliament, winning a seat from Cambridgeshire. Again as before, Charles would dismiss Parliament when it became apparent there could be no reconciliation between Parliament and himself.

When, in 1640, a victorious Scottish Presbyterian army invaded England and defeated the army of Charles in August, it demanded that Charles pay the cost of maintaining this army in the field until an agreement between the Scots and the King could be reached. Having exhausted all other means of finance, Charles was forced to call into being the Long Parliament. Sir Oliver Cromwell would find himself once again elected as a member from Cambridgeshire. During his third term of service in Parliament, Cromwell would become more active and more influential. In May of 1641, Cromwell would initiate the second reading of the Annual Parliaments Bill. He would also prove to be a driving force in the drafting of a Root and Branch Bill calling for the abolition of the Episcopacy.

It would be for his military exploits during the English Civil War for which Sir Oliver Cromwell will forever remain famous. Many times throughout history individuals have been given a sobriquet associated with their deeds. Oliver Cromwell would receive two, being known to history as, "Old Ironsides," and as, "Angry Heavens Flame." A rather surprising honor for a man who had no prior military training other than having served in the "trained bands," the equivalent of a county militia. With the outbreak of Civil War he would recruit a cavalry troop in his Cambridgeshire constituency. He would initially see service at the indecisive Battle of Gainsborough, and by the time of Marston Moor, he would rise to be Lieutenant General of horse.

In terms of longevity and the sequence of events, the English Civil War bears a resemblance to our own, although the issues for which it was fought and the outcomes would be different. Also similar to the two would be the use of conscription, first approved by the Parliament in August of 1643. In the American Civil War conscription would be initiated by the Confederacy in April 1682, with the North resorting to this very unpopular action in March 1683.

In general terms, the armies of Parliament were somewhat larger than those of the royalist and were also better organized and equipped. Parliament also possessed the loyalty of the navy, which prevented the armies of Charles from receiving supplies and armaments from the continent. In addition, there would exist reluctance on the part of local militia to leave the immediate areas of their own homes. Whereas both Charles and Parliament were destitute of funding, the soldiers who fought the English Civil War would always be plagued by the lack of payment for their services.

During the initial series of clashes, the forces of Charles and his Royalist Cavaliers were usually triumphant. At Edgehill in October of 1642, Charles' forces would control the field of battle after an evenly fought contest. Royalist victories would follow in Yorkshire between April and July of 1643, at Stratton in Cornwall, at Landowne near Bath, and again at Roundway Down. A drawn battle would also be fought at Newbury in 1643.

In the aftermath of this series of Parliamentary defeats and narrow escapes, conscription would be authorized by the Long Parliament. In addition, in September of 1643, Parliament would enter into the Solemn League and Covenant. Through this agreement, Scottish military assistance would be assured in return for a Parliamentary assurance of protection for Presbyterianism in Scotland and the later expansion of Presbyterianism throughout Britain. This new agreement between Parliament and the Scots acquired an additional 18,000 infantry and 3,000 cavalry for the Roundhead forces.

To a nation that has existed in various forms for over two thousand years, there exist many battles that could be described as decisive or of great historical significance. Marston Moor must be regarded as one of them. In July 1644, the Roundhead forces, now augmented by the Scots, clashed with the forces of Charles under his nephew Prince Rupert at Marston Moor outside of York. The "Ironsides" cavalry of Oliver Cromwell was to play an important role in this affair, first defeating the Royalist cavalry of Rupert on the right, then re-deploying to help smash the remaining Royalist horse of Lord George Garing who were engaged against the Scottish infantry all the way on the left of the line. As a result of this battle, the North of England would be lost to the Royalist cause for the duration of the war.

Following Marston Moor, there would be several months of maneuvering and skirmishing in the southwest of England. In October of 1644 another major engagement would be fought, this time at Newbury. During this battle, the Parliamentary forces would be commanded by the Earl of Manchester, with Cromwell and his Ironsides as support. Although defeated, due to the incompetence of Manchester, Charles would be allowed to escape and to withdraw his army to Oxford. Sir Oliver Cromwell would now gain control of affairs. Returning before Parliament, Cromwell would rail against the incompetence of Parliamentary generals and urge Parliament to adopt "a frame or model of the whole militia." Such would be the beginnings of the New Model Army.

Much the same as Rome had undergone military reform under Marius prior to the Servile and Social Wars, the forces of Parliament were to undergo the same. In 1645 Parliament would pass a Self-Denying Ordinance, under which members of Parliament would resign from their military positions. Henceforth, soldiering was to be left to the soldiers. Therefore, the Parliamentary army would receive a new commander, Lord Thomas Fairfax, with Cromwell himself as Lieutenant General and Commander of the cavalry. Also, promotions from this point forward would be based upon merit, not blood. Cromwell himself had once declared that, "If you choose Godly honest men to be captains of horse, honest men will follow them... I would rather have a plain russet coated captain who knows what he fights for and loves what he knows, than that which you call a gentleman and is nothing else." Cromwell would himself initiate change within his cavalry. Whereas in the past cavalry had fought in loose ranks and would pursue an enemy to the point of becoming disorganized, Cromwell now dictated that his cavalry would fight almost knee to knee, and would not pursue a broken enemy but would remain organized so as to respond to further needs upon the scene of action.

These changes would be accompanied by other changes as well. Whereas the forces of Sir William Stanley had worn "coats as red as blood" at the battle of Bosworth, which oversaw the defeat of Richard III and the end of the War of the Roses, red was from this point forward to be the desired color worn by all British forces. These red-clad forces were to also be supported by regularized taxation. Initially, there were to be 12 regiments of infantry and 11 regiments of cavalry, plus 1,000 dragoons. Artillery, a branch of service in which the British had long remained behind other continental powers, was to be modernized and reorganized as well.

With this New Model Army, Sir Oliver Cromwell would accomplish great deeds and become the only man in the British history of non-noble blood to rule as sovereign, assuming the title Lord Protector. Before this could take place, he regarded his task as being that of ending the current state of civil war. This mission would be accomplished at Naseby on June 14, 1645. During the battle it would again be Cromwell and his Ironsides who would play the decisive role. Not only did the Ironsides cavalry defeat the Royalist cavalry on the left of Charles' army, they then attacked the infantry of the Royalist center, smashing them and causing most to surrender. By his actions, Cromwell had guaranteed Charles eventual defeat, and also that the Independents within the Parliamentary Party would gain ascendancy in the events to come.

Why is the English Civil War of importance to us today? For several reasons. First amongst them is that our own American Civil War followed a similar course, and much destruction and loss of life could have been avoided if our own leaders had sought council in the pages of history. Whereas the English Civil War began as a contest between small forces from within the ranks of government and the militia-type army then in existence, it would transform itself into a contest at the national level. By wars end 100,000 Englishmen had perished on the field of battle, and entire cities, like Bristol, had been utterly sacked. Also victims of the war were churches and cathedrals, the farms that occupied the countryside, as well as the homes of rich and poor alike.

Our American Civil War would follow a parallel path. Whereas the first battle of Bull Run had been fought between hastily gathered armies, by wars end armies of both North and South would see the service of numbers of men to reach into the millions. The modern effects and the modern needs of the war would see the advent of railroads as means to transport men and supplies; the telegraph would aid communication and the world would see the reincarnation of ironclad warships not seen since the time of Admiral Y. Sung Sin of Korea, who used ironclad warships to destroy the Japanese fleets of Hideyashi and prevent the Japanese conquest of his kingdom in the 16th century. Also, much the same as the English Civil War had engulfed the cities and the countryside, so would our own Civil War, seeing the destruction of many southern cities and the burning of Atlanta.

As the New Model Army was indicative of modern military thought and proof of military reform, our own armies would see similar reform during our War of Secession. Long before the Northern armies would gain ascendancy on the battlefield they would undergo the modernizing influence of new standards of training and organization under the leadership of George B. McClellan. Larger armies would be conscripted during this national struggle, and because of this more men would die, nearly 650,000 during the duration of the war.

There exists one other lesson for Americans as well. The disagreements between the king and Parliament, which led to the eventuality of war, were rooted within a paternalistic state. Taxation by decree according to what the sovereign regarded as his prerogative was in contradiction to taxation by consent of the governed through an elected body. Attempts at "leveling," seeking the even distribution of wealth, were contrary to the economic system of the times. Essentially, prior to the English Civil War the people were over-populated, over-regulated, over-taxed and over-governed. With such stresses and strains in existence, political and civil discord was bound to follow.

The aftermath of the English Civil War would see first a sigh of relief from a war-weary populace, and then a political backlash amongst and between the victors. After the surrender of Charles I to the Parliamentary forces in 1647, the Long Parliament ordered the New Model Army to disband, and ordered the defeated Royalist gentry to pay for it, thus making enemies of both. It then initiated a policy of proscription, especially of Baptist and Independents, who at the time were very prevalent in the army. To further rub salt in the wound, the army was owed a sizeable amount of money. As its pay had been in arrears for some time, this Long Parliament decided not to pay.

These policies would not only raise the ire of Cromwell, they would not sit especially well with his lieutenants, like Henry Ireton, or the army as a whole. The army and its leaders would now feel a need for drastic measures, and drastic measures would be taken. Cromwell's son-in-law Ireton, would seize the king who would now serve as a hostage for the army.

Parliament would become divided, Presbyterians on the one hand ranged against Cromwell and his army council on the other. The events to follow are significant to the history of democracy in the western world. A series of debates would follow, being held at Putney Church from October to November of 1647. All the political views of the disputatious parties were to be aired, including those of the rights of individuals versus the rights of the State, the rights of property against those of community, and the extension of suffrage to all, including women. Henceforth, the new political norm of England would be not the consent of the government, but rather consent by the governed.

Events would now lead to one of the most unfortunate events in English history. In November of 1647 Charles Stuart escaped from his captors at Hampton Court, eventually finding refuge at Carisbrooke Castle on the Isle of Wight. Hearing of the discord amongst the elements of the Long Parliament and the New Model Army, he unwisely courted support from the Scots and from disaffected elements within England toward the renewal of the Civil War. Now regarded as both a threat and a menace by Cromwell and the "Rump Parliament," Charles would be taken to London in December 1648, where he would be brought to trial on charges of treason. When the Rump Parliament was further purged of members during "Prides Purge," wherein some 370 Presbyterian and Royalist sympathizers were removed, the king's fate was sealed.

Shortly thereafter a commission was established to oversee the trial of Charles Stuart, with the proceedings taking place in Westminster Hall. Although Charles was filled with resolve and made every attempt at defense, the results were a foregone conclusion. The commission found Charles guilty of treason, requiring that as punishment his head be severed from his body. On January 30, 1649, the "cruel necessity" of Charles being put to death would occur, although the immediate aftermath of this event would cause the people of England to realize that a terrible deed had been done and would serve also to assist in the eventual restoration to follow.

As the influence of the king had been removed, and in the aftermath of "Prides Purge," further actions would be taken. The left leaning elements of the Rump Parliament would now be suppressed, to include levelers, egalitarians, and any viewed as being religious dissenters. When in May 1649 three regiments of the army mutinied, Cromwell destroyed them at Burford. In the aftermath of suppression of rebellious elements within the army, next would follow censorship of the press.

The cycle of violence would continue. Across the Irish Sea, rebellion would take root amongst the royalist sympathetic Catholics on that island. "Angry Heaven's Flame" would descend upon them. From September of 1649 until May of 1650 Cromwell would engage in the systematic reduction of the fortified strongholds of the Irish. Drogheda, Wexford and Clonmel would all fall victim to Cromwellian forces. At Drogheda, the garrison of the town was invited to surrender. When they failed to do so, Cromwell unleashed the power of his cannon on them. After three assaults the defenses of the fortress would be breached and an all-effacing three-day massacre would ensue. All would be put to the sword, including priest and friar, man, woman and child. The campaign against Ireland would continue for two long years, first under Cromwell and then under his son-in-law Henry Ireton.

No sooner had the axe fallen upon the head of Charles I, than his subjects and many of the sovereigns of Europe considered his son Prince Charles as King Charles II. The estates of Scotland would proclaim his as such and would soon go to war on his behalf. If Cromwell had been un-amused by the actions of Ireland, he would have been even less amused with the actions of the Scots. In a yearlong campaign Cromwell would continue his streak of unabated victories, ending this new threat under Charles II at Worcester on September 3, 1651. The Civil war now ended.

With the end of the rebellion in Ireland and Scotland, Cromwell and his army now turned all of their attention to matters closer to home. To many, the events to follow could almost be predicable. As relations grew worse between the army and the Rump Parliament and as it became obvious that nothing could be accomplished in this atmosphere, Cromwell simply acted as Charles had done before him. On April 20, 1653, after losing patience with the endless shortcomings of its members, Cromwell ordered the Rump Parliament to disband. After referring to them as sordid prostitutes, Cromwell shouted, "Ye are grown intolerably odious to the whole nation. The Lord hath done with you... Go, get out, make haste, ye venal slaves, be gone."

Henceforth Cromwell would rule as Lord Protector of the English Commonwealth. For a time there would exist a barebones Parliament, although when this body proposed the further abolition of many of the instruments of the State, it too would be abandoned by Cromwell. There would also exist a time period wherein the Commonwealth would be divided into eleven spheres, each governed by a military regime under the supervision of a major general. This too would fail, as the collection of a "decimation" tax of ten percent on the estates of former cavaliers would prove to be insufficient to maintain the cost of government.

If the years of the internal fratricide and financial prostration at the hands of large standing armies had not made themselves obvious during the years of the Roman Principate, they would now become obvious to the England of the Lord Protector. It would soon become clear to the English that "an army is a beast that has a great body and must be fed." In the years of the 1650s, the annual government budget was in the vicinity of 2.7 million pounds, three times what it had been under Charles I. Of this, the army alone could cost between 1.5 million to 3 million pounds annually.[41] Added to this financial burden of maintaining the New Model Army was the additional burden of foreign wars. In 1652, after England had dispensed with the campaigns against Ireland and Scotland, a new predominately naval war would soon be fought against the Dutch. To the man known for his increasing chain of victories, Cromwell would find himself within two years as being in a position to dictate terms to the Dutch as well. In exchange for peace, the Dutch States General agreed to recognize English supremacy in the Channel. They also agreed to pay for the right to fish in British waters.

In an attempt to follow the policies once established during the years of "Gloriana," England would now lash out against its former colonial rival, Spain. This time however, the profits would be diminished. Whereas the circum-navigational voyage of pillage and plunder of Sir Francis Drake had netted a 4,700 percent profit for its

---

[41] Ibid, 296.

investors in 1577, this time around there would be no such financial miracles. It would be the continued cost of the war, the continued failure to find a form of Parliament capable of financing these wars, and the death of the Lord Protector himself on the third of September 1658 that would ultimately lead to the return of the Parliament and of monarchy within eighteen months of his death.

To the less violent and more passive elements of society, both his own and that of ours today, Cromwell would be considered as the incarnation of Satan himself. However, this would be false for a man guided by his religious faith and firm in his conviction that only the soldier with his honest intent was capable of protecting society from the evils of over-government, over-regulation and over-taxation. Much the same as Abraham Lincoln had opined in a letter to Albert G. Hodges on April 4, 1864, "I claim not to have controlled events, but confess plainly that events have controlled me," so it was to be with Cromwell. While Cromwell not doubt had his detractors, his actions brought about many benefits to English society. Out of the disputes of who would control England, the Crown or Parliament, a new settlement would be reached: they would rule jointly. Also, the navy upon which the empire was to be built would again be modernized and expanded upon. The Committee of Admirals was created in 1649. This new body would oversee improvements in the quality of food and the regularity of pay for English sailors. During the years of Cromwell, 207 ships would be added to the Royal Navy between 1649 and 1651. In addition, this body would appoint three "Generals at Sea," one being Robert Blake. Also it would be during the most recent war with Spain that England would acquire Jamaica, an island that was to become the center point for English domination of the West Indies. Perhaps it is with some justification that during a 2002 BBC poll that Sir Oliver Cromwell was chosen as one of the ten greatest Britons of all times.

# Chapter 7

¤

# THE SEEDS OF GREATNESS TAKE ROOT

After having endured the reformation and the Counter-Reformation of Tudor England, and with the Civil Wars of the Stuart years behind them, one might reasonably expect that the English nation might be dormant for a generation or so in order to recover its physical and financial strength. Such would not be the case. Much the same as Rome had attained its greatest heights in the aftermath of its Civil Wars under Octavius and through the century of the Antonines, England would over the next two centuries become an empire even greater and more powerful than its ancestor, the Roman Empire.

With the restoration of Charles II as King and in the aftermath of the Declaration of Breda, which offered a general amnesty for all who had partaken in the English Civil Wars, it would seem logical that England would assume a less militant posture. Almost entirely the opposite would prove true. Spurred on by the commercial class who had a vested interest in breaking up the Dutch trading monopolies in North America, Parliament would vote for the expenditure of 2.5 million pounds for the acquisition of 150 vessels for the navy. This expenditure would prove worthwhile in the long run, as in 1653 the Dutch governor of New Amsterdam, Peter Stuyvesant, was forced to acknowledge English dominion over the Dutch settlements on Long Island after the arrival of four frigates in New Amsterdam Harbor. New Amsterdam would of course be renamed in honor of the king's brother, the Duke of York.

The political ineptitude of the Stuart kings would again interject its influence into the internal and external affairs of England. Again also, it would be the Protestant-Catholic rivalry that would cause another serious rift between King and Parliament. In 1670, Charles II would enter into an agreement with the emissaries of the Sun King, Louis XIV, by which France would renew its wars against the Dutch in exchange for a promise to return England to Catholicism when practicable, and in return for a subsidy paid by Louis to Charles. This treaty was reached at Dover, in secret, and without the knowledge or consent of Parliament.

There would of course be repercussions when the conditions of the Dover treaty were made known to the public. From Parliament would come angry denouncement and the Test Act of 1673, which officially excluded all Catholics from public office. Soothing to the Protestant nerves of Parliament was the marriage of James, Duke of York's daughter to the Protestant hero of the Netherlands, William of Orange. It was hoped that this marriage would secure to England a Protestant succession. The problems of monarchal succession would again rear their unfortuitous head. James himself would resign as Lord High Admiral in protest to the Test Act. Furthermore, upon the death of his wife Anne Hyde, he would marry the Catholic Mary of Modena. Parliament would now seek an extension of the Test Act barring James from becoming king. In 1679, Charles would simply dissolve them. On his deathbed in 1685, Charles converted to Catholicism and declared his brother and heir, James, as King James II.

Further Catholic-Protestant discord would continue. After securing his throne against the efforts of the Protestant pretender, the Duke of Monmouth, Charles' oldest illegitimate son, James II would create more problems for himself by staffing the army with Catholic officers, and by packing the Judiciary and privy with Catholic sympathizers. So as to add insult to injury, a declaration of indulgence towards all Protestants was prepared and ordered to be read from every pulpit in the land. When seven bishops refused to do so, James

II had them arrested and tried on charges of sedition. Although acquitted, the damage had been done, and leaders of the recently created Whig party began negotiating with William of Orange, husband of the Protestant heir to the throne, Mary.

The actions to follow are generally regarded in English history as the Glorious Revolution, although occupation by a foreign power might actually be the more appropriate term. For the second time in English history a conqueror named William would launch a full-scale military invasion of the island from mainland Europe. For the second time they would succeed. On November 1, 1688, William of Orange departed Holland, aided by a "Protestant Wind," which would assist in his efforts by keeping the English ships in their harbors. His invasion force consisted of somewhere between 225 vessels and 15,000 men and five hundred vessels, including sixty warships and some 40,000 men.[42] [43] Although the actual size of his force may be disputed, what can be asserted with some degree of authority is that the Dutch-Stadholder engaged in this venture more with the motive of bringing England into the League of Augsburg and using it as a counter to the power and influence of Louis XIV, than with any particular desire to conquer simply for the sake of conquest.

In a political sense, William would claim justification similar to that of Henry IV during his 1399 invasion to overthrow the Plantagenet monarchy of Richard II. A military invasion from a foreign soil would not be portrayed as an invasion at all. It would instead be portrayed as a crusade by a disinterested soul to defend the liberties and properties of the English people from a tyrannical monarch and his despotic government. On his flagship William of Orange would hoist his own colors, along with the flag of England, on which was embroidered the motto, "I will maintain the Protestant religion and the liberties of England."[44]

Crucial also to the success of William's invasion would be the assistance or non-intervention of the army and navy of James II. There

---

[42] Smith, *This Realm of England*, 332.
[43] Churchill, *Marlborough, Vol. 1*, 249.
[44] Ibid, 249.

is evidence of complicity in the events of 1688 as the van of the invasion fleet of William was led by the English Rear-Admiral Herbert. The army of James II did not actively take the field. Most notable amongst those changing their allegiance was John Churchill, the man in command when James II defended his throne against Monmouth at Sedgemoor in 1685. Churchill would later go on to accomplish great deeds for his island nation. There existed also the defection of Lord Cornbury, whose intention it was to carry three regiments of the Royal Dragoons over to the side of the Dutch Prince. In the navy, John Churchill's brother George, in agreement with an ever increasing crowd of sea officers, would deliver his ship, the Newcastle, to William. All in all, there was not to be found much glory in the Glorious Revolution.

Now recognizing that his actions in the past had cost him the support of the army, navy, the church, landowners, and Whigs and Tories alike, and in the knowledge that he could mount no measurable resistance to William of Orange, James II would choose flight over fight. The following spring the new conqueror William would be appointed by approval of Parliament as King William III. His English wife would become Queen Mary II.

It would be upon this stage that one of the all-time greats of English history would arrive on the scene. This is not to say, however, that this individual is one of the best known. By reason of issues not of his own making he is today one of the most obscure of England's great soldiers. This man, John Churchill, Earl and later Duke of Marlborough, would lead combined English and Dutch armies against the greatest military force then known to mankind, the armies of King Louis XIV of France.

Before mention of his accomplishments, it is important to take notice of the improvements and nature of warfare during the years of the eighteenth century. Europe would set the pace in all affairs, both military and non-military. This would be made possible by an irresistible superiority in technology. Within the confines of tiny Europe there would exist five major powers capable of exerting their influence and ambitions on an intercontinental basis, these being

France, Spain, Britain, Austria and Russia. Though less powerful and less populated, Portugal and Holland maintained colonial interest as well. With the exception of Manchu China, Mogul India and the Ottoman Empire of Turkey, there were no other powers of any influence, and these three could not compete with European aspirations, as they could not be considered maritime powers. Whereas armies in the past had consisted of a few thousand or a few ten thousands of men, they would now comprise units at times in excess of 100,000 men. At Malplaquet in September 1709, the army commanded by Churchill consisted of an astonishing 253 cavalry squadrons, 128 infantry battalions, or 110,000 men.[45] Of these, twenty-four thousand would be killed or wounded.

Improvements in the technology of war would be accompanied by an improvement in destructive capacity and fighting methods as well. The eighteenth century would see the rise of such leaders as Frederick the Great of Prussia, John Churchill, Duke of Marlborough of England, Prince Eugene of Savoy, Charles XII of Sweden, Maurice de Saxe of Germany, Peter the Great of Russia, and the two French Marshalls, Claude, Duke of Villars and Louis, Duke of Vendome.

Agriculture was to play an important part in the economy and the military trends of the eighteenth century as well. Much as agricultural inertia had prevented the growth of urban centers in Romanized Britain, it would now affect the industrial and military capabilities of eighteenth century Europe. Being a largely agricultural society, most Europeans of the time were engaged in the raising of crops. However, agricultural production of the time was such that most of the inhabitants of the land could raise enough food to support themselves, with very little left over to support the growing population of the urban industrial centers. Also, when societies resorted to the raising of increasingly larger armies, this meant a resulting decrease in the manpower available to work the land. This should be evident to the American of today, as we are familiar with the problems encountered during the American Civil War, when all

---

[45] Churchill, *Marlborough, Vol. 2,* 604.

the available manpower of the South was taken from the land to fulfill the recruitment needs of the Southern armies. Eventually a tipping point is reached where the land falls into disuse and the men under arms go hungry. Not only would agricultural production have a restraining effect on the size of armies, it would affect their mobility as well, as they always had to remain within a few days march of food supplies.

And yet, with all of these restraints placed upon him, to include the political issues involved with leading an army comprised of soldiers from many nations, Churchill would accomplish great deeds. For ten years he would serve his English monarchs, first William of Orange and then the last of the Stuarts, Queen Anne. He would wage ten campaigns, besiege over thirty towns, and fight four of the largest battles fought to date, at Blenheim in 1704, Ramillies in 1707, Oudenarde in 1708, and finally at Malplaquet in 1709. Never was John Churchill defeated in battle, and he would see the English armies become known as the finest fighting force in Europe. Although England would acquire no territorial gains on the continent, as had happened with the military successes of Edward III and Henry V, the Duke of Marlborough would, with the assistance of his comrade in arms Eugene of Savoy, frustrate both the military and political aspirations of Louis XIV.

Whereas Parliament and Oliver Cromwell had initiated the English Civil War half a century prior to the years of John Churchill, England would now undergo another revolution which would allow it to rise supreme above all its enemies. During the Elizabethan years England had resorted to outright piracy in its attempts to compete with Spain and to finance its ventures in the New World. During the years of William of Orange and John Churchill, agricultural and industrial production had acted as a brake upon the size of armies and on their areas of operations in the field. England would now find a cure all for both of these handicaps. This new revolution, or evolution if you prefer, was the Bank of England. The first banks in England had arisen during the Cromwellian years, when the goldsmiths of London began to accept gold and silver deposits for safekeeping, eventually lending out part of these deposits as interest. Eventually, the receipts given out by these goldsmiths became accepted as a form of currency or paper money. "By 1675 bankers were performing the three essential functions of banking; accepting deposits, lending money, and issuing notes."[46]

This new concept of banking was expanded upon in 1694 with the establishment of the Bank of England. The initial idea for this new creation came from William Patterson, a successful London merchant who had traveled to Holland and had studied Dutch banking policies. His new idea would be seized upon by Charles Montagu, a Whig politician who would initiate the needed legislation and steer it through Parliament. According to the terms of its initial legislation, the newly created bank would lend the government 1.2 million pounds and in return the government would pay 8 percent interest on the money and the bank would be authorized to receive deposits, make loans, issue banknotes, and to sell stock. As an indication of its immediate success, all of the banks initial stock would be sold in twelve days. Also as an indication of its success, whereas the government was restricted to a budget of about 2 million pounds annually during the years of Charles II and James II, during the years of William and Anne it could spend nearly three times as much. This would allow for the creation of a navy second to none and of a new all powerful army.

There would follow the creation of other financial innovations as well. For the first time in English history there would be the notion of a permanent national debt. In the years prior to William of Orange, the monarchs during years of need would secure forced loans from the wealthy of England, pledging repayment by means of Crown revenues as they became available. Such loans were expensive and destructive of future income, which was always needed for future contingencies. In addition, English society would see the birth of the stock exchange and the stock market. The coffeehouses of Exchange Alley would be the unlikely birthplace of these institutions, with

---

[46] Roberts and Roberts, *A History of England, Prehistory to 1714.*

stockbrokers gathering at Johnathan's and Garraway's. Company stocks and government securities were to be sold here, with Parliament in 1697 limiting the number of brokers to 100 and requiring them to register with the government.

Whereas the Glorious Revolution of 1688 had been followed by the successes of English finance and the dominance of English armies under Marborough, the influence of political parties would now tend to combine in order to soften their potential advantages. The Whig and Tory Parties, named after a Scottish fundamentalist and a group of Irish papist bandits, respectively, were initially formed during the years of the Restoration. During the years of Queen Anne, they would now seek to gain ascendancy in the House of Commons. The fact of Party would now become closely associated with the democratic societies of the Western World. Division lists survive for eight different votes taken in the House of Commons during the years of William of Orange. They indicate that 85 percent of the time votes were cast solely on the Whig or Tory side. These division lists are indicative of un-fortuitous tendencies within the western societies. As with the invention of political parties, societies became divided over social issues, with the more important aspects of government assuming a secondary importance. The fact of party would only become more obvious during the years of Anne. Out of 1064 members serving in Parliament between her coronation in 1702 and her death in 1714, only 71 cannot be identified as belonging to either Whig or Tory parties.[47] With collective strength, political parties now had the ability to influence such important matters as the appointment of ministers and such important issues as taxation or the fighting of wars. Political parties now had the ability to divide people over issues not just in Parliament, but also in the shires, cities, towns, churches, and all other segments of society. With the overwhelming landside in the general elections of 1708, another danger would manifest itself through party politics. For many years Queen Anne had attempted desperately to remain free of politics. With an overwhelming Whig

---

[47] Ibid, 420.

majority in the House of Commons, she would have no alternative but to become subservient to it, hence the ability of the party to subjugate the executive branch of government, to be followed eventually by the ability to subjugate the courts as well.

Other repercussions would follow. After decades of faithful public service and unparalleled success on the battlefield, John Churchill, Duke of Marlborough, would himself become the victim of party politics and party tactics. He would not be the last great man to be denied to the public by means of sacrifice at the political altar. Our own American history is also littered with the names of all too many to suffer a similar fate, to include John Jay, Thomas Hart Benton, Sam Houston, Edmund G. Ross, Francis Channing Barlow, etc. Political parties rarely stand on principle; therefore individuals who do usually incur their wrath.

¤

Costly and destructive as they may have been, the years of Cromwell and Marlborough saw many improvements within English society, both in terms of the relationship between Parliament and the Crown and in terms of its influence abroad. These years would also give rise to those instruments that would send England on to even greater heights of glory. The wheellock, which had supplanted the longbow of Crecy and Agincourt, would now be replaced by the flintlock musket with its prepacked paper cartridge and socket bayonet. Not only was the flintlock more reliable than its predecessor, and far less susceptible to the influence of weather, it could also discharge at a rate eight times faster than the wheellock. With the invention of the socket-bayonet, it could also be used as either an offensive or defensive weapon, which, when coupled with the newly developed tactical infantry formations, could be used with devastating effect.

The socket bayonet was of another advantage as well. Earlier types of plug bayonets had been attempted, with the butt of the bayonet being inserted into the end of the barrel of the firearm. This of course rendered the firearm ineffective, as it could not fire a projectile in such condition. With the socket bayonet, the individual soldier now had a combination firearm and bladed weapon. One such weapon, the British "Brown Bess," has become closely associated with the British colonial expansion of the eighteenth century.

Of far greater importance to Britain, were the technological and tactical innovations of naval warfare that would lead it to near domination of the globe. The construction of fighting ships had by this time evolved to the point that the ship of the line with its multi-tiered broadside batteries had long since replaced the galleon. These ships could now average 200 feet in length and could displace up to 2,500 tons. A first-rate ship of the line could carry 100 or more guns on three decks, with a crew of about one thousand men needed to perform all the ship's various functions. There existed six rates of ships in all, with a second rate ship of the line carrying 90 guns on three decks, the fifth and six rate ships carrying as few as 24 to 40 guns all on one deck.

Other naval developments which made the ship of the line more effective as a weapon included the tiller, a beam projecting inboard from the rudder, which allowed for the steering of the ship by means of cables rigged to a steering wheel mounted on the quarter deck. Copper sheathing, attached to the underside of the ship so as to protect it from barnacles and teredo worms was also improved. The seventeenth century English discovery of how to harness a naval gun's recoil by means of ropes, which allowed the gun to be brought to a rest inboard of the gun port so as to facilitate easy reloading also played an important role in Britain's naval supremacy. By expediting the reloading times of these early muzzle-loading naval weapons, the British were always assured of increased rates of fire over their enemies.

The years of the restoration had also seen within the Royal Navy improvements in doctrine, administration and organization. Many of these improvements had come under the guidance of Samuel Pepys, who served as James II's Secretary of the Admiralty. Whereas naval engagements tended to be very confused affairs at this time, with fog, distance, gunsmoke and lack of modern methods of communication all making their effects realized, the English Navy sought to establish a doctrinal procedure for dealing with any contingencies that might arise in battle. While never perfect, these "Fighting Instructions" did give to the English sea captains at least some measure of organization and preparation. Combined with the line-ahead formation, in which each English ship would engage the enemy vessel closet to it while following the course of the English vessel preceding it, this usually allowed the English Admiral a tactical advantage over the opposing enemy fleet.

The English aspiration to establish "Imperium Pelage," domination of the sea, would not come without resistance or at times defeat. The navies of the other maritime powers did possess able ships and capable captains as well. During the Anglo-Dutch wars of the Commonwealth and the Restoration, Holland's greatest sailor, Michiel de Ruyter, inflicted severe damage upon the English fleet during the Four Day Fight of Jun 1 through June 4 of 1666. A year later de Ruyter would brazenly sail up the Medway to Chatham, where he burned thirteen ships and towed away the English Navy's flagship, the Royal Charles. This act was considered by the English people to be an act of humiliation. De Ruyter would not act alone in his defiance of English naval supremacy. The French fighting sailor Jean Bart would administer to the English that which they had earlier administered to the Spanish during the years of Drake and Raleigh. Having fewer ships than the English, Jean Bart would resort to a guerre de course, destroying English ships and damaging English trade in the Channel. Bart's actions would set a gallant example for his successors on how to fight a naval war with limited resources.

It would be the individual commanders, both of ships and of armies, who would be most responsible for the building of the empire to follow. The efforts of Cabot, Drake and Raleigh would be seized upon by men of vision who would learn how to employ the newly developed weapons of war to great advantage. The nature of the wars the new leaders would fight would change as well. Prior to William of Orange, the soldiers and sailors had always fought for issues generally internal to their island, perhaps occasionally spilling over into Northern France during some of the early dynastic disputes. Now they would serve a new master. Wars henceforth would be fought for dominion of the seas, to control distant countries and continents, to establish more and larger colonies, with the accompanying benefit of increased trade and augmented wealth.

During the early years of the eighteenth century, with the increase in maritime commerce, there came about an increase in the numbers of fleet actions between the new maritime powers. By allowing the English fleet to keep the French fleet at Toulon under constant watch, the acquisition of Gibraltar would enable the royal Navy to control the Western Mediterranean for centuries to come. In 1739, England would declare war on Spain during a period known for almost endless turmoil. In this war England would initiate a policy that would have been fully recognizable to Drake and Raleigh. Squadrons would be sent from English ports to attack the Spanish colonies of the West Indies, leading to the capture of important ports. Not the least of which in its importance would be the 1704 capture of the Island fortress of Gibraltar. The taking of this important rock would be accomplished by Admiral Sir George Rooke.

One of these sorties would be led by future Admiral Lord George Anson. His mission was to sail around Cape Horn and attack the Spanish colonies on the west coast of South America. Setting out with an initial squadron of six ships, two would return to England and a third would be lost due to the severities of weather during the trip around the Cape. With his three remaining vessels, he would cruise the South American coast, eventually traveling to Manila where he would capture a Spanish galleon carrying a million and a half dollars in specie. Although not as successful as hoped, this voyage had the advantage of being a public relations gem. With the advent of the war of the Austrian Succession, further hostilities against other fleets would ensue. An English fleet under Admiral Matthews would engage a combined French-Spanish fleet at Toulon in February 1744. Three years later there would be two fleet actions fought between English and French navies, both of them fought near Finisterre, one in May, the other in October. In these battles, Admiral Anson and later Admiral Sir Edward Hawke would severely curtail the fighting strength of the French Navy.

The success of both of the Cape Finisterre actions was attributable to new innovations in English naval tactics. Whereas in the past century sea captains had been restricted in their actions by the "Fighting Instructions" and were required also to fight in a line-ahead formation; Anson and Hawke would be two of the first of England's naval commanders to deviate from them. Henceforth, the English ships would remain in line, as the foremost English vessel came upon the rear most enemy and should be it would bring their guns to bear. They would then proceed to the next enemy ship in line, with the second British ship taking up the action against the rear-most enemy. The success of these new tactics would be telling. In the engagement by Anson, six French warships were sunk or taken. In the action by Hawke, six of eight French warships were sunk or taken and a convoy of 250 merchantmen was forced to flee.

There would be another naval adaptation around this time that would be of strategic importance. Understanding that if naval wars were fought between themselves and the Spanish and French in North America, there came the realization that if England were to win these contests for supremacy, the only chance for success would be a continuous quarantine of the enemy colonies coast. Therefore, a new system of naval rotations was begun. Any ship of the line would be sent to sea for a set time period. Upon its return, it would be replaced by a similar vessel while it underwent repairs and the crew received a period of rest. This system of ship rotations is still employed to this day, especially with the carrier task groups of the U.S. Navy.

These naval developments would be necessary in the years to come and would assist England in the conquest of entire subcontinents. In regard to their colonies in both North America and the Far East, England, perhaps due to its naval supremacy, would expand its colonies much faster than France. In Europe, France held a sizeable lead in population over England. In 1700 France possessed 19.2 million inhabitants. By 1780 this number had increased to 25.6

million. England in the same period rose from 6.9 million to roughly 9 million.[48] Conversely, the British population of North America rose from 265,000 in 1700 to 2.3 million by 1770. In contrast to these numbers, in 1700 there were but 7,500 French and Spanish combined in North America; by 1720 the French population in North America was about 25,000 and by the outbreak of the Seven Years War there were barely 50,000. Given the limited size of its population in North America, and taking into consideration the limits of French naval capabilities, it should come as no surprise that at no time was France able to place more than 5,000 troops into action to defend its North American colonies.

Policies, though necessary, are no good of themselves. Wise and effective policies must be accompanied by the actions of wise and effective men. In this need, England would be extremely fortunate. The alternating and opposite philosophies of two great Englishmen would now come into being and create the further foundation of English supremacy. With the ascendancy to the throne of the Hanovarian dynasty and with the coronation of King George I, a new parliamentary minister would become predominant. His name was Robert Walpole. Initially serving as Chancellor of the Exchequer, he would resign in disgust when England's national debt rose to 50 million pounds.

In 1720 a very speculative and unwise plan to redeem this debt, which stood at 30,000,000 pounds, was brought forward. In 1710, a then Tory ministry had granted a charter for the South Sea Company, and had at the same time arranged for it to assume part of the national debt. This arrangement had initially proven itself so successful that in 1720 its board of directors approached the government with a plan to assume the whole national debt. As presented, the plan was such that if all went well, the South Sea Company could through its investments and profits pay off the entire national debt in twenty-five years. Speculation of projected profits was such that 462 members of the House of Commons and 122 of the peers would become involved

---

[48] James, *Rise and Fall of the British Empire*, 52.

with this scheme by means of their personal investment. It is said that 1,250,000 pounds were spent on bribes to government ministers, members of Parliament, and various influential courtiers. On April 2, 1720, the Bill sanctioning these proposals was approved by the Commons by a vote of 172 to 35. The proposal would sail through the House of Lords five days later by another sizeable margin.

There is an old adage, "If it sounds too good to be true, it probably is." Such would be the case with the South Sea Company. The value of the company's stock soared in three months from 128 to 300. Within fourteen months it would soar to 1050.[49] Unfortunately, these huge initial profits would establish what could accurately be described as a feeding frenzy. Stockbrokers and Stockjobbers would soon be selling shares to crazed investors in any venture or enterprise that sounded even remotely within the realm of possibility. Stocks for inventions such as Puckles Machine Gun or enterprises that involved turning seawater into fresh water, all beyond the technological abilities of the time, were put up for public sale. The resulting crash was inevitable. As more and more of the minor stock bubbles burst, a chain reaction was created. Eventually the South Sea Company would burst as well. To the innocent and the naïve would come the reward of bankruptcy and the loss of life savings. Occasionally there is some justice in this world. The directors of the South Sea Company were arrested and their estates forfeited to an infinite number of creditors. The Chancellor of the Exchequer, John Arslabie, also experienced arrest.

Out of the ashes of the South Sea Company, Walpole would return as Exchequer. His immediate goal was to remedy the issues of finance and cure the problem of national debt. He would accomplish his desired task through a policy of thrift in government spending and the policy of non-intervention in the innumerable wars of the continent. In his financial reconstruction, he would take that portion of the national debt, which had been conveyed to the South Sea Company, and divide it between the Bank of England and the

---

[49] Churchill, *History of the English Speaking Peoples*, 423.

Treasury, now being overseen by a commission. A sinking fund, which he himself had initiated with the sole intent of paying off the national debt, was now placed into action. By these policies, and with the reduction of the debt, the burden of taxation, and especially land taxes, was lowered. There was an accompanying lowering of tariffs and duties on imports and exports that facilitated an increase in trade.

Of course with political success and administrative achievement by one party comes the positive enmity of the other. The attacks against the success of the Whig minister led to his being derisively referred to as the "Prime Minister," no doubt in reference to his girth. His political undoing would arrive after nearly a decade and a half of successfully governing the English nation. His first mistake would be an excise tax passed in 1733 on wines and tobacco, the equivalent of what is currently referred to as a "sin tax." These taxes of course never meet with popular approval. The next act to fall upon the unfortunate minister would be the Tory realization that his policies were successful mostly because he avoided foreign entanglements. Rather than see Walpole succeed, the Tory Party would have England go to war. The excuse for war would be the Spanish policy of stopping and searching English ships unlawfully trading slaves in the Spanish colonies in violation of the 1713 Treaty of Utrecht. Profits in this illegal trade were high, as profits in any illegal trade usually are. Therefore, the merchants in London involved in this trade were to demand that the search by the Spanish be challenged.

With England trying to avoid war and debt, and with Spain itself nearly bankrupt, a settlement between the two nations would be reached with the Convention of Prado in January 1739. In this agreement, Spain would offer concession to the English and Walpole would reduce English claims in return. Success was within the minister's grasp. However, hot heads and a severed ear would lead to failure, and war. An English sea captain, Robert Jenkins, appeared before Parliament with his ear in a jar. His claim was that during the act of search, his ear had been severed by a Spanish naval officer. War, unnecessarily would follow. Soon the era of Walpole would end; in 1742 he lost a motion of confidence and retired to the House of Lords.

He would be succeeded as chief policy maker of England by the brilliant and mercurial William Pitt, or Pitt the Elder. Unlike Walpole, Pitt would not be the head of government, but rather the driving force behind it. His policy in regard to the quarrels of continental Europe was similar to that of Walpole. He believed in restraining the size of armies whenever possible. He differentiated from Walpole, however, on his views toward the struggle for empire and of colonies. On this issue he was very aggressive.

As a lesson to those who believe that honesty is not always the best policy, it would be his reputation for honesty that would lead to his rise in government and his popular support.

It was during the Jacobite rebellion of Charles Edward Stuart, or Bonnie Prince Charlie, that Pitt would first come to public notice. In April of 1746, Pitt was appointed Paymaster of the Forces. In this capacity he was entitled the privilege to carry balances from the payment of forces to his personal account and to further draw interest upon them. This he refused to do. He also refrained from the accepted custom of receiving bribes. When his character and honesty became known to the public, the resulting effect on public opinion was overwhelming. This reputation for honesty was to be responsible for much of his success.

If his success can in part be attributed to his honesty, than his greatness must be attributed in part to affairs external to the island nation and to his possession of a strategic eye. Events well beyond the control of Pitt would initiate a chain of events that would lead to a colonial dispute which was to become the first truly world war.

By the time of the 1750s the continued population explosion of the British colonies in North America and their westward expansion would lead to a dispute with France over the lands of the Ohio River Valley. Believing these lands to be their exclusive dominion, in the summer of 1753 France would begin the construction of three forts, Presque Isle, Le Boeuf, and Machault in an attempt to halt British westward expansion. Robert Dinwiddie, the Lieutenant Governor of Colonial Virginia, would in response send a twenty-one year old major of the Virginia militia on a diplomatic mission to convey to the

French that they must abandon these forts, which he believed to be an encroachment onto English territory. On May 28, 1754, a skirmish would be fought between this English diplomatic mission, under the command of Major George Washington, and a diplomatic party of French under the command of a thirty-five year old ensign named Joseph Coulon de Villiers de Jumonville. There would be a dispute over who fired first upon whom, the end result being that the young French officer was wounded along with thirteen of his countrymen. To further inflame the situation, an English Indian guide named Tanaghrisson would in the confusion after the skirmish murder the wounded French ensign, exclaiming, "Tu n'es pas encore mont, mon pere": Thou are not yet dead, my father.

In the events to follow, the French would send a force of six hundred regulars and Canadian militia to expel the now Lieutenant Colonel Washington and his forces from the forks of the Ohio River. On July 3, 1754, Washington would be forced to surrender his newly constructed Fort Necessity to a French force under the command of Captain Louis Coulon de Villiers, brother of the earlier slain ensign. When word of these events reached London and Paris, the English would respond by sending the Forty-fourth and Forty-eighth regiments of foot to America under the command of General Sir Edward Braddock. Never to be outdone, the French would retaliate by sending seventy-eight companies of regular infantry, the equivalent of six regiments, to Canada.

The ensuing war would not initially go well for England. In the spring of 1755, an English fleet would attempt to intercept the French vessels carrying the aforementioned reinforcements before they could arrive in Canada. This British fleet, under the command of Admiral Edward Boscowan, would only be able to intercept two of the French vessels, Alcide and Lye, allowing the largest part of the French army of these three thousand men to reach Canada. Even worse, in July of 1755, General Braddock in his attempt to capture the three French forts along the Ohio, would be ambushed and decisively beaten at the Battle of Monongahela. In this battle England would lose much of its army and Braddock would lose his life.

The British string of defeats would continue for the following year, although this cycle of defeat would eventually assist Pitt in his efforts. Political friction in England had led to Pitt's removal as Paymaster of Forces in November of 1755. For now, he would be forced to sit on the sidelines. When operations in the war continued in the spring, England would be confronted with naval failure and the loss of its island fortress of Minorca in the Mediterranean. In May of 1756 British Admiral John Byng would be sent with a fleet of 13 ships to recapture the island. In his efforts he would fail to destroy the opposing French fleet and would also fail in his attempt to land the accompanying army battalion to relieve those British forces still holding out on the island. A victim of the Whig-Tory political rivalry of the time, he was sentenced to be shot on the quarterdeck of his flagship as a result of his failure. Pitt would plead before the King for Byng's life, stating, "The House of Commons, Sir, is inclined to mercy." The response from the King, indicative of his disfavor was, "You have taught me to look for the sense of my people elsewhere than in the House of Commons."

Minorca would not be the only British reverse of 1756. In May of that year the French forces in North America received a new commander. His name was Louis Joseph Marquis de Montcalm. Within months he would seize the initiative, cross Lake Ontario and destroy Oswego. His opposite number, the man England sent to oversee the affairs of the North American colonies, John Campbell, Fourth Earl of Loudoun, chose instead to use the year 1756 to attack his English predecessor.

Shortly after Pitt's dismissal in November of 1755, and in fear of a French cross-Channel invasion of England, Britain and the emerging kingdom of Prussia would enter into an alliance. It was the belief of the head of the English government, the Duke of Newcastle, that if the colonial war in North America were to spread to Europe, King George II's other realm of Hanover in North Germany would be easily overrun. Therefore, on January 16, 1756, England and the Prussia of Frederick the Great entered into an alliance with the Convention of Westminster. In response, likewise fearing the growth of Frederick's kingdom, France, Russia, Saxony and Sweden entered into a counter-alliance.

Frederick, finding himself now surrounded and learning of the intentions of his enemies, decided to strike first. In a two-month campaign starting in August of 1756, Frederick would reduce the number of his enemies by one, capturing Saxony and adding its army to his own. The only victory known to England in 1756 would be that of her ally in Prussia. So would end the terrible year of 1756.

The failures of 1756 would lead to the disasters of 1757 and to the return of Pitt. In the spring of 1757, William Augustus, Duke of Cumberland, would be sent by England with an 11,000-man army to defend Hanover and Brunswick. Before the year was over, he would lose both. In North America Montcalm would resume his offensive against the English, capturing Fort William Henry at the head of the Hudson Valley. In the aftermath of this successful siege, Montcalm's Indian allies massacred a column of prisoners who had surrendered and been allowed to depart under the established European rules of warfare.

In a further sign of continued English failures, a planned assault against the French fortress of Louisburg, which commanded the Gulf of St. Lawrence, never got beyond Halifax, Nova Scotia. Much of the failure was due to the commander of this expedition, Lord Loudoun. Additionally, some of the failure could be attributed to the arrival of eighteen French ships of the line, the strongest naval contingent ever sent by France to North America.

As had happened in 1756, the only victories to be seen by the English were those fought by its ally, Prussia, and by an English subject with a conglomerate army in far away India. In India, the exploits of a former clerk would acquire for the British Empire one of its crown jewels. Robert Clive, almost of his own initiative, and with an army of no more than 3,000 men, met and defeated an army of 50,000 troops of the Nawab of Bengal at Plassey on June 23, 1757. There was with this battle, fought by an agent of the world's second great empire, a very striking similarity to the Roman victory of Wattling Street, where Suetonius Paulinus and the 14th Gemina

Legion had crushed the Iceni Revolt against the massive odds of twenty-three to one. In both cases, superior weapons and superior discipline provided to the victor a level of success, which should not have been attainable against such massive odds.

On the continent, Frederick the Great would give the world another well-trained, well-disciplined army. As had happened with Seutonius Paulinus and Robert Clive, his victories would be fought against a foe of numerical superiority and against great odds. In the summer of 1757, Frederick's armies would combine in an attempt to overwhelm him. A French army of 100,000 men invaded Hanover. A second combined Franco-Austrian army 84,000 strong, moved north against Frederick out of Franconia. Two other armies, each in excess of 100,000 men, one Austrian and one Russian invaded Bohemia and East Prussia, respectively. Miraculously, against these overwhelming odds, Frederick would launch a two-month campaign from October to December 1757 wherein he would earn his sobriquet, save his kingdom and defeat two larger armies at Rossbach in the West and Leuthen in the east. Essentially, the abilities of two men would save England and Prussia from unmitigated disaster in the year 1757.

It would be upon this stage that William Pitt would return to action. With colonial opposition to the policies of Lord Loudoun stiffening, the Crown would summon the abilities of Pitt to reverse their sagging fortunes of war. The initiative would be seized immediately. Loudoun would be recalled to London. In his place Major General James Abercrombie would also assume the command of the British forces in North America. So as to cajole their offended sensibilities, Pitt would alter the relationship of the colonial forces raised in America with those of the regular forces sent by Great Britain. Henceforth, colonial officers would only be considered as holding rank junior to regular army officers of similar or higher grades, a deviation of the policies of the past. In a move to solve the perceived injuries of the colonial assemblies, Pitt also agreed that henceforth the Crown would reimburse the colonies for the equipment and provisions for the levies to be raised by the colonies, and that the Crown would also pay for additional expenses in proportion to the "active vigour and strenuous efforts of the respective Provinces."

This complete reversal of policy was a clear indication that Pitt, now serving as Secretary of State, would control the action of the army, navy, diplomatic corps, and govern the direction of war policy. The center points of this policy would be to assist Frederick the Great on the continent by means of greater financial assistance, and to initiate a policy of relying heavily on England's greatest advantage, its navy. In addition, there would be a shakeup in the command of England's ground forces in North America. For a planned expedition to capture Louisburg and then Quebec, the forty-year old Major General Jeffrey Amherst would be in command, with the younger, high-strung Lieutenant Colonel James Wolfe as second in command. For England's overland expedition against Canada, James Abercrombie would be in overall command, the thirty-four year old George August, Viscount Howe to act as his second. Wolfe and Howe would both go forward to achieve fame in the history of the North American continent.

Not only would policy and command structure be altered under Pitt, but the fighting manner of the British forces would also see change. Lord Loudoun's planned expedition against Louisburg had failed in 1757 due to the appearance of eighteen French ships of the line. In 1758, the English would find a remedy to this problem. In 1756 Britain had possessed 130 ships of the line, France 63 and Spain 46.[50] To this overall naval superiority, recent construction added further weight. In April of 1758, Admiral Hawke defeated a large French relief convoy off La Rochelle. In 1758 only six French men-of-war would arrive to defend the waters around Louisburg. The naval blockade was now to become a fact of war, with its negative affects to become known to soldier and civilian alike.

On land, the experiences of "La Guerre Sauvage" and the fighting style of the North American colonists were to come into play. In Europe the armies of Frederick and his opponents would continue to

---

[50] Dupuy, *Encyclopedia of Military History*, 576.

engage in very linear tactics where large masses of men would stand shoulder to shoulder and fire volleys at their enemies at close range. In the forests of America, these tactics simply did not work. Massachusetts Governor William Shirley was largely responsible for the change in tactics to come. In 1755 Shirley had begun recruiting a force of provincial rangers under the command of New Hampshire frontiersman Robert Rogers. This non-traditional force would wear garb more suitable for scouts and raiders. Realizing their effectiveness, Shirley had tripled their numbers and added them to the regular army's payroll.

The young General Howe, noting their abilities and usefulness, initiated a policy of dispersing them among the regular army regiments. They in turn would teach the regular army units how to fight in the woods of North America. When attacked, they would not stand in formation and make easy targets of themselves, as had the army of Braddock in 1755. The first rifles, as opposed to muskets, would begin to be issued to the best marksmen of each unit. So too would begin the nasty habit of deliberately targeting enemy officers during engagements. The long tails of the regular army coats would now be trimmed to allow for easier movement through brush. For the most part, swords would be discarded and replaced by more effective woodland weapons such as the tomahawk. In general, the ceremonialism of Europe was of necessity to be replaced by the practicality of America.

Success would naturally follow, although that success would not be immediate. With the opening of the campaign season in America, British efforts would meet with initial disaster. In July of 1758, General Abercrombie and his subordinate Viscount Howe began the ill-fated overland assault against the Marquis de Montcalm. An army of 16,000 men, the largest ever assembled to date in America, was at their disposal. The initial objective on their path to Montreal was Fort Carillon on the Northern end of Lake George. Over one thousand boats were needed to convoy the English force from its assembling point near the Former Fort William Henry to its debarkation point on the north end of the lake. Almost immediately the young Viscount

Howe would lose his life in a skirmish with French guards near the army's debarkation point. Abercrombie, now shaken, would hesitate; Montcalm would not. Realizing that the British force would in all likelihood have to attack the Fort from the landward side, he and his men constructed breastworks to the northwest of the fort. To further impede the British assault, trees were felled in an interlocking pattern in front of the French works, thus creating a dense abatis through which the British would have to move. On July 8, when Abercrombie finally ordered the assault, the result was disastrous. More than 500 red-coated British troops would be killed and thirteen hundred more wounded during the repeated and futile assaults against the French. French losses were 377 killed and wounded.[51] With his greatest victory and the departure of the British, Montcalm erected at the site of battle an immense red cross with a Latin inscription and its accompanying translation in French. Upon the cross was written:

Christian, behold! Not all the care
that Montcalm took nor this fearsome
abatis, nor all our heroes feats,
have stunned the English here, have
shattered all their hopes: Instead
the arm of God prevailed, the Victor
of this cross. [52]

Little would Montcalm know, that within two weeks of his greatest success in America that the strategic balance of power between his native France and England would shift dramatically and forever when an Anglo-American force captured the fortress of Louisburg on the Gulf of St. Lawrence. In the aftermath of this successful Anglo-American six-week siege, the populations of Cape Breton and Prince Edward Islands and their Indian allies would face fierce acts of retribution. To the Indian allies would go a general

---

[51] Anderson, *The War That Made America*, 138.
[52] Ibid, 139.

policy of massacre "in return for a thousand acts of cruelty and barbarity," as so nobly put forth by the Brigadier Wolfe. For the largely Acadian populations of the two islands, Amherst would demand their deportations to France.

The garrison of Louisburg, denied the honors of war in response to Montcalm's inability to restrain his Indian allies after the English capitulation at Fort William Henry, were to become prisoners of war. They were removed to England to be later exchanged for English prisoners of war held in France. Much credit for the success of Louisburg must go to the young Wolfe, as it was he who led the initial landing of English troops and by his own initiative was responsible for the capture of the initial French entrenchments.

The policies of Pitt would bring to England other successes as well. Fort Frontenac, at the head of the St. Lawrence on Lake Ontario had come under siege on August 26, 1758. Its defense would last nowhere as long as that of Louisburg, as its commander surrendered the next day. In addition, with the fall of Louisburg had come the destruction of the French fleet of ships of the line, which had been sent to assist in its defense. The agricultural issues, so vital to the conduct of wars, would also now begin to turn against France. The years 1756 and 1757 saw the failure of many crops along the St. Lawrence Valley, the virtual breadbasket of New France. When added to this was the diversion of manpower from the fields of agriculture to the fields of war, food supplies had begun to run short. Pitts new policy of naval blockade would take a further toll, so much so that by the beginning of 1758 the average citizen of Quebec was subsisting on fourteen ounces of bread and half pound of horsemeat, accompanied by smaller amounts of pork and codfish, weekly. Worse was yet to come.

The policy of Pitt in regard to assisting his overwhelmed ally on the continent would continue to bear fruit as well. The Prussian army of Duke Ferdinand of Brunswick met a French force at Crefeld on June 23, 1758, forcing them back across the Rhine River. Of even greater importance, Frederick himself defeated a large Russian army at Zorndorf in East Prussia, thereby ending the threat posed to his kingdom from the east and earning himself a brief respite.

If ever a nation had reason to celebrate a given year, such must be the case with England and the year 1759. The number and importance of the British and Prussian victories of that year would cause 1759 to be forever after regarded as the "annus mirabilis," the year of miracles. Pitt would be very largely responsible for the miracles to follow. His plan for the year 1759 included a three-pronged attack to drive the French out of Canada. There was to be a capture of Fort Niagara to sever Western Canada from the St. Lawrence, a second offensive up through the Champlain Valley to the St. Lawrence, and an amphibious assault against the City of Quebec.

Success was almost total as Jeffrey Amherst led his forces north through the Champlain Valley. The French forces would retreat before him, evacuating and destroying the Forts Carillon and Saint Frederick. Both locations would be seized by Amherst, who would order engineering parties to begin reconstruction. To the west, Brigadier General John Prideaux would succeed in capturing Fort Niagara on the southwestern shore of Lake Ontario. With the fall of Niagara, all of France's interior forts were effectively cut off from reinforcement or re-supply. It would be the actions of the young Brigadier James Wolfe, however, that would lead to England's greatest achievement of 1759. Sailing up the St. Lawrence from the captured fortress of Louisburg, Wolfe would lead a landing party up a steep precipice in the dark of night to assemble on the Plains of Abraham, west of the City of Quebec. Accompanying Wolfe up these precipitous cliffs was a battalion of provincial rangers under the command of Colonel William Howe. By the morning of September 13, 1759, Wolfe's entire command of 4,800 men was drawn up in the line of battle before the city. Montcalm, expecting the English assault to come from the east, was caught almost entirely off guard. In the battle to follow, Wolfe and Montcalm would both lose their lives, and France would lose Canada. What remained of the French forces after this very one-sided English victory marched in retreat westward toward Montreal, the last stronghold of France in Canada.

The fact that Wolfe had succeeded in taking Quebec was not of itself an assurance that the English could hold it. Nine weeks later, on

November 25, 1759, the English navy ended any chance of France reinforcing or retaining its Canadian possessions. On that date a powerful English naval force under the command of Admiral Edward Hawke defeated and virtually destroyed a French squadron of twenty-odd ships of the line at Quiberon Bay. This French force had been part of a planned French invasion of England itself, which had been stripped of its forces for the overseas campaign in America. With the destruction of this squadron, the threat of invasion was removed and the Royal Navy was now free to concentrate on commerce raiding and the further economic strangulation of the French overseas possessions.

Whereas Quebec and Quiberon Bay were overwhelming victories for England, there would be other gains as well. Guadeloupe in the West Indies was secured, as well as Goree on the west coast of Africa. In the Far East, French power in India was lost forever, after the French Commodore D'Ache failed to overcome an English squadron under Admiral Peacock in three separate though indecisive actions.

There exists for those of us today a stern lesson in these turmoils of war. In the wake of the English conquest of 1759 and with the accompanying domination of the sea, economic dominance would follow. It is often written that in the year 1760, England had as many as eight thousand sails at sea. Most of these vessels were not ships of the line but were ships engaged in commerce. In England and in America there accompanied the Seven Years War an era of explosive commercial growth. Conversely, rarely if ever did French ships set sail to engage in commerce, and it is said that in the year 1762, France had not a single ship of the line at sea.

The Seven Years War would continue after the losses of Quebec and Quiberon Bay and the English victories in the Far East and the West Indies. Spain, no doubt to its later regret, opted to join France in its naval war against England. On mainland Europe, Frederick the Great would somehow manage to survive against the overwhelming odds. Finally, after all sides had exhausted themselves financially and militarily, a peace treaty was signed at Hubertusburg in February 1763.

During the last years of its now predominately naval war against France and Spain, England seized the initiative so as to add to the already substantial gains of 1759. In the year 1760, Jeffrey Amherst continued his march against Montreal. Without any hope of re-supply from France by sea, the result was a foregone conclusion. On the morning of September 9, the French governor of Canada, Pierre Vandreuil, surrendered the remnants of the last ten battalions of French regular troops in North America. In the details of the surrender, the honors of war were denied to the French troops; their fate was to be a prisoner exchange similar to that suffered by the French forces at Louisburg. Canada was now effectively a possession of England.

In the West Indies, a fleet of nineteen ships of the line accompanied by ten thousand English troops descended upon the French Islands in 1762. In the aftermath of this campaign, Martinique, Grenada, St. Lucia and St. Vincent were added to the existing British possessions of Antiqua, St. Kitts and Nevis.

Some of these islands were to become valuable additions to England's empire; others became bargaining chips for the preliminaries of peace signed at Fontainebleau in November of 1762. The definitive peace agreement ending the Seven Years War was signed the following February in Paris. By this treaty, England acquired all of Canada plus those French possessions east of the Mississippi River except New Orleans. Havana, which had been captured by England during the last year of the war, was returned to Spain, with England receiving Spanish Florida in return. In the West Indies, Guadeloupe and Martinique, as well as St. Lucia were returned to France. In the Mediterranean, Minorca was returned to England; in the Far East, France was allowed to retain her possessions as they existed prior to the war, although she had to agree that they could not in the future be fortified. On the whole, English gains must be considered as overwhelming, due in large part to the foresight of William Pitt and the unchallenged supremacy at sea of the Royal Navy.

There is one other issue of importance that coincided with the multiplication of English power by the end of the eighteenth century. In the century and a half between 1560 and 1720, England had undergone an agricultural revolution. The English farmer of the sixteenth century became more aware of the importance of crop rotations. The practice of permanent tillage, wherein arable land was to lie fallow every third year, was replaced by a new system referred to as up and down husbandry. With the implementation of this new system, arable lands would be used to grow wheat or barley for four or five years, and then rotated into pasture for seven or eight years. The results of this alteration in agricultural practice had the desired effect. By the end of the seventeenth century yields of wheat had increased four fold per acre, and the increase in sheep and cattle populations were even greater.

Other agricultural improvements occurred as well. So as to feed livestock during the winter months, clover and turnip were introduced as field crops. No longer were farmers forced to slaughter animals during the late winter months due to a shortage of fodder. Herds could now be larger, and livestock could be grown to larger populations than before. The use of fertilization became accepted practice with the use of certain sands, lime, and manure being used to increase the fertility of the soil. The concept of selective breeding also was introduced during this time period, thereby bringing about an increase in the quality of breeds available to the farmer. Marginal lands that had once been considered of little or no use were converted into rich agricultural areas. In East Anglia the Fenlands were drained and their rich soils added to those now available for crop production. The cumulative effect of all these improvements in the agricultural sphere were that, whereas medieval agriculture could only support an English population of three million people, by 1700 agricultural output could now support a population twice as large and still allow for the export of some grain.

# Chapter 8

¤

# PINNACLE

The evolution and growth of England had now developed to the point that it stood at or near the pinnacle of its power, not in relation to technological achievement, but rather in terms of qualitative and quantitative advantage over its nearest rival. The economic growth of England was at this time explosive, and no nation or even combination of nations could hope to rival its authority at sea.

The advances of agricultural practices and agricultural sciences had allowed for the sustaining of a substantial population, and had allowed for the birth and growth of modern industries. Politically, England was united. The old contest of authority between first nobles and Crown, and then Crown and Parliament had resulted in the accepted policy of the authority of the Crown through Parliament, a tri-partite sharing of power and mutual respect for authority resting firmly on a constitutional base.

In a purely historical context, one could draw parallels between the England of Pitt the Elder and Imperial Rome during the years of the Antonines. Geographically, the British Empire now stood at or near its Zenith, although in the future there would be geographical shifts with the addition of Australia and the loss of America. In terms of military might, the proficiency of military leadership and the aggressive spirit that accompanied it, we see other historical parallels as well. To Rome, what was the capture of Britannia, the successful siege of Masada, and the leadership of Agricola and Paulinus, Corbulo and Trajan, was to England the Capture of North America, the siege of Quebec and the leadership of Wolfe, Amherst, Nelson and Pitt. The light of the Western World that had been Rome was now the light of England.

There exist with the attainment of the heights of power a curse known alike to the individual and to the nation. When one stands at the top of the pyramid of power, there is but one way to proceed: down. If fortunate, and if economic, military, political and social conditions allow, one may be able to balance at the pinnacle of power for a while. Eventually however, descent must follow. It is in the escaping of this descent where the knowledge of history and the avoidance of history's mistakes may be of particular interest to the individual or nation who attains the pinnacle of power. Chance, luck, and natural or environmental conditions may play their respective parts as well. Those events are beyond the control of individuals. Therefore, the individual or the nation must seek to control those events that are within their power to do so. This is the age of England into which we now enter.

With the astonishing string of English victories after 1759 and the Peace of Paris of 1763, had come a spirit of exuberance among the people of England and those of her colonies. If these same people had been more reflective of the historical trends that follow military success, they no doubt would have been more tempered in their views. As much as overwhelming Roman victories and conquest had been followed by revolt and political discord, so too would those of England. Even before the Seven Years War had ended, Pitt would find himself removed from power. In 1760, King George II of England had died, being replaced by his twenty-two year old grandson who became George III. The simple fact that Pitt was disliked by the new sovereign was reason enough for his removal. Financial issues followed upon the heels of success as well. The cost of acquiring an empire does not come cheap, and the Seven Years War had seen England's national debt rise from 72,000,000 pounds in 1755, to a then unheard of 146,000,000 pounds in 1763.[53] At this level, England's debt required almost one half of the island nation's annual revenue just to pay the interest alone. Obviously, this was a very untenable fiscal situation, and though necessary, any attempts by the government to increase taxes would be met with popular discontent.

There was also the issue of having to deal with England's newly conquered peoples. As Caesar's conquest of Gaul and Claudius' conquest of Britannia had met with resistance, England itself was soon to be confronted with like circumstances. In the fall of 1763, England had embarked on its last enterprise of the Seven Years War: the capture of Manila in the Philippines from Spain. As with other campaigns in the final years of the war, things went remarkably well. A surprisingly small force under the command of Lieutenant Colonel William Draper had invaded and taken the city within a span of just a few weeks. To the British Empire would go 1,300,000 pounds sterling, and a very severe headache. Almost immediately it became obvious that the Filipino people were somewhat averse to conquest, and general insurrection followed. British forces on the island were restricted to the City of Manila and the immediate vicinity. It may have been fortunate for the British that Manila was returned to Spain on May 31, 1764, for a long occupation of the island could only have added to an already immense burden of debt.

Worse circumstances were to follow in the domains recently conquered from France. For decades it had been the policy of European monarchs to gain the alliance of the Indian nations of North America by purchasing their allegiance with gifts of trade goods or generally reducing them to a level of economic dependence. Commodities such as rifles, gunpowder, alcoholic spirits and implements of iron such as axes were beyond the industrial abilities of the American Indian.

With France now departed and England financially exhausted, these gifts were now in increased demand, but of decreased availability. George Grenville, who had succeeded the Earl of Bute as

---

[53] Anderson, *The War that Made America*, 243.

Prime Minister, had instituted initiatives with an eye toward budgetary restraint. As a result, the War Office had been forced to dramatically reduce Jeffrey Amherst's budget in North America. On the heels of budget cuts that had already been instituted in 1761 when the theatre of war had shifted from America to the Caribbean, the results were catastrophic. With the lack of sufficient funding, the practice of distributing gifts to the Indians was dramatically curtailed. In addition, with the French surrender, Amherst had assumed the responsibility of maintaining a string of forts that stretched from Louisburg on Cape Breton Island all the way to Fort Loudoun in present day Tennessee. Simply stated, there were not adequate forces or adequate finances to accomplish this task.

To these issues would be the added problem of the incursion of large numbers of white settlers onto Indian lands. As events continued to unfold, certain things became readily apparent. To General Amherst, it became clear that he could not hope with the limited resources at his disposal to satisfy all the requirements of defending such a vast periphery of forts, or to fulfill all the promises made to the Indian nations of Easton (1758), such as the establishment of trading posts and the prohibition of white settlers onto Indian lands. His immediate response to these issues was an attempt to defuse the situation. Henceforth, the Indian inhabitants under his authority were to be denied two very volatile commodities, gunpowder and alcohol. It was probably his belief that without gunpowder, the Indians could not fight with the white settlers, and without the inducements of alcohol, they would be less inclined to fight amongst themselves. Such would not be the case.

To the Indians, certain things became clear. Primarily, the English could not, or would not fulfill the obligations of Easton or any other treaties entered into with the Indians. Believing themselves without further means of recourse, several of the Indian nations banded together and resorted to violence, launching an all out assault on British frontier posts in the spring of 1763. The leader of this Indian rebellion was an Ottawa war chief named Pontiac. So successful was he in the planning of this uprising that all but three of England's frontier posts fell to him and his allies. The major forts of Detroit, Pitt and Niagara were able to withstand the initial onslaught. With the British garrisons thus neutralized, Pontiac and his followers launched an all out assault on the now unprotected frontier settlements. Given the nature of frontier warfare and the acts of cruelty known to follow, panic spread.

With few resources at his disposal with which to deal with the Indian uprising, Jeffrey Amherst resorted to extreme measures. At the besieged Fort Pitt, he encouraged its commander, Captain Simeon Ecuyer to arrange a truce with the Indians and then to present to them gifts of blankets and handkerchiefs that had been the property of settlers who had previously been infected with smallpox. Given that Native American peoples were without sufficient immune systems to cope with European diseases, the results were deadly. In the end, having few choices and fewer resources available to them, the English resorted to diplomacy. The Grenville ministry recalled General Amherst to England and replaced him with General Thomas Gage. General Gage, with the assistance of his Indian agent Sir William Johnson, entered into negotiations with the Indians, which resulted in British promises to end the restrictions on the trade of gunpowder and rum, and the prohibition of white settlers beyond the Appalachian Mountains. While these arrangements were suitable to the Indians, they would later create issues between British authorities and the white settlers in America.

⌑

It is now that our attention must be turned once again to the negative impact that polemics have upon the affairs of mankind. Although the British tendency toward these polemics was not restricted toward their affairs in North America, it would be there that they would meet with the stiffest forms of resistance and even reciprocity. In the aftermath of the Seven Years War and the rebellions of Pontiac and the Philippine people, it became increasingly clear that the time had arisen to confront England's next enemy: its national debt.

In England itself, the Seven Years War had caused an increase in property tax rates to 4 shillings on the pound.[54] To the landowner of England, trade and overseas colonies were seen as an obvious source of new revenues to alleviate the need for increased property taxes. Whereas the Seven Years War had not even been fought in England, but rather in America and the overseas possessions, it only seemed fair that they should shoulder a portion of England's debt. It therefore became the policy of the Grenville administration that thrift in government spending and an increase in colonial revenues would become the norm. The need for economics even became so readily obvious that Lord Barrington, Secretary of War, began to argue for the removal of all British troops from the chain of Western forts in America, a move that would obviously meet with the disapproval of settlers in these regions.

In the summer of 1763, a treasury report became known to Parliament speculating that Britain was losing tens of thousands of pounds annually in the collection of import duties of foreign sugar and molasses in America, due to collusion on the part of customs officials and to a habit of smuggling made all the easier by the extensive American coastline. It was on this issue that the Grenville administration would find an opportunity to increase government revenues. Accordingly, a new bill in regard to "his majesty's dominions in America" came before the House of Commons in March 1764. One month later it became law. Commonly referred to as the Sugar Act, it reduced the duty on foreign molasses to 3 pence on the gallon, a reduction of fifty percent from the duty imposed by the Molasses Act of 1733. It did however, place duties on certain other foreign goods. The stated purpose of this bill was the necessity of raising revenue from the American colonies for "defending, protecting, and securing the same." In the Sugar Act we find an actual reduction in the duties placed upon Americans. This would not be the only instance of this happening prior to America's War for

---

[54] Simmons, *The American Colonies*, 294.

Independence.

Although the Treasury had investigated possible revenue resources from the import duties of sugar and molasses, Henry McCulloch, a government agent familiar with America reported that there was opportunity for much more revenue by the imposition of a stamp duty on various documents and official papers. In late 1763, preparations for the Stamp Act would begin. By March 1765, the measure had become law, set to take effect in November the following year. Financially and factually, the results of the Sugar and Stamp Acts were negligible in terms of the actual amount of duties they sought to impose. All of the duties collected by means of both acts would result in English taxpayers still footing the bill for one half the cost for North America's defense. This point was never emphasized.

What became emphasized was that the Stamp Act was innovatory and therefore, in the eyes of the colonist, unfair. Other issues made themselves apparent also. The Sugar Act had included provisions affecting duties on the colonies' important wine trade with the nations of Southern Europe. In addition, merchants were required to obtain documentation for their articles of inter-colonial commerce and were required also to purchase expensive bonds on molasses and syrups where smuggling seemed a possible likelihood. Even more irritating to the sensibilities of the colonist, offenders to the provisions of the Sugar Act could be tried by means of "any court of Vice Admiralty which may or shall be appointed over all America." Further provisions established by other acts of Parliament also allowed for navy ships and British troops to aid customs authorities in North America.

Therefore, the disputes between the American colonist and British authorities were issues more of precedent, methods and rights, as opposed to issues of finance. It should be noted that, prior to the global ascendancy of England during the Seven Years War, the colonial aspirations of England had existed as a very threadbare operation. Drake and Raleigh were essentially pirates who initiated a policy of outright pillage against the Spaniards all through the years of the English Civil War, and during the years of the Spanish

Succession all of England's attentions were concentrated on affairs in continental Europe. In the American colonies, the colonists were left more or less to deal with their affairs as they saw fit. While recognizing that they were still a part of the British Empire, they also recognized that they were to a certain extent autonomous. Here we find the roots of discontent.

There may have been other underlying issues as well, of both an economic and agricultural nature. In the years following the Seven Years War, American colonists found themselves dealing with a commercial recession and a time of economic distress. Much of this may have had to do with the war itself. During the war, the British government was pouring millions of pounds into the colonial economy to sustain the war effort. With the removal of war came the resulting removal of war expenditures. An absence of government stimulus was now replaced with government regulations. Regardless if this regulation affected all of the colonists through the use of agents such as the Stamp Act, or even if its effects were localized such as the restriction against using "mast trees," which were regarded as necessary for the Royal Navy and affected only the timber industry of Northern New England, the results were bound to be unpopular.

Whereas Continental Europe had experienced an agricultural revolution in the century and a half prior to the Seven Years War, this same element was lacking in the colonial society of America. It was most certainly not an issue of lack of agriculture in America; during this time period ninety percent of the population made their living by way of farming in one aspect or another. The climate and variety of conditions made possible the growing of everything from rice in South Carolina, to tobacco in Virginia and to corn in New England. The raising of livestock came to be of importance also, with the raising of sheep and dairy animals predominant in New England, and cattle and members of the porcine family in the South. Every possible product from flour, to beer, tar, pitch and turpentine, sawn lumber, hemp, and apples could be found within the colonies. At issue was not variety or quality. At issue were agricultural practices. Even though the American colonists came from Europe, they did not necessarily bring with them agricultural improvements. The rotation of crops was not a regularly followed practice. In some regions the soils simply became tired from misuse. The initial practices of slash and burn agriculture were not always followed up with the spreading of manure on established crop fields.

The very nature of colonial life influenced agriculture as well. With the initial introduction of colonists into the thirteen colonies, there had been an extensive use of the land grant. Traditionally, these grants allowed to each colonist a set amount of acreage, guaranteeing that small farms would be established instead of large plantations. Therefore, the colonies were prone to mixed-use farms, with much of the produce being used to support the settler and his family. When and if there existed a surplus, this would be sold to supply those commodities deemed necessary to colonial life. There simply was not a sizeable profit with which to invest in agricultural implements and technologies. As evidence of this, it is reported that even by the 1760s, only one farmer in twenty owned a plough. It was upon these prevailing economic conditions that England attempted to interject its authority and to extract tax revenue. The results almost could have been predicted. Colonial opposition was almost instantaneous. Given that the colonies were so far removed from the center of government in London, that transportation methods of the day required severe disruptions in communication, and given England's enormous debt, her options were in a sense very limited.

Neither seeking nor wanting rebellion of the nature recently experienced at the hands of Pontiac and the Filipinos, the Grenville administration sought repeal of the hated Stamp Act. This tactical retreat would be masked beforehand by the strategic adoption of the Declaratory Act of March 1766, which stated emphatically that Parliament, "had, hath, and of right ought to have, full power and authority to make laws and statutes of sufficient force and validity to bind the colonies and people of America, subjects of the Crown of Great Britain, in all cases whatsoever." On the same day that this Declaratory Act was passed, the House of Commons also voted, by a margin of 250 to 122, to repeal the provisions of the Stamp Act.

In a sense purely political, this was a victory for the American colonist. No doubt commercial considerations also played their part. During the months of colonial protest to the Stamp Act, many Americans simply initiated a boycott of British goods, no small gesture at a time when 80% of colonial imports came directly from the foundries and factories of England. In *Tyler's Literary History of the American Revolution*, there is reference to the writings of a contemporary to these events: "We would find it hard to overstate the happiness which, for a few weeks, filled the hearts of the American people at the news the detested Stamp Act had been repealed." None other than John Adams would later write in November of 1776, "The people are as quiet and submissive to Government as any people under the sun; as little inclined to tumults, riots, seditions, as they were ever known to be since the first foundation of the Government. The repeal of the Stamp Act has composed every wave of popular disorder into a smooth and peacecalm." Such were the sentiments of the time.

Events were soon to change this sentiment between the colonies and the Crown. George Grenville had been replaced by George III as head of Government for much the same reason as had Pitt, personal dislike by the King. His successor, Lord Rockingham, lasted only eleven months. With few other choices available, William Pitt was recalled in an attempt to rectify the affairs of state. Pitt had earlier displayed sympathy toward the colonist cause. This sympathy was however, limited. While opposed to direct taxation by means such as a Stamp Act, he also believed that England still retained the right of Parliamentary sovereignty over the American colonies. He initiated a new policy. It was his intention to produce a new source of revenue from India in the aftermath of Robert Clive's successes there. He intended to do this by means of reforming the very powerful East India Company, his belief being that once a new revenue source was created from India, the Americans would then become more reasonable in their views and modest sums of money could then be raised in America. Whether or not this would have proven possible was not to be ascertained, as his declining health forced his withdrawal from the occurrence of events, with his resignation coming in September 1768.

With the disappearance of William Pitt from the political scene, it would be left to others to find a solution to the North American problem. Initially these responsibilities would devolve to Lord Shelburne and to Charles Townshend, the Duke of Grafton. Shelburne by his actions had proven himself to be a hardliner. In America, the New York Assembly was vigorously protesting the provisions of the Quartering Act of 1765. The provisions of this act required the colonies to provide for the billeting of British troops and to also provide certain amounts and types of supplies needed by the king's forces in America. To the New York Assembly, this was consistent with a new form of tax, to which they were in opposition. In Shelburne's mind, the solution was clear: strengthen the Declaratory Act so that it became treason to disobey any act of Parliament. Also to be considered treason were the acts of writing, publishing, preaching, or speaking to the effect that the King and Parliament had no right to enforce legislation on the colonies, and offenders should be brought to England for trial. Many in Parliament rejected these proposals as being too harsh. Therefore, in July 1767, a more moderate scheme put forth by Charles Townshend, Chancellor of the Exchequer, became law. Accordingly, this new law suspended the New York Assembly unless it agreed to carry out those provisions earlier established by the Quartering Act.

Other provisions were to follow. In the same spring of 1767, a set of resolves known as the Townshend Acts were submitted to the House of Commons, which sought to impose new duties on items such as paper, lead, glass and tea being imported into the colonies. In addition, there were provisions for the issue of writs of assistance by the colonial courts. These writs could be used as a legal basis authorizing customs officials to enter private homes and search for goods upon which duties had not been paid. One other provision was especially grating to the colonial assemblies. In the past, as a means of protest, the colonial assemblies had refused to vote for payment of colonial governors salaries if they disapproved of the governor's actions. Henceforth, a civil list was to be created whereby governors and other royal officials would receive payment of their salaries directly from revenues created by acts of Parliament. These legislative acts would be passed by Parliament in June 1767.

The response in North America was outrage. In Massachusetts the Assembly proposed a joint petition with other colonial bodies as a means of protest. Further south, the Virginia Non-Importation Association was founded in 1769, George Washington being one of the individuals instrumental in the writing of its covenant. Throughout the colonies the boycott of English manufacturers became the preferred method of resistance to the Townshend Acts. The effects of this policy were telling, so much so that by 1769 British imports to America had fallen by one-half.[55] In 1770 the political kaleidoscope that had prevailed since the coronation of George III continued, with Lord North becoming First Lord of the Treasury in 1770. One of his first acts was to superintend the repeal of the Townshend duties on all items except tea. It appeared, for the time being at least, that confrontation in the colonies had been averted once again.

Having earlier repealed the provisions of the Stamp Act, and having also repealed the majority of the provisions of the Townshend Act, England had demonstrated a tendency toward moderation and the avoidance of confrontation. Within the population of British North America, there was an element that would not reciprocate. No sooner had word reached North America of the repeal of the Townshend duties, then would occur the first instance of bloodshed. In March of 1770, a small group of British regulars involved in garrison duty at Boston were assailed by a crowd of Bostonians who hurled snowballs at them. Somehow, in the confusion that followed, the troops opened fire, resulting in the deaths of five of the Boston citizens. A trial would ensue. During the trial, a Boston lawyer named John Adams attained a great deal of notoriety for his spirited defense and subsequent acquittal of the British troops involved. Once again,

---

[55] Churchill, *History of the English Speaking Peoples*, 451.

a crisis was averted.

Nevertheless, radical behavior in the colonies was to persist. In June of 1772, a British revenue cutter, H.M.S. Gaspee, was seized off the Rhode Island coast, towed to Providence and burned. The cabinet in London ordered an immediate inquiry and instructed General Gage to send troops to Rhode Island if events proved necessary. The Gaspee affair was to prove incendiary in the formation of organized resistance to Crown policies. On March 13, 1773, the young Virginian Patrick Henry and his fellow members of the Virginia House of Burgesses resolved to establish a committee of correspondence to communicate their concerns with the other colonial assemblies. Between May of 1773 and February of 1774, the lower chambers of every colonial legislative body followed suit. The seeds of discontent had now been sown.

The economic conditions of the times, tea, and the earlier American embargo of that product, would now combine to cause the next sequence of events. From June of 1772 through the end of 1773 there raged throughout England and its colonies one of the fiercest financial downturns of the eighteenth century. Banks failed, bringing about a substantial number of personal bankruptcies as well. Businesses were not spared the effects of the financial downturn either. Credit, previously abundant, now became scarce. Creditors, facing hardships of their own, called for payment from debtors who simply did not have the means to pay. This point proved itself hard to the plantation owners of the South. The system of trade between England and the American colonies had always favored the former, to include the mercantile houses of England. As a norm, these agents and agencies typically bought tobacco and other agricultural commodities of the South at prices that were usually unfairly low. In return, the manufactured goods of England were sold in the American colonies at prices that were unfairly high. As a consequence of this unfair method of trade, southern planters found themselves increasingly in debt. Thomas Jefferson estimated that prior to the American Revolution, the planters of Virginia alone owed English creditors over two billion pounds, somewhere between twenty and thirty times as much as was present in the entire colony of Virginia at that time.

The prevailing economic conditions of the time and the previous American embargo on tea had combined to place the British East India Company in a precarious position. In the absence of its North American market, the East India Company had accumulated 17,000,000 pounds of tea in its warehouses. Tea it had; sufficient funds it did not have. Not wanting to see the East India Company go bankrupt, Lord North decided that in the absence of possible financial assistance from the government, legislative assistance might possibly offer an answer. The result was the Tea Act, which guaranteed the East India Company both a monopoly and a market for its tea. The actual import duty to the Americans was reduced, "taking off a shilling duty on a pound of tea, and imposing three pence." Many in Boston could not remember when tea had been so cheap. To the colonist, however, the issue consisted of what they regarded as the violation of a constitutional principle, the right of Parliament to levy taxes upon them without their explicit consent.

The outcome was further colonial protest. On December 16, 1773, Samuel Adams and a group of followers disguised as Indians dumped 343 chests of tea, worth approximately 10,000 pounds, into the Boston Harbor. It is an interesting historical fact and an indictment of human nature that the Boston Tea Party was not carried out by angry consumers due to an increase in cost, but rather that the enterprise was carried out by a group of Boston's wealthy smugglers who stood to loose money due to the importation of much cheaper tea.

In response to the actions of the radical elements of Boston, Parliament put forth and then passed a series of "Coercion Acts." By these Acts, the port of Boston was thenceforth closed, the Massachusetts Assembly was suspended, the colony declared in Crown hands, and in the future all judges were to be appointed specifically by the Crown. Provisions of the Quartering Act were imposed, with troops to be stationed not only in the homes of Boston, but throughout the other colonies as well. In response to the Crown's latest attempts to assert authority over the colonies, the colonial assemblies once again followed the lead of Virginia; they elected delegates for a first Continental Congress. This Congress met in Philadelphia on September 5, 1774. Among its delegates were men such as George Washington, John Adams and Benjamin Franklin. Sources vary in terms of the response by this First Continental Congress. What is generally regarded as a historically accurate is that a Declaration of Rights was dispatched to London demanding that thirteen of the Acts of the British Parliament in regard to restrictions on duties or commerce be rescinded. We also know that the First Continental Congress addressed this declaration directly to the King, ignoring Parliament altogether. Two other provisions were adopted which were more flagrant in their resistance to Crown authority. It was agreed by the signatories that within three months they would abstain from the further purchase of British goods, and that within one year they would refuse to export goods to British ports. The second provision stated that if force were employed against the citizens of Massachusetts, then all of the other colonies should support them in their resistance. The collision of events and peoples was now inevitable.

All are aware of the events of April 18, 1775, of the rides of Paul Revere and his accomplices, and of the resulting acts of bloodshed at Lexington and Concord. No further discussion of them is either warranted or needed. Likewise, any lengthy discussions of the Revolutionary War will be avoided as well. There are however, certain aspects of the war, which are necessary to any discussion of similarities between the growth and the demise of the Roman, British and American republics.

Of primary concern to us is the fact that, with the opening of hostilities between the colonists of British America and Britain itself, America had no established army or navy and no industry to support either of these institutions. All that existed were a handful of citizen soldiers and a few individuals who had attained modest rank within the structure of the British Army. Yet for some unknown reason this newly declared United States of America would entertain thoughts of fighting a war against the largest, most expensively and professionally equipped armed force on the planet. It seems implausible that rational, educated men such as Jefferson, Adams, Washington and others could hope to pull off such a miracle.

Yet there may be a reason for these implausible hopes and beliefs in the success of their endeavor towards a new and independent nation. A portion of their beliefs may have arisen from their historical search of English political thought and English Parliamentary law.

The men who guided America towards its independence were familiar with the arguments of Harrington, Milton and John Locke.

They were also familiar with the actions of the Long Parliament in its dispute with Charles I prior to the English Civil War. It was a somewhat famous quote of Patrick Henry that, "Caesar had his Brutus, Charles I had his Cromwell, and George III might do well to learn by their lesson." Hence, that the brute force necessary for Parliament to overcome the control of the king, Cromwell for instance, was a concept well known to them.

Cromwell was familiar to the colonist for other reasons as well, reasons which would resonate within the ranks of the commercial classes. It had always been Crown policy to discourage manufacturers in the colonies. The colonies were viewed as being a source of raw materials to be exported to England where they would be transformed into finished goods. They could then be exported back to the colonies. Essentially, the colonies were viewed only as a source of raw materials and a market for English manufacturers, though there was one exception to this policy. If we consult the works of Trevelyan, we find that, "Cromwell, with an insight beyond his age, had refused to fetter and discourage the infant commerce of America; and under the Commonwealth that commerce grew fast toward prosperous maturity."

*John Paul Jones, Father of the United States Navy*

Trevelyan goes on to state, "a Stuart was no sooner on the throne than the British Parliament entered on a course of selfish legislation which killed the direct maritime trade between our dependencies and foreign ports, and deliberately crushed every form of colonial manufacture which could possibly compete with the manufacturers of England."[56] How better to make friends than to allow people to become wealthy?

In addition, there were probably other historical lessons that would have been of assistance to them. There is no doubt that England was far superior to any combination of nations on earth in regard to its naval supremacy. If engaged in a war against the colonies, this would be of enormous importance, as the colonists were restricted primarily to the coast of North America and its navy would allow England to both blockade the coast, and to easily transport forces to various theatres of operation. Being Englishmen, the colonists would have been familiar with the actions of England during the time of Drake, when England had but a fledgling navy with which to combat the overwhelming superiority of Catholic Spain. It is interesting to note that the naval practices and policies of the newly declared United States were very much similar to those of England around the time of the Amarda.

Almost immediately after the opening of hostilities at Lexington and Concord, America's new naval policy would take shape. After being appointed as Commander in Chief of the Army by Congress, George Washington arrived to take over the Continental forces at Cambridge on July 15, 1775. In the siege of Boston to follow, recognizing the importance of naval warfare in the new contest, Washington ordered the chartering, arming, and manning of several small merchantmen in order to harass British supply lines. Therefore, in a sense, Washington may be considered as one of the founders of the United States Navy.

In the years to come this policy of naval harassment would continue. Warships with names such as Lexington, Hornet, Wasp,

---

[56] Trevelyan, *The American Revolution, Part I, 1766-1776*, 130.

Ranger, and Bon Homme Richard would go on to give faithful service to the new nation and would serve as the forbearers of the great warships of the future to whom their names would be handed down.

It would be the actions of John Paul Jones and his ship Ranger that would serve as an example of how and to what purpose the new navy would be used to challenge British supremacy. In the spring of 1778, Jones sailed the Ranger to European waters where she would enter into the Irish Sea, engage in raids against Whitehaven and St. Mary's Isle, and capture the British sloop of war, Drake. For these actions, John Paul Jones would become America's first naval hero, and from the British point of view, he and American sailors would henceforth be regarded as pirates. As to the effectiveness of American raids against British commerce, English naval historians generally consider it a fact that by 1778, American privateers had captured nearly one thousand merchant ships valued at nearly 2,000,000 pounds.

Ultimately, the success of the American Revolution would depend upon French naval forces. Although vastly inferior to the English numerically, eighty-six ships of the line as opposed to one hundred fifty, France becoming an ally of America in 1778 carried with it several advantages. It was French naval policy not so much to engage English fleets in combat, but rather to cause them to remain in European waters as a possible deterrent to French ambitions. If England had been allowed to concentrate all of her navy in North America instead of retaining many of them in Europe and along the periphery of its empire, the results of America's war for independence may have been much different.

On land, the contest between British authority and American revolt carried with it a tinge of irony also. When George Washington arrived at Cambridge in the spring of 1775, he was not greeted by a trained, professional force simply awaiting his leadership. What he found before him was an army of men "dirty as pigs." There were no standards of training or discipline, no quartermaster corps to provide for the systematic provisioning of the army, and no established system of leadership either for officers or non-commissioned officers. To his brother Sam Washington he would later write that he had "found a numerous army of provincials under very little command, discipline, or order." Worse would be said of the continentals by the enemy. The loyalist Benjamin Thompson stated that the Continental Army was the "most wretchedly clothed, and as dirty as set of mortals as ever disgraced the name of a soldier." With this army, and little if any navy, Washington was charged with the responsibility of taking on the might of the British Empire.

The answer to Washington's dilemma could be found in the annals of history much the same as the Continental Congress sought answers from British Parliamentary history, and has had the infant navy sought guidance from previous English naval policy. This time the answer was to be found in the annals of Roman history. During the First Punic War, Rome had been confronted with the superior generalship of the Cathaginian Hannibal. In 217 B.C., Hannibal had destroyed the armies that Rome had sent to oppose him, completely destroying one army of 40,000 men at Lake Trasimene. In response, Rome had appointed a dictator, Quintus Fabius, to end Hannibal's dominance and save Rome. Fabius, realizing that time was now the element most essential to Roman success, entered into a campaign and refusal against Hannibal. Fabius recognized that for the time being, the Roman army was not strong enough or well-trained enough to fight against the veterans of Carthage. He also recognized that Hannibal was thousands of miles away from his operational base, and that much of Hannibal's energies would now be needed to simply keep his army supplied and together. For his efforts and tactics, Quintas Fabius would earn himself the name of Cunctator or delayer. His tactics of refusal and delay are referred to as Fabian tactics. With little if any other course of action available to him, George Washington was to adopt these Fabian tactics.

The need to engage in Fabian tactics, but not the desire to do so, would become evident to Washington and his generals in the early stages of the war. After initial success in the siege of Boston from 1775 into the spring of 1776, Washington and his army found themselves under entirely different circumstances at Long Island in the autumn of 1776. Under orders from Congress to defend New York City, and confronted by an overwhelming British army of 32, 000 men, Washington and his army of raw recruits and untrained militia were soundly beaten at Brooklyn Heights and Kip's Bay. In both engagements the colonial militia broke ranks and fled in the face of superior British discipline. From these initial contests, it became clear to the Americans there was but a single course of action available, "a war of post intended to prolong, procrastinate, avoid any general action, or indeed any action, unless we have great advantages."[57] Such were the sentiments of one Joseph Reed, Adjutant General under Washington.

During the English Civil War, Sir Oliver Cromwell had found himself having to deal with local militias who were always very reluctant to leave their home grounds and always eager to return home. George Washington would find himself confronted with a similar problem. Washington would write his brother Samuel, "One half of the year is spent in getting troops into the field, the other half is lost in discharging them from their limited service."[58] Much worse, when their terms of enlistment expired, recruits simply went home taking their weapons with them, no small affair to an army always starved of the materials necessary to make war.

Perhaps even worse than the difficulties of dealing with state militias, were the difficulties of dealing with state legislative bodies. In an infant nation without an established central authority, Washington's army was entirely at the mercy of the state legislative assemblies for money, weapons, supplies and payment of its soldiers. These payments were always scarce, sometimes non-existent. Each succeeding generation of school children are taught of the sacrifices and the hardships endured by the men of Valley Forge during the dreadful winter of 1777-1778. We hear often of how these desperate men starved and froze, as if no other options were available to them. What we do not hear were Washington's repeated pleas to the Continental Congress alerting them to the condition of his men, and

---

[57] McCullough, *1776*, p. 147.
[58] Chernow, *Washington A Life*, 373.

urging their utmost exertions in acquiring assistance from the various state legislative bodies so as to ease their suffering. Also not commonly heard is the part played by the ordinary citizen in the suffering endured by the men at Valley Forge. On December 23, 1777, George Washington wrote to Henry Laurens that without more food his army would have to "starve or disperse."[59] Also included in his letter was that, "not a single hoof of any kind to slaughter and not more than 23 barrels of flour" were available to his army.[60] We read the stories of trails of blood in the snow due to the want of shoes among his soldiers, and of men who passed sleepless nights crouched by open fires for want of blankets.

Conversely, to the men of Lord Howe's army in Philadelphia, conditions were such that, "Assemblies, concerts, comedies, clubs and the like make us forget that there is any war, save that it is a capital joke."[61] Such were the writings of a Hessian captain attached to Howe's army. These opposite conditions were not brought about by the prevailing conditions of war. They were brought about by the prevailing conditions of money and monetary gain. Lacking a strong central government, the only source of revenue to support the Continental Army and Navy was state taxation. The states often proved themselves stingy in this affair and from the time of the opening shots at Lexington in 1775, contributed less than six million dollars or roughly two dollars per capita to support the men fighting in the war. In desperation, Congress would resort to the use of paper money and foreign loans to finance the war. It naturally followed that the Continental currency was bound to depreciate in value, and that while more than 240,000,000 dollars of currency was in circulation, its actual worth was less than 38,000,000.[62] The British pound did not suffer from similar ill effects. Whereas Valley Forge was situated in the heart of an agricultural area where it should have been easy to get provisions, those supplies would not be forthcoming. The good

[59] Ibid, 327.
[60] Ibid, 327.
[61] Ibid, 323.
[62] Nevins and Commager, *Pocket History of the U.S.*, 81.

citizens of the area sold their agricultural surplus to Lord Howe's army in Philadelphia, being paid with the still economically viable British pound; so much for patriotism.

When we speak of the great military commanders of history, certain names come to the forefront: Bonaparte, Caesar and Alexander the Great, to name but a few. Generally, they receive great accolades due to their records of repeated victories. To Washington, victories would be elusive. The successful siege of Boston may be counted as a success, although in large part this victory was due to Henry Knox and the artillery captured by Ethan Allen and Benedict Arnold at Fort Ticonderoga on Lake Champlain. There was also the success of the raid on Trenton, with the remnants of the continental Army crossing the icy Delaware River on Christmas Day 1776. But Trenton was a relatively small affair with but a few thousand troops involved and an eventual return back across the river after defeating British reinforcements advancing from Princeton on January 3, 1777. Washington was also present at the culminating battle of the war, at Yorktown in September and October 1781. This operation was, however, a combined Franco-American effort with Admiral DeGrasse's fleet assuring victory at Yorktown by defeating the British fleet of Admiral Graves at the Battle of the Capes.

To Washington, therefore, would go a reputation of defeats, some tactically, some strategically. At Long Island in 1776, his shortcomings would nearly bring about the end of the war before it had barely begun. There would be defeats at Brandywine, Paoli and Germantown. There would be the ordeal at Valley Forge, where 2,000 American troops would perish from disease and exposure. There would be the loss of New York, Philadelphia, and Charlestown, South Carolina to the enemy. Yet through it all Washington always recognized that British victory could only come with the destruction of his army. Cities did not matter, nor did victories, or even popular support. In order to succeed, all that was required was the survival of the Continental Army. In this venture he was successful. It was Washington who appointed Nathaniel Greene to serve as Quartermaster during the winter at Valley Forge, a task at which

Greene would prove able, allowing the army to somehow survive. It was Washington who allowed Baron Augustus H. F. von Stueben to train the army so that they could meet the British regulars on equal terms, soon to be proven at Monmouth in 1778. In the years between 1780-1781, Washington was somehow able to suppress the effects of six mutinies amongst the troops caused by the lack of pay, the depreciation of Continental currency, and deficiencies of supply. After the disastrous losses of Savannah and Charleston in the south, Washington would appoint Nathaniel Greene, his "right arm," to take command of southern operations. While losing nearly every battle himself, it would be the successful strategy of Greene that would eventually cause Lord Cornwallis to fall back upon Yorktown. On the whole, while having to overcome all the difficulties of the unsteady militia and the unstable state of governments, much credit must go to Washington for America's ultimate success.

And what of England during the American War of Independence? Most people assume that because England lost her American colonies that she must have in fact lost the war. True enough, on one side of the Atlantic the war was ultimately lost, in other theatres however, the results would be much different. In the Far East, the gains of Robert Clive during the Seven Years War would be consolidated. The Governor General of India, Warren Hastings, upon learning of the French decision to enter into war as an ally of America, set in place a plan to capture the remaining French possessions in India. Chandernagore, Pondicherry and Mahe all fell to England. When Holland was later drawn into the war as an ally of France and Spain, Negapatam on the Coromandel coast and Trincomalee in Ceylon were both captured by combined English army and naval forces. To the English would go the eventual domination of the Far East.

Much of the credit for this domination in the Far East must go to the British Royal Navy. On the 13th of March 1778, the French ambassador in London informed the English government that France decided to recognize American independence and to enter into commercial and defensive treaties with them. Shortly thereafter, an all-out naval war would begin between the two nations, with Spain joining France in June 1779 and Holland doing the same in 1781. Against the combined navies of these three nations and with war raging in North America, England seemed to be outgunned. However, such was not to be the case. On July 27, 1778, two fleets of thirty ships of the line, one English, one French, engaged each other at the naval battle of Ushant. Although this battle was indecisive, England would in fact retain dominance of the seas. In 1781, a Dutch fleet under the command of Admiral Zoutman was engaged by the English at the Battle of Dogger Bank. After a few hours of fighting in which both sides were severely bloodied, the Dutch withdrew, again leaving control of the sea to Britain. In the ensuing contest for control of Gilbraltar in the Mediterranean, there would be two naval battles fought off the coast of St. Vincent. To the English would go victory in both affairs, one a victory over a Spanish fleet, the other a victory over a combined Franco-Spanish fleet. In the West Indies, English supremacy would again prove imminent, with Admiral George Brydges Rodney seizing the Dutch colonies of St. Eustatius and St. Martin, along with their merchant fleets worth an estimated fifteen million dollars.

As a whole, England would survive the Revolutionary War, it would survive the naval assault of the greatest rivals in Europe, and it would in the end go forward to achieve even greater heights of power.

The path of England following the American Revolutionary War of 1775-1783 was sure and steady. There would be challenges to its authority on many fronts. Most, if not all of these challenges would be successfully repulsed. Global domination and Empire status would be accomplished by a more liberal thought process. During the nineteenth century, the island nation that had once embraced the use of slavery to expand its colonial empire, now led the effort to arrest that expansion, and then to see its ultimate extinction in the Western World.

Increasingly, Britain's military would become less associated with the defense of the island nation, and more with the expansion and domination of commercial interest throughout the empire.

*Admiral Sir George Brydges Rodney, victor of the Battle of Cape St. Vincent and the first British flag-officer to break with the Fighting Instructions and sail through the enemy's line of battle.*

There would be tremendous levels of success during the Industrial Revolution, with London eventually becoming the financial capital of the world. England was however, entering into a new and previously un-chartered territory in its history. Much as the success of Rome had helped to initiate the events which would bring about its eventual demise, so too would it now be with England.

Ironically, much of the success of England following the American War of Independence was due to its commerce with that new nation. It is said, "to the victors go the spoils," but in this case to the victors – the Americans, would go the need to tax themselves for their own defense. In the fifteen years following the Revolutionary War, American's personal income declined forty-six percent. For the citizen of England, no longer responsible for the defense of the American colonies, taxes declined and income rose. The political breach between mother country and daughter colony was not accompanied by a breach of trade, which soon after the Treaty of Paris returned to and then exceeded pre-war levels.

Agriculture and its influences on population growth and industrial expansion made its effects upon history felt once more. The potato was introduced into the agricultural practices of Ireland, allowing the population of the island to increase to a level of nearly six million souls, or nearly one-third that of England. Eventually, by the year 1800, the policy of treating Ireland as a colonial possession was no longer defensible, and consequently an Act of Union was passed in London merging the English and Irish Parliaments as one. In America, its first elected president, George Washington, encouraged immigration practices that would allow the farmers of the Old World to flock into the New. Washington was especially in favor of allowing the expert farmers of Britain to immigrate to America so as to instruct Americans in new and better agricultural practices. In a land where good farmlands were plentiful and cheap, and where labor was needed, these immigration policies would prove entirely beneficial. Within short order, the Mohawk and Genesee Valleys of New York, the Susquehanna Valley of Pennsylvania, and the Shenandoah Valley of Virginia would become great wheat producing areas, the precursors of the American Midwest.

The inventions of one American were to have a profound effect on the development of England in the nineteenth century. In 1793 Eli Whitney invented the cotton gin, allowing for the rapid cleaning of cotton. This one invention allowed for the expansion of a cotton culture in the American South. This new cotton culture would supply the raw materials needed by England's machine-operated textile mills in Lancashire. The demand for raw cotton was such that it rose from an average of fifteen and a half million pounds in the 1780s to a level of 28.6 million pounds by 1800.[63]

Eli Whitney's second innovation, allowing for the use of interchangeable parts in the manufacture of firearms, would assist England in its further drive toward military and economic dominance in the world. Before Whitney's advance of this process, the size of armies deployed on the fields of battle was often restricted by an industrial inability to produce enough weapons and other implements of war. This restriction was now removed. By the time of England's contest with Napoleon Bonaparte on the continent of Europe, the size of armies employed would reach unheard of levels, with army groups numbering into the hundreds of thousands. It should be remembered that all through England's colonial wars of the nineteenth century, her soldiers almost always fought at huge numerical disadvantages. Yet the mass production of new and better weapons always guaranteed British success over her more primitive adversaries.

While England's technological lead over other nations and the success of its armies on land were responsible for much of its success, its navy would play a starring role and also become historically associated with this success. On the eve of the nineteenth century, one man would step forward to carry on the traditions of Drake and Raleigh, Hawke and Rodney, and would set a new standard for all English sailors to follow until our present times. This was of course Horatio Nelson, whose naval victories at the Battle of the Nile in 1805,

---

[63] Jameson, *Rise and Fall of the British Empire*, 119

and at Trafalgar in 1805 helped put an end to Napoleon Bonaparte's continental aspirations. Much as Drake was afterwards associated with saving England from invasion by destroying the Armada in 1588, Nelson would now forever be linked with saving England from invasion by destroying the combined Franco-Spanish fleet at Trafalgar. It would not be until the rise of Nazi Germany nearly a century and a half later that England would be faced with the possibility of such invasion again. Nelson would also forever after be associated with innovations in naval tactics, through such novel concepts as concentrating his ships to penetrate and break apart the enemy's battle line.

Much the same as Eli Whitney had assisted England's development with his cotton gin and the mass production of weapons with interchangeable parts, French inventors would assist England in further developing its naval supremacy. Eighteen years before the Battle of Trafalgar, the first steamship was launched in France. To a nation that had invested in an enormous fleet of sail-powered vessels, this new means of propulsion was an obvious threat because it had the potential to cancel out all of its hard earned advantages in seamanship. Initially, the limitations of steam, more specifically that the paddle wheels used in accordance with steam were easily susceptible to gunfire, would deliver them from their worst fears. However, John Ericsson's development of the screw propeller in the mid-nineteenth century would guarantee the death of the sail. As a reaction to lessons gained at the naval battle of Sinope during the Crimean War, where new Russian naval ordinance firing explosive shells had devastated a Turkish fleet, France had built a new armor-plated warship, the Gloire. This would force England in turn to build its first armored warship, the H.M.S. Warrior. By the time of Queen Victoria's Diamond Jubilee, the entire English navy had undergone the process of conversion from wood and sail to iron and steam.

These advances in naval technology also brought about changes in the complexion and structure of England's world empire. As a means of producing steam, these new warships needed to burn coal. Because ships had limited storage abilities on board, coaling stations were required throughout the world. These coaling stations would in turn need to be defended in the event of war, so that eventually England found itself in possession of an extensive chain of military facilities around the globe, thus expanding its commercial and military influence and its ability to project power.

Evidence of the extent of English naval predominance in the nineteenth century can be found in the Royal Navy's use as an instrument to end the slave trade. The anti-slave movement itself had started in England around the time of the American Revolution. Much of its driving force came from its two most prominent leaders, William Wilberforce and Thomas Clarkson. The same year that America drafted its Constitution, 1787, a new colony was established in Africa, – Sierra Leone. In the same way as the British East India Company had existed, a Sierra Leone Company was established as well, although the objectives of the two were entirely different. Sierra Leone was to be a social experiment, an attempt to introduce civilization among what were regarded then as crude natives, and to educate them in the practices of agriculture and encourage their understanding of free labor. The experiment proved successful enough that Sierra Leone became a Crown colony in 1808, and its capital, Freetown, would become an extensive naval base used in the suppression of the slave trade. By the 1840s, more than four hundred slave ships would be intercepted off the west coast of Africa. England would employ more than thirty fighting vessels in this naval war against slavery, a force larger than most modern navies of today.

Wilberforce and Clarkson also saw success in their efforts on the home front with Britain abolishing the trading of slaves in the year 1807. Although the Royal Navy was then employed in the Atlantic against the African slave trade, it would later be employed in the Indian Ocean and Persian Gulf in an effort to curtail the Arab slave trade as well. The effort to outright abolish slavery would continue for the next 26 years, with the House of Commons abolishing the use of slave labor in 1833. Old habits and patterns of thought generally die hard. As a solution to the shortage of unpaid labor in the colonies of Britain, the plantation owners resorted to cheap labor instead, hiring large numbers of Chinese and Indian laborers imported into the colonies to cure what was viewed as a new shortage of labor.

If the Royal Navy could be used in the prosecution of inhumane slavery, it could also be used in the prosecution of less noble affairs, such as the opening of foreign markets to British trade by means of outright intimidation. China would be the unwilling and unfortunate recipient of Britain's desire for open markets. As early as 1773, the British East India Company had begun to exploit the British need for tea and the Chinese addiction to opium. Therefore, opium was shipped from India to China, predominately through the Port of Canton, and then tea was shipped back for distribution throughout the Empire. For decades this had proven a very profitable arrangement for the East India Company. To an almost medieval Chinese society, which regarded foreigners with a certain amount of disdain, this trade practice eventually came to be considered as harmful to their interests. In 1839, recognizing the continued harm being done to Chinese interests and the ill-effects of opium addiction to its people, the Chinese Imperial government officially closed Canton to the further trade of the harmful drug. Not only was this action a challenge to the British concept of free trade, it was also a threat to Crown revenues. Throughout the first half of the nineteenth century, the profits received by the East India Company through the sale of opium were used to pay its debts to the government of London. If the sale of opium was curtailed, so too would be the company's payments to the government.

In retaliation to this action on the part of the Chinese government, Lord Palmerston, then Prime Minister, opted to send a combined navy and army expeditionary force to the region. The outcome is known to history as the First Opium War, fought from 1839 to 1842. Armed only with matchlocks and bladed weapons, the Chinese had little chance of being victorious against the powerful ship-of-the-line or the mass volleys of musket fire from British troops. As a result of the inevitable British victory, Hong Kong Island was seized as the site for a future naval and commercial base. With the Treaty of Nanking ending the war, Canton, Foochow, Ningpo, and Shanghai were opened to further British commerce. Shanghai was also to be a naval base and a coaling station for the Royal Navy and the Royal Navy was awarded the right to patrol the rivers and coast of China.

The allowances granted to the British by the Chinese would play a role in bringing about the Second Opium War fourteen years later. In 1856, Chinese soldiers boarded the ship Arrow, which was sailing under an English flag. Their pretense of their boarding was the ruse they were searching for a suspected pirate. After boarding the ship, the English flag was hauled down by the Chinese troops. This incident was seized upon by the British consul in Canton, John Bowring, as a chance to teach the Chinese any lessons they might have failed to understand from the previous war. The outcome was the same, victory for the British. The resulting Treaty of Tientoin legalized the further trade of opium and granted additional concessions to the business interests of the western nations.

While the financial strength of Britain, combined with the exorbitant cost of building and maintaining a navy had acted to guarantee global dominance of the seas for the Royal Navy, conditions on land would be somewhat different. The armies of Great Britain would continue to experience a large measure of success. However, they would also suffer some devastating defeats. British arms in the nineteenth century would now begin to reflect similar tendencies experienced by Roman arms eighteen centuries earlier. Even though England had suffered from the foreign invasions of the Saxons, Danes, and Normans in prior centuries, English armies had always been reflective of the dominant populations and powers on the island itself. The armies that had fought and won the decisive victories on the continent at Crecy, Poitiers, and Agincourt, were recognized as being English in nature. With colonial expansion has come an increasing reliance on locally raised levies. When Braddock marched west in 1755 to confront the French at Fort Duquesne, George Washington and a large contingent of militia marched with him. Throughout the French and Indian War, American colonists were engaged in much of the fighting. When Robert Clive gained his decisive victory at Plassey in 1757, only 900 of his 3,000 troops were

British, the rest being native sepoys. Much as Rome had seen its army transformed from being entirely Roman in the days of the Republic to being only half Roman in the time of Caesar, to being only one percent Roman by the time of the Hadrian, this trend would now begin to gather momentum in the ranks of the British armies. By the later portion of the nineteenth century, specifically the year 1881, the British army in India consisted of 69,647 British troops and 125,000 natives. Conversely, the British army in England consisted of 65,809 British but only 25,353 Irish.[64] Much of this transformation was probably due to financial concerns, as it always tended to be cheaper to maintain an army of natives within their colony than it was to ship troops all the way from England to fight the numerous uprisings found throughout the Empire during the nineteenth century.

Additionally, there were to be found other historical tendencies. At the height of its empire, Roman troops were regarded as the most well-disciplined, best trained and the best-equipped soldiers of their time. The Roman legionary could usually rely on a significant edge of his weapons in regard to those of his enemies. Transportation also played a factor in the legionary's advantage over his foes, with Roman paved roadways such as the Appian Way assuring the rapid movement of troops from one area of concern to another. These features usually combined to guarantee that the Roman soldier would usually prevail over his more primitive adversaries. There were however, occasional disasters along the way. At the Teutoburg Forest in A.D. 9, three legions were completely destroyed by Arminius and his German warriors. In Northern Britain the entire ninth legion would disappear forever from the annals of Rome, their fate unknown but to themselves. Julian the Apostate suffered calamitous defeat at the hands of Sassanid Persia. Finally, at Adrianople in 379 A.D., the myth of Roman invincibility was lost forever.

So Britain would begin to find disaster mixed amid the chronicles of success. Sir Arthur Wellesley, later the First Duke of Wellington, would establish the predominance of English arms during the

---

[64] Brendon, *Decline and Fall of the British Empire*, 143.

Peninsular War in Spain, repeatedly gaining victories over the armies of Napoleon. Combined with the armies of Blucher at Waterloo in 1815, Wellesley would end the power of Bonaparte forever, guaranteeing his exile from the continent. During the War of 1812 in America, British Major General Robert Ross defeated an American army at Bladensburg, then captured Washington, D.C., burning the nation's capital and the White House. There were British successes throughout the world in the nineteenth century, to include India, Africa, and the Far East. In many cases, due to technology and organizational superiority, these victories were very one-sided affairs, such as at Omdurman in the Sudan during the century's last decade.

When defeat came, however, the results could be absolutely disastrous. At New Orleans during the War of 1812, overconfident British regulars would advance against the Americans of Andrew Jackson who were concealed by improvised fortifications. More than 2,100 British soldiers were killed or wounded, including their commanding general. During the first Afghan War of 1839-1842, the British Forty-fourth Regiment of Foot was destroyed almost to the man during its retreat to India after the fall of Kabul in January 1842. Of the fifteen thousand souls who departed Kabul on January 6th of that year, only one completed the journey to safety at Jalabad. During the Anglo-Zulu War of 1879, a force of 1,700 regular troops and native levies suffered a similar fate at Isandlwana. In this defeat the superiority of British arms simply could not overcome the massed attack of a Zulu army of more than twenty thousand strong.

Other issues in regard to the British military would begin to manifest themselves as well. For a number of reasons, republican forms of government tend to be very jealous and wary of strong military institutions. For this and other reasons, these militaries are always placed under civilian control. At issue with this particular trend, is that these civilian governments are subject to political and commercial influence. Therefore, these armies may at times be employed in wasteful foreign wars in order to satisfy political and commercial interest.

There is also the tendency within Republican governments to use a nation's armed forces to acquire popularity and notoriety. Caesar, Crassus, Pompey and other ambitious leaders always used the force of arms against neighboring states as a means of furthering their political aspirations. So too it would be with England. The kings of England who are regarded as successful by history's standards were generally warriors. From the legend of King Arthur to William the Conqueror, Richard I to Henry V, the most popular kings were also those who tended to be war-like. With the creation of the office of Prime Minister, this trend would remain. William Pitt the Elder, Lord Palmerston and Benjamin Disraeli were all ministers who pursued aggressive foreign policies. They are also regarded as being some of the better individuals to hold that office.

These tendencies would contribute to the British army and navy becoming involved in minor conflicts all over the globe. The First and Second Afghan Wars, the Crimean War, The Opium Wars, the Boxer Rebellion and the Anglo-Zulu War are to name but a few of the almost innumerable contests of the nineteenth century. It is ironic that just as there had been almost constant conflict during the Pax Romana, similar situations would exist during the Pax Britannica.

As the nineteenth century had witnessed agricultural, military, and industrial innovations and improvements, English finance would also see a transformation. In the aftermath of England's war with its American colonies, a new government was called into being. At its head would be William Pitt, the Younger. He was to become Prime Minister at the age of twenty-four. Pitt the Younger was an enthusiast of trade, being in staunch agreement with the arguments of Adam Smith, whose *Wealth of Nations* first appeared during the year of America's Declaration of Independence. Pitt the Younger was also averse to the ruinous financial effects of war, and much like Washington in America dreaded the ill effects of foreign entanglements.

Upon his attaining power of the state, he immediately instituted his policies toward financial reform. In 1786 the national debt of Great Britain stood at two hundred fifty million pounds, or roughly two and one half times as much as prior to the Seven Years War. His solution was to implement a sinking fund. Each year, under this plan, a million pounds in hoped-for government surplus was to be invested in stocks, with the interest acquired being applied to the national debt.

During the war with the American colonies, more than forty million pounds which had been approved for war expenditures were simply unaccounted for. As a result, Pitt the Younger fought for the establishment of an audit office within the Treasury Department. In accordance with his beliefs in free trade, Pitt would become involved in efforts to revise the system of customs barriers that had been erected during the years of reliance upon the mercantilist system. To this end, in 1786, the Board of Trade was established. With these initiatives by the government of Pitt, confidence in government was restored, trade revived, prosperity returned, and ten million pounds were removed from the national debt over a period of ten years.

For all of his financial success, Pitt was to become a victim of the effects brought about by the French Revolution. The English Civil War and the American Revolution had not been without their fair share of violence. However, what befell France was beyond expectation, with its after-effects spilling across the borders of Europe for the next quarter century. Although the renewed war with France was not of Pitt's choosing, the consequences of that war initiated Britain's first income tax of two pence on the pound, which was graduated to two shillings for those with incomes of over 200 pounds annually.

Much the same as the French Revolution had helped bring about the Alien and Sedition Acts under the presidency of John Adams, a concerned English administration under Pitt would put in place similar measures. Talk of political reform was regarded as revolutionary, Paines *The Rights of Man*, proscribed. In an act common to many democratic governments under times of duress, the Act of Habeas Corpus was suspended and a new Treason Act implemented. The cumulative effects of these actions caused those in opposition to call them "Pitt's Terror."

If Pitt the Younger had been left unmolested by the effects of the

French Revolution and the subsequent Napoleonic Wars, his policies probably would have done much good for the overall health of Britain. However, in 1806, shortly after Nelson's historic victory at Trafalgar, Pitt died of exhaustion. The government would continue, although under far less capable hands. Lacking the driving force of any outstanding ministerial influence, technological improvements and external influences would now determine the outcome of events. Much as the Appian Way and other transportation improvements had driven the growth of Rome, in the England of the nineteenth century similar improvements would shape future growth.

During the later years of the eighteenth century the construction of canals had assisted industry by allowing the transport of much needed coal, iron ore and other raw materials. By the 1830s the introduction of railways would further expedite this process. Whereas early factories were usually powered by water and were thus restricted to areas where sufficient water flow was available, now factories could be built almost anywhere.

Industrialization was now able to move further inland and into the North. Industrialization, however, carries with it a very sinister side effect. Although it tends to increase the living standards of many, it also consumes both land and labor, which were previously employed in agricultural uses. The population expands, the ability to feed it declines. Eventually this process continues until such time as there arises a need to import food. There is vindication for this train of thought. In the mid-1840s the failure of Ireland's potato crop and the diminishing supply of other agricultural crops led to elevated food prices and even famine. As a result, more than one million Irish people would flee to America by the end of the decade. In desperation, the government in London repealed its earlier 1815 tax on imported grains. While this approach did help lower food prices over time, competition from outside also lowered the prices that English farmers could charge for their produce, impacting their profitability.

The increased industrial capacity of England, along with the resulting increase in population and the higher standard of living, combined to subject England to other ill-effects not recognizable at that time. Industrialization, for all its merits, has a tendency to separate man from nature. The increased reliance upon technical innovations eventually leads to the misconception that mankind is no longer bound by natural laws. With the belief that the restraints of natural law have been abolished comes an accompanying tendency toward liberal thought and liberal governments. The years of the nineteenth century were to bear evidence of this fact. Shortly after the abolishment of the slave trade, the prison system of England was to experience reform. The number of crimes deserving of capital punishment were drastically reduced, and London's metropolitan police force was disarmed. These prison and police reforms were initiated by Robert Peel, therefore these new unarmed constables became known as "bobbies."

Other reforms were to follow. In the 1830s, franchise reform would become the desired flavor of the day. In March of 1831, a reform bill was introduced by Lord John Russell to the House of Commons seeking to eliminate sixty of the old rotten boroughs and redistribute the plural representation of forty-seven others. The then very limited franchise was to be expanded from its base of 400,000 citizens to 650,000. By these acts, the industrial centers such as Manchester and Birmingham were to see an increase in their political capital. After three successive defeats, mostly in the House of Lords, the bill would finally be enacted June 7, 1832 and henceforth be known as the Great Reform Act. Firm in his beliefs of franchise extension, Lord Russell struck again in 1865, this time introducing a bill seeking to allow all males with skilled jobs and ownership of a home to vote. This act would further expand the electorate to over two million. As with the first attempt at reform in 1831, this bill would initially be defeated, leading Lord Russell to resign. In the aftermath of a wave of public protest, the bill was reconsidered, passing in August of 1867. Barely a decade and a half later, the franchise was extended again, this time by the Reform Act of 1887. Voting was now open to all male householders, again doubling the electorate to over five million. When coupled with the forces of mass-market press, a new age was entered into whereupon public opinion became a driving force in the government policies of England.

The more liberal tendencies of thought also affected the institutions of government. Following the English Civil War, the Tory and Whig political parties had been established. In the same way as the Republican party of the United States was born to the nineteenth century out of the ashes of the old Whig party, the new Liberal Party was formed in England from a coalition of Whigs, Peelites and Radicals. William Ewart Gladstone, then Chancellor of the Exchequer, was to become one of its more prominent members, serving as Prime Minister on three separate occasions. Throughout the reign of Queen Victoria (1837-1901), the Liberal mindset of England would continue in its reforming ways, offering legislation to cover issues from child labor laws and poor laws to laws encouraging the promotion of free trade.

Nevertheless, there would a backlash to these attempts at "progress," and the nature of political rivalry would become more intense. Much as in the America of the twentieth century, with higher levels of government becoming restricted to certain families such as the Kennedys, Bushs and Clintons, and the polarizing of the political parties, the later years of the nineteenth century would see the same trend in England. This trend was to make itself evident in the persons of William Gladstone and Benjamin Disraeli. From February of 1868 until 1885, the conservative Disraeli and the liberal Gladstone would alternate in the position as Prime Minister. Not until the 1924 election of Ramsey MacDonald, member of the Labour Party, would an individual serve as Prime Minister who was not either a Conservative or a Liberal. Disraeli was an advocate of an aggressive foreign policy. In a very forward thinking gesture, with an eye to the future defense of India, in 1875 he acquired for Britain nearly half of all the shares in the Suez Canal Company. Although more attuned to the preservation of the empire as it already existed as opposed to the extending of it, the Disraeli years would be marked by England's involvement in the takeover of South Africa's Transvaal Region in 1877, with the Second Anglo-Afghan War in 1878 and the Anglo-Zulu War of 1879. In a move intended to unite the people of India behind the Crown, Disraeli had Queen Victoria proclaimed as Empress of India in 1876. Gunboat diplomacy was not beyond his means either. During the 1877 crisis between Russia and Turkey, he dispatched a British fleet let by the most modern warship in the world, the H.M.S. Devastation, to the Dardanelles. Forever after Benjamin Disraeli would be associated with British patriotism, jingoism, and Empire.

Disreali was capable of attempts at reform as well. His efforts would assist in the passage of an education act, a public housing act, further reforms in labor and factory laws, the repeal of an earlier picketing ban imposed against labor unions, and a public health act aimed at establishing sanitary law. But it would be to his political opposite Gladstone with whom fervor for a more liberal England would become associated. Gladstone was of similar views as Pitt the Younger, who had been an advocate of keeping arms-length away from foreign entanglements. During the Midlothian Campaign, Gladstone had voiced opposition to the policies of Disraeli, declaring them "a vigorous, that is to say narrow, restless, blustering, and self-assertive foreign policy, appealing to the self-love and pride of the community." The disaster at Isandlwana and the massacre of the British legation staff at Kabul in the Second Afghan War were seized upon by Gladstone as why aggressive foreign policies should be avoided.

Gladstone would, during his three alternating terms as Prime Minister, meet with both success and failure. In addition to his attempts to reform the English Civil Service, opening its ranks to individuals according to their ability and not so much political connection, the British army was subject to reform as well. A new Enlistment Act introduced shorter terms of service. In addition, the practice of flogging as punishment was abolished, as was the age-old practice of purchasing commissions. The breech-loading Martini-Henry rife, forever to be associated with Britain's late colonial wars, was adopted for service also. During Gladstone's first term as minister, the Education Act of 1870 was passed, an attempt to introduce more schools into the poorer parts of the industrial cities by means of "board schools." There were also attempts at reform in England's higher levels of education, with admission to the universities open to all students regardless of their beliefs. Along with these successes, there would be setbacks in Gladstone's attempts at reform. Far in advance of the passage of the Eighteenth Amendment to the Constitution in America in 1919, the British government of Gladstone would submit an unsuccessful Licensing Bill, a child of the Temperance Wing of the Liberal Party. Gladstone fought for re-election in 1876 with a proposal to abolish the income tax, which was in place since the time of Pitt the Younger. He was to fail in his attempts. Gladstone was to also meet with misfortune in foreign policy.

In 1881, a thirty-seven year old Messianic holy man named Muhammad Ahmad initiated an uprising in the Sudan. He referred to himself as the Mahdi, with his servants being known as the ansars, or dervishes, as they were known to the British. To crush this rebellion, a well-equipped Egyptian army commanded by Colonel William Hicks was sent south. In November 1883, this force was ambushed and destroyed at Shaykan, with all of its modern rifles and artillery becoming spoils of war for the Mahdist forces. The Gladstone government, believing it would be very expensive and difficult to regain the Sudan and suppress the revolt, decided the wisest course of action was simply to extricate itself and its forces from the region. With much assistance from the press, and with an unrelenting jingoist attitude still prevalent among the general populace, Gladstone appointed General Charles George (Chinese) Gordon to conduct the withdrawal.

However, upon reaching Khartoum in the Sudan, Gordon decided instead to defend the city. Eventually the town was overrun by the Mahdist army, with Gordon fighting to the last. The British press idealized Gordon, while Gladstone was vilified for not sending a relief force soon enough. Shortly thereafter, in June of 1885, Gladstone would resign, thus ending his second term as Prime Minister. England would avenge the death of Gordon with General Herbert Kitchener invading the Sudan in 1897-1898.

*The Battle of Isandlwana as painted by Charles E. Fripp. Just as Rome had experienced disaster at the Teutoburg Forest in A.D. 9, Great Britain would suffer the loss of 1,700 men on January 22, 1879 during the Zulu War.*

On a plain near Omdurman on September 2, 1898, Kitchener's combined English-Egyptian army destroyed the dervish army with its modern weapons killing 11,000 Ansar warriors and wounding several thousand more.

By the end of the years of Gladstone and Disraeli, English society could look back over a century of unparalleled success and advancement. The century that had begun with England helping to prevail over Bonaparte, ended with successes in the Sudan and in South America and with victories over the Mahdist and Zulu armies. During the years of the 1870s England was at the pinnacle of its industrial strength, with its navy at the same time controlling the seas. Reforms in education, housing, suffrage and public health and safety had led to a better standard of living. Technological advance had allowed for the paving of streets, the electrifying of homes, with proper water supply and sewerage disposal. England was at time the leading creditor nation in the world, with London being recognized as the world's financial capital. Below the surface however, the stresses of the Empire were beginning to appear, or at least appear before whose willing to recognize them.

# Chapter 9

¤

# THE BITTER HARVEST

It is perhaps more than just a touch ironic that the Industrial Revolution which allowed first England and then the United States to become the leading industrial nations of the world, was preceded by decades of agricultural expansion. It is also beyond question that these Industrial Revolutions helped bring about massive population growth. An example of this explosive population growth in England can be discerned from the industrial city of Birmingham, whose population rose from 70,000 at the beginning of the nineteenth century to more than 350,000 by the time William Gladstone first came to be Prime Minister.[65] The population of England's other industrial centers experienced similar growth. These numbers are even more astounding when one considers that due to mass emigration from Britain to its colonies that at the birth of the twentieth century nearly 20 percent of the English population lived throughout its dominions. The United States experienced similar growth after the Civil War. In the decade from 1860 to 1870, the number of manufacturing facilities increased in America by 80 percent with a resulting increase in population of thirty-one million in 1865 to nearly seventy-six million by the year 1900. Fifteen million of these people were the result of immigration as opposed to England's emigration.

---

[65] Jenkins, *Short History of England*, 255.

Whereas both of these societies saw similar rates of growth, there existed a difference between them in terms of societal maturity, as the United States still possessed ample space within which to grow, while the land mass of England was by now extensively developed.

The centuries of growth for England were now near their end. While technological progress and industrialization had brought many blessings to England, they were now about to bring many curses. Agricultural decline was to play a leading part in this societal descent. This agricultural decline, which took place in England commencing in the decades at the end of the nineteenth century, bears evidence of a relationship between agriculture and industry, and industry and agriculture. Whereas improvements in agricultural practices at the end of the seventeenth and beginning of the eighteenth century had allowed for increased food supplies and lower food prices, which in turn provided for increased populations and cheap labor to assist industry, events would reverse this cycle. In the 1830s, industry and railroads had provided for an avenue of escape open to those who had formerly worked the land. As the percentage of the population involved in agriculture continued to decline, so would agricultural output. At the completion of the Napoleonic Wars, Parliament had instituted the Corn Law, which introduced a tariff on overseas wheat as a means of sustaining England's farms and farm incomes. By the end of the nineteenth century, these tariffs had to be repealed. Industrialization depended on cheap labor to remain competitive against the growing industrial might of the United States and Germany. Cheap labor depended in turn upon cheap food prices. As foodstuffs are subject to the law of supply and demand, when England's farms had reached capacity and then decline, the only option was to increase supply by importation from America and the dominions. However, increased supply meant lower prices, and lower prices meant less profit and increased difficulty for England's farms. Added to this, the iron hulled steamships and the steam engine decreased shipping cost. Between 1880 and 1900, the cost of importing grain into Britain decreased by 80 percent. These factors could only guarantee a further decline in

England's agricultural output. The importation of food and an eventual increase in food prices were not an option; they were a guarantee.

Whereas England had throughout the nineteenth century been assured of military supremacy due to an extensive lead in industry, the rise of other industrial nations such as Germany and the United States would now see the slow erosion of that supremacy. Henceforward, the expense of maintaining naval superiority and of engaging in wars would combine to almost guarantee England's eventual eclipse as a world power. No sooner had the twentieth century begun than two events would take place to begin this process, the Boer War and the naval arms race. The Boer War in South Africa and the decision by Kaiser Wilhelm II of Germany to enter into a naval arms race against England would initiate the process of financial strain.

The Boer War of 1899-1902 would probably best be regarded as a foretaste of what the United States would experience in Southeast Asia during the Vietnam War of the 1960s and 1970s. The roots of this particular colonial war probably began with the discovery of gold deposits in the region in 1886. Progressively, relations between the British in the Cape Colony and the Boers of the independent state of Transvaal became strained. Also, Prime Minister of the Cape Colony Cecil Rhodes was known to harbor desires of a British imperium stretching all the way from the Cape to Cairo, connected by means of a continuous rail line from North to South. In 1895, Rhodes had laid the foundations of a scheme to acquire the Transvaal by means of an uprising of the British population of Johannesburg supported by an invasion of the Transvaal by a force from the Cape Colony. This raid into the Transvaal was led by Dr. Leander Starr Jameson and consisted of about five hundred men. As events were to transpire, the uprising in Johannesburg never occurred and Jameson and his raiders were captured by the Boers at Doornkop. After years of failed negotiations, President Paul Kruger sent an ultimatum to the British demanding the disbanding of a British military force that was assembling in Natal. His ultimatum was refused by the British.

Recognizing a threat to its own existence, the neighboring Orange Free State agreed to an alliance with Kruger's Boers.

In response to Britain's rejection of the Kruger ultimatum, Transvaal and Orange Free State forces struck first, investing Ladysmith, Mafeking, and Kimberly. The Boer soldier was himself fiercely independent; mounted on horseback, armed with modern Mauser and Mannlicher rifles, and assisted by modern artillery supplied by German sources. He was to prove himself an excellent fighter. It took the British Empire two years and eight months to subdue a Boer army that could field at best 80,000 men. More than one half million British troops were required to put down the Boer resistance, with thirty thousand of them coming from the dominions. British losses were often heavy, as ill-conceived British frontal assaults were usually devastated by the excellent marksmanship of the Boer soldier. Much of Britain's difficulty could be attributed to the fact that for the first time since the war of 1812, British soldiers were confronted by an adversary with the same modern weapons. There were also several defects within the leadership of the British army.

Public opinion would begin to sway as well. The Jingoistic attitudes that had been prevalent throughout the years of Queen Victoria's reign were now called into question. During the Crimean War of 1853-1856, a new creature had been born to the battlefield. This creature was the war correspondent. The Times of London initiated the adoption of the war correspondent, sending William Russell to the Crimea for first hand reports from the front. The reports of Russell, critical of the incompetence of army leadership and of the needless suffering of the troops, were employed to ferment national doubt as to government conduct during the war. Eventually this doubt would cause Parliament to appoint a commission on the conduct of the war, a measure adopted by such a huge majority that it brought about the resignation of the Prime Minister, the Earl of Aberdeen. This commission would actively seek the reform of military administration, and the medical treatment of England's wounded men would also be much improved due largely to the efforts of Florence Nightingale. However, British patriotic fervor was so high that the disastrous charge of the Light Brigade, during which 673 horsemen had charged into the face of Russian guns, losing two-thirds of their numbers, was presented as being an overwhelming success instead of a military blunder. The poet Tennyson and later the actor Errol Flynn would immortalize the charge, which had actually occurred due to misunderstood orders with the Light Brigade actually charging the wrong battery of guns.

By the time of the Boer War, technology and public attitudes had changed. In his attempt to relieve Ladysmith, the British Commander, Sir Redvers Buller, had ordered two assaults against Boer positions. These assaults, at Spion Kop and Vaal Kranz in January and February of 1900, were both repulsed with heavy losses. In these assaults, 408 British soldiers were killed, 1,390 wounded with 311 missing. Boer losses were only 40 killed and 50 wounded.[66] This time around the British would regard failure and loss of life as being just exactly that.

At Spion Kop a young war correspondent named Winston Churchill would pen these words, "A thick and continued stream of wounded flowed rearwards. A village of ambulance wagons grew up at the foot of the mountain. The dead and injured smashed and broken by shells, littered the summit till it was a bloody reeking shambles. Thirst tormented the soldiers, for though water was at hand the fight was too close and furious to give even a moment's breathing space."[67] Such words were to have a telling effect on public opinion.

While the Boer War was settled with the Treaty of Vereeniging, the upcoming naval arms race against the increasing industrial might of Germany was to have far more reaching effects. The Boer War itself had the potential to expand into a contest involving more than just English and Boer participation. The only reason it had not was because England had assembled a large fleet of warships as a deterrent against any nation that might consider interceding on the Boer's behalf. Having viewed this effect first hand, Kaiser Wilhem of

---

[66] Dupuy, *Encyclopedia of Military History*, 854.
[67] Churchill, *London to Ladysmith*, 137.

Germany decided upon a policy of naval construction. This naval expansion was to be ambitious. By 1920, hopes were to have a fleet of forty-five battleships and thirty-two cruisers. These figures were later revised so that it was hoped to have sixty-one battleships by 1928.[68]

Other factors, one factor of their own making, would contribute to the British difficulties in dealing with this threat. In 1906, the construction of the H.M.S. Dreadnought, first of a new design of battleships, was completed. With its entry into service, every other warship in every other navy was rendered obsolete. The recently constructed and much publicized Great White Fleet of Theodore Roosevelt could now be regarded as little better than scrap metal. Of course this presented England with a particular problem as well. Its overwhelming naval superiority virtually vanished overnight, as its own fleet of warships had been rendered impotent as well. To add to this difficulty, the cost of building the Dreadnoughts and the accompanying new design of battle cruisers was nearly prohibitive. Dreadnought herself had required eleven months to construct. She displaced 17,900 tons and mounted ten twelve-inch naval rifles. In response to Dreadnought, the Kaiser ordered construction of Germany's first Dreadnought design, SMS Westfallen.

There is a lesson to be learned from the naval policy of Kaiser Wilhelm. The Kaiser, while ambitious and envious of England's naval might, recognized that he could never hope to build a fleet that could defeat England during a protracted and global war. His hope, and his policy, was to build a fleet capable of doing great damage in the event of war. Essentially, Germany's navy was to be used as a bargaining chip, if you will, leverage to expand Germany's colonial aspirations.

It should not come as a great surprise that with the advent of the war correspondent and with the cost and complexity of weapons becoming more readily apparent, that public sentiment against war would rise, and that the intellectual side of mankind would begin to question the feasibility of modern war. In 1898 a Polish banker and economist named Ivan S. Bloch published a seven-volume book

---

[68] Brendon, *Decline and Fall of the British Empire*, 335.

entitled, *The Future of War in its Economic and Political Relations: Is War Now Impossible*. The gravamen behind this work was the author's belief that the firepower of modern weapons had made war impossible, "except at the price of suicide." This would echo the desires of Hiram Maxim, who created the machine gun with this ultimate desire in mind. In 1910, another work of similar thought was published. This was Norman Angell's work, *The Great Illusion*. Angell had drawn conclusions similar to those of Bloch, that the economic interdependence of nations now rendered war obsolete, as the cost could be catastrophic to the victor and the vanquished alike.

In response to public sentiment against war, the governments of the industrial nations of the world would gather at the Hague Peace Conferences, the first occurring between May and July of 1899, the second from June to October of 1907. At these conferences many of the rules and laws of war would be modified. Although these conferences had initially been called into being under the pretense of controlling armaments, many of the statesmen present were more concerned with assuring national security. In these years the desire for peace existed, the human capacity to make it possible did not.

The German state with which we associate the beginning of two world wars owed its existence in large part to the efforts of Otto Von Bismark. It had been during the years of his Chancellorship that a conglomeration of minor German principalities had arisen and assured itself a place among nations with its victory over France during the Franco-Prussian War of 1870. Bismark himself had advocated that the newly formed state should remain content with power on land, avoiding a clash of interests with England. He had also once made the very prescient statement that, "Some damned foolish thing in the Balkans,"[69] would precipitate the next war.

He would be vindicated in his beliefs. The buildup to the First World War had involved a series of alliances and counter-alliances in an attempt to guarantee a balance of power on the European continent. It was hoped this might serve as a preventative to war. The

---

[69] Tuchman, *The Guns of August*, 89.

results were to be catastrophic. Along with the hopes of peace, there had been an allowance for the planning of war, if and when it came. In Germany, the chief of its general staff, Alfred Von Schlieffen, had prepared a plan of attack that would allow Germany to fight a war on two fronts, against France in the West, and Russia in the East.

Likewise France, still smarting from the loss of 1870 with its accompanying amputation of Alsace-Lorraine, had prepared its own plan of action in the event of war. Plan XXII, as it was known, called for a two-pronged French invasion into Alsace-Lorraine, a move both predicted by and beneficial to the Germans. But for the intervening hand of fate, and the then unappreciated wisdom of General Charles Michel Lanrezac, the First World War might have ended with the defeat of France in the opening campaign.

As events turned out, "some damned foolish thing in the Balkans" actually transpired. There had occurred in the Balkans the First and Second Balkan Wars of 1912 to 1913. Somehow, these affairs had been contained to a regional contest between the Balkan states and Turkey. Soon on the heels of the 1913 Treaty of London, which had ended this affair, the June 19, 1914 assassination of the Austrian Archduke Franz Ferdinand would result in a series of ultimatums and eventual war. The national suicide predicted by Ivan S. Bloch did in some ways occur, with all the participating European nations suffering enormous cost in lives and fortune. In the resulting four years of devastation, France would be "bled white." Russia, in its current form would suffer disaster on the battlefield, as at Tannenburg, and would then undergo the Russian Revolution, leading to the creation of a Bolshevek state. Germany would nearly succeed in its two front war, succumbing only after the entrance of the United States into the war in 1917. England would retain its empire and its mastery of the seas, with the further seeds of its own demise being sown. Germany's ally, the Austro-Hungarian Empire would cease to exist. Turkey would survive the war defeated, although its days as the Ottoman Empire were ended forever.

The First World War provided many valuable lessons to its combatants. It also produced the very causes for yet another world war twenty years later. The American Civil War had presented to the world the notion of modern warfare in which all the energies of the State were required for victory. The farmer and the industrialist were now just as critical to victory as were the soldier and his generals. The telegraph and the railroad had been indispensable tools of the trade in the war of 1861-1865. To these tools, the Great War would add motor transport and the influence of airpower. When Hiram Maxim had invented his machine gun in 1885, his belief was that with its rate of fire, 600 rounds per minute, it would make war obsolete. According to Maxim himself, he had once been advised by a friend, "If you want to make a pile of money, invent something that will enable these fool Europeans to cut each other's throats with greater facility." And so he did.[70]

The rates of slaughter during the Great War were unparalleled. All sides would suffer equally at the hands of the Maxim guns, with modern artillery combining with them to turn the fields of Flanders into a moonscape. At the 1916 Battle of the Somme, the British army suffered 57,470 casualties on the first day alone; 19,240 of these were men killed in action.[71] By the end of this battle, those figures had risen to 419,654 casualties, of which 131,000 were dead. Add to these numbers 204,253 French casualties as well as somewhere between 450,000 and 600,000 German, and one may begin to comprehend the scale of slaughter brought about by waging a modern war.[72]

Other names and other battles would for decades come to be associated with a level of slaughter equal to the Somme. At the Third Battle of Ypres in 1917, also known to the British as Passchendaele, The British army would literally be bogged down, as heavy rains and intensive artillery fire had turned the ground into a quagmire. By the end of the battle, Britain had sustained an additional 300,000 casualties, the Germans slightly less, 265,000. By war's end more than 908,000 soldiers from England and her colonies had been killed. This is no doubt why the youth of Britain slain during the Great War came

---

[70] North and Hogg, *The Book of Guns and Gunsmiths*, 212.

[71] Hart, *The Somme*, 11.

[72] Ibid. 528.

to be known as England's "lost generation."

The Royal Navy, which had played such a dominant role in the creation and maintenance of the Empire, did experience some measure of success during the war. This success would come at a cost. The only major fleet action of the Great War occurred at Jutland in 1916. During this engagement the German High Seas Fleet, commanded by Vice Admiral Scheer, sortied out to challenge the Royal Navy. The British fleet, under the command of Sir John Jollicoe, went to sea so as to respond to this challenge. The English had superior numbers, with 28 battleships and 9 battle cruisers. The German fleet could muster 16 battleships and 5 battle cruisers. As to the engagement itself, Jutland marked the last time a great fleet engagement was fought by opponents who were in eyesight of each other's ships. British seamanship was excellent, but German gunfire was more accurate. The very expensive, yet lightly armored British battle cruisers took a terrible beating, with Queen Mary, Indefatigable and Invincible sinking to the bottom. Germany could claim a tactical victory; they had sunk fourteen British warships while losing only eleven. But the strategic position of the German navy had not changed. In desperation, they would resort to a new campaign of unrestricted submarine warfare, a policy that would lead to American involvement in the war.

The Royal Navy would also see action during the Gallipoli Campaign of January 1915 to January 1916. This attempt to attack the "soft underbelly" of Europe and end the stalemate of trench warfare on the Western Front had been the brainchild of the First Lord of the Admiralty, Winston Churchill. Sound in concept, the overall execution of this campaign was poor. When a British fleet of battleships attempted to force the Dardanelles Strait on March 18, 1915, three of them were sunk. An amphibious assault was then planned, with forces being landed at five beachheads situated along Cape Helles at the tip of Gallipoli Peninsula. British forces were landed successfully, but what followed was a repetition of the trench warfare of Flanders and France, with neither the British nor the Turks being able to overcome the effects of massive machinegun fire.

During the Gallipoli Campaign, 21,255 English, 10,000 French, 8,709 Australians and 2,701 New Zealanders forfeited their lives.[73] Its aftershock would bring about the resignation of the First Lord of the Admiralty, Winston Churchill. While British and colonial losses on the high seas and the battlefield had been great, there were other losses that would impact the British Empire and its health and welfare in the decades to come. It is estimated that each passing day of the Great War had cost England 4,000,000 pounds. By war's end, Britannia had amassed a total war expenditure of 51,975,000,000 pounds, to include shipping losses and property damage.[74] Only Germany, which had borne the brunt of the expenses of the Central Powers and fought a war on two fronts had sustained greater financial losses. In the nineteenth century, with England at the height of its industrial might, this debt would have been difficult to pay. But now both agriculture and industry were suffering the ill effects of foreign competition. Therefore, paying this debt would become even more of an arduous task. If this cloud did have a silver lining, it could only be found in the protectionist policies that had been implemented by Joseph Chamberlain in the years prior to the Great War.

Repercussions from the war were to follow almost immediately. In the aftermath of the four-year slaughter, American President Woodrow Wilson had proposed to Congress on January 8, 1918, what he considered as the "only possible program" for peace. It is known to history as his Fourteen Points Program. It contained policies aimed at open covenants between nations, freedom of the seas in war and peace, the removal of trade barriers, armament reductions, adjustment of colonial claims, as well as a number of provisions to establish or restore the boundaries of Europe's ancient states. The fourteenth of these points provided for the formation of an association of nations to ensure liberty and guarantee territorial integrity of large and small nations alike. If these points had been accepted and adopted, peace may have prevailed in Europe's future.

---

[73] Brendon, *Decline and Fall of the British Empire*, 278.
[74] Dupuy, *Encyclopedia of Military History*, 990.

They were not adopted, and peace would not prevail.

To the untrained eye, Britain had emerged from the Great War further strengthened. It did owe the United States five billion dollars in war debts, although this was less than what France and the other continental powers owed. No battles had been fought on English soil, its factories were intact, its geographical footprint had increased by nearly one million square miles, and 13,000,000 new peoples were now residents of the British Empire. The Middle Eastern lands of what were to become Iran, Iraq, Israel and Jordan were now in British hands. These would prove to be a great asset in a world that was to become more dependent on fossil fuels and oil in particular. The German colonies in Africa and its islands throughout the Pacific were now under British control as well.

Appearances tend to be deceiving. Four months before the Treaty of Versailles was agreed upon, England had already discharged more than 980,000 officers and soldiers from its army. Its military expenditures were also reduced by nearly seventy percent. Long the backbone of its empire, The Royal Navy was to suffer a fate similar to that of the army. The Washington Naval Treaty of 1922 was to do to the Royal Navy what no foreign navy had done since before the time of the Armada. Prior to the Great War, England had been spending twice as much on its navy as any other nation. It had adopted a policy of maintaining a fleet larger than that of any two other nations combined. But now financial restraints and international opinion would combine to alter that balance. As part of the Washington Naval Treaty, the signatory nations had agreed to maintain ratios in terms of the size and tonnage of their respective fleets. England consented to the ratio of 5 (England), 5 (United States), 3 (Japan), 1.75 (France), and 1.75 (Italy). Tonnage restrictions on individual warships were agreed upon as well as the size and caliber of the weapons they would carry. In order to meet the requirements of this new treaty, Great Britain was forced to scrap more than 675 ships. In addition, England agreed to never turn Hong Kong into a naval base.

The United States made concessions as well. In addition to scrapping several older warships, work on the new battleship

Washington was halted when the ship was three quarters complete. A projected class of new battle cruisers was halted as well. Instead they were completed as aircraft carriers. Due to the restrictions of the Washington Naval Treaty, no new battleships would be commissioned into the U.S. Navy from 1923 until the arrival of the U.S.S. South Carolina in 1941. The United States would go to war with an old fleet. In terms of overall numbers, it would appear that England had surrendered more with the advent of the treaty than had the United States. In all likelihood, this was not the case. With its massive war debt, Great Britain simply could not afford to maintain a navy equal in numbers to what it had maintained in the past. The construction of new warships, while still possible, was to be restricted due to shortage of finance. The United States, now the largest creditor nation on earth, was under no such financial restriction. It could, with its massive industrial base and ample credit, build the largest navy on earth. If such had in fact occurred, Japan's course of action in 1941 may have been much affected. England was surrendering ships it could not afford. America was sacrificing ships it could.

The social evolution of England was to also have an impact on its future. Prior to the Great War, the liberal ideas of Gladstone were carried forth to greater heights. In 1908, the Liberal Henry Herbert Asquith came to power as Prime Minister. In his cabinet there would be two future Prime Ministers, David Lloyd George, as Treasury Secretary, and the young Winston Churchill, as Secretary of Trade. These two men, George and Churchill, would be the driving force behind new measures that would lay the foundation of Great Britain's welfare state. Preceding the Great War an old age pension system was created for those over seventy years of age. In addition, a school lunch program was instituted as well as school clinics. The power of the Trade Unions were strengthened by the removal of possible law suits for damages in the aftermath of strikes. Within a few years this provision would see consequences. In 1914, the new power of unions was put into action when major strikes occurred within the ranks of seamen, dockworkers and railway men. To a nation dependent upon the import of foodstuffs and raw materials and the export of manufacturers, a transportation strike was a potential disaster.

The new provisions for old age pensions and school meals needed to be paid for as well. When coupled with the advances of liberal government, instituted under Gladstone, there arose the need for more revenue. In 1909 the income tax was increased. Also, new taxes were implemented on real estate, alcohol, tobacco and petroleum. The sin tax, so to speak, was the creation of England's government, not of the United States government. Lloyd George, who had succeeded Asquith as Prime Minister in 1916, decided perhaps the only thing better than the expansion of liberal government policies, was the expansion of a more liberal electorate. As explained at the time, the right to vote was extended to all males over twenty-one years of age and to all women over thirty as a reward for their service during the Great War. If this move had been intended to guarantee electoral success to the liberal party for years to come, it would fail in its designs. With his departure from office in 1922, David Lloyd George was to be the last liberal to hold the office of Prime Minister, with all subsequent Prime Ministers being either Conservative or Labour Party candidates.

Lloyd George was also to become the victim of a master of his own making. In the aftermath of war, the liberal ideas fostered by Gladstone and Lloyd George gathered impetus. New demands arose on many fronts. The desire for paved streets and public schools were now supplanted by cries for freedom from want, illness, unemployment, and demands for a more equitable distribution of income. The labor unions once championed by Lloyd George now found a new avenue of strength. Public workers, such as police and even soldiers joined miners and railway men in their demands for higher pay and other concessions. More often than not, their increased demands were acceded to.

If the individuals who led the world into war in 1914 could be accused of occasional lack of wisdom, those who led the world out of war in 1918 could be accused of much the same. The Treaty of Versailles had established certain provisions. One of those provisions was that militant Germany was to be disarmed and had to form a new democratically elected government. However, further provisions were that this new, fragile government and its defeated people had to pay war reparations. These war reparations were set at an astounding 56 billion dollars, nearly as much as the now bankrupt nation had spent during the war. The results were predictable. Speaking to the nature of the terms of the Versailles Treaty, the French Marshall Ferdinand Foch wryly remarked, "This is not peace. It is an armistice for twenty years." Winston Churchill remarked that its clauses were "malignant and silly." Even to the far away Americans there were obvious flaws in its provisions, even provocations. General Tasker Bliss had once written that because of it, war would come in "thirty years." Long before its political repercussions were felt, its economic impacts set it. The first tremors of economic instability were felt in 1920 with the appearance of a global recession. Having entered upon a policy of increased social spending, and under the duress of having to pay for its war debts, there existed but one solution: the Geddes axe, named after the coalition minister Sir Eric Geddes, had to fall. Cuts in public spending became a must, with pay cuts to public employees such as teachers, and policemen following.

Economic instability is usually closely followed by political instability. The wounded economy of Britain led to David Lloyd George's political demise. It also allowed for the rise of the political star of Stanley Baldwin, who was to serve as Prime Minister from 1923 to 1924 and from 1924 until 1929. According to author Simon Jenkins, Baldwin "was perfectly cast as a reassuring contrast, the archetypal safe pair of hands, a pipe smoking countryman, sensible, and conciliatory.[75] To others he was far worse. For all of his faults, he did possess a great strength, he knew how to win elections. As events were to become evident, he also knew how to loose subcontinents.

During the final term of Lloyd George, the Government of Ireland Act had made its way through Parliament, to be followed in 1924 by a treaty negotiated by Lloyd George providing for the creation of an Irish Free State. Ireland's first independent elections occurred in 1922.

---

[75] Jenkins, *Short History of England*, 287.

Stanley Baldwin would assist with the further dismemberment of the empire. In 1929, shortly after the stock market collapse of "Black Tuesday," the new Viceroy of India, Lord Irwin, soon to be Lord Halifax, had recommended the attainment of Dominion status for Britain's greatest possession. This was not a new concept. During the Great War of 1917, Lloyd George had declared that British aims in India should be "the granting of self-governing institutions with a view to the progressive realization of responsible government in India as an integral part of the British Empire."

Victor Hugo had once stated, that "more powerful than all armies is the idea whose time has come." Indian self-government was to become a very powerful idea. It was such a powerful idea that the debate on self-rule for India would continue for three years. Leading the opposition of Indian self-rule was Churchill, who simply believed that a land which contained four dominant ethnic strains, Caucasoid, Mongoloid, Australoid and Negroid, and that also spoke 225 different languages, would fall into chaos if British rule were withdrawn. He also believed that chaos would result ultimately in violence. In a land that was also divided along religious lines with Hindus, Moslems, Buddhists, Jains, Zoroastrians, and Sikhs, there existed almost limitless possibilities for religious violence.

As all humans are in the same way products of their environment, and as Churchill's environment was that of Victorian England, Churchill also harbored concerns about what the loss of India would mean to the Empire. India, with its vast population of 400 million, had always been a vast recruiting ground for the army, and Indian troops had long been deployed throughout the Empire in its many conflicts. During the Great War, India had supplied more than one and a half million men for Britain's armies, with nearly 700,000 of these men fighting against the Turks in Mesopotamia.[76] Churchill himself once stated that if Britain were to surrender its Indian possessions, it would be "a hideous act of self-mutilation."[77]

---

[76] Brendon, *Decline and Fall of the British Empire*, 263.
[77] Manchester, *The Last Lion, Vol. I*, 841.

Churchill would initially have two powerful allies in his quest to retain India for the Empire. One was F. E. Smith, known also as Lord Birkenhead. Smith had served as Secretary of State for India and had "deep misgivings about the vast subcontinent." Whereas Churchill led the efforts to defend the Raj in the Commons, Smith had led similar efforts in the House of Lords. Unfortunately in late September of 1929, Smith would pass away while still in his fifties, a terrible blow to Churchill and to the Empire. David Lloyd George had also spoken in opposition to self-rule, which was surprising for the man who had in 1917 actually advocated it. Soon however, ill health would remove Lloyd George from the debate on India as well.

In 1935, the Government of India Act, which was the longest piece of legislation to ever emerge from the House of Commons, was brought forth. By this act, Burma was separated from India and the eleven Indian provinces were afforded self-rule, although this self-rule was in many ways still restricted. This act did not afford India its total independence, as that would not arrive until after the Second World War. As events would turn out, Churchill would be correct in his predictions. With the partition and independence of India at midnight on August 14, 1947, Great Britain completed its Asian Dunkirk. In its aftermath and with the departure of the last British troops from Bombay, more than two million Hindus and Moslems were killed during six months of outright savagery. The separation of Pakistan from India led to further tensions that still exist today.

The economic blizzard of the late 1920s and the early 1930s was to have far greater impacts upon Britain and its outside world. With the termination of the First World War, Britain and the United States as well as other nations had tended to withdraw from the world stage and concentrate on affairs internal in nature. Domestic social programs had taken the forefront and foreign affairs were placed on the back burner. The internal politics of these nations had become more derisive, with mass media playing a key role in this matter. In the United States, the newspaper of William Randolph Hearst now had a circulation of more than fifteen million homes daily.[78] Now also, most of the homes of the two nations contained another technological wonder, the radio. In Great Britain, the newspapers divided themselves along party lines, with Lord Beaverbrooks's *Daily Express* and Lord Rothermere's *Daily Mail*, being decidedly Tory. The *News Chronicle* followed along liberal lines, the *Daily Herald* and *Daily Mirror*, those of the Labour party. The *Times* of London and its editor Geoffrey Dawson would fall into line behind the policies of Stanley Baldwin and Neville Chamberlain. Dawson would prove himself an implacable foe of Churchill; he would also prove himself wrong.

The other great democracy of the western world, that which had been created at Versailles from the remnants of Otto Von Bismark's Second Reich, was the Weimar Republic. Before economic crisis had descended upon the rest of the world in 1929, the Weimar Republic had an economic tremor of its own and suffered through inflationary panic in 1923. This of course should have been expected. With the provisions of the Versailles Treaty demanding massive war reparations and with millions of soldiers returning home from the front to find only alienation and unemployment, economic discomfort was inevitable; so was political instability. As early as 1919, the splintering of the Wiemar's political parties had begun. In that year, a failed painter, then police spy, enrolled as the seventh member of a new National Socialist Workers' Party. No lengthy discussion of Herr Hitler and his policies are needed, as the disastrous effects to follow are known to the whole world. However, what is important to discuss is the nature of the society from which he came, and the fact that Hitler was not a dictator in the truest sense.

With its birth, the Weimer Republic had met with some measure of initial success. Its president was the German hero Paul Von Hindenberg, a figure in whom many Germans placed their trust, and hence trust in his government. The German economy was in the early 1920s, stable, resting firmly on seven billion dollars worth of loans that the United States had granted under terms so favorable as to

---

[78] Ibid, 821.

nearly make them gifts. These were of course the Dawes and the Young Plans, precursors to the Marshall Plan, which was to occur in the aftermath of Europe's next great fiasco. All of this would of course change. In the autumn of 1929 Austria's largest bank, Credit-Anstalt, closed its doors. The repercussions were global and its victims many. The Republic of Germany was a victim, and in many ways the principle victim.

The American loans that had supported the Weimar Republic were immediately cancelled. The most prominent banking institution of the Republic was the Darmstader and National Bank. When that bank failed, it took the majority of other banks with it. Facing economic difficulties of their own, other nations could no longer import German goods, and without the export of their goods, the Republic could not afford imports, even of the most basic commodities such as food. The nation that had once maintained the world's largest armies, now maintained the world's largest armies of unemployed. To most, this was a disaster. To Hitler it was an opportunity. In the aftermath of the collapse, Hitler had himself written, "Never in my life have I been so well disposed and inwardly contented as in these days, for hard reality has opened the eyes of the millions of Germans to the unprecedented swindles, lies and betrayals of the Marxist deceivers of the people."[79]

To the German people, financial failure was to be accompanied by moral failure. The once great nation, Spartan in its habits and militant in its designs, was to become what Paris had been regarded as before the First World War. To quote Manchester from his epic work, *The Last Lion*:

> *Over two million young German women were destitute widows. The more destitute (and attractive) of them became prostitutes, seeking prey near the Hauptbahnhaf. Among them were muscular whores with whips and mothers in their early thirties, teamed with their teenage daughters to offer "mutter and tochter" sex. Tourists*

---

[79] Ibid, 867.

*were shocked by the more infamous night spots; the Kabarett Tingle-Tangle, the Apollo, the Monokel ("die Bar der Frau" for lesbians), and the White Mouse, whose most sensational performer and role model for thousands of German girls in the Weimar years, was Anita Berber, who danced naked, mainlined cocaine and morphine and made love to men and women sprawled atop bars, bathed in spotlights, while voyeurs stared and fondled one another. Anita was dead at twenty-nine. So, by then was the Weimar Republic.*

To Americans today who believe that their own country has set upon some brave new course based upon sexual freedom, I say, perhaps not.

Homosexuality was rampant as well. Stefan Zweig had written of the time that, "along the Kurfurstendamn, powdered and rouged young men sauntered, and in the dimly lit bars one might see men of the world of finance courting drunken sailors," and at the numerous transvestite balls, "hundreds of men costumed as women and hundreds of women as men danced under the benevolent eye of the police." Herr Hitler was to change all that, and although it might be offensive to the human mind to admit, Hitler did not act alone.

It is also important to realize that while there exist the common misconception that Hitler seized power, he did not. Hitler was every bit a politician. From the initial failure of the 1923 Beer Hall Putsch, he went on to seize power by legal means and by political approach. The construction of a party organization had allowed him to build a political base. In 1929 Hitler was supported by only 2.6 percent of the German electorate.[80] In the aftermath of financial collapse, and with the elections of September 14, 1930, the Nazi Party had received 6,409,600 votes, an increase of 690 percent. Other electoral successes were to follow. After his appointment as Chancellor, and five days before a general election, the Reichstag, which was the seat of government, was set on fire by an arsonist. Hitler used the pretext of public safety to have President Hindenburg place the entire country

---

[80] Ibid, 62.

under martial law. What was to follow was one of the bloodiest elections ever seen in Europe. It was also one of the more decisive. The Nazi Party received 17,277, 180 votes. The next closest party, the Social Democrats, received 7,181.629 votes. Soon to follow was the Enabling Act giving Hitler his dictatorial powers. With a huge majority in the Reichstag, this was made easily possible.

One must recognize also that in addition to popular support, Hitler received overwhelming financial support. At a single meeting with the industrialists of Germany's Weimar Republic, the leading Nazi financial agent, Dr. Hjalmar Schacht, had collected more than three million marks. One million of these marks came from Gustav Krupp, much of the rest from the directors of I.G. Farben Ironworks. Krupp and I. G. Farben were manufacturers of weapons; weapons that were soon to be used to tear the world apart.

If any good had come from the Washington Naval Treaty and the subsequent depression of the 1920s and 1930s, it can be found in the fact that it caused the military establishments of Britain and the United States to develop new concepts and to progress along new lines. France, the possessor of Europe's largest and at the time finest army, adopted a very retrograde mentality in terms of military thought and policy. Between the First and Second World Wars France spent hundreds of millions of dollars on a static line of defensive works along its borders with Germany. This Maginot Line would lead to initial disaster in the crisis of 1939 to 1945. In the United States Army Air Service, General Billy Mitchell became a prophet and a proponent of the use of airpower in the next war, if and when it came. On Jun 21, 1921, Army Air Service aircraft bombed the former German battleship Ostfriesland, sinking it after repeated hits. Mitchell would be partially right, proclaiming that warships were now obsolete. For the battleship, the next war would prove this prophecy true. However, the combination of ship and aircraft was to usher in a new era of naval warfare.

The United States would lead the way in the innovation of this new ship and aircraft combination. The concept of the aircraft-carrying warship had arisen even before the Wright brothers' first flight. In the

1890s, a would-be French aviator named Clement Ader had made the first conceptional drawing of such a ship, to include both flight and hanger decks. He even coined a name for such a vessel, "prote-avions." This concept was put into practice to a limited extent on the 14th of November 1910, when Eugene Ely flew his aircraft off a temporary platform constructed on the forecastle of the American cruiser Birmingham. In January of the following year, Ely proved that aircraft could land on a ship as well, bringing his aircraft to a safe halt on a 102-foot platform constructed on the quarterdeck of the cruiser Pennsylvania. The cycle was complete. By 1915, the United States had also introduced the concepts of catapult launching and arrester gear landings.

Active participation in the First World War was to allow the opportunity for England to overcome this American lead in naval aviation. In 1916 the Royal Navy purchased the uncompleted liner Carte Ross, converting it into the world's first flush deck aircraft carrier, H.M.S. Argus. Argus was completed too late in the war to see service, but the ship served as an invaluable test bed for further innovations, such as an island wherein the ships bridge, mast, and vertical exhaust funnel were merged into a single structure mounted on the starboard side of the flight deck. These innovations were incorporated into the world's first purpose-built aircraft carrier, H.M.S. Hermes, which joined the fleet in 1923. She would soon be joined in the fleet by H.M.S. Eagle and the reconstituted H.M.S. Furious. Before the onset of World War II, Britain would also add the two conversions Courageous and Glorius to the fleet, as well as the famous Ark Royal, which at the time was Britain's most modern carrier design.

The United States would begin its carrier navy with the converted Collier Langley, nicknamed the "Covered Wagon." Due to the provisions of the Washington Naval Treaty in 1922, two of its uncompleted battle cruisers were converted into aircraft carriers. The results were the Lexington and the Saratoga, two of the most modern and graceful ships of their time. A "perfectly matched pair of graceful giants," these two ships were 888 feet long, displaced 36,000 tons, could travel at 34 knots and carried up to 90 aircraft. They joined the fleet in 1927 and were an emphatic exclamation to the world of America's new lead in aircraft carrier design. They would soon be joined by the Yorktown class of carriers, Yorktown, Hornet and Enterprise. Two other smaller carriers, Ranger and Wasp, would join the fleet prior to World War II as well.

The creation of the British and American carrier navies was to be an issue of utmost importance. Japan, formerly an ally of Britain and America in the Great War, decided to build a carrier navy of its own. It would also decide in the 1920s and 1930s to enter into a policy of Pacific expansion, by other than peaceful means. Before its attack on the American naval base at Pearl Harbor, December 7, 1941, Japan had built the world's foremost carrier fleet, consisting of six modern full size carriers and four conversions. It possessed the world's most proficient carrier attack groups, the most experienced pilots, and some of the most advanced aircraft types. Without British and American carrier development prior to the war, Japan may have succeeded in its effort.

Whereas most people regard the war of 1939 to 1945 as the Second World War, Winston Churchill always preferred to call it "The Unnecessary War." Unnecessary or not, the war did come about, and there were many reasons for it happening. The Treaty of Versailles included provisions that would cause economic hardship and the festering of ill will in the years after it's signing. Popular history at times tells us that Hitler was responsible, although this in no way explains the events that were to transpire in the Pacific. Others in the Western Hemisphere have condemned Neville Chamberlain for his actions and naiveté at Munich, and for his policies of appeasement. This of course does not take into account the actions of Stanley Baldwin, who held the reins of power in Britain from 1924 to 1937. Baldwin was most responsible for the appeasement policies of Britain, and it was also he who was most responsible for its state of military unpreparedness.

There were others at fault as well. Chief amongst them were the educational institutions of the major participants. The public school systems of the industrialized nations were created with the desire to educate the world's youth, with the objective of allowing them to acquire an education level sufficient to allow them to participate in modern industrialized societies. A higher education allows the individual to attain a higher standard of living; it allows the business and industrial sectors the ability to educate its future engineers and leaders. To those with a well-rounded education there exist the ability to broaden one's own horizons, to become more well versed in music, the arts and literature. Unfortunately, there are always those educators who take it upon themselves to indoctrinate as well as educate future generations.

In the aftermath of the Great War and in the years leading up to its subsequent cataclysm, the educational systems of the major nations provide innumerable instances of this indoctrinal process. In Britain during the early 1930s the undergraduates of the Cambridge Union had voted 213 to 138 for "uncompromising" pacifism. In another indication of the rebellious attitude of English youth, on February 9, 1933, the Oxford Union voted 275 to 153 in favor of a resolution stating, "that this House will in no circumstances fight for king and country."[81] In 1934, the Oxford Tories had invited Winston Churchill to address them and to answer a series of twelve prepared questions. This he did without difficulty. Afterwards, during an informal session of questions, a young German Rhodes Scholar named Adolf Schlepegrell asked Churchill for his views on the proposed plebiscite for the Saar region, which the Versailles Treaty had scheduled for the year 1935. According to the conditions of this plebiscite, the inhabitants of the Saar were to be allowed to decide if they wanted to become part of France or Germany. As the Saar was within Germany's borders, this would be akin to asking the residents of New York if they wanted to be a part of Canada or the United States.

Schlepegrell proposed to Churchill the idea of the immediate removal of French troops from the occupied area. Churchill opposed this concept, believing that French troops should remain in the Saar

---

[81] Manchester, *The Last Lion, Vol. II*, 46

until the appointed time because the Germans had "started the war, plunging the whole world into ruins." When the additional question was put forth in response to Churchill's answer, "Does Mr. Churchill believe that the German people, the men and women who live in Germany today, are responsible for the war?" Churchill was quite firm in his reply, "Yes." To the applause of his fellow students the young scholar bowed to him and then walked out. When Churchill later added that Britain's re-arming was "essential for us to be safe in our island home," he was greeted only by laughter.

When the young Rhodes scholar later returned to his native Germany he was regarded as somewhat of a national hero, a status he would enjoy until it was discovered that his grandmother was of Jewish descent. Eventually Schlepegrell returned to England where he became a naturalized citizen and served as a political officer in the impending war. Indoctrination is therefore a double-edged sword, the edge sharp when events prove true, the edge dull when they do not. On the opposite side of the channel, Adolf Hitler would use the indoctrination of Germany's youth to create his vast armies. Granted, there was a preexisting officer corps and army, but this had been restricted to 100,000 men under the terms of the Versailles Treaty. By the time Hitler was ready to unleash his fury upon France and the low countries, this army numbered more than seven million available troops, much of German's youth, loyal to Hitler himself by a sworn oath. If the educators of England had been less persuasive in their desires for passivity, and those of Germany more ardent in their desire for it, the complexion of mankind may have been negated of one of its more notable blemishes.

The fortunes of war for Great Britain would swing back and forth from one extreme to the other almost as if upon a giant pendulum. Within weeks of its entrance into war, the carrier Courageous would be lost at sea during a submarine attack. In another daring feat of arms, and in a sign of things to come, on the morning of October 14, 1939, German U-boat Captain Gunther Prien was able to navigate through the defenses of Scapa Flow and torpedo the great battleship Royal Oak. Thirteen minutes after being struck by a spread of four torpedoes the old war ship rolled over and sank, taking 833 officers and men to the bottom with her. The repercussions of her sinking would be far greater than the significance of losing one old ship. Recognizing the possibilities and potential of a submarine attack, Hitler entered upon a new policy for his Kriegsmarine (navy). On October 16, two days after the attack at Scapa Flow, it was announced that, "all merchant ships definitely recognized as enemy can be torpedoed without warning."[82] The unrestricted submarine warfare of the First World War was now to become the accepted policy of the Second.

Some measure of revenge was inflicted by the Royal Navy for the loss of Courageous and Royal Oak. In December 1939, the British cruisers Exeter, Ajax, and Achilles combined their weight to force the much superior German pocket battleship Graf Spee to seek refuge in the harbor of Montivideo, Uruguay. In the diplomatic aftermath to follow, the Captain of the Graf Spee, Hans Langsforff, was denied permission to remain in the harbor to repair his damaged ship. He must sail or face internment. Langsdorff would do neither. On December 17, 1939, the Graf Spee slipped her moorings and then was scuttled by her crew near the mouth of the harbor. The loss of Graf Spee, a ship of merely 10,000 tons displacement, was much more of a blow to the prestige of Hitler's navy than it was a great material loss.

Britain was to suffer a worse blow to its naval prestige. On May 18, 1941, the German heavy battleship Bismark would depart Germany on her maiden voyage, a commerce-raiding voyage into the Atlantic accompanied by its small near-twin cruiser Prinz Eugen. In response, several units of the British fleet were sent to find and stop her. Within days, on May 24, 1941, the new German giant would engage the pride of the British fleet and the largest warship afloat, the battle cruiser Hood. In what is known as the Battle of Denmark Straight, at 5:39 in the morning and at a range of 19,000 yards (11 miles), a salvo from the Bismark found its range, one shell plunging through Hood's lightly protected deck in the vicinity of its rear turrets. Within seconds

---

[82] Ibid, 561.

a sheet of flame arose followed by a massive explosion, which tore the ship in two. In less than three minutes the Hood disappeared beneath the sea, leaving only three survivors from a crew of 1,424 men.

The pendulum of bad and good fortune was to swing again. As a result of this blow to the prestige of England, the First Lord of the Admiralty, Churchill, ordered an all out manhunt, or in this case, shiphunt, for the Bismark. In this all out effort to destroy this great ship, Great Britain employed six battleships and battle cruisers, 13 cruisers and 21 destroyers.

Two days after having destroyed the Hood, the Bismark was attacked by a swarm of 15 antiquated Swordfish torpedo planes from the aircraft carrier Ark Royal. One torpedo would strike the aft section of the ship, jamming its rudder mechanism and causing the ship to begin a permanent turn to starboard. On the morning of May 27, 1941, the heavy units of the Royal Navy caught up with the Bismark. The British battleships King George V and the truncated Rodney silenced Bismark's main guns within one half hour. They then closed in for the kill, mortally wounding the German giant with what amounted to point blank fire. Bismark's end followed swiftly, by a combination of British firepower and efforts to scuttle her by her own crew. Only 110 men would survive from a crew of 2,092 sailors.

The naval engagement between Hood and Bismark would establish the tone for Britain's further efforts throughout the "unnecessary war." In April of 1940, Nazi Germany seized its northern neighbor Denmark. The same day that Denmark fell, April 9, German troops also landed along the shores of Norway. Five days later an Anglo-French force of ten thousand troops were rushed to Norway to forestall the Norwegian collapse. This force would eventually be able to gain control of Narvik, but to no avail. With the German Wehrmacht launching an all out offensive against France and the low countries on May 10, 1940, the position of this Anglo-French force could no longer be maintained, and on June 8, and June 9 would be evacuated. British naval might was to be further damaged when the aircraft carrier Glorious was caught by two German battle cruisers, the Scharnhorst and Gneisenau.

Within weeks of the Norwegian disaster there would be further disaster in France. During the Great War Germany's armies were halted by the French and British armies on the Marne. In this war, and with the assistance of ten modern panzer divisions, the Wehrmacht would not be stopped. The British Expeditionary Force in the north would be severed from the French armies in the south. This was accomplished by means of a German armored assault through the hilly, heavily forested Ardennes region. Within nine days German armor reached the English Channel west of Abbeville, France. Miraculously and inexplicably, Hitler ordered his panzer armies to halt their advance against the British and French forces now trapped against the Channel at the Port of Dunkirk. It seems that the head of the German Luftwaffe, Hermann Goering, was of the belief that modern airpower had reached a point in its evolution where it could destroy an unprotected ground army. He may have been right. What he could not count on was the interference of Britain's fighter command on the outcome of events. Outnumbered and foreshadowing the events to transpire in the autumn of 1940, the British fighter pilots suppressed the German air attacks enough to allow the successful evacuation of the allied troops from Dunkirk. In the period of eight days, 850 British vessels managed to evacuate nearly 340,000 men, to include 112,000 French and Belgian troops. These troops would all prove vital in the war to come.

On the same day that the German armies had launched their assault against the low countries and France, the now disgraced Neville Chamberlain resigned as Prime Minister and was replaced by Churchill. Of Dunkirk., Churchill would comment, "We must be very careful not to assign to this deliverance the attributes of victory. Wars are not won by evacuations."[83] With the removal of Britain's armies from the continent, the German juggernaut simply regrouped so as to turn south and finish off the mortally wounded French army. This process was to begin on June 5, 1940. In a mere eight days the German armored formations split the French army into further fragments. By

---

[83] Langworth, *Churchill by Himself*, 273.

June 13, Paris was declared an open city and by Jun 21 the French government agreed to the capitulation of its armies. Hitler had accomplished what the Kaiser could not.

There is a very potent lesson involved with the fall of France in 1940. For all intents and purposes, France was not defeated by German arms. These had served merely to emphasize what was already known. France had defeated itself. During the German occupation of the Rhineland in 1936, France had possessed the largest, best-equipped army in the world. The German occupation of the Rhineland itself had only involved a handful of infantry battalions, without the support of tanks or heavy artillery. If France had decided to mobilize at this time, it possessed nearly 100 fully equipped divisions. The poilus of the French army outnumbered their German counterparts by a ration of ten to one, and they had tanks and artillery. All they needed to do was move forward, and the German troops would have been forced to evacuate the Rhineland. This did not happen because the French government had become passive, a passivity that would infiltrate the ranks of the French army.

From the time of the Rhineland onwards, the ratio of strength between the French and German armies would steadily erode. This slow destruction of military strength was to be accompanied by an erosion of national motivation, although this erosion may have been more of a determined effort than an accidental happenstance. Much of this could be attributed to the political kaleidoscope occurring within the French government. The 1936 French government of M. Albert Garrault was replaced by that of M. Leon Blum. Blum was in turn replaced by Edouard Daladier, who in his turn was replaced by Paul Reynaud. All these changes were to occur within the span of three years. This inconsistency of political thought had an extremely corrosive effect on French national morale. In addition, France in 1940 was a democratic nation with a conscripted army. Under such circumstances, the mood of the people is almost always reflected in the mood of the army. To the casual observer, the French population of 1939-1940 was not imbued with any great deal of faith in its government, and neither was its army, a further lesson to those willing to observe its future effects.

As the first half of the year 1940 had afforded England some of its worst national defeats, the second half of that year would afford it one of its greatest triumphs. The Battle of Britain found the island nation fighting alone against the now combined efforts of Nazi Germany and Fascist Italy. This battle was not to be one between opposing armies or fleets. For perhaps the first time in history, this battle was fought almost exclusively in the air. Against the air fleet of Germany, nearly 2,800 planes in all, England could muster but 650 operational fighters, distributed between 52 squadrons. Fortunately for England, these squadrons were comprised of mainly Hawker Hurricane and Supermarine Spitfire aircraft. In addition, these British fighter squadrons were assisted by the invention of radar and a well-organized and efficient ground control system. This would allow the British fighters to be vectored to the correct altitudes and locations of the incoming German air fleet.

The Battle of Britain began on August 8, 1940. It would be fought in three phases, continuing until October 23 of the same year. In that short three-month period the fate of the British nation would hang in the balance. By the time of its conclusion, 1,733 German aircraft were shot down while British losses were 915.[84] In tribute to the brave pilots of the Royal Air Force, Churchill would exclaim, "Never, in the field of human conflict, was so much owed by so many to so few." In its aftermath, Hitler would unleash his bomber squadrons on English cities during what is often referred to as the "blitz." More than 43,000 British civilians were killed during this aerial assault, with 51,000 others wounded. Great Britain's Bomber Command would retaliate in kind, striking at Berlin, Dusseldorf, Essen and other industrial cities whenever possible. In 1921 the Italian General Giulio Douhet had published his book, *The Command of the Air*. In his book he had elucidated his doctrine of winning future wars by breaking an enemy's will to fight by the unlimited bombing of his cities. His concepts were employed to a limited extent during the Spanish Civil

---

[84] Dupuy, *Encyclopedia of Military History*, 1066.

War of 1936 to 1939 and during Germany's attack on Poland in 1939. The bombing of cities was henceforth to be considered as a necessary accomplice to war.

The ebb and flow of the tides of war continued for England, as well as its allies. In October of 1940, Italy invaded Greece quite unexpectedly. Shortly thereafter, on November 11, 1940, the British aircraft carrier Illustrious was to open a new chapter in naval warfare. On that date twenty-one antiquated Swordfish biplanes launched an assault on the Italian fleet in its harbor at Toranto. The rewards of this attack were enormous. The Italian battleships Littorio, Caio Diulio and Conte de Cavour were rendered hors de combat (disabled). The Italian navy's numerical advantage over Britain in terms of available battleships in the Mediterranean was reversed, from six to five to three to five. Never again during the war would the Italian navy seek an engagement with the Royal Navy if they suspected the presence of a British Carrier.

In the spring of 1941, the British cause would suffer a setback when the island of Crete was captured by a German airborne assault, the first in history of such large proportion. To balance against this loss, Britain would gain two new allies, Russia and the United States. In June 1941, Hitler launched operation Barbarossa, the invasion of Russia. In December of the same year, Japan would emulate the British attack on Toranto with a carrier assault of its own against the American fleet at Pearl Harbor. This Japanese assault was of a much larger proportion than the Toranto attack; all six of Japan's large carriers were involved, their level of success also greater. At Pearl Harbor, seven of the eight battleships present were put out of action. Only the U.S.S. Pennsylvania was spared, as the ship was sitting in drydock where Japanese torpedo planes could not find her.

Within days, the wrath of the Japanese fleet was to be felt by the British as well. Even as the attack against the American fleet at Pearl Harbor was proceeding, similar Japanese assaults were being launched against American, British and Dutch possessions all across the Pacific. The Philippines and Wake Island would be two of the first targets of the Japanese. Also on the list were the warships of the Royal

Navy in the Indian Ocean. The British, in an attempt to disrupt an expected Japanese invasion of Malaya, had dispatched their only two available capital ships in the area, the battle cruiser Repulse and the battleship Prince of Wales in response. The result was disastrous. Three days after Pearl Harbor, these two ships were caught at sea by a force of 34 Japanese bombers and 54 torpedo bombers. Destitute of British air cover, the two ships were overtaken in short order. During a subsequent Japanese carrier strike into the Indian Ocean in April of 1942, the British would also lose the carrier Hermes, plus the cruisers Cornwall and Devonshire.

Worse British losses would follow. The Japanese invasion of Malaya, which Prince of Wales and Repulse had tried to stop, proceeded unabated. This Japanese force of 100,000 soldiers was commanded by Tomoyuki Yamashita, the "Tiger of Malaysia." Landing north of the British colony, the Japanese forces advanced southward, trapping a similar sized army of British, Australian, and Indian soldiers at the naval base of Singapore at the southern tip of the Malay Peninsula. The attack on Singapore Island began on February 8, 1942 when a force of three Australian battalions found themselves under attack from sixteen Japanese battalions. The Australians fought well and inflicted heavy casualties, but against three successive assaults they were forced to give ground. Throughout the summer of 1942 the British would fight to defend the island, inflicting severe losses on the Japanese. On September 15, the British Commander General Percival agreed to an unconditional surrender. What he did not realize was what poor shape the Japanese army was in, with most of its troops now nearly out of ammunition and many of them unfit for duty. The impregnable fortress of Singapore in the end was quite pregnable. Singapore was Britain's greatest defeat, perhaps of all time. In the aftermath, two centuries of respect for the British Empire and its armed forces was swept away as completely as had the respect for those of Rome at Adrianople.

The year 1942 may very well be regarded as a turning point in the history of the British Empire. In 1939, Britain had been regarded as the world's only superpower. This however did not take into account the massive reserves of manpower and natural resources available to its two new allies. From 1942 onwards, the size and scope of Soviet and American military might would reach proportions previously unknown or understood. The Russian armies in the east would grind the German armies and air forces into dust. After the siege of Stalingrad in 1942 and the ensuing Battle of Kursk in the summer of 1943, the only roads open to Germany's Wehrmacht were to the west, in a long arduous retreat from where they had come. Not until June of 1944 would a second front against the Germans be opened, thus relieving some of the pressure on the Russian armies.

In the Pacific, events would follow a similar path, with the disastrous losses of the early campaigns being answered by the overwhelming naval, land and air forces of the United States. The British would return to the Far East to wage war against Japan's Imperial Empire, but their contributions would be negligible until Germany and Italy had been defeated in Europe. British armed forces would play a significant role throughout the war, the eighth army being almost entirely responsible for the defeat of axis armies in North Africa. It had always been the policy of Britain to combine with other nations in its defense against more powerful neighbors, a policy initiated by William of Orange that continued through the years of Pitt the elder and Pitt the younger. This policy was to continue, but now the ratio of power and its resulting relationships would change. During the Seven Years War and the Napoleonic Wars, England had served as the financier of war, usually supplying its allies with the money and the weapons necessary to engage common enemies. Now England was on the receiving end. In 1939 and 1940, Britain had sustained its war effort by means of such policies as borrowing from sterling block countries to include its own colonies, by liquidating overseas assets, and by selling off its gold and dollar reserves. By June of 1941, Britain's gold and cash reserves had dwindled to 150 million dollars. It was now clear that Britain no longer had the ability to finance its continued war effort.

Viewing these events from across the Atlantic, and realizing that America might soon find itself fighting for its own survival, President

Roosevelt initiated the Lend-Lease Act. Under the terms of this Act, Great Britain and its dominions as well as Soviet Russia, were allowed to purchase American weapons and other goods for war in exchange for their pledge to repay these debts at war's end. By war's end these debts were substantial. Britain itself owed more than fifteen billion dollars; combined with its dominions, the debt was more than thirty billion. Six years of fighting were to witness the transformation of Britain from being the world's largest creditor nation, to being the world's largest debtor nation.

As Britain was now dependent on foreign aid to finance its war effort, it would now become increasingly more reliant upon this aid in wartime military operations as well. In 1943, operation "point blank" began. This operation, which consisted of the day and night bombing of Germany's industrial cities, saw British and American bomber forces operating from British airfields. The British and their fleets of Avro-Lancaster and Short Stirlings would bomb by night. By day, vast air fleets of American B-17 and B-24 bombers would practice high altitude precision bombing. The results to German cities would be devastating. During a combined night and day British and American raid on the German city of Dresden February 13-14, 1945, a firestorm was created which killed at least 100,000 civilians in the most destructive bombardment in history.

On land, British forces would continue to combine their efforts with the Americans as well. In June of 1943, the Mediterranean island of Sicily was invaded. More than 160,000 British and American troops would participate, supported by 3,000 vessels and 3,700 aircraft. By the end of August, Messina was captured and the island secured. The invasion of Sicily brought with it other benefits besides securing Mediterranean shipping lanes. The Italian people, already weary of war, toppled the government of Dictator Benito Mussolini. As early as September 3, 1943, an armistice was signed between the allies and the new Italian government under Marshal Badoglio.

The next day, September 9, 1943, allied landings occurred in the Gulf of Salerno, thus initiating the attempt to capture the Italian peninsula. These assault forces, under the command of Lieutenant

General Mark Clark, comprised the British X and American VI corps. The new British-American wartime relationship would initiate the process of British or American forces being under the command of senior officers from the armies and navies of both counties.

The year 1944 brought with it the largest amphibious invasion in history. Operation Overlord would entail the cross-Channel invasion of mainland Europe. Nearly three million men, forty-five combat divisions with supporting units, were moved by air and sea from southern England to the Normandy coast of France, beginning on June 6, 1944. This allied force was accompanied by overwhelming naval and air superiority both in the Channel and over the landing sites. Overall command of the invasion forces was awarded to the American, General Dwight Eisenhower. Over-all command of the land forces was given to British General Sir Bernard Law Montgomery. In terms of the ratio of forces, two-thirds were American, with the other third being the forces of Great Britain and her dominions as well as contingents of Free-French and Poles.

Operation Overlord should provide a certain level of insight into the nature of modern, industrial war. "Total War," as we know it today, requires the almost total industrial output of the belligerent nations. During the assault on Normandy, nearly 4,000 ships were required to transport troops across the English Channel. These were accompanied by nearly 600 warships. Overhead, nearly 2,500 heavy bombers dropped more than ten thousand tons of bombs, saturating the terrain below. More than 7,000 fighters and ground attack aircraft kept the skies free of enemy fighters and restricted the movement of enemy forces on the ground. All of this effort was made without having to curtail operations in other theatres. While all of this was taking place, the fighting in Italy still raged on. The bombing of German cities continued. In the Atlantic, the Mediterranean and the Baltic, the war at sea continued unabated. In the Pacific, enormous fleets brought army and marine forces closer and closer to the heart of Japan. This is the nature of modern war. Advances in technology from the First World War did not end the slaughter of trench warfare; they only modified it and made its effects more lethal.

By the end of 1944, Allied Forces in Europe had fought across France and Belgium and were nearing the very borders of Germany. Control of the air was complete and German industry ceased to be a factor in the war. Soviet armies in the east had destroyed the great panzer armies that had brought so many nations to their knees in 1939, 1940 and 1941. In the autumn of 1944, British General Montgomery brought forth a plan to end the war. This plan was to be known as Operation Market Garden. The plan consisted of dropping three airborne divisions behind enemy lines so as to open a 60-mile-long causeway. The British Second Army would then rush down this causeway and secure bridges across the Meuse, Rhine, and Lower Rhine Rivers. Unfortunately bad weather and a flooded countryside would inhibit total success. At Annhem, more than 7,000 men of the British First Airborne Division were killed, wounded or captured.

Following the outcome of Market Garden, German resistance stiffened. In December of 1944, Adolf Hitler would unleash his final assault against allied armies. The Ardennes Offensive, known also as the Battle of the Bulge, was perhaps Nazi Germany's death rattle. When Hitler had invaded France in 1940, his assaulting army had consisted of 104 infantry divisions, 9 mechanized infantry division, and 10 armored divisions. As an indication of how weakened his armies now were, Hitler's entire assault force, which consisted of everything he could muster, only contained 24 divisions, 10 of them armored. Nazi Germany had thus returned to the state of the Germany of 1918, when Hindenburg and Ludendorff had launched their final assaults against the British and French trenches in a last, desperate effort to end the war. The issue, though hard-fought, was probably never in doubt. Gone were the days of the Panzer and the Stuka, but gone only to be replaced by more terrible times. By the following spring the war in Europe was over, with Germany agreeing to unconditional surrender to take effect at midnight on May 8-9, 1945.

With the surrender of Nazi Germany at hand, Great Britain was able to shift much of its naval and some of its land forces to the Pacific Theatres. Britain had continued it efforts against Japan in the aftermath of the fall of Singapore, but the German threat to its existence had been much greater and hence had consumed much more of its available resources. Therefore, much of the war against Japan had been carried out by American forces, with the almost unlimited industrial capacity of the United States behind them. During the initial phase of the war, the United States had suffered repeated losses and defeats, as had its British, Dutch and Australian allies. Japan had however, made the same strategic mistake as Germany, having to fight a war on two fronts. To its west were the Chinese and the British, and to its east the United States.

As early as June 1942, this error would become increasingly apparent. During that month, the undefeated Japanese carrier force engaged its American opposite during the Battle of Midway. In the initial phase of the battle, the Japanese would virtually annihilate the attacking American aircraft squadrons, fending off no less than five different attacks. Fate would intervene. On the morning of June 4, renewed American attacks caught Japan's four aircraft carriers with their flight decks loaded with planes that were being refueled or rearmed. In less than six minutes the balance of power in the Pacific was shifted forever, with three Japanese carriers being sunk. The next day the fourth carrier, Hiryu, was destroyed as well.

More serious than the loss of four carriers and their assigned aircraft, was the loss of trained pilots and aircrew. Japan had no sufficient training program to provide large numbers of new, experienced pilots. After Midway, the quality of Japan's naval aviators continually declined. Evidence of this came two years later in June 1944. At the Battle of the Philippine Sea, the last of the great carrier vs. carrier battles occurred. On June 19, the first day of the battle, 315 of the 375 planes launched by the Japanese were shot down. American losses for the day were 29 aircraft. The American pilots sardonically named this engagement, "The Great Marianas Turkey Shoot." Japan's carriers also suffered during the battle, with Taiho, Zuikaku, and Hijo finding permanent homes at the bottom of the sea.

In the aftermath of the Marianas battle, Japan found itself in a position in which it could barely defend itself. In response, she would launch the "Divine Wind," kamikaze attacks by individual pilots or planes designed to inflict maximum damage on the American fleets. Their primary targets were the fast carriers of the American task forces, their wooden decks making them especially vulnerable. These new kamikaze attacks first took place during the October 1944 Battle of Leyte Gulf, the largest naval battle ever fought. The Japanese carrier fleet or what was left of it was used as bait to lure the American carrier fleet away from the American beachheads being established on the Philippine island of Leyte. At this late date in the war, Japan's entire carrier fleet consisted of but four ships, capable of putting up 52 fighters and 64 attack aircraft. Japan's hope was that once the American carriers were lured away, Japan's surface combat ships could sail in and destroy the American amphibious fleet. The result was another Japanese disaster. On the early morning of October 25, 1944, the American battleships Maryland, Pennsylvania, West Virginia, California and Tennessee, resurrected after Pearl Harbor, along with the Mississippi, caught the advancing Japanese surface fleet in the narrow waters of Suriagao Strait. In the last battleship vs. battleship engagement in history, these ships annihilated their Japanese foe.

To the north, the American carriers found what was left of Japan's once mighty carrier force, launching massive strikes against them on the afternoon of October 25. The last Japanese carrier still in service to have participated at the Pear Harbor attack was sunk, along with the carrier Zuiho, and the seaplane carriers Chitose and Chiyoda. The hybrid battleships Hyuga and Ise, which had been fitted with improvised carrier decks aft of their superstructure, were heavily damaged. They would struggle back to safety in Japan, only to be sunk within four days of each other in July of 1945. In desperation, on the afternoon of October 25, 1944, the American escort carrier St. Lo came under attack from Japanese zeros during the first of the new kamikaze attacks. One zero would find its mark, smashing through St. Lo's flight deck and exploding its aircraft hanger. The resulting explosion ripped the ship apart, sinking her in 30 minutes.

During the months to come, Japan's kamikaze assault with its "one man one warship" mentality, increased in intensity. During the Philippines campaign, sixteen American ships were sunk and another eighty-seven were damaged. The American carrier Franklin was so severely damaged by a kamikaze assault, that it would limp back to the United States never to see service again. During the American assault against Okinawa from April to July 1945, the kamikaze assaults took the shape of massed attacks, or kikusui. A total of 1,465 Japanese aircraft would participate in this all out desperate assault. Into this scene of mayhem would arrive the cavalry, in this case Great Britain's carrier fleet with their armored flight decks. All four of these British carriers, which served with the U.S. Fifth Fleet, were hit by kamikaze attacks. None however were ever forced to retreat from the scene of action, as the kamikaze hits just disintegrated on their decks and never penetrated into the ships' vitals.

After Okinawa, the combined force of America and British carriers concentrated the fury of their attacks against targets on mainland Japan. So successful were their assaults on the remainder of the Japanese fleet that at the time of Japan's surrender, the only Japanese carrier still afloat was the diminutive Hosho, Japan's first carrier, having been constructed in the 1920s.

Whereas Britain had entered the Second World War being regarded as the only superpower, the financial and military results of the war were to see its status as superpower and empire dissolve almost immediately. When it had become evident to the barbarous tribes that had settled within Rome's borders that the empire was financially and militarily insolvent, they entered into a policy of seeking greater and greater demands from the government, until eventually there existed no stable government from which to make demands. Attilla the Hun had held first the Eastern and later the Western Roman Empire's financial hostages. The last Roman emperor in the west, Romulus Augustus, was deposed by the German mercenary Odavacar. Unlike so many of his predecessors who had met an early and untimely demise, Romulus was fortunate in that he was simply pensioned off to an estate in Campania.

Although Great Britain's head of state was not to suffer the fate of Romulus, the cycle of increased demands from its dominions and in many cases their separation from the Empire to become independent states was similar to that which accompanied the disseverance of Rome. The causes were similar as well. Rome lost its empire for two principal reasons: financially it was broke and militarily it was impotent. In 1945 Britain was much the same. Before it had even had the opportunity to pay its debts from the First World War, Britain had found itself having to finance the Second. Evidence of this fiscal and military decline was most evident within the institution most responsible for Britain's status as an empire to begin with. This institution was the Royal Navy.

During the war years Great Britain built just one battleship, the H.M.S. Vanguard. On VJ Day in 1945, the Royal Navy had ten fleet carriers and eleven escort carriers serving in the Pacific. Five years later during the Korean Conflict, she would have only one carrier left in the Pacific to participate in the UN sanctioned police action against North Korea.

In compliance with the return clauses of the Lend-Lease Act, during 1945-1946 Great Britain was forced to send a large number of its weapons of war back to the United States. During the war Britain had maintained a fleet of 35 escort carriers in its attempts to control the Atlantic shipping lanes. By the end of 1946, all of them were gone. Of its fleet of full-sized carriers, no less than nine of its new carriers were sold or scrapped between 1946 and the last year of Britain's involvement in Korea. Two carriers were transferred to Canada, two others to Australia. One other was sold to France, with an additional carrier going to Holland in 1948. As further evidence of Britain's financial and military decline, some of the British carriers that had been laid down during the war were not completed until many years later. In 1966 the Royal Navy still had five carriers in service, plus two converted commando carriers. Hermes had been laid down in June 1944, but was not completed until November 1959. The laydown and completion dates of the other ships were similar; Ark Royal 1943 and 1955, Eagle 1942 and 1951, Century 1944 and 1953. In addition,

Victorious was still in service, completed in 1941. The development of the British carriers bore evidence of another factor, with inadequate budgets limiting the size of these ships. The American Midway-class carriers, three of which were completed at the end of World War II, displaced 45,000 tons. The British carriers all displaced less than 26,000 tons. This destruction of its carrier fleet was to have enormous impact on post war policy.

Recognizing Britain's now weakened condition, and realizing the significance of their own contributions to the war effort, many of England's colonies now advocated for increased levels of independence from the Empire. Great Britain was also beginning to recognize that the cost of running an Empire was such that it could no longer afford to defend many of its colonies from either external or internal threats. In 1947, budget constraints had forced the elimination of 700 million pounds from defense budgets. These constraints and their effects were not lost on Britain's subject peoples. These effects were most apparent in India. During the year 1946, complaints and a general breakdown of discipline had occurred within the ranks of RAF personnel stationed there. This erosion of morale became contagious, spreading into the ranks of Indian servicemen.

In February 1945, 7,000 ratings of the Royal Indian Navy initiated a four-day mutiny, which started aboard the frigate Talwar in Bombay. The Indian mutineers would use the ship's wireless transmitters to encourage Indian crews on Royal Indian Navy vessels in Madras and Calcutta to join the revolt. This revolt was put down by British and Mahratha troops, but its aftereffects left 223 people dead and over 1,000 wounded.

Recognizing that it would probably require at least five British divisions in India to control events, five divisions that the government simply could not afford and were not available, the decision to abandon India was made. The architect of Britain's withdrawal from the subcontinent was Lord Louis Mountbatton. His arrival in India was accompanied by the further disintegration of public order. With few if any options on the table, Mountbatten recommended the divorce of Muslim India from Hindu India, thus allowing for the creation of a new independent nation, Pakistan. To this the cabinet in London agreed. On August 15, 1947, India and Pakistan became independent. As Churchill had predicted in the 1930s, violence along religious lines ensued, with two million Indians being massacred within six months of Britain's withdrawal.

The departure of Britain's crown jewel of empire further accelerated events elsewhere. Having lost its vast recruiting ground in the east, in an effort to compensate for the loss of the Indian Army, Parliament passed the National Service Act of 1947. Henceforth, all British males aged eighteen were required to serve eighteen months in the armed forces of Britain. With the outbreak of the Korean War, this requirement was increased to two years.

Violence and partition of the Empire reached almost epidemic proportions in the months following the loss of India. In July 1946, Jewish terrorists blew up the British headquarters in Jerusalem, located at the King David Hotel. This act was simply a continuation of the violence which had been present in the region since 1944. Anti-British sentiments were high throughout the Middle East. Upon the termination of the Second World War, the United States had advocated high levels of Jewish immigration into British Palestine. Britain had initially been in opposition to this policy. But Britain's position was weak. In 1947, the United States had initiated the Marshall Plan in an effort to assist the war-torn economies of Western Europe. The plan called for 13 billion dollars in aid. In the first year of this plan, Britain received nearly 700 million pounds in aid. With its options limited, Britain asked the newly created United Nations to find a solution. The UN solution was similar to that which had occurred in India, – Partition. Unfortunately, both the Arabs and the Jews rejected this proposal, the result being that Britain simply withdrew its hundred thousand-man garrison in May of 1948.

As in India, violence followed. A civil war began between the Jewish inhabitants of the region and the Palestinians. Jewish arms and willpower proved superior. The new Jewish state of Israel was born, and more than 720,000 Palestinians fled to Jordan and Gaza.[85]

In rapid succession other British colonies fled as well. In the East, Burma received its independence on January 4, 1948. Within one month, Ceylon in the Mediterranean received the same. What began as a brushfire had now become an all out conflagration. In Iran, Great Britain was a major stakeholder in the Anglo-Iranian Oil Company. Feeling dissatisfied with the initial terms of the agreement reached between themselves and Britain prior to the First World War, Iran sought a reconciliation of the original terms. Already facing continued economic stress, Britain refused Iranian demands for an increase in their annual payment. In response, the nationalist government of Mohammed Mossadegh announced its intent to nationalize AIOC and its refinery operations at Abadan, then the world's largest. On September 26, 1951, Iran issued to Britain an ultimatum, requesting the withdrawal of all British personnel from the AIOC facility at Abadan. With no clear alternative, Britain complied. Shortly thereafter, Egypt began to feel its oats as well. Egypt itself had been a part of Britain's unofficial empire in the Middle East since 1882, when a 25,000-man British army had been landed at Smalia in response to the massacre of fifty Europeans at the hands of an Alexandrian mob. Egyptian troops had fought for the British army during the Mahdist uprising of 1883-1885. Almost half of the 26,000-strong British army that avenged the death of Charles George Gordon at Omdurman in 1898 were Egyptian. However, in the aftermath of World War II, with the fever of independence spreading throughout the Middle East, relations between the English and the Egyptians were very strained. In 1954, future British Prime Minister Anthony Eden had negotiated a treaty with the then Egyptian Prime Minister Gamel Abdul Nasser. Under the terms of this agreement, British troops were to be removed from Egypt by 1956. Within weeks of this withdrawal, and perhaps in response to an American refusal to guarantee Nasser substantial loans for his proposed Oswan Dam project, on July 26, 1956, Abdul Nasser

---

[85] James, *Rise and Fall of the British Empire*, 563.

occupied the strategically important Suez Canal. At this time, foreign investors still had a forty-nine percent holding in the Suez Canal Company.

The response to Abdul Nasser was an Anglo-French attempt to retake the Suez Canal zone by force. Three British aircraft carriers, the Albion, the Bulwark and the Eagle, along with two small French aircraft carriers, were to spearhead the operation. Their first objective was to neutralize Egyptian airfields while simultaneously patrolling the canal itself, the latter effort intended to prevent the Egyptians from blocking the canal by sinking ships into it. What followed was in no way a repetition of the successful raid at Taranto in 1940. While engaged in suppressing the airfields, the resources at hand did not allow for the successful patrolling of the canal. Ultimately the canal was blocked before British and French troops could be landed to seize it, and the operation failed. Much worse, world opinion came down strongly against the operation and British and French military forces were forced to do an about-face. It is an interesting point that just prior to the Suez debacle, Britain had scrapped the carriers Indomitable and Implacable in 1955, had transferred Majestic to the Royal Australian Navy, and had sent Illustrious and Indefatigable to the scrap yard in the months prior to 1956 Suez operation. If these ships and their aircraft had been available for use by the British at Suez, the outcome might have been much different.

The Suez Canal failure was not unique to Britain's efforts to retain its colonies throughout Africa. The plague, which had begun with India and Pakistan, had continued with Palestine, Burma, Ceylon, and Cyprus, now spread to Africa. As early as 1945, a secret organization of Kenyan natives known as the Mau Mau, had initiated a campaign of dissidence, which resulted in violent civil war. Atrocities became common, with blacks and whites, men, women and children becoming victims alike. In October 1952, the violence had become so widespread that Britain declared a state of emergency. In 1953, General Sir George Erskine was dispatched to the region to assume command of British forces in the region. By this time, a force of more than four thousand Mau Mau terrorists had assembled in the

Mt. Kenya forest. Some then thousand British and local troops eventually dispersed them in 1955, but even with their defeat and the arrest of more than 24,000 suspects, it was becoming increasingly obvious that eventual independence would be the end result after such unmitigated violence. In August 1961, the dissident leader Jumo Kenyatta was released after a seven-year prison sentence. He immediately became leader of a pro-independence political party and within two years he was Kenya's Prime Minister. On December 12, 1963, Kenya became an independent state within the British Commonwealth of Nations. In December 1951, Tanjanjika was likewise granted independence, with Uganda also receiving its freedom in October of 1962. On December 10, 1963, Zanzibar received its independence while remaining as a member of the Commonwealth of Nations. By this time any pretense of Empire was long gone, with Britain left to continue its existence in the shadow of the United States.

In the American media of the newly arrived twenty-first century, we often hear reference to what is known as the "welfare state." Great Britain had started along this path prior to the First World War. In the aftermath of the Second World War, the floodgates opened with the people of Great Britain accepting the government's position that somehow it was responsible for the welfare of every British subject, "from cradle to grave." Even before the war in Europe had ended, the Butler Education Act had nationalized every state school within Britain. Far in advance of America's Obamacare, Britain had instituted a National Insurance Act of 1946, which afforded even child allowances and a provision for funeral grants. The Act was supplemented in 1948 by the National Health Service Act, which allowed for a free general practitioner and hospital service for all who needed it. If it was the intention of Britain's government to interject itself into the everyday existence of its citizens, its foot was most certainly by now through the front door. More attempts at nationalization were to follow, with the British government becoming more heavily involved in all aspects of the economy, to include the Bank of England, transportation systems, including both road and rail, coal mines, aviation, and utilities such as gas and electricity. All of this mind you, from a government facing massive national debts and the possibility of bankruptcy.

Once set in motion, there existed no agency with the ability to act as a brake on Britain's new liberal agenda. By the time of the mid-1960s, the Labour Government of Harold Wilson was experimenting with a new program of social reform that included the liberalization of laws regarding such hot topics as divorce, abortion, and open homosexuality. In a clear sign to England's criminal element as to which way the winds of social change were blowing; capital punishment was abolished. By the end of the decade, in 1970, an Equal Pay Act was passed, mandating that women be paid a rate equal to that of men when engaged in similar work.

If a lesson in all of this unfettered liberalism is to be sought after and found, it came to Britain within a few short years of having implemented these many social reforms. In the early 1970s, tensions in the Middle East and the sudden realization by OPEC that they were now in the driver's seat, so to speak, led to a surge in world oil prices. The effect was felt throughout the industrial nations of the world, Britain included. By 1974, the Labour Government, which had instituted so many social reforms, "had nothing to offer beyond increasing the top rate of income tax to 83 percent, plus 15 percent on dividends, the highest peacetime rate ever."[86] Worse was to follow, especially for those who had allowed themselves to become dependent on government spending. In 1976, while Great Britain's former colony was celebrating its bicentennial, Britain herself was forced to accept a 23 billion pound bailout from the International Monetary Fund. As a remediary to this loan, the government was forced to self impose three billion pounds in cuts to its planned domestic spending. In 1944, a government white paper had asserted that in post war England, it would be the responsibility of the government to assist in the creation and maintaining of high levels of employment. By 1976, the realization that the private sector economy

---

[86] Jenkins, *Short History of England*, 321.

could no longer support the weight of the state had set in. At his party conference of that year, Prime Minister James Callaghan had warned party members that a "world where full employment would be guaranteed at the stroke of a chancellor's pen... I tell you in all candour that that option no longer exist."[87]

The devastating effects of Britain's transition to a welfare state were further reflected in the continued demise of its once all-powerful navy. At the Suez Crisis of 1956, only three light fleet carriers were available to an operation that required a much greater effort. France, having been educated by its inability to support its forces at Dien Bien Phu, Indochina, and having lost further colonial prestige during the Suez fiasco, began construction of two modern fleet carriers, the Clemenceau and the Foch. In contrast, Britain disposed of another carrier, Hercules, which it had sold to India. This act is even more ironic given that the Royal Navy was responsible for the invention and innovation of those three elements necessary for the operation of modern carriers, the angled flight deck, the steam catapult, and the mirror landing system.

The trend toward colonial and military decay accelerated as the cold war and the rise of the welfare state continued. In December of 1962, an agreement between the governments of Harold MacMillan and John F. Kennedy allowed Britain to purchase five of America's new Polaris type submarines, with the ships themselves being built in British yards and the missiles and accompanying technology to come from the United States. The England which had once led the world in warship design and production, was now dependent upon the technological lead of its former colony. The acquisition of the Polaris fleet came at a cost: Britain's planned new carrier, CNA01, was canceled. Furthermore, in 1966 the Wilson/Healey Defense White Paper specified that none of Britain's last three carriers, Victorious, Eagle, and the Ark Royal, were to be replaced.

---

[87] Ibid. 322.

*H.M.S. Ark Royal soon after completion, circa 1938*

They were instead sentenced to suffer a slow obsolescence. In the final years of Britain's fleet carriers, further dependence on American know-how could be ascertained by viewing the types of aircraft deployed, with the McDonald Douglas F-4 Phantom serving as the Royal Navy's front line fighter. The tragic end to Great Britain's storied history of fixed wing naval aviation and fleet carriers came in December of 1978, when Ark Royal slowly steamed into Devonport for her appointment with the breakers. In contrast, at this point Britain's ally across the Atlantic was operating a fleet of no less than twelve modern super carriers, to include two of the Nimitz class. In addition, the United States Navy maintained several other carriers in reserve, almost a necessity during times when it can take up to seven years to construct a modern carrier.

It is an unfortunate fact that in modern political states, especially democracies, that an especially virulent political disease eventually causes them to politicize every aspect of their societies, even that which guards their very existence. In the early 1970s the British government decided to construct a major surface vessel for the first time since the end of the Second World War. Throughout the 1960s Britain's defense industries had begun working on a new type of aircraft, the VSTOL, or Vertical Short Takeoff and Landing aircraft. The result was the Harrier "jump jet." The development of this aircraft would offer the Royal Navy a temporary reprieve from having no naval aviation wing. However, the Royal Navy's new surface unit, which was to be designed to operate the new Harrier jump jet, was not to be regarded as an aircraft carrier. Instead, Britain's politicians decided on a new name, the through-deck cruiser. It seems that in England the term aircraft carrier had somehow become politically incorrect. In any case, the H.M.S. Invincible, the lead ship in a new class of light carriers was laid down. Its development would be further hampered by politics. The ship was launched in May 1977, but was not commissioned until June of 1980. Unlike other carriers of its day, the ship was constructed with a massive ski-ramp at the forward end of the flight deck, another of Britain's contributions to carrier development. The Invincible was later joined by a second sister ship, Hermes, with a third ship planned.

In 1982, with Invincible having served in the fleet for barely two years, the politicians struck again. As the last of Britain's fleet carriers had been condemned in the 1960s in order to purchase the Polaris missile subs, the need to upgrade these subs to the newly developed American Trident Missile would initiate the demise of the new class of "through-deck cruisers." In March of 1982, Defense Minister John Nott announced the sale of Invincible to the Royal Australian Navy. Given that the Soviet Union was by this time constructing a fleet of aircraft carriers for the first time in its history, the decision by the British government to destroy the Harrier-equipped Invincibles while still in their infant state can only be seen as a determined effort to rely on the financial and naval strengths of the U.S. military for their defense.

The decision to scrap its modest three-ship carrier fleet may have also had the unintended consequence of sending the wrong message to the right people. On April 2, less than a month after John Nott's decision to scrap the carrier fleet, tiny Argentina invaded the British-held Falkland Islands in the South Atlantic. In response, Britain could intervene only by sending its two tiny Invincibles, carrying a total of twenty Sea Harriers between them. To support these two ships, a mongrel fleet of assorted destroyers, civilian tankers, luxury liners, and commercial transport ships were to accompany them. Operating at a distance of more than 8,000 miles from homeport and facing an enormous disadvantage in numbers of available aircraft, this tiny fleet should have been overwhelmed. Their only support would come from the aging bombers of the Royal Air Force, a fleet of ageing bombers that were ironically to be decommissioned in June of 1982. The first of these aerial missions, codenamed Black Buck I, took place on April 29, 1982, with a fleet of 11 Victor tankers and 2 Avro Vulcan bombers departing from the Ascension Islands for a 16-hour, 8,000 mile round trip. In total, seven of these bombing missions were flown.

The Falkland Islands War would last until the fourteenth of June 1982, with Argentine forces on the islands surrendering. The cost to Britain was excessive, as six modern warships were lost, mostly to the French-designed Exocet air-to-ship missile. The Invincible and the Hermes were largely responsible for the retaking of the Falklands, as their Harriers not only protected the fleet but were also instrumental in assisting the ground assault forces. Their spectacular success against numerical odds and overwhelming distance were followed by the failure of the British government to learn from their lesson. As of 2012, the Royal Navy does not operate a single aircraft carrier, with only the assault ship Ocean bearing any resemblance to such a ship. The British government does plan to build two new aircraft carriers, the Queen Elizabeth Class. Delays in the development of the American joint strike fighter, which the ships are to carry, and further political wrangling have pushed back construction to the point that neither of these ships will enter service until perhaps 2030. In contrast, China, which had never operated a carrier force of any kind, has in recent years purchased four, H.M.A.S Melbourne from the Australian Navy, plus three others from the former Soviet Republics. By November of 2012, the Chinese Peoples Liberation Army Navy had successfully performed carrier landings and takeoffs on the carrier Liaoning, which was the new designation for the former Soviet carrier

Varyag.

Such is the state of England today. The nation that had first attracted the attention of Julius Caesar twenty centuries ago finds itself much diminished from its former status as the world's largest empire of all time. Her evolution from Roman colony to world supremacy had taken eighteen centuries. Along the way men such as Henry Plantagenet had granted her legal institutions, which were to set her apart from the other nations of the earth. Other great men, such as Simon de Montford and Oliver Cromwell had fought against the despotism of kings so as to guarantee her people a level of freedom and self-government not seen before in human affairs. Others, such as Robert Clive and William Pitt the Elder had guaranteed that these laws and freedoms would be spread across the globe, from America to Australia, to a thousand islands and nations in between. For two centuries her navy had dominated the world's oceans, and her fleets of trading ships had opened markets to new products across the globe. Her farmers had been at the forefront of agricultural innovation and expansion and her artisans and craftsmen had helped initiate the Industrial Revolution. During two world wars, her soldiers, sailors, and airmen had helped fend off the forces of brutal militarism. In the end one great man, Winston Churchill, would try to maintain her status as a world power and equal to the great nations of the world. For all his greatness, he would not succeed. Much as Great Britain's famous ancestor could not overcome the internal forces of decay and external forces of conquest, so too would the island nation suffer a similar fate, and from many of the same causes. Now, it will remain to be seen if the offspring of Rome's offspring will be able to avoid the mistakes of the past, and guarantee the continuation of free governments throughout the world.

# Chapter 10

¤

# AMERICA, A NEW BIRTH OF FREEDOM

There has always existed a certain misconception that the United States was founded in 1776. While we may in fact be able to recognize that year as the year of our independence, what we must remember is that our collective history goes back much farther than that. We also tend to assume that the United States Constitution of 1787 marked the beginning of constitutional government in this country. This of course denies the fact that we were an English colony and that we had existed under a similar constitution ever since the time of the first colonies at Jamestown in 1607 and Plymouth in 1620. In this way, we can also recognize that whereas England was a Roman colony that perhaps our history in some small way goes back even further than that.

This shared history should also alert us to similar historical trends and tendencies shared by the world's three great republics, thus far. Each experienced similarities during their formative years, each experienced similarities during their years of explosive growth, and each experienced, and in the case of the Unite States continues to experience, certain similarities while at the height of their power. Therefore, it will be of little if any surprise if in one hundred years hence historians can look back and find similarities during their years of decline, a decline that the honest person must admit we have already begun.

If there is evidence of our connectivity to the republican empires of the past, it can be ascertained in the events leading up to our

Revolutionary War and eventual independence. The very idea of independence and of the rights of man were not our own, they were taken from the Englishmen before us. Many of the great men responsible for our nation's beginnings were both educated and gifted writers. Benjamin Franklin, Samuel and John Adams, Alexander Hamilton, John Jay and James Otis all fall into this category. First they would consult English history and English thought to find the answers they were seeking; then they would wield their pens to spread these ideas to the masses of colonial society. To consult the works of Nevins and Commanger we find that "These colonial writers and pamphleteers hark back to two powerful groups of British thinkers: the group which had written to justify the doctrines of the Puritan commonwealth and the group which had justified the Whig revolution of 1688.[88]

To expand upon this concept further, in the preamble of the Declaration of Independence it is written, "The true remedy of force without authority is to oppose force to it." This concept was expatriated in John Locke's *Two Treatises of Government*. It was Locke's view, and that of many of his American disciples, "that the supreme function of the state is to protect life, liberty, and property, to which every man is entitled."[89]

Even the less educated and more radical elements of society were aware of our ancestral roots in previous English society. During the passage of the Stamp Act Resolves by the Virginia House of Burgesses in 1765, the youthful and impetuous Patrick Henry had declared that "in former times Tarquin and Julius had their Brutus, Charles had his Cromwell, and he did not doubt but some good American would stand up in favor of his country."[90] Popular history has it that the statement was, "That Caesar had his Brutus, Charles I his Cromwell, and George II might do well to learn by their lesson." In either case the references are clear. Tarquin the Proud was Rome's last king, whose reign was ended by the efforts of Lucius Iunius Brutus. Caesar

---

[88] *Nevins and Commager*, 68.
[89] Ibid, 68.
[90] Middlekauff, *The Glorious Cause*, 81.

of course was assassinated by Marcus Junius Brutus and his fellow conspirators. We are well aware also of the fate of Charles Stuart at the hands of Cromwell and his New Model Army. It is therefore apparent from whence many of our founding fathers gathered their thoughts in regard to independence.

Further evidence of the American mindset in regard to Roman history can be found in the actions of army officers when the Revolutionary War was nearing its successful conclusion. Henry Knox, Washington's Chief of Artillery, had spearheaded the formation of a fraternal order of these veteran army officers to be named the society of Cincinnati. The obvious reference here is to the fifth century B.C. Roman hero Lucius Quinctius Cincinnatus, who was summoned from his plow to save Rome from its ancient enemies, the Volscians and the Aequians. Twice elected as dictator, twice Cincinnatus would relinquish his powers to return to his four-acre farm. The first president of this organization was none other than the American Cincinnatus, George Washington, elected to this post by his fellow officers on June 19, 1783.

Further references and comparisons to the Roman hero would continue. In December of 1783, Washington was to pass through Philadelphia on his way home to Mount Vernon. Before his arrival, "the Pennsylvania Assembly had ordered construction of a triumphal wooden arch in the classical style, suspended in the center was an enormous transparency of Cincinnatus, returning to his plow, his brow crowned with laurels."[91] Much of this continued reference to Roman history was probably due to the educational format of the time. The typical colonial curriculum in eighteenth century America consisted of Latin, Greek, Hebrew, Grecian and Roman histories and antiquities, reading, arithmetic-vulgar, decimals and duodecimal, geometry, planometry, trigonometry, surveying, gauging, Italian bookkeeping, and navigation.[92] Little wonder that most colonial Americans were familiar with and able to make comparisons to

---

[91] Chernow, *Washington*, 453-454.
[92] Time-Life, *The Revolutionaries*, 183.

Cincinnatus.

The very foundations of our own government as established in 1787 display a heavy reverence for and reference to Roman and English forms of government. Prior to the adoption of the U.S. Constitution, Alexander Hamilton, John Jay, and James Madison began writing a series of political treatises known as the Federalist. The purpose behind their collective writings was to portray the proposed Constitution as being both coherent and Republican in form, and to encourage popular support for it and ratification of it. The pen name chosen by Hamilton was "Publius," a reference to Publius Valerius, surnamed Publicola, which translates as "friend of the people." Publius had served as co-consul with Lucius Iunius Brutus, the man regarded as being the architect of Roman liberty. Publius had been regarded as a champion of popular liberties during the formative years of the Roman Republic.

To the reader of the Federalist, there are throughout its pages innumerable references to prior attempts at republican government, to include references to the Amphictyonic Councils of Greece, the Republics of Genoa and Venice, as well as the Lycian and Achean leagues. However, most of the historical references in this compilation of arguments in favor of the Constitution came from English and Roman history. Within the pages of the Federalist we find reference to a virtual who's who of Roman and English history, to include James II, Charles II, Cromwell, Brutus, Shakespeare, Sir William Temple, Caesar, and Blackstone, to name but a few. It should come as little wonder that when the Constitution was ratified in 1787 that within its foundations were a senate similar to that of Rome, and provisions for a separation and balance of powers between the Executive, Judicial and Legislative branches of government arrived at through the historical lessons of England's Parliament and Rome's Consular government.

As had been the case with Rome and then England, the firm foundations upon which the American Republic were to be built were its agricultural roots and military systems anchored upon this agricultural populace. The armies of Rome, which had for centuries ventured forth to combat its enemies on the Italian Peninsula and later throughout the Mediterranean world, were composed not of mercenaries or professional soldiers, but rather of farmers. Prior to the military reform of Gauis Marius in the first century B.C., service in the armies was restricted to land-owning Roman males. This may help explain why Roman troops were so resilient in battle, because they were not fighting for pay or for an idea; they were fighting for their homes.

Roman military discipline called for a citizen army wherein all able-bodied males between 17-60 were required to serve. The discipline of the Roman soldier and his legions was outstanding; he himself was physically tough and capable of rapid marches under a combat load of seventy to eighty pounds. Because he was neither a mercenary nor a full-time professional soldier, it cost Rome far less to fight a war during the years of the Republic, and Rome could count on a military manpower reservoir of about 750,000 men out of a total population of just under four million. It is interesting to note that prior to the creation of Rome's army of agrarian soldiers, that in the year 390 B.C., Rome itself was sacked by the Gauls who had migrated into the Po Valley. Rome would not be sacked again until the fifth century A.D., and when it was, there was no Roman army of citizen soldiers, and its agricultural base had been in a steady state of decline for nearly two centuries.

England had experienced a similar fate. During the years of Roman occupation, agriculture had never really thrived, and no native army comprised of land-owning farmers ever took shape. For several centuries, England was ripe for conquest to anyone who wanted to conquer it, to include the Danes, Saxons, Normans and even the Dutch armies of William of Orange during the Glorious Revolution. It was not until a sufficient agricultural base had been established on the island and a new class of free landowners had taken root before English armies had proven predominant during the years of John Churchill. Once these two facets of society had combined, England had set about to become Rome's successor as a great empire.

The roots of the American Republic were the same. As an English colony, industry had been discouraged in the colonies and agriculture encouraged. Although agricultural methods were initially lacking, land was in abundance. It was also cheap. The soil was good, the climate generally salubrious, and hard work and thrift provided for ample reward. When the ships under the command of Christopher Newport had first landed at Jamestown in May of 1607, there were on board a total of 144 men and boys.[93] Initially, growth was slow. But once American agriculture had taken root, population growth was stupendous. In the year 1760, the population of British North America was 1.6 million. Four years after the Declaration of Independence it has risen by an astounding 42 percent, to 2.8 million. Of this population, 90 percent of the people were involved in agriculture.

From this agricultural society came the army and navy that won for America its independence. It is true that during the previous colonial wars that Americans had served with British forces, although always on an inferior basis. The lowest ranking of British officers always held seniority over the highest ranking colonial officers, a situation that existed until the empire-building days of William Pitt the Elder. However, even prior to the outbreak of hostilities at Lexington and Concord in the spring of 1775, Americans had begun to form into militia units, the minutemen for example.

In England there had existed trained bands, the country militia of which Oliver Cromwell had been a part. These trained bands were the basis for the New Model Army that had carried the standards of Parliament into battle during the English Civil War. The companies of minutemen scattered throughout New England would be the embryo for the Continental Army, America's New Model Army of the Revolutionary War. In a way, George Washington would prove to be our Oliver Cromwell – without the crimes.

In the aftermath of Lexington and Concord, and of Bunker Hill, several thousand New England militia laid siege to Boston, Massachusetts. On June 14, 1775, the Continental Congress provided for the establishment of a New Continental Army by the simple act of

---

[93] R.C. Simmons, *The American Colonies*, 12.

"adopting" this New England army. Here we find the official birth date of the United States Army of today. This new Continental Army would suffer a fate similar to that of the Citizen Army of Rome. Failure would arrive more frequently than success, and that failure was often disastrous. However, the long-term results would not be the same, nor would the growth process. During the early years of the Roman Republic, Rome's armies often found themselves surrounded, and on the verge of annihilation. After the first fall of Rome to the Gauls in 386 B.C., Rome was forced to pay a huge indemnity to the invaders. Fortunately for them, Rome's first savior, Marcus Furius Camillus, was able to gather together a new army and drive the invaders from Roman soil.

Soon after America's Declaration of Independence, during the New York-New Jersey campaign of 1776, Washington and his general staff made a series of mistakes which could have led to the end of the Revolution almost before it had begun. In a contest between the amateur soldiers of America and the British professionals, "the amateurs were soon taught a lesson by the professionals, but it was a lesson easier than it should have been. The American officers in general, and Washington in particular, made a series of mistakes that could have ended the Revolution less than two months after the Declaration of Independence, had the British taken full advantage of the errors."[94] In an attempt to defend Brooklyn Heights on Long Island, as well as New York on Manhattan Island, Washington divided his army. The Howe brothers, commanding the British army and navy during this campaign, recognized an obvious opportunity. On August 22, 1776, Lord Howe shifted the bulk of his forces to Long Island. Further realizing that the left flank of the American defenses were not properly secured, he launched an early morning attack in that vicinity on August 27th. The result was an overwhelming British success. Still not recognizing the danger to his divided army, Washington attempted to reinforce an already hopeless position. In the end, this attempt to salvage Long Island would be muted. As

---

[94] Dupuy, *Military Heritage of America*, 86.

British strength on the Island continued to grow, it became obvious to Washington that the only maneuver that could save American arms would be to evacuate his forces from the Island. On the night of August 29-30, Washington and his beaten army carried out this planned retreat, Washington himself being the last man to step into the last boat leaving Long Island. If Lord Howe had caught notice of this operation, he could have easily routed Washington's retreating forces and America would have been retained as a British colony.

Further defeats and failures were to plague American efforts in the concluding stages of the New York Campaign. Having secured Long Island, British forces attacked Manhattan Island from across the East River on September 15, 1776. In the ensuing attack on American forces at Kips Bay, the American forces broke ranks and fled. The British would attack again the next day, this time at the Battle of Harlem Heights. American troops were again driven from the battlefield by the British Army at the Battle of White Plains. Finally, in November of that fateful year, Fort Washington on Northern Manhattan, which overlooked the Hudson River, fell into British hands. With its capture, 2,800 American soldiers and many of the supplies needed to conduct the war were lost to the British. With repeated defeats and near disasters behind them, the American army was forced to retreat southward, with General George Washington leading half the army and General Charles Lee covering the retreat with the other half.

The American Revolution, which had started so auspiciously with the battles at Lexington and Concord, and which had continued with the American success at Boston, was now near collapse. However, just as the Roman farmer-soldiers had displayed such resilience time and time again, American farmer-soldiers were to show themselves capable of equal resilience. With the Continental Army down to a skeleton force of only 2,400 men, Washington and his tiny group of soldiers, now almost completely written off as finished by the British Howe brothers, pulled off a miracle. On Christmas night in 1776, this insignificant little band of soldiers crossed the freezing waters of the Delaware River and attacked a Hessian garrison at Trenton, New Jersey. The American victory at Trenton was as complete as the

American defeat at Kips Bay, but this time the Hessians bore the brunt of the defeat. Much of the credit for this victory should go to Colonel John Glover and his group of Marblehead fishermen, who had manned the boats that ferried the Continental troops across the Delaware. Glover and these same men had saved the Continental troops during the retreat from Brooklyn Heights as well.

Ironic that during that momentous year this group would, in the first instance save the army from utter defeat, and in the second instance provide the means of transport for their utter salvation and ultimate victory. The miracle at Trenton was repeated shortly thereafter with Washington and his men once more crossing the Delaware River to defeat a British force at Princeton. This would happen on January 3 of a new year, 1777.

The initiation of American soldiers during the War would tend to follow the pattern of 1776. Each year, the American forces would suffer numerous defeats and setbacks, only to redeem themselves through Herculean efforts and one or two singular decisive victories. In 1779, the Continental Army under Washington would suffer repeated defeats: at Brandywine Creek, Paoli, and at Germantown. The City of Philadelphia, then home to the Continental Congress, was lost to the British on September 26, 1777. These losses were more than offset by the American victory at Saratoga, which ended British plans to sever New England from the rest of the colonies and would assist America in gaining an alliance to and assistance from France.

The conclusion of the year 1777 would see the remainder of the Continental Army seeking refuge at Valley Forge, in the heart of Pennsylvania's farm country. What should have been a safe haven to the ragtag remnants of America's infant army instead turned into immeasurable hardships and ordeals. The camp at Valley Forge was basically an amalgamation of about two thousand small cabins with dirt floors, fourteen by sixteen feet in dimension and built of whatever materials the soldiers could acquire from the surrounding countryside.

*Examples of the American soldier during the Revolutionary War. Often times the American soldier wore his own clothing and provided his own weapons, much the same as the Roman soldier of the early republic.*

Washington himself agreed to pay twelve dollars to whichever squad of men could complete the first cabin, with a one hundred dollar bounty going to the soul who could devise a method to roof these structures without consuming a great deal of the much-needed wood.

Into these cabins, built along paralleled avenues, would settle what remained of the dilapidated army. Along with them would settle cold, starvation, filth and a host of diseases brought about by these conditions, coupled with a weakened physical state caused by malnutrition. The only circumstances worse than the conditions of the camp were the conditions of the hospitals. At any given time during the winter of 1777-1778, nearly one-third of the army was unfit for duty. Amputations as a result of frostbite were common, as were cases of typhus, typhoid fever and pneumonia. On his inspection of the hospital facilities at Valley Forge, Dr. Benjamin Rush had commented that he found the men there "shivering with cold upon the floors without a blanket to cover them, calling for fire, for water, for suitable food and for medicines, – and calling in vain."[95] In an age where armies traditionally suffered more casualties from disease than from battle, more than two thousand men perished at Valley Forge before the arrival of spring in 1777.

Even more unfortunate than these losses at Valley Forge were the reasons behind it. Located in the heart of farm country, it should have been easy for Washington to feed his army. However, by this point in the war, Continental currency had depreciated to the point of being nearly worthless. The British pound sterling however, was quite solid. Therefore, the patriotic fervor so prevalent after Lexington and Concord now began to disappear. The farmers of Pennsylvania sold their produce not to the hungry Continentals shivering at Valley Forge, but by the wagonloads to the British army at their comfortable quarters in Philadelphia. Washington himself would write, "Is it the paltry consideration of a little dirty pelf to individuals to be placed in competition with the essential rights and liberties of the present

---

[95] *Washington, A Life*, 327.

generation and of millions yet unborn?"[96] Unfortunately the answer to Washington's question is, "yes."

The winter spent at Valley Forge did yield to American arms one very important gain. During that crucial winter, the German volunteer Baron Augustus H. F. von Steuben arrived on the scene to train America's new recruits in the essentials of discipline and to install in them the tactical skills needed to stand up to British infantry assaults. Much as Marcus Furius Camillus had imbued Roman arms with the necessary tactical skills of his day. Having organized the Roman farmers into a new tactical unit, the legion, now von Steuben would endow American soldiers with the same gifts. Handicapped initially by an inability to speak the English language fluently, and having to deal also with an officer corps that initially resented what they regarded to be his interference, von Steuben overcame these difficulties by studying the American soldier both collectively and individually, and making improvements gradually. Given to habits of profanity, he both cursed and cajoled the Continental soldiers until they became more comfortable with and aware of the need for discipline. As Inspector General of the Continental Army, von Steuben appointed other qualified officers to serve as inspectors in each regiment and brigade. He then selected one hundred and twenty men to serve as the Commander in Chief's bodyguards, drilling them until such time as they could become a functional cadre to train other units within the army. By the spring of 1777, the army that left Valley Forge was much more capable than that which had entered it.

Evidence of von Steuben's success in training the Continentals to better conduct themselves in battle became readily apparent. In June of 1778, Washington and his newly trained army attacked British regulars at Monmouth in New Jersey. After being mishandled by the inept General Charles Lee, Washington personally rallied the Continental troops and turned a sure defeat into an American victory. During this battle, the Continental Army displayed a new confidence in itself and its commander, and henceforth proved itself able to

---

[96] Ibid, 329.

withstand British volleys and bayonet charges. In the aftermath of Monmouth, the British General Sir Henry Clinton marched his troops back to New York City, the location from which they had driven the Americans in 1776. Washington himself was to write, "After two years of maneuvering and undergoing the strangest vicissitudes that perhaps ever attended any one contest since the creation, both armies are brought back to the very point they set out from, and that which was the offending army in the beginning, is now reduced to the use of spade and pickaxe for defense."[97] As had happened in the early stages of the war in regard to operations in New England, such was now to be the case of operations in the middle colonies, with Clinton content to remain in New York City while the war moved south for its culmination campaigns.

George Washington and the bulk of the Continental Army would spend much of the next three years containing Clinton in New York. With the fortunes of war going against the American effort in the South, Washington appointed his able associate General Nathaniel Greene to take control of affairs in the southern theatre of operations. His actions and the sequence of events would mirror the efforts and results of Washington during the early years of the war. Opposing Nathaniel Greene in the southern theatre was British General Lord Charles Cornwallis.

British strategy in the southern states was based upon the fact that this region contained a very high percentage of loyalists. Therefore, having failed in their efforts to separate New England from the other colonies, and also having failed to subjugate the central colonies, General Clinton now decided to separate the three southernmost colonies from the other ten. Initially, this effort would meet with much success. In the spring of 1780, after a two-month siege, Charleston, South Carolina fell to a British force. The American garrison of 5,000 troops under the command of Benjamin Lincoln was forced to surrender.

The loss of Charleston was a serious setback to the American cause

---

[97] Dupuy, *Military Heritage of America*, 100.

of liberty. Shortly thereafter, in August 1789, Lord Cornwallis met the hero of Saratoga, General Horatio Gates, at Camden, South Carolina. This time Gates did not have the assistance of the capable Benedict Arnold to help him, and the results were telling. Gates displaced his army in such fashion that the militia ran away at the outset of the battle. The regulars stood their ground, but were outnumbered and outflanked and forced to leave the field to the enemy. Gates himself had fled with the militia, most of whom had never even fired a shot. Four days later, General Gates was 200 miles away, having done, in the words of Alexander Hamilton, "admirable credit to the activity of a man at his time of life."[98] With Gates' defeat at Camden, American resistance in the south largely collapsed, with only the partisan efforts of the "Swamp Fox," Francis Marion and the "Gamecock," Thomas Sumpter to occupy the attentions of British forces there.

Onto this scene would arrive Nathaniel Greene, the unsung hero of Valley Forge, whose efforts during that terrible winter as Commissary General had kept the Continental Army from literally starving to death. Washington would send several excellent junior officers with Greene, who was also greeted by the return to service of Daniel Morgan, whose unit of sharpshooters had proven so valuable during the Saratoga Campaign. Greene himself assumed command of his little army of 1,500 men on December 2, 1780. He was to spend the initial months of his command building up his army to number 2,000 men. Not being restricted by the winter conditions of the north, Greene divided his army, sending Morgan westward from Charlotte with 1,000 men, with Greene himself taking the other thousand southeast to Cheraw, South Carolina. Cornwallis was now forced to divide his own forces, for if he concentrated on either Greene or Morgan, the other would have free reign of the countryside. What happened next was an interesting series of events, further displaying the parallels of American, British and Roman history. In January of 1781, Daniel Morgan engaged a like sized British force at the Battle of Cowpens. It seems that Daniel Morgan was a man of some education,

---

[98] *Life Magazine*, July 1950, 56.

for the displacement of his troops, and the outcome of the battle, bear a striking resemblance to the victory in 216 B.C. of Hannibal Barca over the Romans at Cannae. Morgan, recognizing the inherent weakness of militia and their tendency to flee from the British, organized his line of battle such that the militia was situated in the center of his line, with a river to his rear so that the militia could not escape. In reserve were the regulars commanded by Morgan himself.

As the battle began, all went according to plan. Morgan had told his militia that they only needed to fire two volleys and then they could retreat. This they did, fleeing to the rear where they found themselves hemmed in by the river. While Morgan held off British forces with the well-disciplined regulars, the militia were re-formed by their commander, Pickens, and led back into battle, attacking on the left of the British line. At the same time, Morgan's reserves, consisting of Washington's dragoons, attacked the British line on the right. A double envelopement had been achieved. The British force of Sir Banastre Tarleton was utterly destroyed. Although nowhere near as complex, and not involving anywhere near the number of troops as Cannae, the result of this victory was as decisive. Morgan was now able to rejoin Nathaniel Greene, who would begin a campaign that would be destitute of tactical success, without a single victory to show for his efforts. However, it would be an overwhelming strategic success, in that it would force Cornwallis to eventually retire to the site of his eventual destruction, Yorktown, Virginia.

Initially Greene would avoid battle with Cornwallis, retreating north into southern Virginia, but Cornwallis would pursue. On the other hand, Cornwallis was well aware of his reliance upon supply from the sea. Eventually, he broke off the chase, retiring towards Hillsborough. Greene then followed. On March 15, 1781, Cornwallis turned on his pursuers, defeating them at Guilford Courthouse. One month later, Greene and his army were again defeated at Hobkirks Hill, near the site of the American defeat at Camden in 1780. Ironically, with each victory the British now became weaker and the Americans stronger. Cornwallis himself, realizing he had no hope of controlling the Carolina's, marched north into Virginia. Greene would persist in his efforts to destroy the remnants of British forces south of Virginia. Like Washington, Greene would continue to suffer tactical losses, such as at Eutaw Springs on September 8, 1781, while at the same time accomplishing his strategic objectives of destroying British forces in his theatre of operations.

The stage was now set for the final scene of America's war for independence. After months of inconclusive maneuvering around Virginia, Cornwallis and the remainder of the British Army retreated to Yorktown, on the tip of the Virginia Peninsula. With English naval power supreme throughout the globe, this should have been a safe haven. Nevertheless, weather and human error would now combine to favor the American cause. Recognizing an opportunity to strike a heavy blow to the British, Washington left a covering force in New York to contain Clinton and marched south with his remaining troops. Clinton still had 17,000 troops at his disposal, while the covering force left by Washington was a mere 2,000 men. Why Clinton did not act against them is unknown. When he eventually recognized what had transpired, it was too late. In September of 1781, a French fleet defeated an English squadron under Admiral Thomas Graves at the Battle of Capes, ensuring that Cornwallis could neither retreat nor receive reinforcements by sea. After his defeat, Graves sailed north for New York, thus sealing Cornwallis' fate. The victorious French fleet was then used to transport Washington's army from Baltimore and Annapolis, to Williamsburg in Virginia. Within weeks, 9,500 Continental troops and another 7,800 French army regulars had concentrated near Yorktown to lay siege to Cornwallis and his 8,000 British troops. With the assistance of French Gribeauval field guns, the British defenses at Yorktown were reduced in a two-month siege, lasting through September and October of 1781. With no hope of relief or escape, Cornwallis was forced into terms of unconditional surrender on October 19, 1781. In some ways, this date could be considered as the date of America's birth, as with this defeat hostilities between the Americans and the British virtually ceased. Washington would march back to New York to reinvest the forces of Clinton, leaving the affairs of war to be settled by the negotiating parties of the Continental Congress and the government of Lord North. In the southern colonies, Nathaniel Greene continued to mop up the remnants of the British forces still there, but there were to be no major engagements before the November 1782 Treaty of Paris, by which Britain recognized American independence.

The Treaty of Paris itself was interesting in that whereas it ended hostilities between Britain and her former colony, these conditions were not to take effect until Britain had concluded hostilities against France and Spain in the West Indies. Not until April of 1783 was the Treaty of Paris ratified by Congress. Ironically, at that time the issue of utmost importance to them was to disband the Continental Army, which had won for them their independence. Their haste was telling, as the British forces in New York, now under the command of Sir Guy Carleton, were not to depart until the end of November 1783, a year after the treaty had been agreed upon in Paris. Much as the Roman Senate had always feared Roman armies, the Continental Congress was to establish a pattern of hasty demobilization after the war, which it continued thereafter.

By December 5, 1783, the last transports containing British troops departed from New York. This same day, Washington took leave of those officers who had remained with the Continental Army until the very end. Among these officers were only three Major Generals, Henry Knox, von Steuben, and McDougall, plus one brigadier. The location of Washington's departure from the army was Fraunces Tavern in New York City, the scene somewhat allegorical, no doubt cultivating the image of an American Cincinnatus. This should have come as no surprise from a man who had often during the war used quotes from Shakespearean plays such as Julius Caesar, Anthony and Cleopatra and Henry V. During the frightful winter at Valley Forge, Joseph Addison's play Cato, had been viewed by the future president, a play that was thereafter associated with Washington as the stereotypical stoic Roman. After taking leave of his remaining officers, Washington traveled to Philadelphia, where he formally tendered his resignation to the Congress at noon on the 23rd of December.

The completion of war and the guarantee of American independence were not followed by political harmony. Before the war had ended, in March of 1781, the thirteen states had entered into a loose political union with the signing of the Articles of Confederation. The historian Allan Nevins refers to this confederation as a "league of friendship," as opposed to a form of central government. This was no doubt due to Article III of the document, which stated, "the said states hereby severally enter into a firm league of friendship with each other." However, this new confederation and the articles governing it had several serious drawbacks. Under the articles, Congress could not levy taxes, enlist troops, enforce treaties, or generate a sufficient level of revenue so as to pay America's war debt, estimated at 36,500,375 dollars.[99] There were serious disagreements ranging from state borders to the issuance of currency. With thirteen states all distributing different currencies, commerce between the states was difficult, as was commerce within the states. With many of the state legislatures eventually passing measures, that allowed for the printing of paper currency or rag money, the value of these various currencies fell, sometimes dramatically. This made it harder for the people, ninety percent of whom were farmers, to pay mortgages and taxes. In Massachusetts the distraining of land and foreclosures of farms actually led to violence. In 1786, a veteran of Bunker Hill named Daniel Shays led an uprising or rebellion against these foreclosures. Although the rebellion was contained, it became obvious that a more centralized federal government was necessary.

This idea of and need for a stronger form of central government had been especially important to the Continental Army during the war. Always in arrears of their pay and generally without adequate provisions, there had been numerous mutinies in the army throughout the war. In January 1783, with rumors of mass resignations in the air within the officer corps, a three-man delegation of Continental officers traveled to Philadelphia to present Congress with a list of grievances. This delegation of officers met with two men

---

[99] Time-Life, *The Revolutionaries*, 183.

who were to play a predominant role in the formation of a new government: James Madison and Alexander Hamilton. Hamilton was familiar with the hardships suffered by the men in the army, as he himself had served as an aide to Washington during the war. He was entirely familiar with the difficulties of collecting money from the states so as to support the army's needs. Even at this early date, Hamilton saw the possibilities of using the army's discontent to stir Congress from its perpetual state of inaction and as a means of eventually expanding federal powers.

Although Alexander Hamilton is closely associated with the Federalist Papers, this effort towards a strong form of central government and the adoption of a new constitution was not his first. In September of 1780, Hamilton had written a seventeen-page exposition on the need for a constitutional convention. Never one to sheath his own pen, in the seven years prior to the Constitutional Convention, he had written numerous letters, public and private on the subject. He even published a series of newspaper articles entitles, "The Continentalist," in which he urged for a new government to be suited not to "the narrow colonial sphere in which we have been accustomed to move," but rather "that enlarged kind suited to the government of an independent nation."[100]

Commerce would be the cause for this eventual convention in 1787. In 1785, Maryland and Virginia became engaged in a quarrel in regard to navigation of the Potomac River. That spring they sent delegates to Mount Vernon to discuss and debate their opposing positions. Out of this debate arose the concept of inviting neighboring states to become involved in this dispute, with the result being an enlarged commission that would meet in September of 1786 at Annapolis, Maryland. The outcome of this Annapolis commission was a recommendation to Congress for all thirteen states to send delegates to Philadelphia to discuss the future trade and commerce of the United States. This report from Annapolis to Congress was written by none other than Alexander Hamilton.

---

[100] Drincker, -Bowen, *Miracle at Philadelphia*, 8.

In response to the Annapolis Commission and its recommendations, Congress had in February of 1787 sanctioned the Philadelphia Convention "for the sole and express purpose of revising the Articles of Confederation." It seems that the states were still very wary of a strong centralized government that could intrude on their authority, for when the convention finally met on Monday, May 14, 1787, the only delegates present were those from Virginia and Pennsylvania. It would take another eleven days before enough delegates were in attendance to represent a quorum of seven states. Of the fifty-five delegates who were to eventually participate, twenty-one had served in the army during the Revolutionary War. The years of suffering and neglect at the hands of the previously impotent Congress were to now be rectified with a new form of government that would hopefully be better equipped to deal with national difficulties in the future. Eight members of the new convention were signatories of the Declaration of Independence.

Notable by their absence were two of the Declaration's signatories, John Adams and Thomas Jefferson. Adams and Jefferson were in Europe at that time, tasked by Congress with securing foreign loans and arranging treaties of commerce. In their absence other capable minds would come to the forefront, most notably James Madison, who would in the future be regarded as the father of the American Constitution. The time involved for debates and writing of the Constitution would take from the end of May until the following September. Almost immediately after the first meeting, the delegates tacitly agreed that they would not simply revise the Articles of Confederation, but rather write a whole new constitution. They were aided in their efforts by the rules of secrecy, which kept their discussions amongst themselves and free from the influence of the press. As they had during the years prior to the Revolution, they looked to history for solutions to their problems. They studied the histories of the Amphictyonic Councils, and the Helvetic and Dutch Confederations as well. They also referred often to English history, and to the federal system, which had existed within Britain's government prior to 1763. They also referred to some of the more recent treatises of government, including John Adams' *A Defense of the Constitutions of Government of the United States of America*, published in 1787.

The result of the Constitutional Convention of 1787 was a new national machinery. During the convention, two plans of government had been put forth, the Virginia Plan, and the New Jersey Plan. These two plans were centered around arguments of proportional representation of the states in the national legislative branch. If the members of the new lower house were elected along the lines of population, than obviously the larger states such, as Virginia, Massachusetts and Pennsylvania would always have an unfair advantage over the smaller, less populated states, such as New Jersey or Georgia. For this reason, the small states wanted an equal vote in Congress; the larger states a proportional one.

There were of course other issues involved beyond those of representation in the national legislature. However, proportionalism in the legislature was a major sticking point. What was needed was a solution, and what was found was a compromise. On Monday, June 11, 1787, Roger Sherman of Connecticut proposed "that the proportion of suffrage in the first branch should be according to the respective numbers of free inhabitants, and that in the second branch, or Senate, each state should have one vote and no more." While this proposal was initially rejected, it was to be the foundation of what came to be known as The Great Compromise, The Connecticut Compromise, or the Sherman Compromise.

When the framing of the Constitution was completed that September, there were many novel concepts within its framework. There were provisions for a bicameral legislature, as well as an executive and judicial branch. There were provisions for a system of checks and balances so that no one branch could reign supreme over the other two. Provisions were set forth to create a location for the seat of government, to be referred to as the "Ten Miles Square." Another important compromise during the convention arose over the issue of slavery. With southern states dependent upon slavery economically, and with many northern delegates violently opposed to the continuation of it, a provision was contained in the draft, which would allow for the importation of slaves until the year 1808, after which time it was to be disallowed. On the whole, the United States Constitution is a remarkable work, one that probably could not be duplicated in our time due to the rampant factionalism and fact of party known to our modern society. Nicholas Gilman, delegate from New Hampshire had written on September 18, 1787, "It was done by compromise, yet not withstanding its imperfections on the adoption of it depends (in my feeble judgement) whether or not we shall become a respectable nation, or a people torn to pieces by intestine commotions, and rendered contemptible for ages."[101]

On Monday, September 17, 1787, delegates from twelve states gathered together during the last meeting of the Constitutional Convention to sign this new document. Of the forty delegates present, only three refused to sign. Many, including Franklin and Hamilton, alluded to the fact that even though there were parts of this new document of government with which they did not agree, they believed that the members should trust in the judgment of the body of delegates as a whole, instead of standing firm in the belief that they were themselves infallible. Franklin himself made reference to the painting on the wall behind the president of the Convention's chair, which depicted half a sun. In regard to this painting Franklin stated, "I have often and often, in the course of the session, and the vicissitudes of my hopes and fears as to its issue, looked at that behind the President, without being able to tell whether it was rising or setting; but now, at length, I have the happiness to know that it is a rising, and not a setting sun."[102]

With the document finally drafted and signed by the delegates, all that remained was the ratification by the various states. It was agreed during the convention that nine of the thirteen states would need to ratify the Constitution before it became law. The contest over ratification by the states was waged in the various state legislatures,

---

[101] Ibid, 94.
[102] Nevins and commager, *Pocket History of the U.S.*, 112.

as well as the press. The Federalist Papers of Jay, Hamilton, and Madison were of course instrumental in their arguments for ratification, to be countered by the arguments of the Anti-Federalists. Out of these arguments for and against ratification would come the genesis of America's two-party political system. Before the year 1787 had passed, three states had ratified, Delaware being the first. The following year six more would decide in favor of ratification, with New Hampshire being the ninth. Shortly thereafter, George Washington and James Madison's home state of Virginia had decided in favor of the new Constitution as well. Soon after ratification, plans were made so as to have the new form of government up and running by the following year, 1789. To fill the office of Chief Executive, there was but one obvious choice, George Washington. Therefore, on April 30, 1789, the man who had resigned his commission to Congress at the close of the Revolutionary War in 1783 now became the republic's first President.

Within short order, a very busy and successful first Congress had provided for another first as well. Sitting in New York City, the nation's first Capital, Congress rapidly established a Department of State, a Department of War, and a Department of Treasury. These departments were headed by Thomas Jefferson, Henry Knox and Alexander Hamilton, respectively. The First Congress also established a system of federal courts, with the passing of the Judiciary Act of 1789. At a time before the distractions of political parties became prevalent, the First Congress was also able to enact a Federal Bill of Rights. As further evidence of America's ties to its English past, the concept of a bill of rights had been borrowed from the English Bills of Rights of 1628 and 1689. Though different in form, and extended to include the rights of freedom of speech, of religion, of assembly, and of the press, the concept was similar and not unique to our new nation. With a firm foundation now in place, next would come the process of economic, agricultural and military growth.

# Chapter 11

¤

# THE SEEDS OF GROWTH

In the aftermath of the American Revolution and with the adoption of the Constitution, America found itself in a position for rapid expansion and growth. The basis for and process of this growth would again show striking similarities to those of Rome and England. Much as the birth and growth of Rome came at the hands of farmers who were also soldiers, this same relationship could be found in post-revolutionary America. When consulting a list of modern American presidents, most of them would be regarded as professional politicians, with a background possibly in law or political science. Many have served as governors or senators. However, within the group of the initial American presidents, many had listed their professions as "planters." Washington, while generally regarded as a soldier, had spent most of his life when not employed in war, building and expanding his estate at Mount Vernon. Thomas Jefferson also chose to regard himself as a planter, as did many of the members of the "Virginia Dynasty," that earliest group of the founding fathers who came from the "old dominion."

Whereas Washington and Jefferson had close ties to the earth in respect to their agrarian pastimes, they also maintained similar views on how their newly created society should proceed into the future. During a time when ninety percent of the population made its living off the land, both men assumed that the nation would, and should, remain agriculturally based. Equally important, both of them regarded wars with foreign nations as being unnecessary and expensive distractions that should be avoided at all cost. We find evidence of this written within the policies employed during their respective presidencies. With the new Constitution in effect and still in its infancy, the possibility of renewed war with England began to emerge during the early years of the 1790s. In response to these possible threats of war, Washington sent the very able Chief Justice John Jay to London in order to establish a new treaty to settle disputes between the governments and thus avoid war. The resulting document, Jay's Treaty, was an agreement that kept the United States out of a war it could neither win nor afford, but for which Jay and Washington would receive much criticism from an unwise public. Further evidence of Washington's views can be found within his Farewell Address of 1796, in which he remonstrated against entangling alliances and foreign wars. He would also write:

> *Our detached and distant situation invites and enables us to pursue a different course. If we remain one people, under an efficient government, the period is not far off when we may defy material injury from external annoyance; when we may take such an attitude as will cause the neutrality we may at any time resolve upon to be scrupulously respected; when belligerent nations, under the impossibility of making acquisitions upon us, will not lightly hazard the giving us provocation; when we may choose peace or war, as our interest guided by justice shall counsel.*[103]

Thomas Jefferson, while of more Anti-Federalist leanings than his fellow Virginian, Washington, was of similar views and of similar policies. The war between Britain and France, which had erupted in 1793, had long held the possibility of American involvement. First Washington, and then his successor John Adams had been able to avoid this involvement. Jefferson was to pursue a similar path. As the war between England and Napoleonic France continued, the

---

[103] Heffner, *A Documentary History of the U.S.*, 67

unintended victim turned out to be American shipping. Britain, with its overwhelming navy of more than 700 ships, determined that a very powerful weapon was at hand to destroy France by means of a naval blockade. In return, Bonaparte retaliated with his Berlin and Milan decrees, intending to deny commercial trade to his rival. British and French naval vessels were therefore ordered to seize ships attempting to trade with the enemy. Because the British and French navies controlled most of Europe and the West Indies, commerce for the Americans became nearly impossible.

To make matters worse, in order to maintain the size of its navy, The British fleet resorted to the practice of impressment. As the British tar of this period was ill-paid, ill-fed, and ill-treated, not to mention pressed into service against his will, many sailors fled at the first opportunity. The sailing ships of other nations were always a means of escape, and with the removal of a language barrier, American ships in particular were popular refuges. Therefore, the British Navy initiated the policy of stopping and searching American vessels and seizing anyone they suspected of having fled from British service. The British policy was so strictly enforced that the English refused to believe that a Britain could become a naturalized American citizen. This course of action opened up impressments to an entirely new class of seamen.

To resolve this infringement upon American ships, Thomas Jefferson convinced Congress to authorize the Embargo Act of 1806. Jefferson's immediate goal was to bring the 20,000 to 30,000 American seamen home from troubled European waters and to save America's 2,000 ships and eighty million dollars worth of commerce from capture. He also had hopes for certain long-term effects, which indicated a transition in America's mindset. Whereas he initially believed in an agrarian America, he now began to formulate ideas of a more self-sufficient state. "I trust the good sense of our country will see, that its greatest prosperity depends on a due balance between agriculture, manufacturing, and commerce, and not in this protuberant navigation which has kept us in hot water from the commencement of our government."[104] Here we find the American concept of a more commercial and industrial economy, as advocated by Jefferson's long time political rival, Alexander Hamilton.

Jefferson's Embargo Act was very detrimental to America's frail and infant economy. In New England, the shipping and commercial classes were especially hard hit, to the point that there was talk of New England seceding from the union. The South was hurt as well, as farmers became unable to sell most of their cotton and tobacco crops. With mounting opposition to the Embargo Act from the citizens of both North and South, Congress repealed the Embargo Act and replaced it in 1809 with a Non-Intercourse Act. Within this Act we find another transformation within the American mindset. Whereas our Constitution had been established with a desire toward popular government, we now find the influence of the commercial class upon government policy much the same as the commercial class had become more influential in England with the growth of the mercantile class in early Angevin England.

As the actions of foreign governments had caused a transformation in Jefferson's thought process in regard to an agrarian state, these same external forces were beginning to change the American mindset in regard to its armed forces. The founding fathers had exhibited a deep-seated fear of an entrenched military in America. Concerning civilian control of the Continental Army, John Adams once said, "We don't choose to trust you generals with too much power for too long a time."[105] Nevertheless, as the war between Britain and Revolutionary France had become more manifest in its effects on American commerce, there became a gradual change in how Americans viewed the need for a strong military. Ironically, it was during the years of the Adams Administration that a fledgling United States Army would begin to develop along more modern lines, ending the previous reliance upon state militias for national defense.

---

[104] Brodie, *Jefferson, an Intimate History*, 418.
[105] Drincker-Bowen, *Miracle at Philadelphia*, 6.

One of the principal architects of this new army was Alexander Hamilton, who was chosen to serve as Inspector General. Curiously, as war with France seemed imminent during the Adams Administration, the former president, George Washington, was selected as the individual to command the new army. Washington, although reluctant to accept this position, agreed so long as Alexander Hamilton, Henry Knox, and Charles Pinckney were commissioned as Major Generals under him. After becoming Inspector General, Hamilton set about the task of establishing this new army with his usual zeal. Everything from manuals of drill to design of uniforms came within his gaze. He, along with Secretary of War, Patrick McHenry, was responsible for submitting to Congress "a Bill for Establishing a Military Academy." Hamilton would even be largely responsible for choosing the site of its eventual location, West Point, New York.

The United States Navy would also begin its process of gestation. It should come as no surprise that a new nation, largely of English descent, with two great oceans bordering it, initially the Atlantic and eventually the Pacific, would become a maritime power. In the aftermath of the American Revolution, the high financial cost of the war had forced the sale of the Continental Navy, with the Alliance being the last ship sold, in August of 1785. Within weeks of this sale, two American merchant ships in the Mediterranean were seized by the Barbary corsairs. Coupled with the advent of British and French intrusions against American commerce in the early 1790s, it became obvious that the new nation would in fact be required to maintain a naval presence throughout the world. The end result was that on March 27, 1794, Congress authorized the construction of six frigates that were to become the nucleus of a new navy. It is an interesting contradiction that while fearing a large army, John Adams was to write that, "a navy is our natural and only defense."[106]

One of these six frigates would become involved in an incident that would in some ways lead to an eventual return to hostilities with

---

[106] Naval Historical Foundation, *U.S. Navy, A Complete History*, 10.

Great Britain. On June 23, 1807, the frigate Chesapeake was intercepted by the British warship Leopard. The Leopard's captain demanded the right to search the Chesapeake for British deserters. The American captain refused this request. In response, the Leopard fired three broadsides into the unprepared Chesapeake, killing three American sailors and wounding eighteen others. The Chesapeake, her decks covered in blood, struck her colors. Four sailors – one British deserter and three Americans, were taken away; one to be hanged and the other three forced to serve in the British Navy. The American public was outraged.

The atrocities against American shipping by the corsairs and against the Chesapeake by the British were to be avenged, while at the same time giving to America some of her first national heroes. Without a sufficient navy in the Mediterranean to protect its commerce, America had for years been forced to pay protection money to the Pasha of Tripoli in order to guarantee the safety of American commerce. In 1801, the Tripolitans upped the ante, declaring for higher protection rates. Thomas Jefferson took action by sending a small American naval squadron to the area. In 1803, the new American naval commander in the Mediterranean, Commodore Edward Preble, initiated a new policy, to hunt down these Tripolitans or Barbary corsairs. In 1804, the young Lieutenant Stephen Decateur boldly sailed into Tripoli harbor to destroy the American frigate Philadelphia which had run aground and been captured by the Tripolitans. One year later, Commodore John Rodgers sailed the U.S.S. Constitution into Tunis and forced the Bey of Tunis to make peace with the U.S., thereby ending payment of tribute to the Tunisians.

With war against England almost inevitable, the youthful U.S. Navy was forced to suspend its operations against the Tripolitan corsairs. However, in 1815, now Commodore Stephen Decateur would return to the Mediterranean with a fleet of ten American warships. He would show the corsairs little if any mercy. Sailing directly into Algiers Harbor, at cannon mouth, he forced the Algerians to release any and all Americans they held captive. He ended all further payments of U.S. tribute, and forced guarantees against further acts of piracy against American vessels. Decateur also forced similar guarantees from the corsairs of Tunis and Tripoli. The former roles of predator and prey were irrevocably reversed.

Further evidence of the importance and influence of naval affairs on America's future can be found in the roots of the War of 1812. The American declaration of war against Great Britain on June 19, 1812, was ostensibly to defend the doctrine of "freedom of the seas." Being the decidedly weaker of the two nations, this war declaration exhibits another change in the American pattern of thought. Gone already were the precepts of Washington's Farewell Address and of the efforts of both John Adams and Thomas Jefferson to keep America out of war. There was something else that was beginning to make itself obvious to the observer of American thought. This was the idea of expansion. Immediately after the June war declaration, America began the planning of a three-pronged invasion of Canada, an invasion that collapsed even before it began due to events elsewhere. But the very idea of seizing Canada from Britain is an indicator of what was on the American mind.

As to the War of 1812 itself, it would generally be a muddled affair with both sides gaining victories and suffering defeats intermittently. Within months of the opening of hostilities, British armies captured Fort Dearborn (present day Chicago) and Detroit. The American commander at Detroit, with a larger army than his British counterpart, surrendered without firing a shot. As a further indication of American military incompetence, in October of 1812 an American expedition into Canada at Queenston was defeated when American militia refused to cross the Niagara River to assist the American regular troops who were pinned down on the other side. In this one-sided battle, the Americans lost more than one thousand troops by death or capture as opposed to the loss of fourteen British troops killed.

At sea, the six frigates of the early navy made their presence known. In August 1812, the U.S.S. Constitution under the command of Captain Isaac Hull defeated the warship H.M.S. Guerriere. In

October of that same year, the U.S.S. Wasp smashed the similarly sized Frolic off the Virginia coast. In that same month, Captain Stephen Decateur aboard the U.S.S. United States defeated the British man-of-war Macedonian, which was seized as a prize, re-commissioned, and sent back to war to do combat against her former flag. In December 1812, the U.S. Navy would close out its year of success when the U.S.S. Constitution defeated the British frigate Java off the coast of Brazil. By years end, American sailors and ships had proven that in any ship-for-ship contest, the American ship design was better than that of the British, and the American seamanship and gunnery capability were superior as well.

The year 1813 brought better fortune to American ground forces. During this year we find the beginnings of a close level of army-navy cooperation that would reap huge benefits for American arms in the two centuries to come. In September of 1813, an American naval squadron under the command of Oliver H. Perry met and defeated a squadron of British ships on Lake Erie. When his own ship, the Lawrence, was lost during the battle, Perry transferred to another by rowboat while under fire. Eventually, his squadron was able to break the British line of battle. By late afternoon, all of the British vessels had struck their colors. Reporting his actions to the land commander and future president William Henry Harrison, Perry began his message, "We have met the enemy and they are ours." Perry's victory at Lake Erie marked a turning point in the fortunes of war for the American forces engaged in operations around the Great Lakes.

With Perry having gained control of Lake Erie, William Henry Harrison was now set to launch an attack to retake the fallen Detroit. With a force of 7,000 troops, to be transported across the lake by Perry's ships, Harrison initiated his assault. On September 29, 1813, British forces withdrew from Detroit with the approach of this much larger American force. Harrison did not relent, choosing to pursue the British and their Indian allies instead of simply acting as an occupation force. On October 5, Harrison met his foe at the Battle of Thames. Harrison himself led the American infantry assault, while his cavalry force charged the right end of the British line. The result was an overwhelming American victory. During this battle, the great Shawnee war chief Tecumseh was killed, ending the dream of an Indian confederacy and removing the Indians from the war as an ally of Britain.

The ebb and flow of the War of 1812 was to continue throughout 1813-1814. At sea, the tiny American navy that had started the war with but 14 serviceable vessels continued its fight against the supreme Royal Navy, which possessed 1,048 seaworthy vessels. In February of 1813, the U.S.S. Hornet defeated the H.M.S. Peacock along the Brazilian coast. In September of 1813, the U.S.S. Enterprise defeated the H.M.S. Boxer off the coast of New England. Conversely, the ill-fated U.S.S. Chesapeake was less fortunate. In June of 1813, the Chesapeake was challenged by the H.M.S. Shannon, reputed to be the most battle-effective ship in the Royal Navy. Within minutes of the beginning of this action, the Shannon had raked the decks of the Chesapeake with such devastating fire that nearly one-third of its crew were killed. The Chesapeake's captain, James Lawrence, himself mortally wounded, implored his remaining crew, "Don't give up the ship." His pleas were to no avail. Chesapeake was captured, taken to Halifax as a prize of war, and used by the Royal Navy for many years to come.

In 1814, two new forces would make their way onto the stage of war. One would be large numbers of British regulars freed up from Europe with Napoleon's defeat in Spain. The other would be Andrew Jackson, initially a major general of militia, later a major general in the regular army. As for the British regulars, they were employed in operations against Washington, D.C. and Baltimore. In August 1814, in a near repeat of the disastrous American defeats of 1812, a British army under General Robert Ross defeated an American army at Bladensburg, Maryland. Furthermore, in reminiscence of the disgraceful events at Detroit and Queenston, the American militia under William Winder ran away, leaving the defense of the nation's capital to a miniscule force of 400 sailors and marines. Against a force of nearly 5,400 British regulars fresh from combat against the armies of Napoleon, the outcome was never in doubt. On August 24-25, the

British occupied Washington, D.C., forcing President James Madison to flee, and burning several government buildings, including the White House. This was done in retaliation for the American burning of York (Toronto) earlier in the war.

Ross and his regulars then sailed away to destroy Baltimore. This city, unlike the capital, would not fall. The American militia was able to contain the British regulars along their path of advance, with Ross himself being mortally wounded. During a war known for memorable and patriotic phases, the British naval bombardment of Fort McHenry failed in its efforts, inspiring Frances Scott Key to write *The Star Spangled Banner*. Having met with defeat, British forces departed from the area in October of that year.

The same war that would launch William Henry Harrison toward his eventual presidency would do so for another individual as well. In July 1813 the Creek Indians of Alabama allied themselves with England and attacked Fort Mims, which was located about 30 miles north of Mobile. In the ensuing melee, the Creek's massacred about half of the 500-man garrison, along with a large number of refugees. Andrew Jackson in response organized a large militia and punished the Creek tribes for their transgressions. When the Indians persisted in their frontier attacks, Jackson took to the field again, severely defeating them at the battle of Horseshoe Bend in March of 1814. As a reward, he was commissioned into the regular army and given command of the Gulf Coast area. When in November of 1814 a combined British-Indian attack was mounted against Fort Bowyer from Pensacola in Spanish Florida, Jackson defied government orders not to enter Florida and seized Pensacola.

Andrew Jackson was never to be outdone. With Pensacola secure, he departed for New Orleans to deal with a planned expedition against that city, which the United States had acquired from France with the Louisiana Purchase in 1802. He would arrive in New Orleans on December 1, 1814 to take charge of American defenses there. Five weeks later, and two weeks after the Peace of Ghent had been signed ending the war, the Battle of New Orleans was fought. The result for the British was an unmitigated disaster. Safe behind their earthworks, the American troops inflicted grievous losses on the British troops, who had attempted a frontal assault. News of the Treaty of Ghent had not reached the states until after the Battle of New Orleans.

More than 2,100 British were killed or wounded during the Battle of New Orleans, as opposed to American losses of 8 dead and 13 wounded. Andrew Jackson became a national legend, although a slightly poorer one. In the weeks preceding the battle, Jackson had imposed martial law over the city in defiance of a writ of habeas corpus, even going so far as to jail the federal district judge who issued the writ. For this, he was of course fined to the sum of 1,000 dollars.

At sea, the events of the last years of the war were to cause the American navy to resort to the tactics employed by the English during the years of Francis Drake and Sir Walter Raleigh. By 1814, the British blockade of the American coast had so devastated U.S. trade and American manufacturers that many private citizens were ruined and the United States Treasury nearly bankrupt. In retaliation, the few U.S. naval vessels still in action, as well as a number of privateers, engaged in a naval Guerre de Course against British shipping throughout the world. Some measure of success was achieved. The U.S.S. Essex, during a seventeen-month cruise throughout the Pacific, captured more than forty vessels before finally being cornered and destroyed at Valparaiso, Chile. The U.S.S. Wasp experienced similar success, destroying or capturing thirteen merchant ships and defeating the British warships Reindeer and Avon. The U.S.S. Constitution met and defeated both of the British warships Cyane and Levant. On the down side, Stephen Decateur met his first serious setback when his frigate U.S.S. President was forced to strike its colors in January of 1815. It should be noted however, that in this contest Decateur was facing five British vessels with just the President, and even still he was able to disable the British frigate Endymion.

Did America succeed during the War of 1812? When considering that America declared war against Britain under the pretext of defending its rights to freedom of the seas, the answer must be in some respects, yes. The Treaty of Ghent, signed December 24, 1914 at

Ghent, Belgium, ended the war but basically ignored this issue. However, in the aftermath of this war, the final confrontation between England and her former colony, the Royal Navy never did employ its highhanded tactics at sea against the Americans again. Likewise, the United States never sought to conquer Canada again. There were other benefits for the Americans as well. The U.S. Navy had proven itself on the high seas, and America's fear of a standing regular army abated in the aftermath of the failures of the militia at Detroit and again at Bladensburg. During the war, James Monroe had been promoted to act as Secretary of War subsequent to the burning of Washington, D.C. His name will forever be associated with the change in America's foreign policy after the war. He would also be one of three men to attain the presidency after having served at high levels of participation during the War of 1812.

The years between the War of 1812 and the American Civil War are not generally regarded as being of huge importance to American history. To the average American citizen of today, they probably know less of the history of these years than they do about the Italian Renaissance. This is unfortunate because it was during this time period that America would see explosive growth, the repercussions of which we feel within our society today, if we choose to look. Within the same year that the War of 1812 ended, Stephen Decatur returned to the Mediterranean to continue his chastisement of the Barbary corsairs.

Within three years of the war, Andrew Jackson would be back in the field of action, this time waging war against the Seminole Indians of Florida. Using the raids of the Seminoles against U.S. citizens as a pretext, he led an army of nearly 8,000 men into Spanish Florida. In April of 1818, Jackson and his army occupied the Spanish post at St. Marks. One month later, he would seize Pensacola for the second time in his life. It was during the taking of St. Marks that Jackson almost single-handedly brought America back to war against England. Finding two British subjects there who were assisting the Seminoles, Jackson had them court-martialed, convicted, and executed. When the Spanish governor of Florida fled to Fort Barrancas, Jackson had this post shelled until it surrendered. Highhanded as Jackson's actions may seem, they did bear results. As had happened during the War of 1812, the Spanish post was returned to Jackson's forces. However, this time negotiations were begun to obtain all of Florida for the United States. This goal was accomplished by means of the Adams-Onis Treaty of 1819, resulting in the United States receiving Florida for five million dollars. The treaty also defined the boundary line of Spanish Mexico, to extend from the Sabine River in the Gulf of Mexico, northwest to the Pacific Ocean.

James Monroe, who had served as War Secretary during the War of 1812, had succeeded James Madison as President in 1817. Monroe is considered to have been the last of the founding fathers to serve in this capacity. During his annual message to Congress in 1823, Monroe put forth the concept of a new doctrine in regard to non-colonization and non-intervention by the European nations in the Western Hemisphere. Although much of the credit for this doctrine is due to John Quincy Adams, this new idea was to forever become known as the Monroe Doctrine. Henceforth, any attempts by the European powers to interfere in the affairs of the nations of North and South America were to be regarded as acts unfriendly to the United States. This doctrine would define United States policy for the next one hundred years.

Whereas Thomas Jefferson had doubled the territory of the United States by means of the Louisiana Purchase, American policies toward expansion were now assuming a nature more consistent with those of Republican Rome and England. In Florida, the army had led the way to the American acquisition of that area. This undeclared war of acquisition would continue, a war fought predominately to seize the lands of Native Americans for the next three quarters of a century. Initially, with vast unsettled lands to the west still available, this undeclared war revolved around the concept of a general removal of the Eastern Indians to the Great Plains west of the Mississippi. Some of the first victims of this concept, initiated during the years of James Monroe but generally associated with those of Andrew Jackson, were the Sac and Fox tribes of Illinois and Wisconsin. Under the pretext of a treaty, more than fifty million acres were ceded by these tribes to the U.S. Government. After having been forced west of the Mississippi by means of threat and intimidation, these Indian peoples sought to return east in 1832 after finding the western lands less suitable to the raising of corn. The result was the Black Hawk War, which was more of a massacre than a contest between rival combatants.

Further south, the Five Civilized Tribes, the Choctaws, Creeks, Cherokee, Seminole and Chickasaws, were all gradually forced from their lands. The Second Seminole War lasted for seven years and became the nation's largest and most expensive Indian War, costing an estimated thirty-five million dollars. On December 29, 1835, The Treaty of New Echota was signed between the U.S. Government and representatives of the Cherokee Nation. The problem was, those Cherokees who signed the treaty were not authorized to speak for the nation as a whole. Therefore, many Indians under the leadership of Chief John Ross, simply ignored it. By the year 1838, which had been chosen as the final date for removal of the Cherokees west to Oklahoma, most had not departed their lands. Therefore, the army was employed to remove them. During this forced exodus, known as the Trail of Tears, "an estimated 4,000 of the 16,000 Cherokees who were forced out of their lands died along the way."[107] Perhaps more appalling than the actual removal, were Jackson's comments in regard to it. In his farewell address of March 1837, Jackson stated, "the philanthropist will rejoice that the remnant of that ill-fated race has been at length placed beyond the reach of injury or oppression, and that the paternal care of the General Government will hereafter watch over them and protect them."[108] One had to wonder what the Cherokees were thinking of this.

By this point in the development of the United States, American thought patterns had crystallized under the slogan of "Manifest Destiny," which was the belief that America had the "right" to absorb

---

[107] Meachsam, Andrew Jackson, 318
[108] Ibid, 318.

North America all the way to the Pacific Ocean. As had happened with the Roman and British expansion in their times, much of the stimulus for American expansion at this time was the search for and desire to accrue wealth in the new territories. In the early nineteenth century, the fur trade would lead to further development of the west. During the presidency of Thomas Jefferson, Meriwether Lewis and William Clark had been commissioned by the government to explore the western frontier all the way to the Pacific Ocean. Shortly after his return, Clark became instrumental in founding the Missouri Fur Company. In time it grew to be a very prosperous adventure. Shortly thereafter, the American Fur Company was established by John Jacob Astor. His intent was to establish a trading post at the head of the Columbia River. Therefore, in 1811, he sent a ship south, around Cape Horn, and then north again until it reached the mighty Columbia. Here, at the mouth of that river, he established his new trading post.

In 1822, a St. Louis militia general named William Ashley founded the Rocky Mountain Fur Company, which recruited adventurous young men to head west along the Missouri River and to remain there trapping their own furs for a period of one to three years. Many of these aptly named "mountain men" were employees of this company, men like Jedediah Smith and Kit Carson. Not only was the west a place of wealth, it was to be a place of adventure as well.

The further desire for profit and trade would also lead to the establishment of two very important avenues to the west coast. In the south, the Santa Fe Trail was opened up in the early 1820s as a pathway west to facilitate trade with the inhabitants of Spanish Mexico. In the north, by the 1840s, settlers had begun to navigate the trail leading to Oregon, which was earlier blazed by the fur traders. Traffic along this Oregon Trail began as a trickle, but by 1849 this traffic had so populated the Northwest that Oregon was organized as a territory. The massive influx of settlers into the new territory also led to the establishment of a boundary being drawn between the United States and Canada. On June 15, 1846, a long-standing Anglo-U.S. border dispute was settled by the Oregon Treaty. American intransigence on this issue was evident by the popular slogan of the time, "Fifty-four forty or fight." It was America's contention that the U.S. boundary extended north 54 degrees 40 minutes north latitude. When the dispute was settled, the United States gained control over land lying between 42 and 49 degrees north latitude (present-day Washington, Oregon, and Idaho as well as parts of Montana and Wyoming, while Great Britain was granted territory between 49 degrees and 54 degrees 40 minutes north latitude as well as Vancouver Island.

It was to be the Santa Fe Trail and not the Oregon Trail that would become instrumental in America's next war of territorial aggrandizement. In 1821 Stephen F. Austin established the first Anglo-American settlement in the territory of Texas, which at that time belonged to the newly established Republic of Mexico, which had freed itself from Spanish rule after years of revolutionary struggle. By the early 1830s, enough Americans had traveled west along the Santa Fe Trail to establish a significant population within the territory of Texas. Disagreements between these settlers and the weak Mexican government were inevitable.

In June of 1830, armed insurrection in Texas broke out between the American settlers living there and the Mexican government. Initially, the settlers did not do well against the sizeable Mexican army under Antonio López de Santa Anna. In February and March of 1836, 188 Texans held out against the Mexican Army at the Alamo in San Antonio. Eventually, all 188 were overpowered by the larger army of Santa Anna and killed. It was written that "Thermopolae had its messenger of defeat; the Alamo had none."[109] On March 2 of that year, while the Alamo still held out, Texas was proclaimed a republic. Interesting that Texas had initiated the war, then declared independence before the war was won, much as the United States had done. Following the battle at the Alamo, Santa Anna's army took Goliad, killing another 300 Texans who were defending that location. Shortly thereafter, the indomitable Sam Houston surprised the much larger Mexican army at San Jacinto, defeating it and capturing Santa

---

[109] Nevins and Commager, *Pocket History of the U.S.,* 189

Anna himself. As a precondition of his release, Santa Anna was forced to recognize Texan independence, an act that was later repudiated by the Mexican government. Sam Houston, the hero of San Jacinto, was elected as the new republic's first president. On July 4, 1836, the United States formally recognized Texan independence.

After nine years of being on its own, the Republic of Texas requested to become part of the United States. Initially, this request was refused. However, due to "pocket motives," the issue was again raised during the election of 1844. In this election, the expansionist candidate James K. Polk won, and on March 1, 1845, the Republic of Texas became the Lone Star State. By this act, war between Mexico and the United States became inevitable. Mexico had long claimed the Nueces River as its border with the Texas Republic. The United States now claimed that border to be further south along the Rio Grande. On April 25, 1846, an American reconnaissance force of 63 dragoons was overpowered by a Mexican force of 1,600 men just north of the Rio Grande. The very next day, a veteran of the Seminole War and future president, Zachary Taylor, announced the commencement of hostilities.

During the first week of May 1846, a Mexican army nearly 6,000 strong, crossed the north side of the Rio Grande and attacked the American outpost named Camp Texas. The American Major Jacob Brown was killed in this action, the name of this site eventually being named Brownsville.  On the eighth and ninth of May, two more battles between the army of Taylor and the Mexican army of Mariano Arista were fought, Taylor being victorious at both Palo Alto and Resaca de la Palma. The American declaration of war would come on May 13, 1846, after these two engagements had already been fought.

The newly declared U.S.-Mexican War was to last a relatively short two years. However, the impact of it on American history would far outweigh its brief longevity. The war itself was characterized by smaller U.S. forces defeating the usually larger Mexican forces. In addition, with the outbreak of the war, Brigadier General Stephen W. Kearney was ordered west from Fort Leavenworth, Kansas to occupy New Mexico and California. After initially occupying New Mexico,

Kearney moved west to join a naval force that had landed in California under Commodore Robert F. Stockton. In December of 1846 and January of 1847, these forces would overpower Mexican-Californian resistance at San Pascual, San Gabriel and Mersa. Kearney would, in the aftermath of these victories, occupy Los Angeles.

Further south, in the main theatre of operations, the army of Zachary Taylor was joined by another army under the command of General Winfield Scott. This military force was to conduct an amphibious landing near Vera Cruz, and then march inland to capture Mexico City while Taylor's army held the remainder of the Mexican army at bay. Former general and now president of Mexico, Santa Anna, learned of this plan and decided to attack the 5,000-man army of Taylor with the 20,000-strong Mexican army. He attacked Taylor at Buena Vista in February of 1847 and was narrowly defeated by the much smaller American force.

During the spring and summer of 1847, Scott led his army toward Mexico City, defeating Mexican forces along the way at Cerro Gordo, Contreras, Cherabusco, and Molina del Rey. By September of that year, the Americans had taken the fortified hill at Chapultepec, the last major defensive obstacle before Mexico City. On September 14, Mexico City was captured, virtually ending Mexican resistance. The end result of Mexico's utter defeat was the initiation of peace negotiations that were to drag on for four months. Finally, on February 2, 1848, the Treaty of Quadalupe Hidalgo was signed. By this treaty, the Rio Grande became the agreed-upon boundary between Texas and Mexico. In addition, Mexico transferred to the United States ownership of the region now comprising California, Utah, Nevada, the largest parts of Arizona and New Mexico, as well as portions of Wyoming and Colorado. As had happened with Spanish Florida, the United States agreed to pay Mexico fifteen million dollars for these territories, in the aftermath of virtual military occupation. To the casual observer of history, the American seizure of Mexican territories by virtue of feats of arms should be viewed as being no different than Caesar's occupation of Gaul, or Robert Clive's taking of India. In all these cases, much smaller military forces were able to acquire vast amounts of territory by use of superior technology over a less organized foe.

With the acquisition of vast areas of the North American continent now assured, it was time for an expansion of the American agricultural base that would lead ultimately to the post-Civil War industrial explosion. Technology was to be important in this agricultural expansion. During the years of Angevin England, the simple invention of the horseshoe and the padded horse collar had allowed English farmers to pull plows with horses instead of oxen. Although an ox is as powerful as a horse, it is slower and has less endurance. Over time, when coupled with new practices reclaiming wastelands, an increase in agricultural productivity was achieved.

With the Mississippi Valley becoming increasingly more populous, two technological developments would assist this region in becoming the breadbasket of the United States. In 1831, the Virginia farmer Cyrus H. McCormick had invented the reaper, a device used in harvesting grain. This new mechanical apparatus increased harvest rates by a dozen-fold margin. By 1848, McCormick had built his factory in Chicago, which, using the interchangeable parts established by Eli Whitney, could produce 5,000 machines per year. Shortly thereafter, McCormick was joined by John Deere, who had invented the steel plow. By 1856, Deere was producing more than 13,000 machines per year. McCormick was also responsible for the agricultural explosion of the Midwest by means of an advertising campaign that grew out of the invention of his reaper. The advertising campaign put forth by McCormick was responsible for the phrase, "Westward the course of empire makes its way."

The second invention necessary for the mid-nineteenth century agricultural explosion was the railroad. This new source of transportation could be regarded as the modern rendition of ancient Rome's Appian Way. The railroad was of course not America's first attempt at transportation improvements. During the presidency of Thomas Jefferson, the highly successful Secretary of the Treasury Albert Gallatin had proposed spending a portion of the federal budget on the construction of a turnpike. Then of course there was the success of the Erie Canal, completed in 1825. This 363-mile long waterway made possible the shipping of goods from the Great Lakes eastward to the markets and factories of the east coast. By 1830, however, the railroad began to supercede other modes of transportation with the initial success of the Baltimore and Ohio Railroad, a thirteen-mile stretch of track built by a group of Baltimore businessmen. The initial success of these railroads owed much to an advantage of speed over their rivals. The earliest and most primitive steam locomotives could travel at six miles per hour, the canal boat only four. Within a decade, improvements were such that locomotives could move at the increased speed of fifteen miles per hour. As these railroads spread west, they would combine with the reaper to make America the most agriculturally advanced society on earth. By 1854, "Seventy-four trains a day ran into Chicago, which already boasted itself the largest grain market in the world."[110]

What began as a trickle in railroad construction would eventually turn into a flood. Whereas the United States could boast but 9,000 miles of railroad tracks in 1850, by the time of the American Civil War this total would exceed 30,000 miles. The vast majority of these railroads and rail centers were concentrated in the industrial North and the agrarian Midwest, a factor that would contribute much to the success of the Union during the approaching Civil War. It is important to note, that as these railroads moved west, they were accompanied by another invention, the telegraph.

The Mexican-American War would prove beneficial to the United States for reasons other than those of an agricultural nature. Even before the Treaty of Guadalupe Hidalgo was signed, gold had been discovered in the foothills of California's Sierra-Nevada Mountains, resulting in the California Gold Rush. In the year 1849 alone, more than 100,000 persons would migrate into the territory in search of easy riches. As compensation for a war that had cost the United States 98 million dollars to finance, the mines of California had yielded nearly five hundred million dollars in gold by the year 1853.

---

[110] Ibid, 181.

Napoleon Bonaparte had always believed in the policy of making war pay for war. If this is a measure of success, the Mexican War and the acquisition of California was an overwhelming success.

This success was to be accompanied by certain unintended consequences of a very negative nature. With the rapid expansion of acquired U.S. territories, nearly two million square miles acquired from Mexico alone, there arose the issue of these lands being organized into territories and eventually being admitted to the nation as states. As the federal constitution had curtailed the slave trade but had not abolished slavery itself, sectional rivalries along the lines of free state vs. slave state began to arise. By the year 1850, it became apparent that California, Oregon, Utah, and Minnesota would soon be eligible for statehood. As they would likely be admitted as free states, the South became increasingly alarmed that the legislative scales in Washington would increasingly be tilted away from them. The result of the free state/slave state rivalry was the Compromise of 1850, or Clay's Compromise, in reference to the great Senator Henry Clay of Kentucky.

The provisions of Clay's Compromise were many and varied. Although far from perfect, they did succeed in preventing the outbreak of war for a period of ten years. Under the Compromise, California was admitted as a free state, while Utah and New Mexico were organized as territories without legislation for or against slavery. In addition, the slave trade in the District of Columbia was abolished, a new system for allowing for the return to the South of fugitive slaves was established and compensation to Texas for portions of land ceded to New Mexico were called for. In this time of crisis, America was fortunate to possess the abilities of some very great men, among them Henry Clay and Daniel Webster. Unfortunately, they were soon to be replaced by a group of leaders who were far more obdurate in their political beliefs.

The drift toward civil war in America had actually begun long before the Compromise of 1850 and its after affects. In the months leading up to the War of 1812, there had been talk of Federalist New England seceding from the Union. During the years of Jacksonian

Democracy, the doctrine of "nullification" had been brought forth by John Calhoun in response to the ultra-high tariffs on raw materials passed by Congress. As these tariffs were especially tough on the South, Calhoun proposed in his South Carolina Exposition and Protest, that the tariffs were unconstitutional and that their implementation into law could motivate his state to secede from the Union. His thoughts on the subject were to linger for an entire generation.

By the 1860's the economic and philosophical differences between the industrial north and the agrarian south were widening over the issue of slavery. In opposition to the fugitive slave laws brought about by the Compromise of 1850, many northern states simply refused to enforce them, or sought legislative means to circumvent them. In 1853, President Franklin Pierce concluded the Gadsden Purchase of 45,000 square miles of territory along the Arizona and New Mexico border with Mexico for ten million dollars. With this purchase, a new route was opened for a transcontinental railway traversing the south. This southern railway and its options for the further spread of slavery west brought the slavery issue to the forefront again. In 1854, Senator Stephen Douglas suggested that in two of the territories to be traversed, Kansas and Nebraska, the people of the territories be allowed to decide if they would be free or slave-owning states. Thus the concept of "popular sovereignty." In May of 1854, the Stephen Douglas-sponsored Kansas-Nebraska Act was passed by Congress and signed into law by Franklin Pierce. Within a year, an undeclared guerilla war would break out in Kansas with the pro-slavery raid on the free-soil town of Lawrence and John Brown's retaliatory raid during the Pottawatomie Creek Massacre as evidence of the extent of this violence.

In 1857, the judicial branch of government would become embroiled in the slavery issue as well. In its ruling during the case of Dredd Scott v. Sandford, the majority of the U.S. Supreme Court ruled that because Scott was a slave, and therefore not a citizen of the United States, he had no legal right to bring a suit against any party in a federal court. In its ruling of the Dredd Scott case, the court went even further in its verdict declaring that the Missouri Compromise was unconstitutional. Even though the Kansas-Nebraska Act had voided the 1850 Compromise, the Supreme Court now held the position that Congress could not exclude slavery in any state or territory, and that slavery could not be abolished by any territorial government affirmed by Congress. Essentially, the concept of popular sovereignty was now dead.

The political divide in the United States was now all too great. Most of us are familiar with the events leading up to the Civil War. Many had recognized that the war would be inevitable. Thomas Jefferson had once declared that slavery should be wiped out by a combination of emancipation and deportation, stating, "I tremble for my country, when I reflect that God is just."[111]

Justice would come, and it was to come with an interesting shift. In the years prior to the Civil War, with the admission of Michigan, Iowa, Minnesota and Wisconsin as new states, a political region was established to compete with the old polar opposites of North and South. With this new "middle border" region, comprising eight million residents, Senator Stephen Douglas of Illinois stated that it would become "a swelling power that will be able to speak the new laws of this nation."[112] During the contest for the Illinois seat for United States Senate, this political shift became more evident with the Lincoln-Douglas debates drawing national attention to both candidates. By the year 1860, with the election of Abraham Lincoln to the presidency, it became clear that the Industrial Northeast and the Antebellum South were now to have less influence in the future affairs of the nation. This shift, also earlier exhibited to a lesser extent with the election of Andrew Jackson, was similar to the political shift seen in ancient Rome in the post Antonine years when future emperors traditionally came from the Roman colonies such as Spain, Iberia, Gaul, and eventually Great Britain. This process had started within a century of the death of Augustus, when Trajan, who was

---

[111] Ibid, 160.
[112] Brinckley, *American Heritage History of the U.S.*, 183.

born in Spain, ascended to the throne in A.D. 98. Eventually this trend became so common, that for whole decades no Italian Romans became emperor.

As for the Civil War itself, no great discussion of the campaigns is either necessary or possible, as they themselves could fill entire volumes of books. Nevertheless, there were trends during and after the war seldom mentioned or recognized, simply because they were overshadowed by the campaigns themselves. The American Civil War in many respects could be considered as the first truly modern war. With the war's first battle at Bull Run in 1861 came the use of the railroad, which could rapidly shift troops from one theatre of operations to another. If not for the ability of the Confederacy to transfer the forces of Joseph E. Johnston from Winchester and the brigade of Kirby Smith from 43 miles away in the Shenandoah Valley to the scene of battle, no Confederate victory could have been possible. With the introduction of the railroad during the Civil War, the concept of strategic mobility was reborn.

Also important to the war effort and the ultimate Union victory was the agricultural disparity between the opposing sides. It is generally regarded by many that the South was the more agrarian of the two antagonists. However, southern agriculture was generally based upon crops such as cotton, tobacco and sugar. While important cash crops, they were of little value in feeding an army and sustaining a wartime populace. Although the South did have the all-important Shenandoah Valley, breadbasket of the confederacy, its close proximity to the scene of conflict made it as much a liability as an asset. In contrast, the North could feed large armies for a sustained period of time, with its control of the Midwest grain belt.

The importance of industry made itself apparent with the advent of this new form of total war. During the years of Napoleonic Europe, the size of armies was limited by the ability of the various warring nations to feed and equip them. The army of Bonaparte that had invaded Russia in 1812, consisted of about 200,000 French soldiers, the available manpower of the entire nation. When this Grand Army disintegrated in the retreat from Moscow, there were no resources available to replace it. With an available population of twenty-two million men, the Union possessed the ability to field armies of a size not yet seen anywhere. By war's end, the number of men who had worn the blue uniforms of the Union had soared into the millions.

The telegraph and the observation balloon also made known their presence during the war. Union General George Thomas, the "Rock of Chicamauga," was one of the first to fully comprehend the importance of the telegraph. Thomas had the first mobile command post in the U.S. Army, a specially equipped wagon with desk and file drawers for documents and telegraphers to send and receive dispatches to and from other units and commanders.

At sea, the use of ironclad warships would initiate the demise of wood and sail. Americans did not invent the initial ironclad warship; that distinction must go to the Korean Admiral Y. Sung Sin and his tortoise ships of the late 16th century. However, when the C.S.S. Virginia met the U.S.S. Monitor off Hampton Roads on March 9, 1862, it became clear that the turreted ironclad warship held the key to the future of naval warfare.

It is interesting that whereas technology brought forth several innovations in the way that wars were fought, an age-old implement would surpass them in terms of its importance. With the advent of the rifled musket and the breach loading repeating rifle, the arcane tactic of ranks of armed men exchanging volleys of lead at close range became obsolete. In order to survive these new levels of modern firepower, troops were forced to seek cover. By war's end, Robert E. Lee would earn for himself the sobriquet "King of Spades." This particular phrase was no doubt a result of the kind of defensive works Lee had constructed during his defense of Petersburg in 1864. A war that had begun with battles fought along the lines of a Napoleonic contest, would conclude in a fashion similar to World War I.

The casualty list at the end of the war would be lengthy, with casualty totals surpassing all the previous wars in which America had fought. The North would suffer 370,000 dead, the South 260,000 dead. These numbers do not take into consideration the number of troops who went home as amputees or otherwise inured. Financially the cost was great as well, with the national debt of 90.6 million dollars in 1861, skyrocketing to 284 million after four years of war. Between the two opposing governments, Union and Confederate, a total of 5.2 billion dollars was spent.

There were to be financial and emotional costs suffered by the noncombatants as well. With the introduction of "total war" in 1864, the civilian populace of the South officially became a target. The one hundred thousand-man army of William Tecumseh Sherman burned Atlanta to the ground in September 1864. Writing to the mayor of Atlanta in the aftermath of its fall, Sherman stated, "You cannot qualify war in harsher terms than I will. War is cruelty, you cannot define it."[113] After the sack of Atlanta, Sherman turned east on his "march to the sea." By the time he emerged from his march at Savannah, his army had cut a sixty mile-wide swath through the State of Georgia, destroying everything in their path. Not satisfied, Sherman then turned North, capturing Columbia, South Carolina, a city that was to suffer a fate similar to that of Atlanta. The concept of total war was applied to the Shenandoah Valley as well. In that theatre, Cavalry commander Philip Sheridan destroyed the valley so thoroughly that it was said, "a crow flying over it would have to carry his own rations."[114] The accumulated effects of Confederate losses on the battlefield in the last half of the war, its inability to support itself agriculturally and industrially, and the overwhelming superiority of numbers possessed by the Union Army, would drive the South to eventual defeat. On April 9, 1865, Robert E. Lee was forced to surrender the 28,000-man shadow of the once great army of Northern Virginia to Ulysses S. Grant at Appomattox Courthouse. Seventeen days later the army of Joseph E. Johnston surrendered to William T. Sherman in North Carolina. This surrender would mark more than the end of the American Civil War. It would serve as a demarcation line in the history of America. The old way would soon pass by and the path would now be cleared for a less democratic, omni-competent

---

[113] Ibid, 225.
[114] Nevins and Commager, *Pocket History of the U.S.*, 225.

federal government. With the end of the Civil War in April of 1865 came also the end of America's era of innocence. In the years prior to the war, the newly created Republican Party put forth a platform based upon high tariffs to protect American industry, free farms to spur agricultural expansion, land grants to the growing railroads, as well as other internal improvements. Prior to the war they did not have the ability to pass legislation toward this end. When the South seceded from the Union, their representatives, mostly Democrats, left the halls of Congress. With their departure, the Republicans found themselves with an open road to pass any legislation they saw fit. The flurry of legislative activity which occurred during the war, would make possible the explosive growth of the post war years. With the conclusion of the war in 1865, Congress repealed wartime taxes on raw materials such as coal and iron. To spur the westward expansion of the railroads, one hundred million acres of public lands were given as grants to the railroad companies. As a further stimulus, the railroads received over sixty million dollars worth of federal grants.

The result of these initiatives was astounding. Between 1860 and 1870, the number of manufacturing firms in the United States increased by eighty percent. The value of goods manufactured increased by one hundred percent. In the Midwest, Chicago would become one of the great meat packing centers of the world. St. Louis and Milwaukee became known for their breweries, Pittsburg became an iron and steel manufacturing giant, while the twin cities became renowned for their cereal products. Pennsylvania and Ohio were to become the homes of many of the nation's new oil refining facilities.

There were, nonetheless, other explanations for this industrial explosion. Success in industry is dependent upon other issues, such as cheap labor, which is in part dependent upon cheap food. Much as agricultural expansion was responsible for the expansion of Roman and British societies, so too it would assist in the expansion of America. Once its power became firmly established, the Republican Party re-enacted the Homestead Law, a law earlier vetoed by a Democratic president. In accordance with this law, any eligible citizen could claim 160 acres of land simply by agreeing to cultivate it for a period of ten years. With millions of acres of virgin soil available in the west, hundreds of thousands of farmers took advantage of this provision in the law. In addition, Congress passed the Morrill Act, granting several million acres of publicly owned lands for the creation of agricultural and industrial colleges through the states.

The results of these land opportunities were telling. Between 1860 and 1880, the production of grain crops doubled, as did the number of domestic swine, cattle and sheep. The earlier inventions of Cyrus McCormick and John Deere allowed for higher crop yields and faster rates of harvest. The demand for agricultural implements in turn soared, further aiding the industries engaged in the production of them.

There existed as well another factor essential for the industrial explosion of the late nineteenth century. Abundant natural resources are an absolute must for any nation seeking to further its industrial advantages. Whereas Thomas Jefferson had acquired the Louisiana Purchase with the intention of expanding an agriculturally based society, what he could never foresee were the massive deposits of natural resources below the surface of the ground. Similar statements can be made in regard to the acquisitions made from the Treaty of Guadalupe Hidalgo and the Gadsden Purchase. Although there were vast amounts of natural resources within the original thirteen colonies, there were far more resources to the west. Beneath the earth in the states of Kansas, Texas, New Mexico and Colorado were nearly inexhaustible amounts of coal. Similar reserves of petroleum could be found below the sands of Texas, Oklahoma, California, Illinois and Kansas. With massive deposits of iron ore located deep beneath the ground all around the rim of the Great Lakes, The United States was set to become the world's leader in the production of iron and steel. Further to the west another valuable metal, copper, was found in abundance. In 1882, the Anaconda Mine was opened in Montana, touching off a contest for an industrial monopoly that in many ways was reflective of the California Gold Rush of 1849. Assisting the nation's ability to finance much of the industrial expansion of the late nineteenth century was the discovery of large silver deposits in

Colorado, Montana and Nevada.

There was at the disposal of the growing nation another natural resource, which may at the time not have even been regarded as such. In colonial America many of the infant industrial facilities had relied upon water and the waterwheel to propel the early mills and machine works. With territorial expansion had come the acquisition of great rivers such as the Tennessee and Columbia Rivers. As the technologies became available, these rivers and others would be dammed and harnessed to generate the power necessary to support America's industrial explosion. Overall, it might accurately be stated that the United States was granted the natural advantage of having more available natural resources than any other nation on earth, with the possible exception of Russia.

In regard to Russia, it would be from this nation that the U.S. would obtain the next great acquisition of territory. William Seward, serving as Secretary of State, brokered what at the time was regarded as "Seward's Folly." For the price of just over seven million dollars, or roughly two cents per acre, Seward was able to acquire an area twice the size of Texas. Alaska would in the future prove to be resource-rich, a fact probably not comprehended until the "oil shock" of 1973 when OPEC nations of the Middle East imposed an embargo of oil on nations friendly to Israel and quadrupled the price of oil to all other markets.

Seward's 1867 purchase of Alaska was followed two years later by an event that in many aspects changed the culture of America. Much as the Roman Appian Way and England's dominance of the world's sea routes had allowed them to become economic powerhouses, on May 10, 1869, the Central Pacific and the Union Pacific railroads were joined together at Promontory Point, Utah. Grenville Dodge, once Union Major General turned railroad engineer, stated in the aftermath of the driving of the final track spike, "then it was declared that the connection was made and the Atlantic and Pacific were joined together, never to be parted."[115] In all, within the span of half a

---

[115] Brinckley, *American Heritage History of the U.S.*, 250.

century from the inception of railroad building, the United States was to develop a transportation system with nearly 250,000 miles of new track.

The importance of this new transportation system in regard to industrial growth cannot be overstated. In some ways, it would also transform the very culture of American society. Before the United States engaged in its Civil War, the nation had possessed a population of 31.5 million people and 17 million cattle. During the post-bellum years, a cattle culture developed in the west when it became possible to ship these cattle east to the larger metropolitan areas and their hungry inhabitants. The same livestock that would be sold in Galveston, Texas for six dollars per head could be driven north and then shipped east to sell for a price ten times as high. Chicago and Omaha, as rail centers, would become cattle capitals. By the 1870s, with the invention of the refrigerated boxcar, men such as Philip D. Armour and Gustavus Swift became cattle barons, and Omaha and Chicago would become home to vast slaughterhouses as well as railway centers. Within decades, the number of cattle being shipped east nearly quadrupled, thus initiating a process by which the industrial east would become economically intertwined with the more agricultural west.

The last half of the nineteenth century could generally be regarded as a time when the lifestyles and standards of living were improving for most Americans. During the years between 1869 and 1914, the gross national product of the United States more than quadrupled, and the per capita income increased by 250 percent. For the Native American, events would cause them to suffer a less fortunate fate. Already having been driven from their lands and homes in the east, the coming of the railroad would be accompanied by the end of their nomadic way of life. First to go was the American bison, or buffalo, upon which many of the Plains Indians were dependent. A herd that numbered in the tens of millions in mid-century would number only 549 animals by 1889, just one more testament to the un-teachable nature of mankind.

Just prior to the Civil War, the U.S. government had initiated a policy of removing Indian tribes from their traditional homes and relocating them to much smaller areas known as reservations. The government also intended to socialize them by forcing them to exchange their nomadic lifestyles for a more agriculturally based way of life. Some would accept this way of life. Others, predominately the 200,000 members of the tribal nations of the Northern Plains, resisted the taking of their lands and the changing of their ways. The response to this challenge to government authority was to be armed intervention.

Between the years of the end of the Civil War in 1865 and the beginning of the Spanish American War in 1898, the U.S. government conducted 12 different campaigns against the Indian nations, a total of 943 separate actions or engagements. The nature of these wars could be brutal, with women and children often becoming victims. The Plains Indians themselves, to include the Sioux, Comanche and the Cheyenne, were especially effective as light cavalry and probably as good as the world had yet known. They would inflict numerous defeats on the U.S. Army, most notably the defeat suffered by G.A. Custer in June of 1876 at the Little Big Horn. On that fateful day, Custer and his entire command of 212 officers and men were massacred.

Barely a year after Custer's defeat, the U.S. government attempted to force the Nez Percé Indians from their homelands in the Wallowa Valley of Oregon. After an initial clash with an army detachment at White Bird Canyon in June of 1877, the Nez Percé Chief Joseph attempted to move his entire tribe of 700 people away from the army in search of a new home. For the next four months Chief Joseph would both elude the pursuing soldiers of the U.S. Army and at times turn and inflict losses on them. Finally, after a four-month trek of nearly 2,000 miles, Chief Joseph and his people would be cornered and forced to surrender in the Bear Paw Mountains, a mere thirty miles from the relative safety of the Canadian border.

The last major engagement of the Indian Wars occurred on December 29, 1890. This confrontation, known to history as the Battle of Wounded Knee, was more an act of indiscriminate killing than of battle. The Minneconjou Sioux of Chief Big Foot were to all intents and purposes the victims of a purported misunderstanding between the 7th Cavalry of Colonel James Forsyth and the three hundred and fifty members of Big Foot's tribe, who had been ordered by the government to return to their assigned reservation. The details surrounding the initial shots fired during this engagement vary, the end result being the deaths of nearly 300 Indians, including the pneumonia-stricken chief himself. The 7th Cavalry, which had earlier suffered an unmitigated defeat under Custer at the Little Big Horn, lost a total of 25 men. The incident at Wounded Knee Creek marks the terminal point of the nomadic culture of the Plains Indians, a culture whose only crime was that it stood in the way of progress and profit.

While it may be obvious to many that the year 1890 had brought with it the end of the Indian Wars, this same period in American history would also bear signs to a changing of American society in other areas. The 1890 census conducted by the U.S. government revealed that for the first time in U.S. history, the value of manufactured goods was greater than the value of the produce raised on America's farms. The balance between farm and factory was to be thenceforward altered.

Beginning in the 2nd century B.C., the former Roman Republic had seen the rise of latifundia, which were large slave worked agricultural entities. The process by which a republic of robust and independent farmers came to be displaced by these "latifundia," had transpired for various reasons, such as small Roman farm owners being away serving in the legions and practices involved in the taxation of land. During the years of the late nineteenth century, the American farmer was to suffer this same fate. Industrial and technological improvements were partly to blame. The Homestead Act had created provisions for the establishment of 160-acre farms. In a time of manual labor, this proved sufficient. The reaper invention of Cyrus McCormick, improvements in the design of plows, plus the innovation of the threshing machines and combines, reduced labor requirements and cost for harvesting corn by a full half, to one tenth

*The transformation of American agriculture that would help lead to explosive industrial growth, with 40 acres and a mule being replaced by 400 acres and a tractor.*

the cost for oats, and to a twentieth of the cost for wheat. [116]

However, to pay for the initial cost of acquiring these machines, one had to farm an area much larger than the 160 acres provided for in the Homestead Act. The cycle was begun whereby the larger, more profitable farms were able to drive out and acquire the farmland of those who could not afford these new technological wonders.

There existed another fault that could be attributed to these new machines. Because they were so efficient, they brought with them over-production of agricultural goods. With the law of supply and demand taking effect, the price of agricultural commodities fell by more than half between the end of the Civil War and the year 1896.

Speculation also began to take its toll on America's agricultural base. The railroads, once the friend of the farmer, now began to charge increased rates to ship farm produce east, so much so that by the end of the century it could cost more to ship some of the products than their market value was worth. The railroads were not the only enemy of the western farmer; other factors also contributed to the farmer's plight. Banks, for example, could choose to lend money or withhold

[116] Ibid, 259.

it. Then there was the issue of foreign competition, which in the late nineteenth century began to make its presence felt.

Into this scene of industrial expansion and the beginnings of agricultural demise stepped an agency more closely associated with English growth and expansion than with that of the United States. During the Civil War the U. S. Navy had adopted policies that very much emulated those of the English Royal Navy between 1775 and 1783, and 1812 to 1815. A naval blockade was initiated so as to starve the Confederacy into submission. In response, the Confederate Navy initiated policies of the Continental Navy of 1775 to 1783, and the U.S. Navy of 1812 to 1815, the guerre de course.

With the surrender of the Confederacy in April 1865, Secretary of the Navy Gideon Welles reduced the size of the fleet from its wartime high of 700 vessels, all the way down to a post war skeleton of 120 vessels of all types. Whereas the war had brought about an explosion of technological advances, the post-bellum U.S. Navy was to revert to an age of sail.

In a prelude to the Great White Fleet of Theodore Roosevelt, the ironclad warship Miantonomoh and the side-wheel gunboats Augusta and Ashuelot were sent to Europe on a ten-nation goodwill tour. By the time of their return, they had steamed more than 17,000 miles. Less peaceful expeditions would be sent forth to other nations. In 1853, Commodore Matthew C. Perry had first visited Japan. One year later he returned to Yokohama, where the March 31 Treaty of Kanagawa had opened commerce between the U.S. and the Island nation of Japan. During the 1868 Meiji Restoration, which restored imperial rule to Japan, the United States Navy would intervene and protect U.S. interests there on several occasions, with landings occurring at Nagasaki, Yokohama, and Hiogo. The gunboat diplomacy of the Royal Navy was now an established fact of American relations with its foreign neighbors.

Whereas the four decades of the post-bellum navy would find the condition and size of the U.S. fleet in a constant state of neglect and disrepair, these same years would bear witness to the emergence of the naval thought and doctrine which would lead it to become the world's mightiest navy within a few short decades. In October of 1884, Secretary of the Navy William Chandler signed a Navy Department General Order establishing the Naval War College at Newport, Rhode Island. Its first president, Commodore Stephen Luce, intended that its purpose was to be "a place of original research on all questions relating to war and to statesmanship connected to war, or the prevention of war."[117]

In 1886, Luce would be succeeded as president of the Naval War College by Captain Alfred Thayer Mahan. Having initially served as the institution's first instructor in naval history, Mahan would go on to write the two-volume *Influence of Sea Power* series, which would lay the groundwork for modern American naval thought. It is interesting to note that it would take Mahan five years to find a publisher for his work, now regarded as a classic, and the basis for naval study in nations other than our own. The year of publication is also interesting, 1890, the same year as the termination of the Indian Wars and the same year when the worth of industrial output first exceeded the worth of agricultural output. In this work, Mahan essentially redefined the mission of the Navy, writing, "It is not the taking of individual ships or convoys, be they few or many, that strikes down the money power of a nation, it is the possession of that overbearing power on the sea which drives the enemy flag from it. This overbearing power can only be exercised by great navies."[118]

The doctrines set forth by Mahan would coincide with those of another individual and would drive America towards its next round of conquest. In 1893, the University of Wisconsin scholar Frederick Jackson Turner proclaimed the end of manifest destiny and the western frontier and the need for new areas of conquest now that much of North America had been conquered. Turner also espoused the idea that to stop expansion would create severe difficulties for the American farmers, as they would be forced to contend with higher prices and higher taxes due to the increased demand for less available

---

[117] Naval Historical Foundation, *U.S. Navy, A Complete History*, 25.
[118] Ibid, 244.

land. These ideas, put forth at a Chicago meeting of the American Historical Society, would be considered by many as suggesting a need for a new American frontier, which could only be found overseas.

The agent of this "new frontier" would be the U.S. Navy. In the early 1890s the U.S. government began to modernize its antiquated fleet. In the year 1895, the U.S. Navy commissioned the first two modern battleships, the U.S.S. Maine and the U.S.S. Texas. Relying on new coal-burning boilers to create steam for propulsion, and containing main batteries of modern naval rifles housed in rotating turrets, they were the epitome of the modern warship. These ships were shortly followed by three Indiana Class Battleships, and by the U.S.S. Iowa in 1897. It would be the fate of the ill-fated U.S.S. Maine to bring America into its first war with a foreign nation since the 1846-1848 war with the Republic of Mexico. Under the pretext of protecting American interests on the rebellion-torn island of Cuba, and as a show of support to the Cuban citizens whose human rights were often encroached upon by their Spanish overseers, the Maine was dispatched to Havana Harbor, where she arrived on January 25, 1898. After an uneventful three-week visit, the ship suddenly blew up on the night of February 15, 1898. At the time, the cause of the explosion, which claimed the lives of 266 sailors, was unknown. A hastily convened Court of Inquiry determined that the ship's forward magazines had exploded as result of a mine placed under the ship by saboteurs, the nineteenth century term for terrorist. Fueled by an American press, the American public demanded war against Spain, a war, which was granted by Congress in April of 1898. Of interest, just prior to the commencement of the war, Congress passed what was known as the "fifty million bill," authorizing the expenditure of fifty million dollars to build up the nation's defenses. Nearly half would be used for the construction of battleships. The Spanish-American War was another of history's truly needless conflicts. Prior to its outbreak, the aging Spanish empire made every possible concession in an attempt to avoid it. Therefore, much of the blame for it can be attributed to a public frenzy created by the newspapers of Joseph Pulitzer and William Randolph Hearst.

The war itself was to last but a matter of months, being ended by the Treaty of Paris, December 10, 1898. This "splendid little war," as it was referred to by the future Secretary of State, John Hay, was of enormous consequence. Two naval engagements were fought, both resounding U.S. victories. On May 1, 1898, Commodore George Dewey and the ships of the U.S. Asiatic fleet engaged a much inferior and much older Spanish fleet in Manila Bay, the Philippines. The entire Spanish fleet was sunk while U.S. ships received no hits. Two months later, a second Spanish fleet would suffer a similar fate at Santiago Cuba, where the ships of the U.S. Navy's North Atlantic Squadron destroyed or captured every single Spanish vessel. On land, an army force of regulars and volunteers under General Wesley Merritt captured Manila in the Philippines. In Cuba, fifteen regiments of regular army troops plus three regiments of volunteers, to include the Rough Riders of Theodore Roosevelt, were able to defeat Spanish forces at San Juan and El Caney in July 1898. Less than one month later, a small American force under General Nelson A. Miles evicted Spanish forces from Puerto Rico.

Brief and one-sided as the war may have been, the Paris Treaty of December 1898, which ended the war was to bestow upon the United States a new global empire, although an empire still dwarfed by that of Great Britain. Having gone to war with Spain with the stated intention of freeing Cuba, American forces had somehow managed to find themselves in Puerto Rico, the Philippine Islands, Samoa, Guam, and various other islands of the Pacific. By means of the Paris Treaty, the Philippines were ceded to the United States for twenty million dollars. Even before the war's end, on July 7, 1898, the United States had annexed the Hawaiian Islands. In the end, William McKinley would annex everything except Cuba, which essentially became a U.S. protectorate. Much of America's success in this war was due to its navy, and in the war's aftermath, naval construction would begin anew, so much so that within two decades American naval might would equal, and eventually surpass, that of the British Empire.

America's victory of 1898 would soon afford to the nation a lesson learned centuries earlier by both Rome and Britain. While it may be

347

possible to conquer a Gaul, it is not always possible to conquer the Gauls. Whereas it may be possible to defeat enemy armies and to conquer foreign soils, it is often expensive and difficult to subjugate the newly conquered peoples. In the aftermath of the American conquest and annexation of the Philippine Islands, hostilities would break out between American occupational forces and those of the Philippine insurgent Emilio Aguinaldo. Although less violent than the Philippine Insurrection, American fighting men and dollars would also be used to interject American influence into Cuba, Santa Domingo, Haiti and Nicaragua, as well as in China during the Boxer Rebellion.

As evidence of America's desire to flex its newly found muscles, in December 1907 sixteen U. S. battleships with their hulls freshly painted white would sail forth on a 42,227-mile, 434-day cruise around the globe. This "Great White Fleet" was the brainchild of President Theodore Roosevelt. This naval cruise was intended to impress the American people and to win from them the political support vital to further expand the Navy. It served also as a warning to potential future enemies. This support was to be necessary, as the 1906 commissioning of Great Britain's Dreadnought had already rendered the ships of the Great White Fleet obsolete.

Roosevelt himself would be the greatest advocate of this new navy. On April 2, 1903, during a speech in Chicago, Illinois, Roosevelt declared, "There is a homely old adage which runs, 'speak softly and carry a big stick' you will go far. If the American nation will speak softly, and yet build, and keep at a pitch of highest training, a thoroughly efficient navy, the Monroe Doctrine will go far." Within months in October of that same year, the General Board issued a secret document calling for the construction of forty-eight battleships.

Roosevelt was responsible for another initiative involving naval might. With fleets stationed on both the East and West coast of the United States, it became obvious that there existed a need to find a shorter route to connect them other than by sailing all the way around South America. This need became apparent during the Spanish-American War, when the battleship Oregon required sixty-seven days, traveling 14,000 miles from San Francisco to Florida to join the Atlantic fleet. The apparent solution was a trans-isthmus canal across Panama, which at that time was a possession of Columbia. In 1881, a French company had attempted this task but had failed. Initially, Columbia refused to grant America the rights to build such a canal, but a Panamanian Revolution in early 1902, resulting in the U.S. recognition of Panama as an independent nation, provided Roosevelt with his chance. In November of that year, the Hay-Bunau-Varilla Treaty granted the U.S. a zone through which to build a canal, in exchange for ten million dollars and an annual stipend of $250,000. Construction was to take a decade, with the canal opening in 1914.

As a further indication of the new American mindset and its more aggressive international posture, on December 6, 1904 Theodore Roosevelt issued the Roosevelt Corollary to the Monroe Doctrine, which stated "As a mere matter of self-defense we must exercise a close watch over the approaches to the Panama Canal, and this means that we must be thoroughly alive to our interest in the Caribbean. The Monroe Doctrine may force the United States... to the exercise of an international police force."[119] To put an exclamation point on this new corollary, the following March Congress authorized the further construction of two of an eventual ten new battleships. By the end of 1910, the United States would have in service a fleet displacing 712,000 tons with an additional 824, 000 tons under construction, placing the United States second in the world in terms of the size of its navy. Only Britain's Royal Navy would displace greater tonnage.

With the acquisition of new extra-continental territories, there was a change in the American mindset that would initiate changes in American foreign policy. The early American leaders, Washington and Jefferson in particular, had always advised against becoming involved in the affairs of foreign nations. Territorial expansion, with its accompanying sense of vulnerability coupled with the increased influence from corporations involved in foreign trade would continue to change all of this.

---

[119] Ibid, 299.

*The Great White Fleet of Theodore Roosevelt, impressive for their time, these ships had been rendered obsolete with the launching of the H.M.S. Dreadnought in 1906.*

During the late nineteenth century the railroad magnate James Hill had made a fortune with his Great Northern railroad line. Upon reaching the Pacific, he looked even further west, creating trade routes to and from the Orient and to its 500 million potential new customers. Trade to that region would soar. Total exports to Asia of 26 million dollars in 1896 climbed to 135 million by 1905. Imports also saw an increase from 95 million dollars to 175 million over this same time period.[120]

The results of these changes in societal and government thought resulted in the "Open Door Policy" of 1900. Secretary of State John Hay, recognizing the importance of Oriental markets and those of China in particular, sought agreements from the industrialized nations who controlled spheres of influence in China not to restrict

---

[120] Brinckley, *American Heritage History of the U.S.*, 254.

trade or interfere with Chinese territorial or administrative integrity.

The Panama Canal of Theodore Roosevelt increased America's influence in Central America. When William Howard Taft succeeded Roosevelt as president, he initiated his "dollar diplomacy." The precept of Taft's new diplomacy was that the United States should expand its investments overseas, and that it had the right to protect these investments. In some cases, such as the unstable government of Nicaragua, U.S. troops would be used to replace unfriendly governments with those more willing to accept the American viewpoint. In others, American businessmen would take over the operations of foreign banks and even customs services. These were of course dramatic shifts in U.S. policy.

Then of course, there were those shifts in policy that occurred due to external events. With territorial expansion and the increased cost of maintaining global power status comes the need for increased revenues. During the last year of the Taft Administration, Congress, with the approval of the states, ratified the Sixteenth Amendment to the Constitution, allowing for the collection of income taxes. During the first year of its existence, this new law allowed the government to collect 28 million dollars in new revenue.

In 1912, Woodrow Wilson became only the second Democrat to win the presidency since the inauguration of Lincoln. Ideologically opposed to the concept of Taft's "dollar diplomacy," Wilson initially attempted to rely on "moral force" when dealing with foreign policy issues. Ultimately, events would force him to resort to military force. In 1913, a group of generals under the leadership of Victoriano Huerto had seized power in neighboring Mexico, a move Wilson regarded as being both illegal and immoral. Upon learning that a German munitions ship was about to dock in Vera Cruz to provide Huerto with arms, Wilson, in response, sent a force of U.S. Marines to occupy this foreign city. Violence would ensue, during which 126 Mexicans and 19 Marines were killed. Worse was to come. In August 1914 the Huerto regime was overthrown, being replaced by the Constitutional Army of Venustiano Corranzo. Further instability led Corranza to split with two of his rebel leaders, Francisco "Poncho" Villa and

Emiliano Zapata. Still believing Corranza to be the head of Mexico's legitimate government, Wilson chose to recognize the Corranza regime. Consequently, Villa began to conduct terrorist-style raids in Mexico, and eventually against American border towns. In March of 1916 Villa and his rebels raided Columbus, New Mexico. Twenty American citizens were killed and the town was razed to the ground. With events now beyond his control, Wilson was forced to send an American expeditionary force into Mexico under the command of General John "Black Jack" Pershing. Pershing and his 6,000-man army would pursue Villa for nearly a year, until events in Europe would force his recall in order to deal with much more important matters.

With the outbreak of general warfare in Europe in late summer of 1914, the initial stance of the United States was much the same as the one followed during Europe's other great wars, – neutrality. Shortly after the outbreak of war, on August 19, 1914, Woodrow Wilson declared to the Senate that, "The United States must be neutral, in fact as well as in name... We must be impartial in thought as well as in action."[121] Whereas the expressed position of the U.S. government was neutrality, the commercial reality of the time was that U.S. arms manufacturers were willing and able to reap huge profits by selling weapons to the belligerent nations. Due to England's superior Royal Navy and its blockade of the Central Powers of Germany, Austria, Hungary and the Ottoman Empire, The U.S. manufacturers simply ended up being a quartermaster to the Allied Powers of Britain, France, Italy and Russia.

With nations now embroiled in the fighting of a total war with their very existence at stake, a condition of one-sided trade simply could not be tolerated. While for centuries England had controlled the seas around Europe, technology had provided to Wilhelmine Germany a counter to the authority of the Royal Navy. The submarine, first invented during the American Revolution, had now become a modern, effective weapon of war. In response to the Royal Navy's blockade of Germany, Germany began a counter blockade of

---

[121] Ibid, 343.

Britain. One of its principal victims was the British passenger liner Lusitania, which was sunk by a German submarine on May 7, 1915. The sinking of this ship resulted in the death of 128 Americans. This disaster began to shift American public opinion away from its original stance of neutrality.

American hackles would be further raised in March of 1917 when the U.S. State Department released a note intercepted by the British in which the German Foreign Minister to Mexico, Arthur Zimmerman, had alluded to an alliance between Germany and Mexico with the intention of allowing Mexico to reacquire the territories it had lost during the Mexican-American War of 1846-1848. By April, public sentiment was such that Wilson went before Congress to ask for a declaration of war against Germany. This declaration was passed by the Senate on April 4, 1917, and by the Congress two days later.

No lengthy discussion is necessary regarding America's combat operations during World War I, other than to say that eight military divisions fielded in Europe by the end of the war helped tip the balance of scales away from Germany and toward the allies. During the summer and fall of 1918, American troops were vital to the success of the St. Mihiel and Meuse-Argonne Offensives, which would lead to the collapse of the German Army on the Western Front.

Issues not recognized at the time would prove far more important in the post-war world. In 1914, Great Britain had gone to war as the world's strongest nation, with Germany and France laying claim to empire as well. After four years of stalemate in the trenches of the Western Front, all three had expended much of their manpower strengths and had run themselves to near bankruptcy. This is not to say that the war was inexpensive to the United States, as America spent 32.7 billion dollars on its participation in the war, more than the total amount spent by the federal government from 1791 to 1914.[122] However, by the spring of 1919, the United States would find itself in a position to become the leader of the free world.

On the eve of the American declaration of war, Wilson had

---

[122] Ibid, 346.

predicted that the United States would become a less tolerant nation, and that "The spirit of ruthless brutality will enter into the very fiber of our national life, infecting Congress, the courts, the policeman on the beat, the man in the street."[123] Wilson himself would attempt to rise above intolerance, and his Fourteen Points that were proposed in January 1918 would seek to establish a better post-war world. In his message to Congress recommending the declaration of war Wilson had stated:

> *We have no selfish ends to serve. We desire no conquest, no material compensation for the sacrifice we shall freely make. We are but one of the champions of mankind… we enter this war only where we are clearly forced into it, because there are no other means of defending our rights.*

America would enter the war with moralistic tones. It would exit the war with something quite different. During the years of the Jefferson Administration, America had first found itself interjecting its influence across the globe. Affairs such as the Tripolitan War continuing through the Spanish-American War had been relatively local issues. Subsequent to World War I, the concept of total, global war was born. For the United States, its involvement would mean the need to supply two million fighting men at the end of a three thousand mile line of communications. In addition, these men would require the new weapons of war, everything from machine guns to heavy artillery, to aircraft. It was during this time that the military industrial complex was initiated. In the years prior to the war, Roosevelt, Taft and Wilson had assailed the practices and unlimited growth of American industry. Now, Wilson would be compelled to forge a close bond with them. In order to supply the needs of war, Wilson appointed one of Wall Street's leading men, Bernard Baruch, to be chairman of a new War Industries Board. This board would be given nearly dictatorial powers over the U.S. economy and wartime

---

[123] Ibid. 347.

production. Existing factories would be converted from producing peacetime products to the goods of war. Once established, this new military industrial complex was to become a fixture of American society with an ever-increasing influence on the affairs of state.

This new military industrial complex would provide for the United States a military power now capable of dealing with any adversary in the world. On the day America declared war on Germany, The United States Army consisted of 200,000 men, 65,000 of whom were National Guard.[124] By the end of the war nineteen months later, this army had grown to twenty times its original size. Having entered the war late, by the time of the Armistice of November 1919, the number of American troops on the Western Front actually exceeded the number of British troops with the width of the front held by U.S. troops also exceeding that of the British.

The U.S. Navy was to experience explosive growth as well. Although the major surface units of the Navy saw little service during the war, American destroyer forces would become actively engaged in submarine warfare, hunting down the U-boats of the German fleet and acting as escorts for the trans-Atlantic convoys. As early as May 4, 1917, six U.S. destroyers were operating in European waters. By war's end, that number had risen to seventy-nine. In terms of the overall ships available to the Navy, 774 ships were listed on the Navy Register by war's end, more than twice the number available when the U.S. had entered the war nineteen months earlier.

Perhaps another important aspect of American involvement in the war would be the experience gained by future leaders of the next war. Most associate the "liberty ship" as being an invention of the Second World War. However, during World War I, the need for destroyers to combat German U-boats led to the construction of Liberty Destroyers, a prelude to the cargo vessels of World War II. America would gain its first experience in aerial combat, with pilots such as Lieutenant Frank Luke achieving "ace" status and leaders such as Colonel William Mitchell gaining the needed experience in organizing and

---

[124] Dupuy, *Military Heritage of America*, 358.

overseeing large-scale aerial campaigns. In the trenches on the Western Front, men such as Eisenhower, MacArthur, Patton, and many others would gain needed combat experience, which would enable them to conduct the campaigns of the next war.

Much as post-bellum America had experienced massive growth and extensive social transformation after the Civil War, America would experience similar changes after World War I. Unfortunately, this transformation would come with a price. Agriculture, so vital to the health and welfare of any country, would experience a major decline in the years after the Great War. This decline would be so dramatic that during the 1920s America's farms saw their share of the nation's pool of wealth reduced by half. Much of this resulted from the removal of wartime price supports for grain and wheat and from reduced demand from foreign markets such as in Europe where large armies no longer had to be fed and where millions of soldiers were returning home to work the farms of their native countries. There were also contributing factors beyond the control of both farmers and government. Crop yields, after centuries of increase, began to decline. Manmade factors such as overgrazing and deforestation would begin to take their toll. Natural factors such as flooding and drought would continue to plague farmers, just as they had since the dawn of organized farming. For all of man's technological innovations, he still could not overcome the forces of nature.

As another indication of America's agricultural health, the United States Census of 1920 revealed that for the first time in U.S. history, more Americans lived in urban-metropolitan areas than in rural areas. No doubt much of this was the result of the wartime industrial economy, and could also be attributed to the continued disparity between industrial and agricultural wages. Indicative of this trend, between the years of 1920 and 1929, Americans would experience an almost 26 percent increase in real earnings, at a time when agricultural wealth was continuing to decline. Just as the Punic and Civil Wars of Rome had affected a decline in Roman agricultural fortunes, the First World War and America's future wars with their accompanying social changes would begin to impact U.S. agriculture.

If America's agricultural fortunes began to decline, its financial fortunes would see an opposite trend. The years of the early twentieth century would see America transformed from the world's largest debtor nation, to the largest creditor nation. During the First World War and the years of its immediate reconstruction, the United States would lend ten billion dollars to allied nations. Private sector investors would add to this with ten or twelve billion of their own. Added to American military and industrial might would be the new factor of financial might. Many might choose to underestimate this financial might, but in the years after the Great War, American policies would have a dramatic effect upon the financial and military stability of the world.

With the entry of America into World War I had come Woodrow Wilson's Fourteen Points, with an eye toward future security and peace. In the aftermath of the war had come Wilson's initiatives toward a lenient peace, so as not to incite future enmity. If enacted, these policies would no doubt have gone far toward these ends. Nevertheless, leaders of the European powers and members within the U.S. Senate would fall victim to an almost adamantine stubbornness and much of Wilson' sage advice would go unheeded. Thence, America would drift toward isolationism. Even worse, it would drift toward protectionism. As early as 1920, Republicans in Congress were seeking to enact artificially high trade barriers. These initial attempts would be vetoed by Wilson, who added, "If we wish to have Europe settle her debts, governmental or commercial, we must be prepared to buy from her. Clearly this is no time for the erection of high trade barriers."[125] With the departure of Wilson from the White House and complete control of the government by the Republicans under Warren Harding in 1920, the Fordney-McCumber Tariff was enacted. By this act, European nations were effectively prevented from selling their goods to America. In 1928, and on the very eve of global depression, the Smoot Hawley Tariff was enacted, bringing with it the highest tariff rates in U.S. history. Henceforth, the

---

[125] Nevins and Commager, *Pocket History of the U.S.*, 404-405.

only way for European nations to pay off their debts or to buy American goods would be through further acts of borrowing.

With little if any resort open to them, European nations would retaliate, imposing barriers on American manufacturers as well. The economic instability brought about by these measures would contribute to the political turmoil of the times and affect U.S. international policies. Germany, defeated in war and further ruined by the "malignant and silly" terms of the Treaty of Versailles, became almost entirely dependent upon the United States for its survival. Through the Dawes Plan of 1924, Germany was afforded an economic respite, with war reparations being scaled downward, and large loans being afforded to stabilize its economy. Five years later, the Young Plan was put forth to further ease Germany's economic distress. By this time, 1929, the victors of World War I were actually providing more money to Germany as loans than they were receiving in war reparations.

Other repercussions from the economics of this time period would become evident in social change. When big business had come to the forefront of American society during the last half of the nineteenth century, there had come with it an element of society opposed to its negative impacts. Referred to as "muckrakers," this new band of journalists exposed much of the graft and corruption of the period. In his work *The Jungle*, Upton Sinclair exposed the excesses and abuses of the Chicago meatpackers. In response, Congress passed the Meat Inspection Act and later a Pure Food and Drug Act. Theodore Roosevelt once stated that, "The great development of industrialism means that there must be an increase in the supervision exercised by the Government over business enterprise."[126] The chosen instrument for this Government supervision would be the Sherman Anti-Trust Act, which Roosevelt would use during his assault on the Northern Securities combination as well as the tobacco and oil trust.

It would only be natural that in the ebb and flow of events, big business would respond to this assault on their growth and

---

[126] Ibid, 353.

prosperity. In 1915, the first full-time public relations firm was established by Edward Bernays. Advertising would now be accompanied by attempts to groom and promote a more positive image to the American public. Technology would assist big business in its efforts. In 1903, the first feature film, *The Great Train Robbery*, would become available to the public, using the inventions of Thomas Alva Edison. Originally regarded as more of a novelty than a means of mass media, by 1924 America would be home to 20,000 movie theatres and by the end of the decade, between eighty and one hundred million Americans went to the movies every week. Furthermore, the invention of Guglielmo Marconi, the radio, would afford to big business and government an additional means to influence societal thought. Just as the motion picture industry had started as a novelty before its meteoric rise in popularity, so too would the radio. In 1925, a national radio network had been established by the Columbia Broadcasting System (CBS), soon to be joined within two years by the National Broadcasting Company (NBC). By the year 1930, more than 12 million American households would possess at least one radio.

The importance of these new advances, the motion picture and the radio, were that they allowed for the creation of a new consumer-based economy. Of itself, this was probably not a bad thing. However, this new consumer-based economy became heavily dependent on the use of credit. With the 1920s being accompanied by the rapid electrification of homes and the accompanying increase of electrical appliances, with the ownership of automobiles increasing from 25 percent to over 60 percent, the need for credit only increased. Events would soon show that easy credit and the rapid extension of installment buying, when coupled with other economic factors, could be very unhealthy for a national economy.

It may well be more than a little ironic that just as a nation's agricultural health could be a positive indicator of future industrial and commercial growth that the economic collapse of 1929 was preceded by an agricultural collapse during the 1920s. Between the years of 1920 and 1932, farm income declined from fifteen and one half to less than five and one half billion dollars. The value of crops dwindled as well. The 1920 crop of wheat, some eight hundred million bushels, was valued at one and a half billion dollars. A similar crop in 1932 was worth less than three hundred million. Much as Roman agriculture began its decline after the Antonine years, American agriculture would begin to experience similar signs of distress. By the year 1930, more than forty percent of American farms were operated by tenant farmers, and during the years of 1927-1932, more than ten percent of American farms would experience foreclosure. This is not to say that American agriculture would not experience future growth, but it was an indication that it was showing signs of economic dry rot.

It would be the never-ending cycle of human violence that would lead to the next series of challenges for American society. Although the U.S. Senate refused to ratify the Treaty of Versailles and declined also to commit America to the League of Nations, the U.S. still maintained an interest in international affairs. During the Harding Administration, the world's major powers, with the exception of the Soviet Union, met in Washington in a vain attempt to prevent future war. Several treaties were signed, the two most important being one which limited armaments, the other guaranteeing the sovereignty of China and reaffirming the "Open Door" policy in regard to Chinese trade. The Washington Naval Treaty of 1922 set restrictions on the size and number of heavy warships to be allowed to each of the major powers. This was done according to a simple ratio, with the U.S. and Britain being allowed 525,000 tons of new capital ships, 315,000 for Japan and 175,000 tons each for France and Italy; thus the ratio, 5:5: 3.1: 1.75: 1.75.

Although well intended, the problem with this pacifistic treaty was that the United States, now the largest and wealthiest nation on earth, agreed to sacrifice ships it could afford to build while the other nations agreed to scrap or sacrifice ships they largely could not afford to build. This was especially true of the Royal Navy and the French Navy, whose nations emerged from the First World War economically prostrate. The full outcome of this treaty would not be understood until the after effects of December 7, 1941, when it became evident that Japan's decision to attack America rested partly within Japan's belief that in a short war it could tip the balance of the scales and defeat America.

Further mistakes were made as well. In the absence of U.S. participation in the League of Nations, the countries of Europe sought security by means of alliances, their memories so ephemeral so as not to remember that alliances were a major contributor to the mistakes of 1914. In addition, with the fear of modern weapons such as the airplane and chemical weapons on the rise, many of Europe's nations seized upon the Kellogg-Briand Pact of 1928 as an opportunity to renounce war. Unfortunately, this pact only banned aggressive warfare, which would be hard to define, but there existed within the pact no provisions to punish nations in violation. Kellogg-Briand was a tiger with no teeth.

With a dither of pacifistic dreams driving the nations of the Western World toward disarmament, all that would be needed to drive the world into its next violent convulsion was a period of economic instability and social unrest. On October 29, 1929 this period would be ushered in with the collapse of the New York Stock Market. Not entirely understood at the time, or perhaps even now, this collapse was accompanied by similar events in Europe. Having made the critical error of believing that a shattered German economy could be harnessed to pay their war debts, all that was needed to begin a domino effect within the debt-ridden economies of the victorious nations of World War I was a small push. That push came with the closing of the Credit-Anstalt, Austria's largest bank. The aftershocks were felt around the globe.

In the United States, few realized or believed that October 29, 1929, also known as Black Tuesday, would be of lasting effect. However, in the ten days prior to Christmas of that year, one million Americans were told they no longer had jobs. By the end of the first week of 1930, that number would increase to four million. It is both interesting and revealing that President Herbert Hoover took a hands-off approach to this economic crisis. His reasoning and his fear was that government aid would turn citizens into government dependents who would in turn favor whichever candidate or party, that promised them the greatest benefit at election time. The Roman poet Juvenal had written of this phenomenon during the first century in his work, *Satires*.

In Germany, the economic collapse was complete. When economic conditions in the United States became such that aid to Germany was no longer possible, Germany in turn was no longer able to pay its debts. The German mark sank to an all-time low of five million to the U.S. dollar. It then sank completely out of sight, its only real value perhaps as a substitute for wallpaper. No longer being able to pay its debts to Britain and France, these two nations found themselves struggling to pay their own debts to the United States. In turn, the United States could no longer afford to lend money to Germany to support its failed economy. The dominoes were falling.

With Germany's Weiman Republic becoming one vast soup kitchen, the stage was set for any number of demagogues to step forward with promises to save the nation. Promising to restore Germany to its pre-war glory, the political star of Adolf Hitler would begin to rise. In the aftermath of the burning of the Reichstag, and following the very violent elections of 1933, which were won by Hitler and the Nazi party by a more than two to one margin, Hitler would push through the Reichstag the Enabling Act of March 23, 1933, granting to himself the authority to control budgets, make laws, and to make treaties with foreign governments; a clear and clever transition from democracy to dictatorship by legal means.

Having been granted these sweeping powers, Hitler would then unleash a reign of terror on his own people, with the clear intent of destroying Germany's Jewish population and of driving the intellectual elements from German society. The ferocity of this campaign of terror would initially be denied by the outside world, until its effects and Hitler's intentions began to spill across German borders and into the ancient states of Europe surrounding the Third Reich. Eventually, after German ideas had spilled across its borders, German armies would follow. This new German viciousness and militarism would be accompanied by equivalent policies in Italy and Japan, with Italy attacking the nations of the Mediterranean rim and Japan eventually attacking China and the island chains on the Pacific rim.

Needless to say, these events would eventually lead the world into its Second World War. These events would also impart a valuable lesson in regard to foreign policy: that wars are not contractual affairs, and they need but one nation's consent. There would be another lesson as well. During America's formative years, in the aftermath of each conflict, U.S. armed services were reduced to skeleton forces, auspiciously under the guise of financial constraint. However, now having been thrust into a role of world leadership, this reduction could be catastrophic during an age of total war. The numbers prove especially revealing, with German, Japanese, and Italian armies numbering in the millions. On the eve of World War II, the United States army numbered only 118,750 regular enlistees plus a 20,000-strong officer corps. The Army Air Corps at that time numbered only 17,000 officers and men with but 1,700 aircraft of all types. Many of these aircraft were used for training purposes or they were so obsolete so as to be rendered useless in the event of war.

The U.S. Navy, the pride and joy of Theodore Roosevelt and purveyor of American might, was large, having fifteen battleships and five aircraft carriers, thirty cruisers and two hundred twenty-six destroyers. However, because of the Washington Naval Treaty, only five of the battleships were of post-1919 construction, and nearly two thirds of the destroyers were also of First World War vintage.

This lack of military preparedness was not unique to the United States. Similarly, Great Britain had a large navy but had allowed its army and air force to dwindle. Only during the late 1930s was this trend reversed, with airpower and air superiority becoming a near obsession with England's future wartime leader, Winston Churchill. The reliance of the United States on a policy of neutrality and the misconception that the two great oceans to our west and to our east would allow us time to prepare for war, would be especially costly. Modern war does not ask, but rather demands, a total economic effort from the nations involved. Modern weapons require a lead-time in their production; failure to afford this lead-time could in the future be a major hazard to a nation's very existence.

With the volume of war and the size of armies reaching new limits, the stockpiling of weapons and the proper allocation of natural resources became vital elements to the war effort as well. In effect, modern warfare mandates that nations must regulate and convert their entire peacetime economy to survive a modern contest between nations.

The Second World War would begin much the same as the First World War, with the exception that this time Germany would first strike to the east, against Poland on September 1, 1939. The U.S. would adopt a stance very similar to that of the earlier conflict; neutrality with public sentiment largely in favor of the allies. Even after the war in Europe had been waged for more than two years, and Japan's war against China for nearly ten, pacifist waves still washed over America's shores to the extent that in 1941, the U.S. House of Representatives voted in the affirmative on a continuation of the 1940 Draft Act by a majority of only one vote. Victims of our own wishful thinking, on December 7, 1941, America would suffer a fate like that of the once sleeping nations of Europe who eventually awoke to the fury of the Third Reich.

America's involvement in the Second World War would come only after the Japanese attack against Pearl Harbor. While generally considered as being one of America's worst military defeats, the Pearl Harbor attack would grant to the United States one major advantage. The outcome of the Versailles Treaty of 1919 had rendered Germany prostrate. While it was the intention of the victors to place Germany in a weaker position by virtue of stripping it of its arms, what they actually brought about was a new Germany forced to discard the weapons of the prior war to concentrate on newer, more efficient weapons, which is one reason for the huge success of German arms during the initial stages of the war. With Japan's attack at Pearl Harbor, much of America's battleship strength was destroyed, with four ships being sunk and three others severely damaged. From that point forward, the U.S. Navy would be forced to rely on its aircraft carriers to conduct the bulk of the fighting in the Pacific campaign. Unwittingly, Japan had created a virtual Frankenstein's monster; a fleet that would rely upon the striking power of aircraft and their much greater range, instead of the big guns of the battlewagons.

The misguided belief of Japan that its Navy and Air Force could deliver a knockout blow to the United States in a speedy war would prove fatal in its consequences. It would also provide to the United States, the Soviet Union, and to the world, a lesson in the importance of logistic and mass manufacture in modern war. This logic would hold especially true due to the technical advances in armored and air warfare. When Germany had attacked Poland in September of 1939, German panzer armies would encounter Polish Cavalry. In the air, Germany's new Luftwaffe would first secure air superiority, and then turn its full attention to an all out assault on Polish ground forces, limiting their ability to operate efficiently. This new German concept of combined arms assault, or blitzkrieg, would sweep all before it in the initial years of the war. It would not be until Hitler assaulted Soviet Russia that it became evident that for all its fighting skill, the German army could never overcome the vast manpower and industrial reserves of Soviet Russia. Japan would learn the same lesson, as American industrial might simply overpowered them during a long protracted war.

The size and depth, and technological improvements in American arms are the principal indicator of this phenomenon. With much of its military strength destroyed at Pearl Harbor in December 1941, by war's end the strength of the Navy was established at 18 battle ships, 3 battle cruisers, 27 fleet carriers, 70 escort carriers, 31 heavy and 48 light cruisers, 367 destroyers, 296 destroyer-escorts, and 200 submarines.[127] In contrast, Japanese naval construction following the attack on Pearl Harbor consisted of no battleships, 7 aircraft carriers, two of which were conversions from passenger liners, no cruisers, 14 destroyers, 31 destroyer escorts, and 76 submarines. In a protracted

---

[127] Crescent Books, *Jane's Fighting Ships of World War II*, 254.

war spanning the great distances across the Pacific, the outcome was inevitable. Not only were American weapons available in superior numbers, they were of superior quality as well.

If American industry could far outstrip that of its naval rival in the Far East with warship production, its capacity to produce warplanes would correspondingly outstrip that of both Japan and Germany in the air. When Germany initiated the war with its attack on Poland, American aircraft production for the year 1939 stood at 5,856, less than one-half the combined totals for Germany (8,295) and Japan (4,467). Five years later, American aircraft production would reach the undreamed of total of 96,318, whereas the combined total of Germany and Japan was 67,987, a difference of nearly 30,000 aircraft for that year alone.

Much of this difference was of course due to a disparity in industrial output, and it may be very much true that the axis powers never had any real chance of attaining parity with the much larger economies of the United States and Russia. Much of the disparity may also be attributed to long-term strategic thinking. Undoubtedly Germany and Japan had a qualitative superiority in aircraft types in 1939. However, both nations expected a short war, so that not enough attention was given to the design or production of future aircraft types. Both mistakenly believed that the aircraft types in service at the beginnings of hostilities would be sufficient to finish the war. Hence, fighters like the Messerschmitt Me-109 of Germany and the Mitsubishi A6M Zero of Japan would remain mainstays of their respective air forces throughout the war. In contrast, American fighters like the Curtis P-40 Warhawk in service at the time of Pearl Harbor, would be replaced by more capable aircraft such as the P-51 Mustang and the F-6 Hellcat, and in much greater numbers.

Other such numbers were indicators of the rapidity of the United States military buildup during the war. In November of 1942, when U.S. forces had invaded North Africa during operation "Torch," the three different landing forces consisted of 109,000 troops transported on 120 landing craft and escorted by a predominantly British force of warships.

*Instruments of victory in the Pacific War of 1941 to 1945:*
*The American aircraft carrier Hornet underway in September 1944.*

Less than two years later, the initial wave for the June 6, 1944 invasion of France would consist of 176,000 troops and their equipment transported on 4,000 ships and landing craft, supported by 600 warships. In the skies overhead, some 2,500 heavy bombers and more than 7,500 fighter aircraft would support these landings. Granted, this invasion was multi-national with allied troops from other nations constituting a major force. However, there is no doubt that U.S. manufacturing provided much of the material needs for this invasion.

With the beginning of the last year of the war in 1945, America had been able to mobilize a force such that no nation in history had ever been able to exercise as much power over as wide an expanse of the globe, and with as much efficiency. The United States of F.D.R. and Harry Truman had attained the status of the Rome of Octavian. This is not to say that it was the world's only power, as Soviet Russia was a definite power as well. America however, could dominate the seas and the skies as well as the land, whereas Soviet Russia was predominately a land-based power.

There was also the issue of financial power. Its nearly four-year involvement in the war cost the United States nearly 350 billion dollars, an amount equal to that spent by Russia, Britain and France combined. This figure was also equal to that spent by Germany (200 billion), Japan (100 billion), and Italy (50 billion). As the world's largest creditor nation, the United States could easily afford this total. The other nations, Britain in particular, could not, with future financial constraints limiting their global influence.

As a further indicator of a new U.S. global dominance, the U.S. military of a few hundred thousand active and reserve servicemen had grown to an establishment of 14.9 million. Only Soviet Russia would mobilize more forces, nearly 20 million. However, by war's end the United States had a monopoly over the world's most destructive weapon, the atomic bomb. In the B-29 super-fortress, it also had an aircraft capable of delivering it to almost any point on the globe. After nearly one hundred and fifty years of growth, the United States now found itself at the pinnacle of global power.

# Chapter 12

¤

# ZENITH

With the termination of the Second World War in September of 1945, the United States would find itself an inhabitant of a new bi-polar world in a nuclear age. This new period of American culture and world history would be ushered in with the realization that man had discovered the power of self-destruction. There were other realities to face as well. Even before the war had been won, the process of military demobilization had begun, so much so that by June of 1946, U.S. forces had shrunk from 12 million men to 2.9 million men. In so much as Octavian had realized that there was such a thing as too much military power and had reduced his army to twenty-five legions, the U.S. now discovered this same need.

The transition from a wartime to a peacetime economy would also generate economic issues. With the sudden curtailing of wartime production, factories did not have sufficient time to convert back to the production of peacetime goods. Consequently, by the end of 1946, consumer prices had risen by nearly thirty percent. Having accepted wage restraints during the war years, laborers began to demand pay raises when wartime economic controls were lifted and consumer prices rose sharply. In the year 1946, labor-management relations were so poor that U.S. unions conducted over 5,000 labor strikes, involving nearly fifteen percent of the total labor force.

Even though the end of the war gave rise to the influence of internal forces in American society, by and large it would be external forces that would dominate the attention of not only American society, but the societies of many other nations as well. With the defeat of axis armies across the globe, the expectation was that peace would bring stability around the post-war world. Unfortunately, quite the opposite would hold true. In the world's most populous nation, the absence of Japanese armies would only lead to a continuation of civil war, with the Communist forces of Mao Zedong gaining control of that nation by 1949. With Britain and France greatly weakened by the war, many of their former colonial possessions sought independence. In September of 1945, ideologue Ho Chi Minh announced the formation of the Democratic Republic of Vietnam, which France would initially recognize, and then attempt to regain. In war-torn Europe, relations between the Allied Armies of the western nations and those of the Soviet Union would cool rapidly, so much so that the now alienated nations would enter into what statesman Bernard Baruch referred to as the "Cold War." Always the master of words, Winston Churchill would best describe the situation during a March 1946 speech in Fulton, Missouri declaring that, "From Stettin in the Baltic to Trieste in the Adriatic, an Iron Curtain has descended across the continent."[128]

The confrontation between the Democratic West and Communist East would spread across the globe. Korea, initially promised its independence, was divided with Russia controlling the North and the South coming under the protection of the United States. By 1947 the Soviet domination of Eastern Europe threatened to spread south to Greece and Turkey. Recognizing the inability of the British Empire to sustain these nations, President Harry S. Truman asked Congress for 400 million dollars in aid to support these two ailing economies, arguing, "I believe that it must be the policy of the United States to support free people who are resisting attempted subjugation by armed minorities or by outside pressures. I believe that we must

---

[128] Langworth, *Churchill by Himself*, 10

assist free people to work out their own destinies in their own way."[129] This new doctrine was to become known as the Truman Doctrine.

Perhaps as a response to this new American foreign policy, the Soviet Union continued its aggressive posture in Europe. In February 1948, Following a Communist coup d'etat, the Soviet Union assumed virtual control of Czechoslovakia. Four months later, the Soviets would initiate a blockade of Berlin by closing all land routes to the city. The American response was both calculated and massive. To supply Berlin, the United States and its allies initiated the Berlin Airlift, an around the clock strategic airlift, which would last 321 days and carry approximately 877,864 tons of supplies to the besieged city. Even before the Berlin airlift was successfully completed, the United States and eleven European nations entered into the North Atlantic Treaty Organization, or NATO, a defensive alliance intended to blunt any Soviet military threat westward. Finally, to assist Europe in its post-war recovery, the U.S. initiated the Marshall Plan, named after Secretary of State George C. Marshall, which would pump 13 billion dollars into the European recovery between the years of 1948 and 1951.

September of 1949 would prove to be a month of momentous implication for future U.S. foreign policy. During that month, Harry Truman announced that the U.S. had incontrovertible evidence that the Soviet Union had detonated an atomic bomb. To the United States would go a new lesson: as Rome had discovered with the Barbarians and Sassanids, and as England was to find in the wake of the First and Second World Wars, there is no respite or time out for a superpower. To attain a dominant status is only to invite challenges from rivals, great and small. In the aftermath of repeated Soviet threats, the post-war draw-down of American armed forces would need to be reviewed. Accordingly, the Truman administration would initiate a reorganization of its armed forces. On July 26, 1947, Truman signed into law an act placing the Army, Navy, and newly

---

[129] Brinckley, *American Heritage History of the U.S.*, 464.

independent Air Force into a new Department of Defense. The first Secretary of Defense was to be James Forrestal, with each branch of the three services to have their own Secretary subordinate to him.

In Addition, this new defense administration was to have a new home, the Pentagon. Other subordinate agencies would also emerge, including a Research and Development Board and a Central Intelligence Agency, intended to gather information about arms and activities of foreign countries. Organization of these innovations in national security would not come without a price, and that price would eventually soar into the hundreds of billions of dollars annually.

Not readily visible or recognized at the time, the enemy from without would eventually find an accomplice by means of an enemy from within. Rivalries, both inter-service and between the manufacturers of arms, would begin to have an impact on how much the U.S. would spend on defense and weapons and to some extent where and when these weapons would be employed. Much as Claudius had invaded Britain in the first century to garner public approval and win the support of his legions, the now enhanced military-industrial complex would begin to influence U.S. foreign policy.

The weapons of the Cold War would even begin to assume a new dimension in American society. Ancient Rome is always closely associated with the centurion, the legionary, the gladius, and the lorica segmentata. Beginning in the 1950s, the super carrier and the strategic bomber, especially the B-52, would begin to be associated with American military might, just as they are to this day. When the atomic bomb of the late 1940s was superceded by the Hydrogen bomb of the 1950s, the importance, complexity, and cost of weapons would increase dramatically. Military strength would also come to be closely associated with numbers. The B-29 Superfortress, which dropped the atomic bombs on Hiroshima and Nagasaki in August of 1945, would be replaced with the B-36 Peacemaker. Following the continued development of jet propulsion, the Air Force would acquire its first all jet strategic bomber, the B-47 Stratojet, of which nearly 2,000 were built. Its successor, the B-52 Stratofortress, even larger and more capable, would become the backbone of the American strategic bomber force, still serving in that capacity today. Nearly 750 of them would be purchased.

The United States Navy, regarded as an instrument of American power since the time of Theodore Roosevelt, would assume a role of even greater importance in the new Cold War. At its peak during the Second World War, the Navy numbered 6,768 ships of all types, dominating the oceans of the world. In the late war years vast carrier fleets had roamed the Western Pacific with near impunity. By 1950, this carrier presence had been reduced to a single flattop, no doubt under the mistaken belief that the end of the war and the advent of atomic weapons had spelled the end of any further need for a carrier navy. In 1949, when Secretary of Defense James V. Forrestal had resigned and was replaced by Louis A. Johnson, one of the new Secretary's first acts was to cancel construction of the navy's first post-war aircraft carrier, the U.S.S. United States. What followed is commonly referred to as the "Revolt of the Admirals," which resulted in Congress holding public hearings over the Air Force B-36 program and the status of U.S. Naval aviation.

In April of 1950, the Navy began carrier tests on the AJ-1 Savage, its first aircraft designed specifically as a carrier-based attack bomber. The further need for conventional carrier forces would be realized when North Korean forces crossed the 38th parallel into South Korea on June 25, 1950. For the next three years the Cold War would be a little less so. With few other military assets in the region, America's only carrier in the Western Pacific, the Valley Forge, would begin air strikes against North Korean targets. During three years of hostilities she would be joined in Korean waters by her sister ships the Essex, the Boxer, the Leyte, the Philippine Sea, and the Princeton.

While the efforts of the navy during the Korean War were of great importance, events away from this theatre of operations would hold far greater importance for the future of naval operations. On June 17, 1952, the U. S. Navy's atomic era was born when the keel was laid for the submarine Nautilus, the first nuclear-powered vessel in the world. Exactly one month later, the keel for the Navy's first super carrier, Forrestal, was laid at Newport News Shipbuilding and Dry Dock Company in Norfolk, Virginia. By these two acts, the future of two of the Navy's most important weapon systems and means of power projection were set in stone. Also of importance to future naval operations, the year 1952 would see the initial test firing of the sidewinder air-to-air missile in September, and the test firing of the Regulus assault missile from the test ship Norton Sound in November. Missile warfare was to be an integral part of future naval operations, thus increasing their effectiveness and their cost.

Additionally, the year 1952 would be of great importance in regard to new American initiatives in foreign affairs. In March, the United States and Cuba would enter into a bilateral military agreement, although this would be terminated in 1959 after Fidel Castro overthrew the government of Fulgencio Batista. In May of 1952, the United States First Fleet Commander in the Far East Vice-Admiral Arthur Struble would hold meetings with his British and French counterparts to discuss joint strategy on the defense of Southeast Asia. A further meeting in Washington with the Commander of French forces in Indochina, General Jean deLattre de Tassigny, would result in U.S. aid to French forces fighting Viet Minh guerillas in the region. This event would mark the beginning of the U.S. Involvement in Vietnam, an involvement that would last until the Nixon Doctrine and the withdrawal of American combat forces in 1972.

In the wake of the Egyptian Revolution of July 1952, the United States was drawn into the power vacuum caused by the decline of British and French influence in the Middle East. Having already demonstrated a policy shift in the region by recognizing the independent State of Israel in 1947, the U.S. would now offer Point IV aid to Egypt, Lebanon, Jordan, Turkey, Iran, Iraq, Israel and Saudia Arabia. The cost of Point IV assistance was 4.5 billion dollars throughout the region, with an additional 40 million dollars worth of economic assistance going to the new Egyptian government of

Mohammed Naguib. These policies of national defense through foreign aid show a striking similarity to those of Imperial Rome, whose stated policy was "keep your weapons short, and your frontiers long." England had adopted a similar policy at the height of its power, often relying on the manpower of its Indian Army as well as those of its other colonies in Australia and South Africa. However, this policy always comes with a price, as the United States would continue to find out.

The 1952 election of Dwight Eisenhower as President of the United States would be followed by an extension and revision of the Truman Doctrine. The new Eisenhower Doctrine was far more generous than the former, even going so far as to offer military and economic assistance to any nation that was thought to be in danger of Communist invasion or subversion. Paradoxically, while making additional pledges of military assistance, the first months of the Eisenhower administration would see cutbacks in U.S. defense budgets. The Air Force budget was reduced by 5 billion dollars and the level of manpower for the U.S. Navy was cut 55,000. In addition, 40,000 Department of Defense workers were let go and the number of manufacturers of weapons reduced. As had Rome with its Foederati, America was going to arm its allies, while reducing the size of its own military. This policy of course denies the possibility that regime changes in foreign countries could mean the prospect of U.S. weapons eventually being used against America. There is also the issue of new technology being lost to America's enemies by means of changing alliances. Proof of this very issue was to follow soon.

Having agreed to supply French forces in Indochina with weapons and necessary supplies, 400 million dollars worth in 1953 alone, when French forces were overpowered at Dien Bien Phu in 1954, all of this equipment was lost. Furthermore, after signing an armistice with the Viet Minh on August 11, the French National Assembly revealed to the world that the United States had financed nearly eight percent of the cost during the Anti-Communist fighting that took place in Indochina. If financing a war is a detriment to the state of a nation's finances, financing a losing war is much worse.

The financial burden of arming foreign nations so as to contain Communist expansion would continue. In January 1955, the Eisenhower administration appropriated an additional 216 million dollars in aid to Cambodia, Laos and South Vietnam. Placing further strains on American military resources, the U.S. also pledged to defend the Island of Taiwan, a pledge that would lead to demands by the Peoples Republic of China for the removal of U.S. naval forces from the seas around Taiwan. In June of that same year, Secretary of State John Foster Dulles announced to the world that the U.S. had accumulated a stockpile of 4,000 nuclear weapons, four times as many as the Soviet Union. Accompanying this announcement was the adoption of the policy of massive retaliation.

Moreover, in 1956 Dulles announced a new policy of "brinksmanship," which simply means going right to the brink of war without actually getting into a war. This was naturally a very dangerous policy, given that the most likely adversary of the U.S. was the Soviet Union, with the ability to field 175 army divisions as compared to 14 for the U.S., and being in possession of the world's largest submarine fleet. This new policy of brinksmanship loomed especially large during and after 1958. In that year, the U.S. Navy's first submarine capable of launching Regulus guided missiles was commissioned. With the commissioning of the submarine Grayback, the concept of a submerged deterrent was born. In addition, by 1958 the Air Force had enough B-52 bombers armed with nuclear bombs to guarantee a continuous airborne presence while other aircraft were on the ground being serviced.

The nuclear arms race would gather speed again in 1959 and 1960. In December 1959, the navy's first ballistic missile submarine, the George Washington, was commissioned. Eleven months later it would set sail on the open seas for the world's first underwater missile patrol, armed with 16 Polaris thermonuclear missiles. In regard to the land-based portion of America's nuclear "triad," in 1960 the Air Force began installing the first Minuteman Inter-Continental Ballistic Missiles at launching sites in Montana. Able to strike a target 6,000 miles away, with a warhead equal to 500,000 tons of TNT, the Minuteman was a further attempt to close what was perceived as a "missile gap" with the USSR. By 1962, a force of 126 liquid-fueled Atlas, 54 liquid-fueled Titan, and 20 solid-fueled Minuteman missiles were active, at a cost of nearly seven billion dollars. Their presence would soon be needed.

Ironic it is that the very same man who presided over these extensive and expensive military upgrades would be prescient enough to recognize their future implications. Much as Washington had warned an infant nation against the perils of entangling alliances, foreign wars and extensive debt, Dwight Eisenhower would warn a mature nation of somewhat similar evils. During his farewell address on January 17, 1961, Eisenhower would state:

> *In the councils of government, we must guard against the acquisition of unwarranted influence, whether sought or unsought, by the military industrial complex. The potential for the disastrous rise of misplaced power exist and will exist.*[130]

Whereas external affairs such as the Cold War and the power vacuum created by the dissolution of British and French colonial power would attract much of America's attention in the aftermath of the Second World War, there would also be an increase in social legislation. While it had been written in the Declaration of Independence that "we hold these truths to be self evident, that all men are created equal," much of the nation's early years would see legislative efforts toward this end being employed only in general terms. Although, the post antebellum years would see the passing of the Thirteenth, Fourteenth, and Fifteenth Amendments, guaranteeing the end of slavery, the right of citizenship, and the right to vote, these were gains only in a general sense, making no mention of gender-based equality. After the First World War, suffrage was granted to women, although initially very few used this new

---

[130] Ibid, 495.

freedom to vote. In fact, during the election of 1920, only 49.2 percent of the electorate actually voted, the lowest percent since 1824.

The volume and nature of social legislation would change after the 1942-1945 war. During his first term in office, Harry Truman would initiate a legislative program referred to as the New Deal. Among its many proposals and provisions was a federal Fair Employment Practices Act, an end to poll taxes, an anti-lynching law, and a bill to end segregation in interstate transport. Furthermore, Truman put forth proposals for a new health insurance program, increases in Social Security payments as well as a higher minimum wage. It would seem that Herbert Hoover's earlier warnings about "bread and the circus" were to now become a part of the new national political landscape.

In the same way as Rome had sought to reward the veterans of her legions with land grants and other rewards, the U.S. Congress in 1944 would pass the G.I. Bill of Rights, granting veterans money while they sought employment, low-cost mortgages, and college assistance and support. Although there can be no denying that the men who fought the war deserved these privileges, no one could guess the ramifications of this legislation. One year after the end of the war, America's colleges and universities were teeming with two million students, nearly half of which were veterans. As Rome had its veterans' colonies, America would have hers too.

With nearly fifteen million men and women having served during World War II, their return home to establish families would forever alter the American landscape. There would be a boom in the building of new houses, facilitated by available veterans' administration mortgages that required no down payment to eligible veterans. Many of these houses would be built in planned communities, giving rise to the "suburbs." By 1960, more than half of the U.S. population would live in "suburbia" rather than urban or rural areas. As an unintended consequence of these build-for-profit policies, large tracts of land formerly used for agricultural purposes would be removed from the agricultural sphere. In addition, as land tends to be affected by the law of supply and demand, the same as any other commodity, land would become more expensive. Naturally, this would adversely impact the farmers.

The combined march toward a more urban and suburban society would be followed by social changes. It should be remembered that both the Roman and British empires were subject to social evolution. Traditionally as these empires expanded, there was an exportation of true Romans and Englishmen into conquered territories followed by an influx of immigrant peoples into Rome and England. This was usually followed by an increase in privilege and rights when these new immigrant or conquered peoples possessed enough political capital to either demand or legislate these changes. In post Second World War America, there would be a similar increase in social change.

Following the events of World War II, focus would be directed toward racial matters. Harry S. Truman would desegregate the U.S. Armed Forces; no longer would there be all-white or all-black units within the Army. In February of 1960, a simple sit-in at a Woolworth's lunch counter in Greensboro, North Carolina, would help to inspire the civil rights movement of the 1960s. In time, this movement would gain impetus and become more organized, culminating with the founding of such organizations as the National Association for the Advancement of Colored People, and the Congress for Racial Equality. Given the fallacies of human nature and its tendencies toward self-interests and political dominance, there would be resistance to these attempts at change. In 1961, Attorney General Robert F. Kennedy employed 400 federal marshals to protect CORE director James Farmer and his "freedom riders" from mob violence while they engaged in a bus tour from Washington, D.C. to New Orleans. Robert Kennedy would also be instrumental in the civil rights movement during other incidents.

In September 1962, Kennedy would force Mississippi Governor Ross Bennett to allow registered black student James Meredith to enter his dormitory at that state's university. In June of 1962, Kennedy would again become involved in a race dispute during the attempt of Alabama Governor George Wallace to prevent two black students from registering at that state's university.

Generally speaking, as a society we tend to associate the civil rights movement of the 1960s with attempts by African-American citizens to right old wrongs. Perhaps this is due to the influence of individuals such as Martin Luther King Jr., whose stand against segregation in Birmingham, Alabama in 1963, and his march on Washington, D.C. in August 1963, both led to his arrest. However, it must be remembered that America is a nation with many minorities, so that the efforts of Robert Kennedy and Martin Luther King Jr. would be destined to go much further than just ensuring rights for the black segment of society. They would eventually guarantee a continuing shift in political power away from rural America and toward the increasingly influential urban and suburban areas of the country.

Although the administration of John F. Kennedy in the 1960s would begin with tangled domestic issues, it would be the larger world stage that would force the new president away from the lofty idealism of his inaugural address. Upon taking office, Kennedy had inherited from the Eisenhower administration a covert plan by the CIA to overthrow the Communist regime of Fidel Castro in Cuba. This plan, which entailed the landing of 1,500 trained and heavily armed Cuban exiles on the island nation at the Bay of Pigs, would be launched on April 13, 1961. Poorly planned and poorly executed, it would take but three days for Castro's forces to kill or capture this CIA-sponsored effort, ending in a severe blow to American prestige.

In June of 1961, perhaps emboldened by the Bay of Pigs fiasco, Soviet Premier Nikita Khrushchev began making demands that East and West Germany be unified within six months, and that the partitioned city of Berlin become demilitarized with all access routes leading into the city to be controlled by the German Democratic Republic, or East Germany. In the spirit of John Foster Dulles' policy of brinksmanship, Kennedy authorized an increase in U.S. troop strength in West Germany to 200,000 men. He also allocated an additional 3.5 billion dollars for the purchase of new weapons. Furthermore, U.S. Attorney General Robert Kennedy advised Soviet

Ambassador Mikhail Menshikov that President Kennedy regarded the Berlin issue as one worth going to war over. War would not be the result, however. At 3:00 am on August 13, 1961, the border between East and West Berlin was closed, with a barbed wire fence sealing off West Berlin from the rest of the world. Ten days later, construction of a permanent wall was begun, a wall that would stand for twenty-eight years.

Whereas the Berlin issue raised the issue of a possible conventional war, events in Communist Cuba would bring the world to the brink of nuclear war. During a conference on July 12, 1960, Khrushchev had declared that the American Monroe Doctrine "has outlived its time and has died a natural death." He further added that it had been used by the United States "to perpetuate the reign of colonialism and monopolies in Latin America."[131] The implications of these declarative statements were not realized until October 14, 1962, when an American U-2 spy plane detected the presence of 40 Soviet medium and intermediate range nuclear missiles in Cuba. They were accompanied by Soviet nuclear-capable JL-28 aircraft, both clear threats to American national security. This discovery would touch off the 13-day Cuban missile crisis.

With mankind having developed the technology to destroy itself, the art of saber-rattling had attained new heights. The reaction by Kennedy was immediate. Elements of the First and Second U.S. Marine Divisions began arriving at Guantanamo Bay Naval Base on October 21. Large numbers of military reservists were recalled to duty and a naval "quarantine" of Cuba was initiated. This maneuver would be enforced by a contingent of more than 60 vessels, a considerable number.

Fortunately for the world, the Soviet ships carrying more missiles to Cuba did not attempt to run the blockade. In a peace settlement, Khrushchev agreed to dismantle the missiles in Cuba if Kennedy agreed not to invade the island or attempt to destroy Russian armaments there as long as they were removed within thirty days.

---

[131] Anderson, *U.S. Military Operations, 1945-1985*, 102.

As an aside to the agreement, the U.S. unofficially agreed to remove its intermediate 744-mile range Jupiter missiles from Turkey. The aftershocks of the October missile crisis would have far-reaching effects. Having learned how sensitive the handling of nuclear arsenals had become, the U.S. established the National Military Command System. Henceforth, there would be a sea-borne command center at all times. Three C-135 aircraft were converted to airborne command centers, plus a number of subterranean command posts were constructed. During the year 1962, the cost of research and development for defense and for the emerging space race totaled 12 billion dollars, a figure greater than that spent on research and development for defense from the period of the American Revolution until the end of the Second World War.

These new peacetime controls were intended to prevent an accidental launch of nuclear weapons, as well as to ensure that if the U.S. fell victim to a first strike, there would exist a command structure able to control a massive retaliatory response. These controls would be needed. By the first year of Lyndon Johnson's administration, the U.S. nuclear arsenal had in service 10 Polaris submarines, 20 more in the building stages, plus 108 Titan and Titan II ICBMs, 129 Atlas ICBMs, plus 350 of a planned 950 solid-fueled Minuteman ICBMs. In addition to that, the Strategic Air Command of the Air Force had its fleet of B-47 and B-52 bombers.

Not all of Lydon Johnson's attention would be devoted to the Cold War. In the wake of the assassination of John F. Kennedy, Lyndon Johnson inaugurated a legislative agenda and series of domestic social programs that came to be known as the "Great Society." Two of the first acts in this new liberal program were to increase the minimum wage and to increase Social Security benefits. If there ever existed sure-fire legislation that would attract the attention of voters in the next election, these two Acts would surely be those acts. An additional voter incentive came with the Tax Reduction Act in February 1964, which reduced tax rates on corporations and on those individuals with lower incomes. In a democratic society, these two groups – big business and the less wealthy, would be sure to look favorably upon lower tax burdens. Johnson's "Great Society" went even further. Medical care for the elderly, a legislative item long sought-after by the American Medical Association, passed both houses of Congress by sizeable majorities. Also passed by Congress was a far-reaching educational bill, which helped to underwrite education at all levels from pre-school to graduate school.

This Great Society first proposed by President Kennedy and carried to legislative success by President Johnson may well have attained a large level of success. Contrary to the economic policies of the Democratic Party of the twenty-first century, Johnson was able to increase the standard of living, as well as the incomes of private citizens and corporations, alike through reductions of income, corporate, and excise taxes. Far-reaching as this new legislative agenda may have been, it was doomed to failure simply because it was under-funded.

And the cause of this under-funding? – The Vietnam War. Ever since the Communist forces of Ho Chi Minh had evicted the French from Indochina in 1954, the United States had maintained some level of support for South Vietnam, newly created by the Geneva accords in July of that year. Initially, this support was monetary or in the form of military advisors. On March 23, 1961, America would suffer its first casualties of the coming war, when an SC-47 intelligence aircraft was shot down over the Plain of Jars. In a delayed response to this incident, President Kennedy would send General Maxwell Taylor with a group of advisors to the troubled nation. According to Air Force General T. R. Milton, this mission had "no clear-cut objectives – just go over there and straighten things out."[132] In accordance with the recommendations of this advisory group, and in accordance also with Defense Secretary Robert McNamara's new policy of "flexible response," which had replaced the earlier "Massive Retaliation" policy of John Foster Dulles, President Kennedy decided to expand military assistance to South Vietnam in December 1961. This

---

[132] Ibid,113.

increased assistance would initially arrive in the form of two companies of U.S. helicopters and pilots to transport South Vietnamese troops into combat. The following February, as a demonstration of American resolve to support the South Vietnamese government, the U.S. Military Assistance Command (MACV) was established.

President Kennedy would begin to have doubts about the prospects of American success in Vietnam. Early in 1963, the President sent Roger Hilsman, head of the State Department's Intelligence Division, along with Mike Forrestal, the State Department official most responsible for Vietnam, to Saigon for a new appraisal of the ongoing war. Upon returning they would report that in their opinion, the U.S.-backed South Vietnamese were "probably winning, but certainly more slowly than we had hoped." Their belief was that the war would "last longer than we would like, cost more in terms of both lives and money than we anticipated, and prolong the period in which a sudden and dramatic event would upset the gains already made." Given the ultimate course the war was to follow, including the 1968 Tet Offensive, the assessment of Hilsman and Forrestal was spot on.

In May of 1963, Kennedy apparently concluded that the best course of action would be to avoid an escalation of U.S. involvement in a war we could not win. His appointments secretary, Ken O'Donnell is said to have remembered a conversation between the President and Montana Senator Mike Mansfield after which Kennedy stated that he "now agreed with the senator's thinking on the need for a complete withdrawal from Vietnam. But I can't do it until 1965 – after I am re-elected."[133] Furthermore, just prior to his trip to Dallas in the late autumn of 1963, Kennedy is reported to have remarked to Vietnam aide Michael Forrestral, "I want to start a complete and very profound review of how we got into this country, what we thought we were doing, and what we now think we can do.

---

[133] Dallek, *An Unfinished Life, JFK 1917-1963*, 668.

I even want to think about whether or not we should be there."[134]

Unfortunately, in the case of the Vietnam War, the fate of a nation was to be closely bound to the fate of one man. With Kennedy's assassination in November 1963, the possibility of an American withdrawal from Southeast Asia probably died with him. With his removal from the scene, the fate of American involvement in Vietnam would pass to Lyndon Johnson. It is curious to note that as a party leader in the U.S. Senate in 1954, Johnson had helped block U.S. intervention in French Indochina during the last desperate French stand at Dien Bien Phu. Upon assuming the role of Commander in Chief, Johnson would send General William Westmoreland to Saigon to direct American military affairs. He would also authorize the use of U.S. Air Force and Navy aircraft reconnaissance missions over Laos, and the use of South Vietnamese torpedo boats in raids along the coast of North Vietnam. It would be this last authorization that would eventually lead to a retaliatory raid by North Vietnamese torpedo boats on the destroyer U.S.S. Maddox, engaged in intelligence gathering missions in the Gulf of Tonkin. This incident, which occurred on August 2, 1964, was followed three days later by Johnson's announcement that "Hostile actions on the high seas" had forced him to order an American military response. Consequently, carrier-based planes from the aircraft carriers Constellation and Ticonderoga bombed the oil storage facilities at Vinh, a harbor facility north of the 17th parallel in North Vietnam.

Prior to this action, American involvement in Vietnam had been essentially hidden behind CIA-directed operations that engaged in such tactics as using military aircraft wearing the insignias of other nations, U.S. military personnel being termed as advisors, and mislabeling equipment so as not to violate the conditions of the 1954 Geneva Accord. Yet even more dangerous ground was now to be tread upon. On August 7, 1964, the U.S. government passed the Gulf of Tonkin Resolution, an endorsement of Johnson's decision to order an overt U.S. military action against the North Vietnamese.

---

[134] Douglass, *JFK and the Unspeakable*, 183.

Henceforth, Constitutional controversies would arise as to this type of resolution being a sidestepping of Congressional authority to declare war. The resolution passed in the House by a vote of 416-0, in the Senate by a vote of 80-2. Oregon Senator Wayne Morse, in opposition to the resolution, declared the United States had become "drunk with military power."

During the years of the Kennedy administration, U.S. troop strengths in Vietnam reached a peak of 16,000. By June 27 of 1965, General Westmoreland had command of more than 115,000 troops in Vietnam, a number that would continue to rise. America was to encounter the Sassanid Persia of Rome, the Afghanistan of Great Britain. As events continued to escalate, the North Vietnamese, instead of being intimidated by the U.S. military force, only stiffened in their resolve. On Jun 27, 1965, one of the deadliest weapons in the U.S. arsenal, the B-52 Stratofortress, was unleashed on the North Vietnamese. Soon airborne and airmobile units would join the fray as well. By December of 1968, U.S. troop strengths in Vietnam stood at 536,040.[135] This number would eventually increase to 625,866 by March of 1969. Armed with the B-52 and the super carrier, and with ground troops better equipped and supplied than their enemies, military success was almost universal. Between January and April of 1968, when 20,000 Communist troops attempted to overrun 3,000 U.S. marines at Khe Sanh in Quang Tu Province, there was to be no repeat of the 1957 French disaster at Dien Bien Phu. United States military power would prevail. However, again as Caesar had discovered in Gaul, to conquer Gaul, is not to conquer the Gauls. A little wisdom from one of our founding fathers may have gone a long way in preventing the tragedy of Vietnam. In the wake of Lexington and Concord nearly two hundred years earlier, Thomas Jefferson had written in regard to British attempts to quell American fervor by force of arms:

*This may perhaps be intended to intimidate into acquiescence, but the effect has been most unfortunate otherwise. A little*

---

[135] Dupuy, *Encyclopedia of Military History of the U.S.*, 585.

*knowledge of human nature and attention to its ordinary workings*
*might have foreseen that the spirits of the people here were in a state*
*in which they were more likely to be provoked than frightened by*
*haughty deportment.*[136]

If the words of Jefferson could have served as a preventative of the war, then the war itself would serve as a lesson to the new American psychology towards war. Prior to World War II, America's wars could be viewed as being the forces of good against the forces of evil. After World War II, these delineations became much more blurred. With daily images of the war being carried into almost every American home via television, public opinion was now a critical issue. Therefore, Washington politicians began to sanitize the war. During the war in Korea, officials in Washington objected to General Matthew Ridgeway's use of the term "Operation Killer." In Vietnam, when General Westmoreland called for an operation to be called, "Operation Masher," there were similar objections. Likewise, the tactical term "search and destroy" was eliminated in favor of the less offensive "reconnaissance in force."

In addition, the weapons of the war and how they were employed have much to convey. The use of the B-52 Stratofortress as an anti-personnel weapon, the employment of the armored personnel carrier and the wearing of body armor by ground troops tells of a change in the American viewpoint towards war. During the years of Roman military dominance, the legionary had been transformed from being a citizen soldier who was generally lightly armored, into a more mercenary professional who wore the Imperial gallic helmet and the lorica segmentata. Eventually, as Rome's enemies became more numerous and Rome's legions less capable, there would be a further transformation to heavily armed cavalry wearing chain mail, known as cataphracts. Even more heavily armed were the units of Clibinarii, heavy cavalry who wore suits of segmented armor, which could cause one to think of the armored knight of the Middle Ages. This

---

[136] Sterne Randall, *Ethan Allen*, 24.

transformation may be reflective of two circumstances. First of all, as societies become more affluent, their citizenry place a heavier importance on life, and are therefore less willing to accept casualties. Secondly, there is the issue of finance. Professional soldiers require greater amounts of training, and more expensive weapons. When a soldier is lost in battle there is a greater financial strain placed on society. As evidence of this increase in the cost of soldiers and armies between the end of the Second World War and the beginning of the Korean War five years later, the cost of equipping a single infantry division had risen from 19 million dollars to 91 million. An armored division had seen a similar rise, from 40 million to 293 million. With such expensive toys, a nation is always hesitant to lose them.

Certain years can be long associated with great shifts in the affairs of mankind. To Roman history there are years of importance such as 753 B.C., 44 B.C, and 476 A.D. To England there is 55 B.C., 1066 A.D., 1215 A.D., and 1769 A.D., the annus mirabilis. To the United States there is 1776, 1860, 1929 and 1941. To this list could be added the year 1968. In Vietnam the 1968 TET Offensive would prove that we were involved in what was to become a war we could not win. As a result, anti-war protests would soon become the norm. In 1968 the nation would lose two important leadership figures, Robert F. Kennedy and Martin Luther King, Jr. It would have been a very contentious presidential election in which Lyndon Johnson chose not to run for re-election. That same year also saw increasingly visible civil and women's rights demonstrations. There was also something else evident that year. Long before the advent of the "Tea Party" of the early 21st century, there was the success of George Wallace's American Independent Party Campaign. This movement displayed a far-right reaction to the far-left events so prevalent throughout the decade of the 1960s. As evidence of just how politically fragmented American society had become, the winner of the 1968 election, Richard M. Nixon, received but 43.4 percent of the popular vote, the lowest total since Woodrow Wilson's victory in 1912 over a fractured Republican party.

Social decline was accompanied by agricultural decline as well.

The industrial explosion of the late 19th century had been assisted by an explosion in the number of family farms brought about by the Republican re-enactment of the Homestead Law. In the century following that time, this trend had reversed itself. With the help of government subsidies, enormous agri-businesses had accelerated a decline in the number of both family farms and farmers in general. As evidence of the impact of these agricultural subsidies, during Richard Nixon's first term in office, the wealthiest seven percent of farms received about 63 percent of total government farm subsidies.[137] Much as the latifundia had overtaken the small farm of Rome, this process of government subsidies saw fewer farms, although the acreage of each farm increased from 215 acres to more than 380 acres.

In Vietnam, the fate of America's legions would begin to change. By 1969, the total of combat deaths would exceed those of the Korean War nearly twenty years earlier. Politically, the war would become increasingly unpopular at home. Evidence of this could be found among the 250,000 young men who refused to register for the draft, as well as the 50,000 of them who fled to neutral countries such as Canada to avoid military service.

With the North Vietnamese refusal to resume peace talks, in December of 1972 President Nixon ordered an air offensive known as Linebacker II. Nearly100 B-52 bombers flying in cells of three aircraft would fly from bases in Guam and Thailand for saturation bombing of North Vietnamese targets. They would be joined in their efforts by carrier-based F-4 Phantom fighter jets of the U.S. Seventh Fleet. Following a final raid on December 29, 1972, the United States and North Vietnam would sign a peace accord. By the time of cessation of hostilities, American war dead numbered 56,379. The financial cost of the war would linger for many years to come, affecting U.S. spending both at home and abroad. The psychological impact of the war would be telling as well. In an even more technologically advanced and politically fractured world, not only

---

[137] Nevins and Commager, *Pocket History of the U.S.*, 585.

would Americans change their views toward the world, but the world would begin to changes their views of America.

In January 1964 when a group of American teenagers raised an American flag over a high school in the Panama Canal Zone, a seemingly minor incident would touch off an international incident. Within days of the incident, Panamanians both young and old would arise in protest, to the extent that armed mobs would march through downtown Panama setting fire to U.S. owned businesses. During an armed clash between Panamanians along the border of the Canal Zone, six U.S. soldiers would be wounded by snipers before U.S. troops returned fire, killing several of the snipers.

The violence would escalate. By the time the gunfire had ceased, three U.S. soldiers would be killed and another eighty-five wounded. Panama claimed that American troops had killed twenty Panamanian citizens, while wounding more than 280. By May of 1964, in a direct challenge to the U.S. policy since the time of James Monroe, Panamanian President Roberto F. Chiani ended diplomatic relations with the United States and called for a revision in the terms of the 1903 Panama Canal Treaty. In June of 1967, a revision in those terms would be made with an agreement that would give Panama "effective" sovereignty of the Canal Zone.

More trouble would follow in the Caribbean. Following the 1961 assassination of dictator Rafael Trujillo, the Dominican Republic saw seven years of turmoil. In April 1965, Colonel Francisco Caamano Deno led a revolt of junior army officers with the intent of restoring reformist leader and former president Juan Bosch to power. Many of the pro-Bosch rebels were members of the "14th of June Movement," a leftist organization which had been named after an aborted Castroite invasion of the Dominican Republic in 1959. In response to this crisis, President Lyndon Johnson announced, "I will not have another Cuba in the Caribbean," and followed this announcement by sending more than 31,000 military personnel to the troubled nation.

It must be remembered that this military commitment came at the time of the U.S. involvement in Vietnam, and when the U.S. was also heavily engaged in the Cold War; further crisis, further cost.

In an added sign of open defiance to U.S. military might, in January of 1968, the intelligence-gathering ship U.S.S. Pueblo became the first U.S. ship to surrender to an enemy since the 1807 surrender of the frigate Chesapeake to the British Royal Navy. This incident occurred reportedly in international waters off the coast of Wonson, North Korea. The American ship with a crew of 83 would be captured by a group of North Korean warships 16.3 miles from the North Korean shore. After the ship's capture, its captain, Lloyd Bucher and his crew would remain captives for a period of 11 months. Upon their capture, eleven months of drawn-out and frustrating negotiations for their release would ensue.

External involvement would lead to internal discomfort and a new form of economic warfare following the Yom Kippur War. On October 6, 1973, Egypt initiated this war by sending 200 attack aircraft, 70,000 troops and 600 tanks across the Suez Canal for an attack on Israel during its traditional Day of Atonement. Syria would attack Israel shortly thereafter. With the Soviet Union supplying arms to Egypt and Syria, the U.S. would be forced to begin re-supplying Israel in an attempt to stabilize the region and guarantee the future of the Jewish nation. Israel would eventually prevail over the invaders, but in response to U.S. aid to that nation, the Arab nations of the Organization of Petroleum Exporting Countries (OPEC) imposed an embargo on petroleum sales to all countries friendly to Israel. Oil prices quadrupled across the board. Especially hard hit by the embargo were Japan and Western Europe, which relied on the Middle East for nine-tenths of their oil supplies. To a nation that had existed for two centuries under the protection of nearly inexhaustible resources, the concept of resource depletion and its economic impacts hit home extremely hard.

War debts had done much to undermine the stability of both Roman and British Empire status. Now, much the same would happen to the United States. America's ten year involvement in Southeast Asia had cost the nation nearly 140 billion dollars, money that no doubt would have done much good if spent on internal issues. War debt when combined with the impacts of the oil shock and soaring inflation would lead to the worst economic conditions since the depression of the 1930s. Its continued effects on the American economy would give rise to a new economic term, "stagflation." As a hopeful response to this economic malaise, in 1971 President Richard Nixon declared a national ninety-day freeze on both wages and prices to be followed by other federal controls until the economy would begin to rebound. Nixon would also make the decision to end compliance with the Bretton Woods Agreement of 1945, and would take the U.S. off the gold standard, much the same as Churchill had taken England off the gold standard during his tenure as Chancellor of the Exchequer.

Another of history's great ironies was about to come into play. Having once declared, that "No man can set himself above the law in the name of justice,"[138] the nation's Chief Executive would do just that. Perhaps due to a growing sense of paranoia, and in response to those who would challenge his policies, Nixon would establish an extra-legal investigative force to conduct espionage against his political foes. Illegal wire-tapping, burglarizing of private files, and taping of reporter's phone calls were now being authorized by the President. What's more, there were other issues. In response to the 1972 presidential election, the Committee for the Re-election of the President had collected a campaign chest of nearly sixty million dollars, some of which had been illegally laundered through oil, airline and other corporations.

Much of this would probably have never come to light, had it not been for other circumstances. However, on the night of June 17, 1972, a team of five intelligence operatives on the payroll of the Committee to Re-elect the President were apprehended while breaking into Democratic National Headquarters at the Watergate Hotel in Washington, D.C. This was an event initially dismissed as being only a "caper" by the presidential press secretary Ronald Ziegler. However, it would escalate into a political scandal that would define the decade of the 1970s and would lead to the eventual resignation

---

[138] Ibid, 590.

of Richard M. Nixon.

In a historical sense, the Watergate affair may be indicative of something much larger than itself. When those few chosen societies eventually attain greatness, such as Imperial Rome and Great Britain, eventually governments become larger than the societies they represent. There are enormous amounts of power and wealth centralized in the hands of a few. Along with this wealth and power comes an enormous temptation. The Watergate scandal of Richard M. Nixon is no different to American history than were the intrigues of Stilicho and Aetius to the history of Rome.

Of itself, the Watergate incident did much to damage confidence in government. It should be remembered, however, that during the occurrence of Watergate, the nation's Vice President Spiro Agnew had also come under investigation in Maryland for having accepted payoffs on state contracts while serving as governor of that state. When brought to trial, he would plead nolo contendere to a charge of tax evasion. His resignation from office in disgrace would follow. On December 6, 1973, Agnew would be replaced as Vice President by Michigan Lawmaker and House Minority Leader, Gerald Ford. Within a year, upon Richard Nixon's resignation from the office of President on August 8, 1974, Gerald Ford would assume the mantle of leadership for a nation with a crisis of confidence in public government.

Gerald Ford would occupy the Oval Office for but two years. His tenure there would lead to a display of political courage rarely seen in modern governments. Recognizing that the nation was suffering from a decline of public confidence in government, Gerald Ford would attempt to remove Watergate and the Agnew resignation from the public mind and to set the nation toward progress once again. Acting according to what he regarded as the "laws of God and the needs of the national interest," Ford would pardon former President Richard Nixon exactly one month to the day after his formal resignation. To the public mind, this pardon was premature, and the Ford administration would be dogged by the persistent public belief that his pardon was but another instance of presidential cover-up. Public resentment of government may have been aided by the after effects of the Vietnam War still being fought to its conclusion in Southeast Asia, and by a continued decline in economic health accompanied by spiraling inflation.

The American mind of the early 1970s would be forced to come to grips with other unpleasant issues. Ever since the time of Alexander Hamilton and his Society for the establishment of useful manufacturers, Americans had viewed industrialism as a positive force to increase the financial health of a growing nation. Now, after two centuries of explosive growth, the mythology of perpetual economic growth would begin to be challenged by the realization that the nation's natural resources were finite, not infinite. This issue would for the first time manifest itself due to the increased pollution of water, soil and air. Recognizing this fact, however, was not always accompanied by attempts to find solutions to the problem. For example, with unemployment already high and being fearful of additional layoffs, President Ford would bow to pressure from Detroit, postponing until 1976 the implementation of the reduction of ninety percent in auto emissions called for by the 1970 Clean Air Act. Hence, the need to find a new balance between economic comfort and long-term national health would be governed by human self-interest and not necessarily by wise decision making.

In the realm of foreign affairs, there was to be found a new and possibly more dangerous shift. In 1940 Franklin Roosevelt declared that in response to the challenges of Fascism and Nazism, the United States should become the arsenal of democracy, ensuring a sufficient supply of arms to the free nations of the world. During the years of the Ford administration, Henry Kissinger would expand this philosophy. With the Cold War still raging, and in pursuit of national security, the U.S. would begin to court more repressive allies such as General Pinochet in Chile and General Park of South Korea. In 1975 Kissinger would urge passage of a 4.7 billion dollar military aid package to support these two nations.

In the Middle East, which had known nothing by instability and violence since the end of the Second World War and the evacuation of British authority, the United States would now attempt to offset oil cost and guarantee the continued flow of oil by a policy of arms proliferation to the area, including large sales of arms to Iran and Saudi Arabia. This policy would not only prove to be expensive, but would result in placing new strains on American military resources. For instance, with the outbreak of the Yom Kipper War in October 1973, the U.S. initiated an immediate re-supply to Israel. This supply effort included M-48 and M-60 tanks, as well as F-4E Phantom jet fighters. The problem was that the former Nixon Doctrine had called for a reduction in U.S. military production; only three Phantom jets were being produced per month and only one factory remained that produced tanks, at a rate of only 3 per month. As Israeli losses during the war escalated, the United States was forced to cannibalize its stockpile of weapons that were committed to its support of NATO in Europe. This strain on American military resources nearly led to the dissolution of the quarter-century-old Atlantic Alliance.

As the nation began to celebrate its two-hundredth anniversary in 1976, issues concerning its military strength would reveal other future issues. With the election of Jimmy Carter to the office of President in 1976, there would be a shift in U.S. defense policies. Upon taking office, Carter would veto production of the B-1 bomber program and cancel the building of a new Nimitz class aircraft carrier. He would also grant pardons to Vietnam-era draft evaders, defer production of the neutron bomb, and cancel SR-71 surveillance flights over Communist Cuba.

To many, these changes would convey a softening of the U.S. military resolve. The global events that were to follow would also indicate a perception by our adversaries that such was the case. In the autumn of 1978, it would be discovered that the Soviet Union had placed advanced Mig 23 fighters in Cuba, plus a brigade of around 3,000 combat troops. On November 4, 1979, militant students who were supporters of Iran's Ayatollah Khomeini stormed the U.S. Embassy in Teheran and seized 66 Americans as hostages, demanding the return of the deposed Shah to stand trial in that nation. This crisis would define the Carter administration. As if these crises were not enough, in December of 1979 more than 50,000 Soviet troops would invade Afghanistan, an act which placed the Soviets 350 miles closer to the Arabian Sea and within easy striking distance of the flow of oil to the United States and its Western allies.

On balance, and with the failed attempt to rescue the Iranian hostages by means of a military raid in April of 1980, it would appear that President Carter had presided over a decline in American military prestige. But there may be more to it than that. Although Carter had eliminated the B-1 and the carrier, he also approved production of a mobile MX ballistic missile as a nuclear deterrent. He also authorized the establishment of a new Rapid Deployment force of 200,000 soldiers, sailors, marines, and airmen. Two thousand years before Jimmy Carter, Rome had wasted away its legions in far away campaigns in Armenia and North Britain. Two hundred years before that, England had begun to squander its Royal Navy controlling the world's oceans at great cost. Perhaps Jimmy Carter had an eye to the past as well as the future. Events would come to prove him right. In Afghanistan, the Soviet army would fritter away its strength in an unwise war, suffering the same fate as American forces in Vietnam. Eventually, after the expenditure of many lives and much treasure, they would be forced to retire from that hostile nation.

The concept of the rapid deployment force however, would bear validity as time went on. Reflecting back to the Ford administration, an American vessel on the high seas was seized by Cambodian Khmer Rouge gunboats. This event, known as the May 1975 Mayaguez incident, would imply a future that would be given to acts of terrorism. Beginning in 1978, there would be a chain of more than 20 terrorist attacks on U.S. Embassies and diplomatic personnel within one year, with the ultimate act of terrorism being that which occurred during the 1979 storming of the embassy in Teheran. As evidenced by the events of September 11, 2001, war would now devolve from a competition between nations to random acts of violence perpetrated by the few against the many. The Rapid Deployment strategy would become essential to the military establishments of all industrial nations.

There may have been something else that Jimmy Carter recognized as well. Due to their increased technological complexity, weapons of war had attained unheard of cost. When the nuclear-powered aircraft carrier Nimitz (CVN-68) was commissioned in 1975, the cost of construction was a staggering 1.88 billion dollars. This did not include the cost of its air wing; the cost of each of its ninety aircraft ranged into the tens of millions of dollars. When the first B-52s had been purchased for the Strategic Air Command in 1951, each aircraft cost six million dollars. The B-1 bomber, at the time the most expensive combat aircraft in history, had an estimated unit price of 77 million dollars. With plans calling for a force of 241 aircraft, the price tag for this new force of bombers was a staggering 18.6 billion dollars. As a naval academy graduate, Jimmie Carter might have had a more keen realization of what the future would hold in regard to the nature of weapons needed to act as a nuclear deterrent.

Rather than spend massive amounts of money on the B-1 program, Carter opted instead to retain a force of upgraded B-52 bombers equipped with the newly developed AGM-86 air-launched cruise missile, a weapon that would allow each B-52 to attack targets from as far away as 760 miles. As of 1977, the striking force of the Strategic Air Command consisted of 13 wings equipped with 165 B-52G and B-52H model aircraft. With each aircraft capable of carrying up to 20 missiles, this third leg of the strategic triad remained a potent striking force.

In terms of American naval strength, while President Carter was opposed to the "big deck" carrier concept and had canceled construction of a new Nimitz class carrier, it was during the Carter years that the new Ohio class of ballistic missile submarines, armed with Trident sub-launched ballistic missiles, came into being. The first of these new ships, the U.S.S. Ohio, was laid down on April 10, 1976. Plans called for the eventual construction of 27 of these new submarines, each capable of carrying 24 missiles. Eventually a total of eighteen would be built, joining the fleet between 1981 and 1997. Difficult to detect and nearly impossible to destroy before launching their weapons, the Ohio class nuclear missile submarines were to become one of the most essential weapons in America's nuclear deterrent arsenal.

# Chapter 13

¤

# SEEDS OF DECLINE

In January of 1981, President Ronald Reagan assumed control of the administration of the U. S. government. Generally speaking, Ronald Reagan is considered to have been an above average President. He is regarded as having been a successful concensus builder and legislator, and his years in office are often regarded by the American people as having been prosperous years. There were however, issues coming to the fore that would affect American society in the decades to come. Some of these issues were within the control of the Reagan administration and some were not.

Agriculture, so vital to the growth and expansion of Roman and English societies, would continue to experience a downward spiral during the years of the twentieth century. As earlier noted, the impact of government subsidies on agriculture had made itself readily apparent during the years of the Nixon administration. But there existed another issue, quite literally below the surface, which was to have a greater future impact on American agriculture. As the initial thirteen American states had expanded westward, the American Midwest had become an agricultural Mecca. However, this region, which largely overlies the Ogallala aquifer, is an area that does not always have adequate precipitation or perennial surface water for diversion to crops. For years, the region had been prone to crop failures brought about by cycles of drought. This cycle of crop failures had culminated with the dust bowl of the 1930s. There was, nevertheless, a way to remedy the problem. The solution was to tap into sub-surface water supplies for the irrigation of corn, wheat, and soybean crops, and to ranch substantial herds of cattle.

This process of groundwater extraction from the Ogallala aquifer was begun in 1911. Large-scale water extraction from this aquifer was to begin in the late 1930s. However, the cost involved with the mechanics of groundwater extraction would initially serve as a brake on the amounts of water withdrawn. This was to change dramatically and irreversibly following the Second World War, when new and less expensive technologies made the large-scale extraction of groundwater more affordable. The rate of withdrawal from the aquifer would soar, so much so that by the year 2000, withdrawals would total nearly 21,000,000 acre feet annually. For obvious reasons, crop yields would increase also.

As usually happens many times when we tamper with nature, there was a serious side effect with these groundwater withdrawals. Present day recharge of the Ogallala aquifer occurs at an exceedingly slow rate, suggesting that paleowater, the water contained in the aquifer's pore spaces, may have been deposited there during the last great ice age, perhaps even before that. Being part of the High Plains Aquifer System, one of the world's largest, nearly seven percent of the irrigated land in the United States overlies this aquifer, which yields 30 percent of the groundwater used for irrigation in the United States. Add to this the fact that as of 1990 nearly 2.3 million people were dependent upon the aquifer for drinking water as well. Thus, a recipe for the future makes itself readily apparent. Current predictions are that with withdrawal rates exceeding rates of recharge by such drastic amounts, the volume of water remaining may last as little as twenty-five years. Of even greater concern, center pivot irrigation and the use of groundwater for the irrigation of crops is a practice widely used in other areas of the free world, such as Australia, New Zealand, and Brazil.

While the Reagan administration largely had little if any control of American agricultural practices, the new President would initiate new policies regarding American military doctrine and foreign affairs. These policies would in turn affect fiscal practices and finance. Reaganomics would eventually become the term most closely associated with these new policies, which would call for an increase of four billion dollars in defense spending during his first year in office, while trimming non-defense spending and taxes by nearly ten times this amount. Coming into power after nearly two decades of military operations and diplomatic policies that had proven indecisive and inconsistent, Reagan would now attempt to reassert American influence around the globe with a new military, strong enough to back American policy.

This of course was not a concept new to history. During the years of Imperial Rome, numerous emperors had sought to rekindle the greatness of Rome following cycles of decline by means of military strength, Claudius, Marcus Aurelius, and Julian notable amongst them. England had known such policies as well, as evidenced by a host of individuals ranging from Henry V after the Black Death and the social revolt to Disraeli during the years of Great Britain's colonial wars. Within months of taking office, Reagan would call for a long range defense buildup to include plans for a 600-ship navy, the re-introduction of the B-1 bomber program, and the production of 7,000 of the newly designed M-1 main battle tanks. In strategic terms, the Reagan administration would also divest itself from the policies of Jimmy Carter. During the Nixon years, the U. S. had entered into negotiations with the Soviet Union to limit the production of nuclear weapons. The outcome was the 1972 Strategic Arms Limitations Treaty (SALT). President Carter had hoped to improve on this treaty and to actually begin the elimination of such weapons. In June of 1979, the President had joined the Soviet Premier Leonid Brezhnev in Paris to sign a new treaty, SALT II. This new treaty was to result in the Soviet Union actually reducing the number of warheads in its nuclear stockpile. However, in the aftermath of the Soviet invasion of Afghanistan in 1979, ratification by a more hawkish U.S. Senate appeared unlikely, and President Carter withdrew the proposed treaty from Senate consideration.

After his 1980 election, President Reagan decided to shift U.S. military doctrine away from its previous reliance on a nuclear deterrent. Instead of basing war plans on a 30-day exchange of nuclear weapons with the Soviet Union, new U.S. military doctrine would be based upon the ability to fight two or more long-term conventional wars at the same time. The procurement of weapons during the years of the Reagan administration was especially reflective of this new trend. For the U.S. Navy, there were to be 15 carrier battle groups, and the four Missouri class battleships were to be upgraded and returned to service. On the other hand, the Trident nuclear-powered submarine program was to be truncated to allow for this expansion in the fleet of carrier battle groups. With a cost of 250 million dollars per Trident-armed submarine, the Reagan Defense Department opted to cancel orders for 19 of the proposed 27 submarines and curtail production of the Trident missile as well.

In terms of the projection of American airpower, the ambitious Reagan five-year plan to rebuild the nation's military would receive another blow. Although Ronald Reagan had decided to reverse the Carter administration's decision to scrap the proposed B-1 bomber, when Congress mulled the 40-billion dollar price tag for 100 aircraft, it decided that it was far too much expenditure for an aircraft not expected to see service for nearly ten years. For, in that time it might not even be able to penetrate enemy air defenses in light of rapid advances in Soviet anti-aircraft technology. Fortunately, the B-1 bomber would eventually join the arsenal, with the first B-1B squadron becoming operational in 1986 and the last of 100 production aircraft being delivered to the Air Force on May 2, 1988.

The Reagan years would see the addition of two other weapon systems to the American nuclear arsenal. Complementing the Trident missile submarines and the B-1 bomber in the nuclear triad, the Boeing Peacekeeper Inter-Continental Ballistic Missile would officially enter service in December 1986. The Northrop Gruman B-2 Spirit Bomber would make its presence known to the world in November 1988. Both weapons were developed and deployed at enormous expense. While the Carter administration had initially called for several hundred of the Peacekeeper missiles, ultimately only fifty would enter service, all deployed at F. E. Warren Air Force Base in Wyoming. As for the B-2 Spirit, the USAF initially planned to procure 133 of these aircraft, but due to the enormous cost of these planes only 21 were manufactured.[139]

The addition of the Trident missile submarine, the Peacekeeper ICBM, and the B-1 bomber would indicate a change in policy from the Nixon and Carter administrations. Effectively, President Ronald Reagan was adopting a far more hawkish line toward the Soviet Union, to include scrapping of the SALT II Treaty and the building up and overhauling of America's military arsenal. The introduction of these weapons also gives evidence that the long standing Cold War and its accompanying arms race would now be transformed, no longer driven by numbers of weapons, but rather by technological advances. This would of course require the Soviet Union to follow suit, at an expense that would ultimately prove to be too much for the aging Soviet empire. When those weapons that had actually been deployed were coupled with the threat of those that were not, such as Reagan's proposal for an anti-ballistic missile defense shield, the result was inevitable. Although Ronald Reagan could never be accused of starting the Cold War, he may in fact be given some measure of credit for helping to end it, as Soviet military power would begin its precipitously steep decline by the end of the 1980s.

If the Reagan years were successful in helping to bring about an end to the nearly half century-old Cold War with Soviet Russia, they would also make known the fact that as a military superpower, for a time the sole military power, that the mere existence of this force and the system of foreign alliances would require their employment at times and under circumstances not favorable to the United States. During the Reagan years, Central America would become an area of focus, as evidenced by the increase in U.S. military advisers in El Salvador in 1982, the deployment of the aircraft carriers Ranger and

---

[139] Miller, *The Illustrated Directory of Modern American Weapons*, 40.

Coral Sea off the coast of Nicaragua in 1983, and the October 1983 invasion of the Island of Grenada. Central America was not unique in seeing the use of U.S. military resources during the Reagan years. Following the April 2, 1982 Argentine invasion of the British Falkland Islands in the South Atlantic, the United States would offer Britain the use of aerial refueling aircraft to assist British bombers en-route to the South Atlantic. The U.S. also provided use of U.S.A.F. C-5A transports to ferry supplies and munitions, and the Royal Air Force was given permission to use Ascension Island airbase for forward operations.

Whereas the Grenada invasion and British operations in the Falkland Islands proved successful, there existed the much less fortunate use of American forces in Lebanon in an attempt to prevent an all out war between Israel and Syria. Eventually, U.S. involvement as part of a multi-national peace-keeping force would lead to the October 23, 1983 suicide bombing of the U.S. Marine headquarters in Beirut, during which 241 American servicemen were killed and 71 others injured. Although not the first incident of terrorism in history, this act could be viewed as a sort of indoctrination for America of what the nature of warfare would be in the future, and of the price that a global power must pay for intervening in the affairs of fractured societies.

The greatest testimony to the military buildup of the 1980s may be the events that followed in the years after Mr. Reagan's departure from office. During the presidency of George H. W. Bush, Ronald Reagan's Republican successor to the Oval Office, America's new weapons of war would be tested in the aftermath of the August 2, 1990 Iraqi invasion of Kuwait, a move that placed the Iraqi army of Saddam Hussein on the northern border of Saudi Arabia. Within five days of this act, the aircraft carriers Dwight D. Eisenhower and Independence would be operating in the Gulf of Oman. The striking power of these two carriers would be but the tip of the spear, as by the 16th of January 1991 more than 425,000 military personnel would be in the theatre for the beginning of Operation Desert Storm, the liberation of Kuwait. No fewer than six American aircraft carriers would launch strikes against Iraqi military targets. The striking ability of the U.S.A.F. provided U.S. ground troops with complete air cover and suppressed much of the retaliatory ability of the Iraqi combat formations.

The ground assault against Iraqi forces in Kuwait, Desert Sabre, began on February 24, 1991. So devastating was the coalition assault against the Iraqi Army that a suspension of offensive action was declared by March 2, 1991. In a mere 89 hours of fighting, the U.S. Army's VII Corps would destroy as many as 1,350 enemy tanks and 1,223 armored vehicles.[140] In all, by war's end, more than 3,847 Iraqi tanks and 1,450 armored vehicles would exist only as burnt-out wrecks lying in a desert wasteland. Much of the success during this overwhelming victory can be attributed to American air power and to the M-1 Abrams MBT, which could engage Iraqi tanks under all weather conditions and at distances of 2,500 meters. The Russian-built Iraqi Main Battle Tanks could not acquire targets at ranges any greater than 1,500 meters. The victory of the American-led coalition forces over Iraq was probably as predictable and as great as that of Rome over Carthage during the Third Punic War.

Throughout history, success on the battlefield may sometimes lead great nations into a state of complacency. The overwhelming victory of American arms during the Gulf War of 1991 was followed shortly thereafter by the December 25, 1991 resignation of Soviet President Mikhail S. Gorbachev and his declaration that the Soviet Union no longer existed. This is the date generally accepted as the end of the Cold War. With it, there would be an almost immediate change in American military and foreign policy. Believing itself now the world's sole military superpower, the United States initiated a dramatic draw down of its armed forces. From the end of Desert Storm to the end of 1994, the active duty strength of the U.S. Army was reduced by more than 200,000 troops. In addition, the National Guard was reduced from 458,000 to 397,000, the Army Reserve from

---

[140] Giangreco, *United States Army, The Definitive Illustrated History*, 452.

335,000 to 260,000.[141] This recognition of superiority was reflective of Octavian's decision to reduce the armies of Imperial Rome to 25 Legions, of England's decision in 1968 to allow its carrier fleet to wither and die, and an acknowledgment that even great empires are faced with budgetary constraints. However, the breakup of the Soviet Union led to a chain of events similar to the events that followed World War II, with the removal of British influence from much of the world. No longer living under the cloud of nuclear war, the world became a much more fractured place. American deployments did not decrease. Instead they increased to incendiary spots in Africa, Eastern Europe, South America, the Caribbean and Southwest Asia. Particularly troubling were the U.S. involvements in war-torn Somalia in 1993-1994 and in Haiti in 1994-1995. When coupled with American involvement in Bosnia, Macedonia, and Kosovo in the mid 1990s, it became readily apparent that the post-Cold War role of the United States military would be that of a modern police force.

Not only would new President William Clinton seek to alter the role of the U.S. military in the 1990s, he would seek also to use it as an instrument for social change. On April 28, 1993, Secretary of Defense Les Aspin lifted the ban on women flying combat missions and promised to end barriers prohibiting women from serving on combat vessels. Ultimately, President William J. Clinton would sign legislation on November 30 of that same year allowing women to serve on combat ships. By June 9, 1998, women would not only serve on combat vessels, they would begin to assume command of such ships. And then there is the issue of sexual preference within the armed forces. The presidency of William Clinton would also see a different approach in this regard with the institution of the famous "don't ask, don't tell" policy. These shifts could be regarded as dangerous precedents, as it should be obvious that these decisions were politically based attempts to sway the electorate and were not always based on any inherent level of wisdom or of military need.

These changes also indicate something else. In the aftermath of the

---

[141] Ibid, 465.

victory over Iraq in 1991 and the subsequent decline of the Soviet Union, the American psyche seemed to develop the belief that the United States had attained a status that no other nation or other people had achieved. Yet it must be again remembered that wars are not contractual affairs; they need only one willing participant. It must also be remembered that, the way a potential enemy views a nation's military, as being either cohesive or weak, may determine whether or not that enemy chooses the path toward war. In the third century A.D., Imperial Rome reorganized its legions, lessening their strength to 1,000 men instead of the usual 4,500. They created the limitanae, formations of troops of lesser quality, with less discipline and lower standards of training. Then, to deceive their enemies, they created lists with more, and at times fictitious legions to convince the enemy of their strength. Nevertheless, they did not deceive their enemies; they simply deceived themselves. Shortly thereafter, any man in any tribe throughout Europe would pick up a spear or sword and the empire would find itself revealed as a paper tiger.

Within years of these changes in policy, the United States military and the society it protects would find themselves as targets for a new kind of warfare. On October 12, 2000, the U.S. destroyer Cole would fall victim to a terrorist attack while refueling at Aden, Yemen. Seventeen sailors would be killed and thirty-nine wounded by terrorists utilizing an inflatable speedboat packed with explosives. Damage to the ship was so extensive that it had to be returned to the U.S. by means of a Norwegian-owned semi-submersible heavy lift ship. The U.S.S. Cole would not return to duty with the fleet until October 2002.

The attack on a U.S. combat vessel in a foreign port by terrorists could only be perceived as an indication of things to come. The September 11, 2001 attack by terrorists on the twin towers of the World Trade Center, New York and the Pentagon in Washington, D.C., were not only attacks against U.S. commercial interest and the defense establishment, they were a clear message that henceforth, Americans were subject to attacks against the civilian populace. If America thought that Desert Storm and the end of the Cold War had made for a more secure world, America was as mistaken as the Roman citizens during the times of Hannibal or Attila; same violent world, just different tactics and techniques. It is also noteworthy that the terrorist cells that launched these attacks, using civilian airliners as guided missiles, chose to use Afghanistan as a base of operations. Of course Afghanistan has long been a graveyard for invading armies, as learned by the British during the Anglo-Afghan Wars of the nineteenth century, and the Russians during the Twentieth. Perhaps someone involved in these attacks was familiar with military history.

The American reaction to this 911 attack was predictable. American military forces and American military expenditure would return to the Middle East and Southwest Asia on a massive scale. In less than one month, on October 7, 2001, the U.S. initiated Operation Enduring Freedom, launching air strikes against Taliban and Al Qaeda targets in Afghanistan. Initially, Secretary of Defense Donald Rumsfeld would hold to the airpower theories of Giulio Doulet as put forth in the 1920s and 1930s, that airpower itself would in the future have the ability to determine the outcome of wars. With an arsenal of precision guided bombs and Tomahawk cruise missiles, an initial attempt to win the new global war on Terrorism would be carried out along these lines. However, in March of 2003, the administration of President George W. Bush would decide to extend the war on terrorism into Iraq. Operation Iraqi Freedom would find U.S. forces actively engaged in two wars. This of course leads to the question, is it better to have a large military and use it, to have a small military and refrain from using it, or is the best policy to have a large military and refrain from using it. No doubt, the wars in Afghanistan and Iraq have had and will continue to have a dramatic effect on U.S. budgets, both military and discretionary, for years to come.

At this time, the war in Iraq has largely ceased, with nearly all of America's armed forces having been withdrawn from that nation. America's longest war, that in Afghanistan, would continue even after the death of Osama Bin Laden. One thing is certain, that technology, though helpful and at times necessary in war, is not always a guarantor of success. Whereas the Roman soldier of the legion was always better equipped than his foe, as was the British soldier of the Victorian era, victory was not always a certainty. Rome had its Andrianople, Britain its Isandlwana, both resulting from overconfidence. What defeat might await American forces if Americans become complacent, and what does the future hold for American military fortunes? Much will be decided by the nation's ability to sustain the military financially. There will also be the issue of how other nations tend to structure and finance their militaries. The final issue may be one of how this nation's political institutions tend to employ the armed forces, as well as their continued insistence on using the U.S. military as an instrument for social change.

Of these factors, available financing may prove to be the single greatest threat to America's military institutions, as will the cost of increased technology. For instance, when the second nuclear-powered aircraft carrier, Nimitz, was completed in 1975, its cost to build was 1.88 billion dollars.[142] As of 2013, the estimated cost of the newest Gerald R. Ford class nuclear aircraft carriers was in excess of 11.4 billion dollars.[143] This of course does not include the cost of such a ship's air wing. When the F-14 Tomcat became the U.S. Navy's principal fighter aircraft in the late 1970s and the early 1980s, the cost of each aircraft was a staggering 25 to 28 million dollars. Today, this cost is minimal when compared to the estimated cost of a fifth generation fighter aircraft such as the F-35 Lightning, where the unit cost is expected to reach at least 118 million dollars.[144] As expected, the consequences of such skyrocketing cost are fewer aircraft. For example, during the initial stages of the Cold War, the U.S. Air Force was able to acquire a fleet of nearly two thousand B-47 stratojets to serve as its nuclear component of the strategic triad. With the advent of the B-52 and its nearly 6 million-dollar per aircraft price tag, production was limited to 744 aircraft. The eventual successor to the B-52, which would only supplement and not entirely replace it, the

---

[142] Salamander Books, *The U.S. War Machine*, 118.
[143] Cropsey, Mayday, *The Decline of American Naval Supremacy*, 241.
[144] Key Publishing, *Combat Aircraft Monthly*, 16.

B-1B, was limited to a production run of 100 aircraft.

The B-2 stealth bomber, of which the air force initially intended to purchase 133 aircraft, was limited to a production run of only 21 aircraft. As the B-52 Stratofortress has a service life of 30,000 hours, the B-1B only 10,000 hours, it appears that the B-52 will probably outlive its successors, the B-1 and the B-2.

If spiraling production costs are to affect the ability of America to project air superiority around the globe, we can expect the same in regard to American naval supremacy. For instance, when the George Washington-Ethan Allen-Lafayette classes of ballistic missile submarines entered service in the 1960s, a total of 41 ships were built. The successor class to these ships, the Ohio class, was intended to be produced in similar numbers. However, due to the enormous cost of these ships and the Trident missiles they carry, only eighteen were produced, with nine being based at Bangor, Washington, and nine at Kings Bay, Georgia. Since 2002, four of these ships have been retired, and plans are to reduce the size of the SSBN fleet to 12 in number.

The surface fleet may also suffer this same withering effect. The newest class of destroyer sought by the U.S. Navy, the DDG-1000 class, has an estimated cost of 3 billion dollars per ship, more than the cost of the first Nimitz class carriers in the 1970s. Initially, the Navy intended to purchase thirty-two of these vessels. With the price per unit having exploded, current plans are to purchase only three. The less expensive alternative to these ships, the Arleigh Burke class, will cost 1.5 billion dollars each. Similar costs are expected for all other types of vessels as well. The relatively small littoral combat ships will cost 550 million dollars per ship, the new Virginia class attack submarines 2 billion dollars per ship, and the new class of LHA 3.4 billion dollars per ship, not including the cost of each ship's aircraft.

In essence, the cost factor can be expected to reduce the size of the U.S. Navy much as it did the British Royal Navy in the years following World War II. As evidence of this conclusion, by the early 1980s, the size of the U.S. Navy was only half that of the U.S. Navy of the early 1960s. During the presidency of Ronald Reagan this trend was to be temporarily reversed. Much of this reversal of trend and increase in the fortunes of American naval forces could be attributed to Secretary of the Navy, John F. Lehamn, Jr., a naval flight officer with an Ivy League PH.D. As the sixty-fifth Secretary of the Navy, Lehman would see the size of the Navy increased from 521 ships in 1981 to 594 ships in 1988. Also under Lehman, America's carrier strength would rebound to fourteen carriers with fourteen active and two reserve carrier air wings, an impressive accomplishment during an age of soaring cost and increasingly expensive technology.

In the post-Lehman years, the downward spiral in the fortunes of the navy has returned. The fourteen-carrier fleet of John Lehman has been reduced to ten as the older conventional carriers have been retired, as has the nuclear-powered CVN-65 Enterprise. With the soaring cost of building these ships and the seven or more years required to complete construction, it is estimated that within twenty years the carrier fleet will be further reduced to a total of eight. As for the submarine fleet, current proposals suggest reducing the number of ballistic missile submarines from the current level of fourteen to twelve.

The force of attack submarines is to become truncated as well. Between 1976 and 1996, sixty-two of the highly successful Los Angeles class attack submarines were built, one of the most expensive of all defense programs undertaken during the nearly fifty-year Cold War. The successor class for these ships, the Sea Wolf class, was to consist of 29 units, of which only three have been built. The newest class of attack submarine, the Virginia class, is to comprise a total of twenty ships. Cost for these ships has soared as well. The first Los Angeles class ship cost 221 million dollars in 1976, the last ship of this class costing nearly 1 billion dollars. The last of three Sea Wolf ships, the U.S.S. Jimmy Carter, cost 3.2 billion and each of the Virginia's will cost between 2 and 3 billion dollars. It becomes apparent that the United States Navy will probably suffer the fate of the Royal Navy in the post-World War II era. Fewer ships and greater cost shall become the norm. With an enormous national debt forcing proposals to reduce defense spending by 1 trillion dollars over the next decade, additional armed forces reductions become apparent as well.

If American's cannot see the implications of these cuts and reductions, other nations can. Perhaps doubting future American resolve or strength, Great Britain has begun construction of two new fleet carriers of the Queen Elizabeth class. These will be the first full-size carriers deployed by Great Britain since the retirement of the H.M.S. Ark Royal in 1978. Japan, perhaps hearing the heavy footsteps of nearby China, has decided to increase the size of its submarine fleet by thirty-seven percent in the next four years, with Australia announcing plans to double the size of its submarine fleet as well. India intends to add stealth frigates to its emerging fleet. Most importantly of all, China, the emerging economic powerhouse of the twenty-first century, has begun sea trials and deck landings on its new aircraft carrier, Liaoning. It is obvious that China intends to add more carriers to its fleet. In essence, America's future weakness has become apparent to friend and foe alike.

The issues confronting the United States are no different than those that confronted Imperial Rome two thousand years ago, or those that confronted Great Britain two hundred years ago. As a democratic society where the direction or misdirection of government will be determined by popular vote, and hence human nature, the outcome may not be good. In the aftermath of recent popular elections, it is becoming readily apparent that in the United States the electorate has decided to vote not necessarily along party lines, but rather along lines of gender or ethnicity. With a burgeoning population, with almost unrestrained immigration, and with each new assault against societies most conservative institutions viewed as some sort of victory, the traditional enemies of the United States may prove to be correct in the assessment that Imperial Japan had made in regard to the United States just prior to its attack on Pearl Harbor in 1941, that American society was soft and to some extent corrupt. We may seek to deny this view of America, yet our own actions as a society continue to lend to these views continued support.

In the years prior to the Great War of 1914 to 1918, it is generally regarded that civilization may have removed itself too far from nature, or had become too independent upon the forces of technology. Violence was the result. In the years prior to 1914, no less than six heads of state were assassinated by an anarchistic tendency to reject the new society of the age. Much the same can be seen today, where the terrorist attack targets the many, instead of the few. Resource depletion may prove itself an enemy to mankind in the future, and the competition between industrial nations for these resources is replete with the potential for bloodshed. As the strains of modern society continue to increase on the individual, persons of all nations tend to bond together along lines of race or ethnicity, as they have for thousands of years. The United States of the 21st century may become more like the Balkans of the nineteenth century, or Africa of the twentieth century. Nevertheless, one thing remains certain, that the fortunes of agriculture, industry, commerce, and the military are interwoven and inseparable, just as they were to the Rome of Vespasian or the England of Henry Plantagenet. If we deny these basic truths, it will be to our peril.

# Bibliography

Anderson, Fred, *The War that Made America, New York*, 2005.

Anderson, Kenneth, *U.S. Military Operations, 1945-1985*, Connecticut, 1984.

Brendon, Piers, *The Decline and Fall of the British Empire 1781-1997*, New York, 2007.

Brinkley, Douglas, *American Heritage History of the United States*, New York.

Brodie, Fawn M., *Thomas Jefferson, an Intimate History*, New York, 1974.

Chernow, Ron, *Washington, a Life*, New York, 2010.

Churchill, Winston S., *The Gathering Storm*, New York, 1948.

Churchill, Winston, *A History of the English Speaking Peoples, abridged*, New York, 2011.

Churchill, Winston, *London to Ladysmith and Ian Hamilton's March*, London, 1900.

Churchill, Winston, *Marlborough, His Life and Times, Book One*, University of Chicago Press, 2002.

Churchill, Winston, *Marlborough, His Life and Times, Book Two*, University of Chicago Press, 2002.

Crocker III, H.W., *The Politically Incorrect Guide to the British Empire*, Washington, D.C. 2001.

Cropsey, Seth, Mayday, *The Decline of American Naval Supremacy*, New York, 2013.

Dallek, Robert, *An Unfinished Life, John F. Kennedy 1917-1963*, New York, 2003.

Dando-Collins, Stephen, *Legions of Rome*, New York, 2010.

Dorman, Dr. James E., *The U.S. War Machine*, New York, 1978.

Drincker-Bowen, Catherine, *Miracle at Philadelphia*, New York, 1966.

Dupuy and Dupuy, *The Encyclopedia of Military History*, New York, 1977.

Dupuy, Ernest R. and Trevor D. Dupuy, *Military Heritage of America*, New York, 1956.

Ellis, Joseph J., *American Creation*, New York, 2007.

Ferguson, Niall, *Empire*, London, 2002.

Giangieco, D.M., *United States Army, The Definitive Illustrated History*, New York, 2011.

Gibbon, Edward, *The Decline and Fall of the Roman Empire*, Random House, Toronto, 2003.

Goldsworthy, Adrian, *How Rome Fell*, Yale University Press, New Haven, 2009.

Goodspeed, M. Hill, *U.S. Navy A Complete History*, Hong Kong, 2003.

Hart, Peter, *The Somme*, New York, 2008.

Heather, Peter, *The Fall of the Roman Empire*, Oxford, 2006.

Humble, Richard, *Aircraft Carriers, The Illustrated History*, Herts, England, 1982.

James, Lawrence, *The Rise and Fall of the British Empire*, New York, 1994.

Jenkins, Simon, *A Short History of England*, New York, 2011.

Keegan, John and Homles, Richard, *Soldiers*, London, 1985.

Koch, H.W., *The Rise of Modern Warfare, 1618-1815*, London, 1981.

Langworth, Richard, *Churchill by Himself*, Philadelphia, 2008.

Mahan, Alfred Thayer, *The Influence of Sea Power Upon History, 1660-1805*, New Jersey, 1980

Manchester, William, *The Last Lion, Vol. II*, New York, 1988.

Manchester, William, *The Last Lion, Volume I*, Boston, 1983.

Matyszak, Philip, *Chronicle of the Roman Republic*, London, 2003.

McCullough, David, *1776*, New York, 2005.

McNab, Chris, *The Roman Army*, Oxford, 2010.

Meacham, Jon, *American Lion*, New York, 2008.

Middlekauff, Robert, *The Glorious Cause*, New York, 1982.

Miller, David, *The Illustrated Directory of Modern American Weapons*, Connecticut, 2002.

Mommsen, Theodor, *The History of Rome*, New York, 1958.

Nevins, Allan, and Henry Steele Commager, *A Pocket History of the U.S.*, New York, 1981
North, Anthony and Ian V. Hogg, *The Book of Guns and Gunsmiths*, London, 2004.

O'Donnell, James J., *The Ruin of the Roman Empire*, New York, 2008.

Potter, David, *Emperors of Rome*, London, 2007.

Preston, Anthony, *Jane's Fighting Ships of World War II*, Random House Publishing, 1994.

Purkiss, Diane, *The English Civil War*, New York, 2006.

Randall, Willard Sterne, *Ethan Allen, His Life and Times*, New York, 2011.

Roberts, Clayton, Roberts, David, *A History of England, Prehistory to 1714*, New Jersey, 1980.

Rodgers, Nigel, *Ancient Rome*, London, 2006.

Simmons, R.C., *The American Colonies from Settlement to Independence*, Toronto, 1976.

Smith, Lacey Baldwin, *This Realm of England*, Lexington, MA, 1992.

Time-Life Books, *The Revolutionaries, Alexandria*, Virginia, 1996.

Trevelyan, Sir George Otto, *The American Revolution, Part 1 766-1776*, Norwood, MA, 1899.

Tuchman, Barbara W., *The Guns of August*, New York, 1962.

Willmott, H.P., *World War I*, New York, 2003.

Zelizer, Julian E., *Arsenal of Democracy*, New York, 2010

CPSIA information can be obtained at www.ICGtesting.com
Printed in the USA
BVOW08s2254180416

444711BV00001B/12/P